Disability and Political Theory

Although disability scholarship has been robust in history, philosophy, English, and sociology for decades, political theory and political science more generally have been slow to catch up. This groundbreaking volume presents the first full-length book on political theory approaches to disability issues. Barbara Arneil and Nancy J. Hirschmann bring together some of the leading scholars in political theory to provide a historical analysis of disability through the works of canonical figures, ranging from Hobbes and Locke to Kant, Rawls, and Arendt, as well as an analysis of disability in contemporary political theory, examining key concepts such as freedom, power and justice. *Disability and Political Theory* introduces a new disciplinary framework to disability studies, and provides a comprehensive introduction to a new topic of political theory.

Barbara Arneil is Professor of Political Science at the University of British Columbia and the author of *John Locke and America* (1996), *Feminism and Politics* (1999), *Diverse Communities: The Problem with Social Capital* (Cambridge University Press, 2006), and a co-edited anthology entitled *Sexual Justice/Cultural Justice* (2006). Scholarly recognition includes the Harrison Prize (best article published in *Political Studies*), the Rockefeller Fellowship in Bellagio, C. B. MacPherson Prize (shortlist), and Killam Research and Teaching Prizes.

Nancy J. Hirschmann is Professor of Political Science at the University of Pennsylvania and has published many books and articles in feminist theory and disability theory, including *The Subject of Liberty: Toward a Feminist Theory of Freedom* (2003), *Gender, Class and Freedom in Modern Political Theory* (2008), and *Civil Disabilities: Citizenship, Membership, and Belonging* (2015), co-edited with Beth Linker. She has held fellowships from the National Endowment for the Humanities, the American Council of Learned Societies, and the Institute for Advanced Study.

Disability and Political Theory

Edited by

Barbara Arneil

University of British Columbia

Nancy J. Hirschmann

University of Pennsylvania

CAMBRIDGE
UNIVERSITY PRESS

University Printing House, Cambridge CB2 8BS, United Kingdom

One Liberty Plaza, 20th Floor, New York, NY 10006, USA

477 Williamstown Road, Port Melbourne, VIC 3207, Australia

314-321, 3rd Floor, Plot 3, Splendor Forum, Jasola District Centre, New Delhi - 110025, India

79 Anson Road, #06-04/06, Singapore 079906

Cambridge University Press is part of the University of Cambridge.

It furthers the University's mission by disseminating knowledge in the pursuit of education, learning and research at the highest international levels of excellence.

www.cambridge.org
Information on this title: www.cambridge.org/9781316617052
DOI: 10.1017/9781316694053

First published 2016
First paperback edition 2020

A catalogue record for this publication is available from the British Library

ISBN 978-1-107-16569-4 Hardback
ISBN 978-1-316-61705-2 Paperback

For Carter McGuigan and Jasbir Uppal, two former students who have taught me so much about disability, both in practice and theory. BA

In memory of Nancy Hartsock and Dick Flathman, with gratitude and love. NJH

Contents

Contributors

Barbara Arneil (PhD, London) is interested in the areas of identity politics and the history of political thought. She has published a number of books including *John Locke and America* (1996), *Feminism and Politics* (1999), and *Diverse Communities: The Problem with Social Capital* (Cambridge University Press, 2006). She has published articles on the role of disability in political theory and is about to publish a book on Domestic Colonies with Oxford University Press. Scholarly recognition includes the Harrison Prize (UK PSA award for best article), Rockefeller Foundation Fellowship, the C. B. MacPherson Prize short list, and Killam Research and Teaching Prizes.

Eileen Hunt Botting is Associate Professor of Political Science at the University of Notre Dame. She is most recently the author of *Wollstonecraft, Mill, and Women's Human Rights* (2016).

Sue Donaldson is an associate researcher at Queen's University, Canada, where she helped to establish the Animals in Philosophy, Politics, Law and Ethics research group (APPLE). She is the co-author (with Will Kymlicka) of *Zoopolis: A Political Theory of Animal Rights* and of numerous articles exploring the place of animals in political theory.

Kathy E. Ferguson teaches political science and women's studies at the University of Hawai'i. Her main areas of interest are contemporary political theory, particularly feminist political theory and anarchism. Her most recent book is *Emma Goldman: Political Thinking in the Streets* (2011), and she is currently writing two books: one on the role of the letterpress printer in the anarchist movement and the other on women's participation in anarchism.

Nancy J. Hirschmann is Professor of Political Science and Director of the Alice Paul Center for Research on Gender, Sexuality and Women at the University of Pennsylvania. Her books include *The Subject of Liberty:*

Toward a Feminist Theory of Freedom, which won the Victoria Schuck Award for best book on women and politics, *Gender, Class and Freedom in Modern Political Theory*, and *Civil Disabilities: Theory, Membership, and Belonging*, co-edited with Beth Linker. She has held fellowships from the Institute for Advanced Study, the National Endowment for the Humanities, and the American Council of Learned Societies among others.

Will Kymlicka is the Canada Research Chair in Political Philosophy at Queen's University. His books include Contemporary Political Philosophy, Multicultural Citizenship, and most recently, *Zoopolis: A Political Theory of Animal Rights*, co-authored with Sue Donaldson.

Lorraine Krall McCrary is a Visiting Assistant Professor in the Department of Political Science at Wabash College. She writes on the intersection between ethics of care feminism and disability studies, in addition to the relationship between the family and politics. She draws on literature in her research, including Marilynne Robinson's approach to disability in her novels.

Theresa Man Ling Lee is Associate Professor of Political Science at the University of Guelph in Canada. Her research covers contemporary political theory (continental philosophy, Marxism and critical theory, feminism, postmodernism, philosophy of social science, psychoanalysis, multiculturalism, human rights, modern Chinese political thought, and comparative political theory. Lee has published on a wide range of subjects in these areas, including intercultural pedagogy and is the author of *Politics and Truth: Political Theory and the Postmodernist Challenge* (1997).

Lucas G. Pinheiro is a doctoral candidate in the Department of Political Science at the University of Chicago. His research deals with historical themes concerning capitalism, politicized identity, empire, and aesthetics in modern political thought. His contribution to this volume is part of a project on disability in the political theories of Locke, Rousseau, Kant, and Nietzsche.

Stacy Clifford Simplican is a Senior Lecturer in the Women's and Gender Studies Program at Vanderbilt University. She is the author of *The Capacity Contract: Intellectual Disability and the Question of Citizenship* (2015).

Rogers M. Smith is the Christopher H. Browne Distinguished Professor of Political Science and Associate Dean for Social Sciences at the University of Pennsylvania. He is the author of many articles and seven books, most recently *Political Peoplehood: The Roles of Values, Interests, and Identities*. He is a member of the American Academy of Arts and Sciences, the American Academy of Social and Political Science, and the American Philosophical Society.

Deborah Stone is Distinguished Visiting Professor in the Heller School for Social Policy and Management at Brandeis University, where she had previously held the Pokross Chair in Law and Social Policy. She is author of *The Disabled State and of Policy Paradox: The Art of Political Decision Making*, which won the American Political Science Association's Wildavsky Award for an Enduring Contribution to Policy Studies. She has held fellowships from the Guggenheim Foundation, Harvard University, the Robert Wood Johnson Foundation and the German Marshall Fund and has written regularly for American Prospect, Nation, New Republic, and Boston Review.

Joan Tronto is a professor of political science at the University of Minnesota. She is the author of *Moral Boundaries: A Political Argument for an Ethic of Care* (1993), *Le risque ou le "care"?* (2012), *Caring Democracy: Markets, Justice and Equality* (2013) and *Who Cares? How to Reshape a Democratic Politics* (2015) as well as numerous articles on care, care ethics, and democratic theory.

Foreword

Deborah Stone

When I was growing up in the 1950s, I knew disability as a boy with cerebral palsy. Robbie was in a wheelchair, very disabled, able to talk but in a way that took some getting used to, like a thick foreign accent. His father worked at some kind of professional engineering job and, as far I could tell, spent all his free time carrying Robbie and designing what we'd now call adaptive devices so Robbie could feed himself and even type. His mother spent all her time tending Robbie and teaching him in a way we'd now call home schooling. She had to do that, she told us neighborhood kids, because no school would accept Robbie. Not public school, not private school.

I could see and feel how isolated Robbie was. He couldn't play with kids unless the kids decided to go to his house to play with him. He couldn't even call us to invite us over unless his mother dialed and held the phone for him. I could see and feel how his mother's life had been hijacked by the need to provide for Robbie what society provided for the rest of us and we took for granted. I understood the family's isolation too, because I caught how uncomfortable adults were around them and how our parents avoided them, while subtly praising us kids for spending time with Robbie. I knew that we were somehow letting them off the hook. I sensed the injustice of Robbie's exclusion from school. And yet, in spite of all that I saw and felt, disability wasn't something political for me. It was just a tragic birth accident, bad luck for Robbie and his family, their burden to bear.

When Barbara Arneil and Nancy Hirschman first told me about a book on disability and political theory, I thought to myself, this is one of those topics so obvious, so staring us in the face, how can it possibly be that political science has virtually ignored it? Then I remembered Robbie and my total obliviousness to disability as a political issue. It was the 1950s, the time of the Cold War, and politics, I gleaned, was about elections and wars, not personal troubles. Only now, looking back through the lens of disability rights and my own scholarship, can I see the cultural obliviousness we all shared.

It wasn't until halfway through graduate school, while I was researching German national health insurance for my dissertation, that I first noticed disability as a policy category. Something in the German healthcare cost figures jumped out at me: half of all health insurance expenditures went to pay wage replacement for people unable to work because of illness or disability. Doctors, in addition to treating their patients, were the gatekeepers to this vast economic redistribution system. They held the power to certify patients as unable to work, or in the colorful phrasing German exudes, doctors "write people sick." This was the early 1970s, when the US was going through one of its periodic spasms over the welfare rolls. It dawned on me that German doctors were presiding over a cash welfare system as vast as the American one, and I thought, how strange that physicians, not social workers, were empowered as its arbiters.

Eventually, I wrote a book to figure out that puzzle for myself (Stone 1984). Because *The Disabled State* was the book on which my tenure case hinged, I was haunted by departmental ghosts whispering, "What's political about disability? Where's the political science in it?" There was good evidence for the existence of my ghosts, beyond the usual tenure neuroses. Several years earlier, I had gone on the academic job market with a dissertation on health insurance. After every job talk I was asked, "What's political about medical care? Why would a political scientist study it?" Thankfully, with the Reagan purge of the disability rolls in the air and the winds of the disability rights movement at my back, disability-as-political was an easy case to make.

Alright, disability as a *policy* issue now seems obvious, but what about as an issue for *political theory*? I had been teaching John Stuart Mill's *On Liberty* for many years before I noticed the passage that could exclude people with disabilities from the right to liberty. Mill famously put forth the guiding tenet of classical liberalism and, arguably, contemporary American libertarianism: government is never justified in interfering with individual liberty except to prevent harm to others. Then he went on: "It is hardly necessary to say that this doctrine is meant to apply only to human beings in the maturity of their faculties. We are not speaking of children and very young persons… *Those who are still in a state to require being taken care of by others* must be protected against their own actions as well as against external injury." That all seemed pretty natural and unremarkable to me, especially in light of Mill's subsequent exception for "those backward states of society in which the race itself may be considered of nonage" (Mill 1974 [1859]: 69). As a child of the civil rights era, race was the exclusion that grabbed my attention.

I don't know whether Mill was thinking of people with disabilities when he mentioned the need for care, but in the context of my new-found disability-rights consciousness, those words conjured up Robbie and people like him. And in the context of my post-1970s feminist consciousness, those words conjured up Robbie's mother and people like her. In no sense did disabled people and their caregivers, whether unpaid relatives or poorly paid wage workers, enjoy the freedom to set their own life goals and pursue them, to live the good life as the giants of political theory imagined the ends of government. While I and my siblings and friends were worrying about where we'd like to go to college and what we'd like to do with our lives, Robbie lived in perpetual dread of the life plan he saw as his fate: when his parents were no longer able to care for him, he'd be placed in an institution.

As the authors in this book show, political theorists have shunted disabled people aside with a scarcely an intellectual hiccough, the same way society once packed them off to warehouses where they wouldn't bother anyone's glorious, if deluded, sense of autonomy. There have been many critical victories in the disability rights movement, and surely this book is another one. These authors are asking all the right questions and unmasking ableist assumptions left and right. No longer will political theorists be able to consider the big questions of citizenship, justice, equality, and freedom without caring about and for people with disabilities.

Still, our work isn't done. As feminists have long argued, and these authors as well, the real victory will come when "people who still need taking care of" aren't treated as a separate category, different from everybody else. We all need help, and we need it all the time, not only when we are young, elderly, or disabled by injury and illness. That's what's so wrong with the movement idea that the world is divided into people with disabilities and the "temporarily able-bodied." We live constantly in webs of helping relationships, some people more than others, but no one lives without being helped, all the time, in everything we do. Every time you walk in a pair of shoes, read a book, use a computer, ask a friend for advice, drive a car, borrow a tool, make hot oatmeal for breakfast, send a text, use your bank account, or vote in an election, you are being enabled by the thousands of people who made such activities possible for you, some of them no longer living, some of them living on the other side of the planet, some of them people you might not dream of inviting to your home. They're all helping you and you couldn't live your life without them, any more than Robbie could live his without his parents' help.

This is the continuing challenge for political theory, politics, and public policy. We need to go beyond understanding "the universality of dependence," as this book does so compellingly, to acknowledging that mutual care and help are the air and water of our human existence.

Distinguished Visiting Professor
Heller School for Social Policy and Management
Brandeis University

Disability and Political Theory: An Introduction

*Barbara Arneil and Nancy J. Hirschmann**

The study of disability is experiencing significant changes which have affected all of the social sciences, but relatively little attention has been devoted to this subject by political scientists.

(Hahn 1985)

When political scientist and disability scholar Harlan Hahn wrote this sentence in 1985, he seemed to expect the field of political science to take the lead on many of the issues he addressed in his essay. Yet, 30 years later, political science has actually fallen behind other disciplines in analyzing disability in our society. In the subfield of political theory, the problem is even more acute. While philosophers, historians, sociologists, and literary scholars have all recognized the importance of disability to their disciplinary inquiries, political theory has for the most part ignored it. The pre-eminent journal in the field, *Political Theory*, has published only one article on disability (by one of the editors of this volume). The *American Political Science Review*, the flagship journal in the discipline, has published no articles from a theoretical perspective; and while some political theorists include disability along with gender, race, and class as categories of exclusion, they do not present any sort of analysis of disability itself. The Americans with Disabilities Act of 1990 (ADA), the ADA Amendments Act of 2009 (ADAAA), and the United Nations Convention on the Rights of Persons with Disabilities (UNCRPD), adopted by the UN General Assembly in 2006 and ratified by 127 countries (although not the United States), all of which raise issues of rights, citizenship, entitlement, and justice, are rarely if ever mentioned in political theory journals or books.

One might well ask: Why should political theorists care about disability? The first reason is a basic demographic one – disability is not a

* We are indebted to the Social Sciences and Humanities Research Council of Canada for providing funding for this research through an Insight Grant to Barbara Arneil, the two anonymous reviewers who provided extremely helpful suggestions for revising the manuscript, Julie Jenkins who helped us to articulate some of the cross-cutting themes and central ideas within this introduction, Kelsey Wrightson and Sarah Munawar who helped with final editing, and Zachary Willis who assisted with research and editing.

phenomenon limited to a small minority, but a significant social issue. It was recently estimated that in the United States alone, 51.2 million Americans are disabled, as defined by the Americans with Disabilities Act, approximately 18 percent of the population, and United Nations Enable estimates around one billion people or 15 percent of the world's population are disabled, as defined by the World Health Organization's International Classification of Functioning, Disability and Health (Steinmetz 2002). Disability affects people of all races, ages, religion, ethnicity, nationality, class, gender, and professions. Simply stated, one out of every five or six individuals (including political theorists!) is likely to be disabled; when we include family members, particularly children and elderly parents, and add the number of people closely affected by disability, this figure rises further. Moreover, with an aging population worldwide, the rates of disability are also increasing, thereby making disability a social problem that will affect even those who do not have an immediate experience of it.

But beyond simple demographics, there are substantive reasons for political theorists to take up disability as a central concern of their analyses. Those engaged in liberal and democratic theory who depend on "reason" and "capacity" to underpin their analyses of citizenship and even personhood will, by definition, exclude a certain number of the disabled from both categories either explicitly, as several of the key canonical thinkers have done, or implicitly, as is more often the case in contemporary theory. If the objective of any liberal or democratic theory in today's world is to create a universal theory that is fully inclusive, the very terms of the debate as currently defined simply make this impossible as shall be discussed in several of the chapters in this volume. For more critical political theorists who use a poststructural, postmodern, or postcolonial framework for their analyses, despite the fact they are engaged in theorizing power, disability has also been ignored and the power exercised over the disabled, including discursive power, has simply not been addressed. The failure of political theorists to engage this subject is particularly obvious when we compare our subdiscipline to the work done by colleagues in the disciplines of English literature, history, and philosophy.[1]

[1] It would be impossible to document fully, but for good overviews in history, see Longmore and Umansky (2001) and Kudlick (2003). In philosophy, Nussbaum (2006) and the journal *Ethics* published a special issue in 2005, *Symposium on Disability* (vol. 16, no. 1, October, 1–213) with articles by prominent philosophers such as John Deigh, Eva Kittay, Lawrence Becker, Anita Silvers, David Wasserman, and Jeff McMahan. In English, two leading texts are Thomson (1997) and Siebers (1995). Many of the works cited throughout this chapter, the reader will note, are by scholars of philosophy, history, and English including Shelley Tremain, Alasdair MacIntyre, Jonathan Wolff, Anita Silvers, C. F. Goodey, Mark Jackson, James Trent, and Lennard Davis.

As our philosophy colleagues in particular show us – and some philosophers, such as Martha Nussbaum and Eva Kittay, are cited widely by political theorists – disability involves theoretical questions of justice, power, entitlement, care, and freedom, whether that means allocation of resources to provide care, accommodation or medical treatment, alteration of the built environment to facilitate access to public space and avenues of public participation, or setting public policy and legislative agendas to support caregiving and receiving in a way consistent with equality and dignity of all. And as Foucauldian philosophers have shown, disability can also be theorized through an alternative theory of power (Tremain 2002). These issues, and how they are dealt with, in turn impact the citizenship status and empowerment of disabled individuals.

Put simply, to the degree that many liberal and democratic political theorists adhere to fundamental modernist notions of freedom and the basic moral equality of all human beings, these questions, and scholarship that reveals the ways in which the disabled are excluded in substantive terms – much like analysis around gender, race, class, and sexual orientation challenged previous theory – are relevant to political theory. Political theorists regularly attend to issues of recognition and inclusion, membership and citizenship for various marginalized peoples and disabled people simply need to be included in these studies and incorporated into theorizing the intersecting nature of inequality and/or oppression rather than (if at all) as an afterthought or add-on. Similarly, postmodern or poststructural political theorists have as much reason to attend to disability, as our colleagues in literary criticism, critical philosophy, and new historicism show us. Questions of the relationship of the body and 'rational' mind to subjectivity and identity, the ways in which minds, bodies, and bodily experience are interpreted by and through medical and social discourses, and the ways in which "disability" as a concept and category is produced through relationships of power are all significant questions for political theorists.

As many of the chapters that follow will illustrate, the history of political thought displays a close correlation between abject definitions of disability and exclusionary understandings of citizenship and rights. Disabled identities are deployed to delimit and define citizenship, freedom, equality, and rationality, raising the question: how can we redefine disabled subjectivity and politics in order to facilitate the inclusion of disabled persons in society as full citizens; indeed, as full persons under the Enlightenment ideals of natural freedom and equality? Correspondingly, how can we redefine citizenship and the foundational concepts within politics to be more inclusive of disabled identities? Several promising answers are given in this collection of articles that engage not only a redefinition of disability but also a redefinition of the principles of political theory such as equality, freedom, justice, right, and citizenship (Hirschmann and Linker 2015).

Political theorists bring a unique set of scholarly tools to this field of study. Often missing from analysis by philosophers and disability scholars from other disciplines is a complex understanding of politics and the workings of power. The study of power is where political theory particularly excels, and this is key to why we maintain that political theory has a distinct contribution to make, beyond that of mainstream philosophy, by enlarging our understanding of the different ways in which the subject's relationship to public space, public resources, and public power are expressed, compromised, enabled, and restricted. The tools, texts, concepts, and arguments that several of the authors make in this volume are generally familiar to political theorists, even if they use them in a different frame and put them to different use, pertaining to the specific subject of disability as opposed to other forms of oppression and discrimination.

Thus, while political theorists ought to be engaging in disability for both demographic and substantive reasons, what makes this volume important at this particular historical juncture is the fundamental shift over the past 40 years in the definition of disability from an individual medical defect to something that is, wholly or partially, in the social and political domain. Within disability studies, what is known as the "medical model of disability," in which disabilities are viewed as individual defects arising from flawed bodies or minds, and must be "prevented" through reproductive technologies or "fixed" through surgery, drugs, or other medical interventions, has been challenged by a "social model of disability" in which "impairments" or "health conditions" such as blindness or paraplegia only *become* "disabilities" due to particular kinds of linguistic, physical, and political social arrangements that favor the certain kinds of bodily attributes that are considered "normal" or "able-bodied" and penalize or exclude other kinds of bodies and abilities. Disability in the social model is not simply about biology or physicality or even bodies, but rather about power and politics.

For example, it is not the fact that I am unable to walk that disables me from participating in society – such as entering a building to take a class, attend a meeting or go to work – but the fact that the building has stairs instead of ramps or that the elevator is not working today. Similarly, it is not the fact that I cannot hear that disables me from using a telephone at work, but the fact that my company refuses to install TDD technology. These social arrangements are a function of power and constitute, as Mairian Corker (1999: 631) says, "a form of social oppression" since it is these structures, rather than whatever health conditions or impairments one might have, that prevent the individual from being a full participant in his/her own life and in the wider society. In addition to these two examples of visible disabilities, the emergence of "invisible" disabilities create an additional set of power relations and social structures that make the transition of impairment to disability more complicated as the necessary accommodations may not be as apparent or seemingly necessary (Hirschmann 2015).

The introduction of the social model of disability pushes disability squarely into the arena of politics, both in relation to the broader notion of power relations in society but also the degree to which states provide the accommodations necessary to remove barriers to the full inclusion and participation of disabled persons. Ultimately, as the definition has evolved to the current understanding of disability as the *interaction* between the particular physical conditions of individuals *and* the environment they must navigate in their daily lives, it only underlines the fact that political theorists have much to learn about and contribute to these new debates.

Ultimately, the political implications of what we have been arguing leads us to believe not only that disability is a critically important subject to incorporate into political theory, but also that political theorists have important specific contributions to make in theorizing the meaning of citizenship, freedom, equality, and rights on the one hand, and the constitution of power on the other. Such theorizing has a broad scope, including the constitution of disability as a category of political identity and conceptual meaning and the distribution and constitution of public goods and resources in the social/political realm in response to the changing understanding of disability that political theory can enable. Such theorizing should in turn help contribute to the ongoing political project of theorizing "diversity" and "difference" within the democratic polity by helping produce a broader theory and practice of politics in relation to the full diversity of human minds and bodies.

Thus, this book is a clarion call and, we hope, a catalyst to the discipline of political science and in particular to the subfield of political theory to fully engage in disability in the fundamental and sustained way that we have begun to engage in the politics of gender, race, ethnicity, multiculturalism, indigeneity, colonialism, and sexual orientation over the past half century, and put this understudied but critically important issue at the center rather than the margins of our studies of citizenship and power. To this end, we have invited some of the leading political theorists working in the discipline today to think about and develop their own insights on disability and political theory rooted in their theoretical and methodological perspectives, along with a few emerging political theory scholars, part of a younger generation entirely focused on disability, to contribute chapters to this volume. Between these two groups, we believe this volume not only spans a generation of scholars but also brings new insights from a variety of perspectives.

Finally, the co-editors of this volume are feminist scholars who have published in the area of gender and political theory, and we have been struck in our own research and in developing this volume, how the second-wave feminist adage "the personal is the political" is as true of disability as it is of gender politics. One cannot present a paper at a conference on disability without experiencing, in the questions or conversations that follow, individuals talking about their own or their family's experience with disability. For one of us, the experience of living with diabetes and other impairments and the accommodations necessary to ensure equity, full participation, and individual health are very much part of the impetus and shaping of this book. For the other, watching, as many of us do, the last few weeks of her father's life as he became increasingly disabled – largely physically but eventually mentally – raised profound questions for her about the nature of care, human dignity, and accommodation within a hospital and hospice setting that sometimes reinforced insights gained from the disability community and in other instances raised different questions. The point is that disability is both political and personal; and it is in a very real sense universal, as we are all likely to face disability at some point, either ourselves or in our families, within our lifetime. But while the experience of disability may be in some ways universal, we are equally cognizant of the adage, "nothing about us without us,"[2] meaning it is also critically important that the voices of those who are living with disability are included in this volume. To this end, some contributors have disabilities or have family members, specifically children, who are disabled.

The essays that follow, although dealing with the largely unfamiliar (to our subfield, that is) topic of disability, engage very familiar approaches and strategies, ranging from analysis of canonical figures to engagement with contemporary theory and topics and application of theoretical concepts and categories to contemporary political issues. We have sought to bring together a range of scholars who deploy analytical, historical, critical, and/or liberal theoretical approaches to address a broad array of topics ranging from the social contract and citizenship to care for disabled persons to the meaning of central political theoretical concepts to

[2] This phrase is one often used by disability advocates and activists and refers to the long history of non-disabled people speaking on behalf of the disabled and defining for them what they need and want. See Charlton (2000).

strategies of alliance between disabled persons and other groups. The range of topics is certainly not exhaustive given space limitations but also because, as articulated earlier, few political theorists view disability as a significant topic for consideration. In particular, we think it is critically important to take up the issue of intersectionality in relation to disability, which while included in this volume at various points deserves much greater study and elaboration. Exactly because political theory lags behind other disciplines, however, there is less diversity in approach than we would want, and we therefore hope this volume will serve as an invitation to other scholars to take up the study of disability from every possible vantage point.

In the narrative that follows, we lay out the order of the essays in a way that hopefully draws the reader in through some familiar approaches to the broad diversity of topics that are possible within a political theory approach to disability. Two major concerns emerge in the chapters that open the volume. The first is the problematic binary constructed through modern political theory between rights and charity, independence and dependence. The citizen, as a presumed signatory of the "social contract," has rights guaranteed through the principles of justice, freedom, and equality, but is constituted in opposition to disabled dependents, outside the contract, who have needs that must be attended to as determined by the principles of charity or welfare. The second related concern is the centrality of reason to modern political thought and its impact on the disabled. If reason is crucial to central political theory notions such as consent, freedom, justice, equality, and the will, as the first several authors maintain, then it follows that these central ideas will be constituted in opposition to the cognitively disabled in society, sometimes explicitly and other times implicitly (and sometimes including the physically disabled as well). If the key concepts in the modern canon have all been built on ableist assumptions that in their very definitions excluded the cognitively disabled from them, then political theorists will need to fundamentally rethink the meaning of such concepts in ways that include disability.

In the first chapter, "Disability in Political Theory versus International Practice: Redefining Equality and Freedom," Barbara Arneil contrasts the definitions of disability found in such key canonical thinkers as John Locke, David Hume, and John Rawls with those proposed by modern disability advocates and in recent international disability documents. Arneil argues these key founders of Western political thought developed principles of citizenship that explicitly excluded people with both mental and physical disabilities, and indeed used these excluded persons to create the boundaries for their key concepts of freedom, equality, and justice respectively. These exclusions in essence established a binary between the rational and physically able autonomous public citizen with rights governed under the principle of freedom, equality, and justice in opposition to and mirrored by the mentally and/or physically disabled dependent person with needs governed under the principle of charity. Arneil maintains that this binary is rooted in a naturalized idea of disability as a pre-political individual negative defect within the body or mind caused by nature, thereby precluding (1) a social model that locates disability in the environment, (2) disability being simply one component of human diversity, and (3) the possibility of disabled persons being capable of citizenship and rights. Thus, Arneil juxtaposes the assumed why, what, and where of disability in the history of political thought with current international practice to show how the premises precluded by political theory are now foundational to international documents. This suggests that contemporary political theory needs to pay greater attention to international disability practice if they are to avoid perpetuating previous exclusions and contradictions.

Lucas Pinheiro echoes Arneil's critical analysis of disability in the history of political thought in his chapter, "The Ableist Contract: Intellectual Disability and the Limits of Justice in Kant's Political Thought." Framed as a critical intervention in contractarian theory, Pinheiro critiques the exclusionary logic of Kant's *Metaphysics of Morals*. Following in the tradition of Carole Pateman's sexual contract and Charles Mills' racial contract, Pinheiro argues that social contract thinkers simultaneously construct an "ableist contract" that explicitly excludes disabled identities from citizenship because of their impairments. Focusing on Kant, he argues that the exclusion of disabled identities from modern political theory was not a mere omission or procedural mishap but the result of deliberately constituted definitions of the disabled as delimitation on the key principles of citizenship. Against their negative accounts of disabled identities as the embodiment of a "lack" of reason and "failure" of morality, Kant is able to constitute his vision of freedom, personhood, and morality. Second, Pinheiro critiques the false binary constituted in political theory that holds autonomy and reason in the civic realm situated in opposition to dependency and charity in the realm of nature. Third, Pinheiro argues that this relegation of disabled identities to an unidentified natural space outside the social contract naturalizes impairment and precludes a social model of disability. Kant's social contract fails to actualize universal justice for all, since his definition of persons is predicated on the exclusion of disabled identities, which in turn allows for their further marginalization and abjection on the margins of political theory and citizenship.

Pinheiro does not conclude that we must throw the baby out with the bathwater and dispose of the social contract altogether in Kantian theory. Rather, the question is how to disband the *ableist* contract, and the answer seems to lie in challenging the naturalization of disabled identities in order to constitute the citizen. Pinheiro also draws a clear line between Kant and Rawls, claiming both early and later contract theory exclude the disabled in the same way and for the same reasons. Pinheiro argues while Kant *explicitly* excludes disabled identities through his overt definitions of the disabled subject, Rawls does so on procedural grounds.

By contrast, Stacy Clifford Simplican's chapter, "Disavowals of Disability in Rawls' Theory of Justice and his Critics" challenges Pinheiro's assertion that Rawlsian exclusion is procedural and argues that Rawls' reliance on "compulsory capacity" to define the subjects of justice necessarily excludes those who do not match up to a Rawlsian conception of 'normal'. Clifford's "double disavowal" analysis suggests that Rawls intentionally omits disabled identities, first when he evokes disability to delimit the "normal" intellectual capacities of moral agents, and second when he in turn excludes disabled people from social membership and claims to justice.

According to Clifford, evoking compulsory intellectual capacity as the basis for inclusion in the social contract stigmatizes disabled identities and fails to propel political theory beyond a hierarchical understanding of human abilities toward one that values diversity both among individuals and throughout lifespans. The legacy of this disavowal parallels the critical interventions on Rawls' political theory by contemporary gender and race theorists but adds another critical dimension to their critiques. Clifford uses feminists' and critical race theorists' critiques of Rawls as a model for her own analysis, but also critiques them for failing to eschew their own ableist assumptions, upholding notions of citizenship that hinge on an ideal universal intellectual capacity that is not reflective of the reality of diversity.

Like Pinheiro, who does not think the social contract should be dismissed entirely, Clifford does not conclude that Rawls' theory of justice is irredeemably flawed. Rather, she argues that its reliance on compulsory capacities creates a fictional ideal account of the citizen that deliberately and effectively allows so-called citizens to continue to disavow disabled identities, and thus continue to marginalize them. Thus, a radical rethinking of Rawls' reliance on compulsory capacities is called for. An inclusive foundation for citizenship would not be based on ideal theory, but rather on the diversity of human abilities and the universality of dependence. Thus, while Pinheiro and Clifford disagree about *how* Rawls excludes disabled identities, they both arrive at the same conclusion that social contract theory can be salvaged and put to better use for all citizens, as Arneil argued that the modern concepts of freedom and equality might be salvaged if imagined in different ways that are fully inclusive rather than exclusive of disability.

Nancy Hirschmann's chapter, "Disabling Barriers, Enabling Freedom," also seeks to disrupt the idealized notion of the independent, autonomous individual so central to the Western canon of political thought. Starting with standard accounts of "negative" liberty from Hobbes through Berlin and Flathman, Hirschmann critiques the juxtaposition of freedom and ability, and considers how the social model extends the notion of "external barriers" to include aspects of the built environment, such as stairs, and ableist attitudes against disability, that most able-bodied people consider "normal" and not barriers at all. Political theory's shortsightedness in its conceptualizations of the concept of freedom, the free subject, and ideas concerning what constitutes an "obstacle" or "barrier" to freedom leads to consideration of the meaning of "the will," a key element of the modernist mind/body duality. Hirschmann critiques both Hobbes and Locke for upholding the Cartesian mind/body dualism that causes us to reject the will of our body or see it at odds with reason, and thereby at odds with freedom. The modernist association of the mind with reason and the body with irrationality denies freedom to disabled bodies and thereby further marginalizes disabled identities. In contrast to standard feminist approaches that value emotion and the non-rational, however, Hirschmann expands the definition of the will to include *both* rational and physiological desires, and in doing so bridges the gap between "normal" and "disabled" identities.

All of these chapters in the first part of the volume illustrate that past and current definitions of disability within modern Western political theory are problematic for many reasons. Moreover, problematic definitions are shown to have dire consequences for the political rights and membership of disabled people. But other chapters take up how disability might be reframed, moving beyond "defect" toward a positive capability – or simply another aspect of human diversity. Eileen Hunt Botting's chapter draws on Hobbes and Wollstonecraft to consider the place of "anxiety" in disability discourse. As a universal state that is nevertheless framed differently for women and men, Botting particularly considers how the medical community's contemporary understanding of anxiety might negatively influence how women approach their struggles with it, preventing women – and indeed, thereby all "patients" – from recognizing anxiety's productive potential. Her chapter disrupts the contemporary narrative, which warns of a rising "epidemic" of female anxiety, as well as negative definitions of anxiety deployed by the medical community, and argues that women's anxiety in the context of patriarchy might be understood as a strategic emotional and political capability, and a rational response to the challenges women face in patriarchal society.

Understood this way, anxiety and other disabilities can be revalued as positive, strategic, and rational responses to unfavorable social circumstances. While Botting acknowledges that disabilities constitute real embodied experiences that can be negative, she also argues that embodied experience need not be understood as solely irrational or pathological, and depend as much on the medical and social context that defines them as it does on individual experience. If anxiety is appreciated as both rational and emotional, it might be used and valued by people as a tool that enables caring for others and coping with uncertainty while challenging the power relations that helped to create them in the first place.

Kathy Ferguson's "Dyslexia Manifesto" offers a similar perspective on both the interactive nature of disability and a reimagining of disability as positive using the case of dyslexia. If understood as a failure of educational institutions rather than a failure of impaired learners, dyslexia could be reframed from a disability to an aspect of neuro-diversity that is, once again, not necessarily defective as it is commonly understood but simply different. Once seen as part of the diversity of human experience, the solution changes. No longer must we seek to 'fix' dyslexia, as a medical model would promote, but rather we need to 'fix' our educational technologies and institutions to reflect the needs of a more diverse population. The universality of disability comes through Ferguson's article in that her "manifesto for dyslexia" could just as easily be applied to a variety of other non-standard learning styles. If the education system were universally able to rethink the way it approaches different kinds of learners, and if learning problems were seen as much a function of institutional arrangements as of individual brains, then her manifesto could have universal application to children in public education.

Even as they articulate a more positive understanding of both anxiety and learning disabilities, both Botting and Ferguson recognize there could be a trade-off between positively re-evaluating disability and developing the tools that allow participation in the broader community. For Ferguson, too strong positive evaluation might lead to isolation and further marginalization, even potentially leading some to think it is not necessary to challenge the exclusionary impulse of society. In this sense Ferguson's and Arneil's interactive definitions of disability come with caveats with respect to the idea of rehabilitation or specific techniques that allow individuals to participate better in the wider society; namely the tendency, if one sees disability *only* through educational or rehabilitative techniques that one may inadvertently reinforce existing power relations. As Arneil notes, "'rehabilitation' as a term is not problematic if understood as a tool to support and facilitate the disabled in their daily lives." Rather, it "becomes so when it is the sole paradigm by which disability is governed." Ferguson's social model likewise acknowledges the lived experience of frustration and failure that many people with dyslexia experience due to their disability, especially if understanding it as difference may lessen the political impetus to challenge all of the various forces of marginalization in society.

In "Rethinking Membership and Participation in an Inclusive Democracy: Cognitive Disability, Children, Animals," Sue Donaldson and Will Kymlicka build upon the insights of Ferguson, Botting, and Hirschmann by pointing out that people with cognitive disabilities may be able to exercise agency through their unconscious or "irrational" physiological desires. Recognizing those desires as an expression of the will assigns agency and freedom where political theorists have not seen it before, and expands the inclusionary grip of political theory. Although Donaldson and Kymlicka do not propose a new definition of disability per se, they borrow from disability scholarship to develop a theory of citizenship that is inclusive of identities traditionally understood as lacking the full capacity to reason, and are therefore excluded from traditional models. These include people with disabilities, children, and domesticated animals. Donaldson and Kymlicka take up a liberal rights model to argue that all members of society have a right to membership and participation. This right to membership is grounded in the fact that all individuals in a given community – including children, people with disabilities, and domesticated animals – exist within complicated webs of interaction and trust with others. Thus, our citizenship rights are grounded not in individualized universal capabilities or minimum capacities to reason, but rather in the "webs of trust, communication, and cooperation with others." Donaldson and Kymlicka do not believe mere membership in society is enough, therefore. Rather, people with disabilities also have a right to participate in the decisions that shape their individual lives and their societies. This definition of citizenship as active and participatory necessitates that we understand people with intellectual disabilities as full participants in society rather than excluded based on a lack of rational capacity. This reimagining in all three cases begins with eschewing "reason" as a requirement for citizenship. Instead, citizenship entails the democratic right of the individual (and a corresponding duty of the state/society) to be consulted on all decisions that affect their lives, both private and public.

Donaldson and Kymlicka offer a two-part conceptualization of agency: the right to both "micro-agency," or decision-making power over everyday choices such as what they will wear, what activities they will participate in, and where they will live, as well as "macro-agency," or the right to influence the structure and rules of the political world in which we live. Thus, as several other authors in this volume argue, citizenship requires taking seriously the preferences of people with severe cognitive disabilities to move beyond a paternalistic charity model toward one where people with disabilities have political power to shape their own lives and ensure their interests in the community. In turn, participation presupposes the active involvement of the state in removing barriers to and actively facilitating participation in ways that are appropriate for each individual.

Lorraine Krall McCrary similarly wants to get beyond specific, and often ableist, requirements for citizenship by considering Arendt's argument for "natality" as a useful entrée for disabled persons to establish "their right to have rights" and even their right to exist as human beings, let alone as citizens. Arguing that dominant understandings of disability – even those struggling to make positive representations – fall short because they at least implicitly assume and depend on a certain level and kind of ability that is influenced by an ableist perspective, McCrary argues that Arendt offers a more open-ended and inclusive notion that is useful for disability. However, she points out that Arendt, too, falls short in her insistence on the importance of the political realm, since many disabled individuals express their natality, their individuality, and their abilities through activities that are not – and that Arendt would certainly not consider – political. Moreover, the intellectualism of Arendt's conception, not to mention her stress on labor as a key aspect of humanity, poses multiple problems for a disability perspective. So, like other canonical figures that are utilized by the essays in this volume, Arendt may not provide a perfect solution to the question of disability inclusion within the polity. But McCrary shows us that Arendt's theory nevertheless holds more potential for political theorists to develop than other popular frameworks such as the capabilities approach.

Theresa Man Ling Lee's chapter explores the connection between mental disorder and political order, like McCrary, through a consideration of the work of Hannah Arendt but in conversation with Frantz Fanon and Karl Jaspers. At the core of her argument is the centrality of intersubjectivity in maintaining both mental health and political order. As a political thinker and a psychiatrist, Fanon offers the direct connection between the two by focusing on colonization as a form of political disorder – violence, torture, and armed conflict – whereby the colonized are denied the capacity and the context to connect with their fellow citizens. Jaspers and Arendt, however, when taken together provide a subtler but no less powerful connection. Jaspers' writings on psychiatry show the limits of science and the relevance of philosophy (specifically, phenomenology) in apprehending the relation between the patient and the doctor, between the narrative and the interpretation, between experience and observation. His analysis establishes intersubjectivity as the foundation for "understanding," which is essential to treating, caring for, and possibly healing psychological disorder. While Jaspers has forcefully argued for the importance of social context and situatedness to mental condition, he does not address its connection with politics.

To examine this critical link, Lee turns to his student Hannah Arendt, whose work centrally displays themes inherited from her teacher. Although Arendt never directly talked about psychopathology as her teacher did, her study of totalitarianism shows how mental disability and political disorder are inextricably related. Arendt described the prototypical follower of totalitarian movements as the "mass man" – someone who is in complete isolation from others. To Arendt the emergence of the "mass man" represents the breakdown of intersubjectivity, thereby disabling the possibility of politics as "action," including the vital activity of debate between citizens. Totalitarianism in turn disconnects citizens through a deluded sense of connectedness and what Arendt called "ideological thinking": a self-contained system of thought that does not speak to the concreteness of human experience. In sum, according to Lee, the three thinkers point to the direct bearing that political order has on mental health. Stated more poignantly, political disorder disconnects us from each other, from ourselves, from our humanity.

Joan Tronto takes up the critically important issue of violence against the disabled as another kind of disconnection between people. Well-known for her work on the ethic of care, Tronto considers violence as the flip-side of care, insofar as it demonstrates a lack of care, or even a hostility to care, which is so central to the human condition and a morally informed political theory. We are familiar with sensational cases of violence against disabled persons in institutional settings, such as the *New York Times'* exposé of the Oswald D. Heck Developmental Center, which revealed that attendants regularly abused its residents, all developmentally disabled, and eventually killed a 13-year-old boy (Hakim 2011). There are other twentieth-century horror stories, such as Willowbrook, which then-Senator Robert Kennedy liked to a "snake-pit," and the historical treatment of the mentally disabled in the Huronia Regional Center, which resulted in a $35 million settlement (in 2013) by the Ontario provincial government in Canada to compensate former residents for the abuse they endured.

But Tronto points out that violence against disabled persons takes many forms beyond these high-profile institutional cases, ranging from active physical abuse to selective abortion and genetic counseling to hostile and derogatory attitudes and language. Moreover, she identifies three distinct sites for the location of violence: institutions are only the most obvious. But violence occurs in the public sphere, and in the private sphere as well, in the home among family members. From so-called "mate crimes," where disabled persons are falsely befriended so as to exploit and hurt them, to the profound psychological and emotional abuse – not to mention physical harm – that stems from neglect, to outright physical assault, the victimization of disabled persons turns them from potential citizens into at best targets of pity, at worse targets for abuse.

Creating a sense that even your own body does not belong to you generates an alienation from self and society so profound as to cast in doubt the possibility for imagining membership, much less claiming it. Violence, as an effect and symptom of hatred and oppression, ensures that harm extends well beyond individual moments or incidents of violence into the social construction of what it means to be disabled: less than human, not a real person, certainly not a citizen. The principle of violence, woven into the fabric of the ableist vision of "reality," may unconsciously or implicitly accept various practices of violence as "normal," a function of being disabled rather than of its perception and treatment. Capturing this in the notion of "the bereft subject," Tronto grapples with the difficulties of addressing violence against the disabled, because it requires a profound shift in hateful and discriminatory – even violent – attitudes toward the very idea of disability. Ending with a call for pluralism, she holds out hope for the ideas of tolerance and respect for difference as an entry point for bringing disabled persons back into the human community in non-violent ways.

The risk of talking about disability in only positive terms in many of the essays in this volume, although a reasonable a response to the highly negative way it has been treated historically, is that it can become "just another difference" to be protected and preserved as either positive or neutral in relation to the human condition. But disability does have distinct qualities that make it different from other kinds of differences, in that there are often physical facts faced by persons with specific impairments that no amount of accommodation can overcome. A person who is paralyzed from the waist down will take longer to get dressed for work every day than a person who is fully mobile, for instance: that might seem a trivial difference, and certainly it is a difference that could potentially be reduced as technology improves, but the fact is that many persons with disabilities are not only different but, in many instances, either face additional burdens or suffer from their impairments in ways that social rearrangement cannot address: pain, or difficulties in navigating relationships with others, or unavoidable biological reactions of the body, such as incontinence or low blood sugar or seizures, even under the best conditions.

Thus, as much as many of the chapters in this volume have rightly sought to correct the tendency in previous political theory to see disability as *only* negative or tragic, the final chapter in this collection, like Tronto's chapter on the reality of violence in the lives of people with disabilities, seeks to remind us that disability is not *only* difference. Consistent with feminist disability scholars' arguments of recent years, Nancy Hirschmann and Rogers Smith argue that we must take seriously the embodied nature of disability as well as the social barriers to the disabled.[3] They take a different approach to challenging the bifurcation of medical and social models, and to bringing those models together, by seeking to rethink the idea of "curing." "Cure" is a term that is frequently demonized, or at least viewed with suspicion by the disability community, because of its long association with medicalization, torturous (and ineffective, if not harmful) treatments, and a refusal to accept the possibility that impairments may simply just be differences, and even valuable ones, rather than signals of inferiority, defect, and inhumanity.

Accommodation, accordingly, has been a primary focus of disability activists in the era of the "social model," on the basis that if disability is created by a hostile built environment or social attitudes, then changing architectural structures, technology, and attitudes will end disability – or at least make certain impairments less disabling. But Hirschmann and Smith point out that even in the most supportive environments, physical effects of various impairments remain for many disabled people. These hardly diminish the value of the person experiencing them – an attitude found so commonly throughout history that disabled persons might be overly invested in denying or downplaying then. But Hirschmann and Smith argue that the problem does not lie in the pursuit of cures per se but in the way such pursuits have become overly politicized in opposing directions when they should instead be complementary. Examining the various arguments for and against cures, they particularly challenge the ways in which cure and accommodation are set against one another, and suggest that we must reject an ableist notion of resource limitation

[3] Susan Wendell (1996), for example, argues it is necessary to find a "middle ground" through which the "social model" might "integrate the personal experience of the impaired body afresh" rather than deny these bodily differences altogether in the interest of focusing on social and physical structures. See also Morris (2001).

on how much can be spent on disability and illness. Such limitations take disability out of public discourse, or assign it an inferior status. Hirschmann and Smith argue that a different way of framing the relationship between accommodation and cure, both theoretically and ethically, allows a different political approach to cures and accommodation, as well as a more inclusive disability theory.

As is typical for political theory, there is a great deal of critique in these essays; critique of specific theorists, critique of concepts and frameworks, as well as critique of social categories and assumptions that have led to exclusion of persons with disabilities, just as political theory has critiqued in comprehensive and myriad ways the exclusions of non-white, non-Western, non-straight-male persons. But in these essays there are also positive visions for alternative futures that we, as political theorists, can start building today, in the present. While there are obviously many different topics and foci taken by the essays presented here, and even further variations on topics that might superficially seem the same, a few central themes emerge from these chapters.

The first is the interactive nature of disability. If the medical model (which most of modern political theory seems to follow) sees disability as being contained wholly within the specific conditions, defects, or limitations of an individual's mind and/or body, the social model often sees disability as *entirely* within the social environment; physical, linguistic, social, political, and legal barriers to participation and inclusion become the sole causes of what makes a particular condition a "disability." But what several chapters in this volume suggest is that we need to embrace the definition championed in the UNCRPD[4] and by a growing number of disability scholars where disability is understood to be the *interaction between* the body/mind and the social context. Disability thus exists in the *interactive processes* of bodies living in social space – between the health conditions of individuals and how society facilitates, supports, and cares for the disabled or not; between the physical and mental capabilities of particular persons and the language, architecture, structure, layout, rules, customs, assumptions, and expectations that exist in the world in which those persons live. And if disability involves an interactive process between bodily conditions and the larger environment, it is reflected back in the interactive relationship between accommodation and cure, as Hirschmann and Smith argue.

[4] The preamble states: "Recognizing that disability is an evolving concept and that disability results from the interaction between persons with impairments and attitudinal and environmental barriers that hinders their full and effective participation in society on an equal basis with others." UNCRPD, www.un.org/disabilities/convention/conventionfull.shtml, preamble, paragraph e.

A second theme is the shift from understanding disability in the canon of political theory as negative and even tragic to seeing it as more positive, which in many instances can enhance political life. Without denying the embodied experience of disability can be frustrating, painful, and even tragic for some individuals and/or their families, the history of seeing disability as *wholly* negative and tragic is challenged. Thus, all of the chapters in this volume express a continued commitment to the social model within the interactive definition described above to provide the theoretical basis for seeking continued opportunities to adapt the environment to minimize barriers to disabled persons' full inclusion in society as much as possible.

A third theme, related to the second, is the role of canonical political theory in setting out the terms for how we understand disability today. Not only have such theorists written about disability itself – often in pejorative and limiting terms – but they have drawn on disability as the "excluded other" to shape the parameters and limiting conditions of the concepts they develop, a fact that we have never acknowledged as a field. Arneil, Botting, Clifford, Hirschmann, McCrary, and Pinheiro all show the ways in which canonical figures from Aristotle to Rawls have profoundly shaped our thinking of disability as something outside the realm of politics while at the same time basing the essence of our political theoretical framework on disabled bodies.

Relatedly, then, a fourth theme is how many of the standard "essentially contested concepts" that are the bread and butter of much of political theory are themselves intimately tied up with disability, and how making disability an explicit framework for analysis not only reveals this but also changes how we must think of those concepts. From Donaldson and Kymlicka on citizenship and rights, to Arneil on the language of freedom and equality, to Hirschmann on freedom, to Tronto on violence, to Clifford and Pinheiro on the social contract, to Ferguson on positive duty, to the interweaving of autonomy, interdependence, justice, and particularly rationality throughout the volume, every one of the essays helps us rethink the standard concepts of political theory.

A fifth and final theme is the centrality of the body to politics: disability indeed makes literal the idea of the "body politic" for it brings bodily difference, and the disadvantages it faces due to the way social relations and institutions are structured, into the political arena, demanding recognition, attention, and response, as Ferguson, Botting, Donaldson and Kymlicka, and Hirschmann and Smith show. Similarly, Hirschmann's place of the body in the will, Tronto's place of the body in the process of violence, both receiving and generating, all place corporeal experience and limitations in the lived experiences of people with disabilities and stress the need for political theorists to theorize how these lived physical experiences are interpreted through our social understandings of the body.

At the risk of sounding immodest, we believe the essays gathered here provide nuanced, sophisticated critiques of existing political theories of citizenship and power, and in turn offer alternative definitions, principles, and theories that are more inclusive of and responsive to disabled identities. Ironically, these alternatives repurpose the language of modern political theory – rights, citizenship, equality, freedom – that they also critique. While arguments vary and feature several points of agreement and disagreement, the message is simple: while core principles of modern political theory, especially the ideal notion of the rational, atomistic individual, must be discarded to make way for a disability-inclusive political theory, the principles of equality, freedom, and justice for all remain within an understanding of individuals embedded in communities of care. While communities and environments have long been the source of physical and intellectual barriers, these articles help out the hope that the disabled can be incorporated as citizens and repurpose the community as a vehicle of empowerment over their own lives.

1 Disability in Political Theory versus International Practice: Redefining Equality and Freedom

Barbara Arneil

While there is a growing literature in moral philosophy, law and sociology on disability, little has been published in political theory on the subject,[1] notwithstanding the fact that most of the key scholars in Western political theory often refer to people with disabilities,[2] albeit briefly and only to exclude them from such key concepts as freedom, equality and justice (Arneil 2009). This lack of attention to disability in political theory is even more puzzling given how many contemporary disability scholars and advocates use citizenship and rights, the very stuff of political theory, to frame their own analyses. In this chapter, I briefly examine how disability is defined in modern political theory before analyzing the very different definitions of disability found in contemporary international documents, including the *International Classification of Functioning, Disability and Health* (2001), the *International Convention on the Rights of People with Disabilities* (2006) and the *World Report on Disability* (2011).[3]

Based on an analysis of the shifting 'where, what and why' of disability, I argue the international practice of disability that has developed in response to disability scholars and activists is far more advanced with respect to the full inclusion of people with disabilities as citizens in

[1] The journal '*Political Theory* has published only one article on disability; the *APSR* has published none from a theoretical perspective' (Hirschmann 2011).

[2] There has been an enormous debate over the appropriate language of disability within disability scholarship and advocacy, in particular whether 'people with disabilities' versus 'disabled persons' is the better term. There are important considerations at play here including the degree to which one follows a civil rights versus social oppression model of disability, but for purposes of this chapter, I simply use both terms.

[3] I use *international* documents to articulate a 'new' definition of disability, as opposed to *national* documents (such as the ADA) for two reasons: (1) being international, they incorporate, by definition, a diversity of perspectives from different cultures around the world; (2) because they are more recent than many national documents, they better reflect a social model of disability (which has gained ground in recent years) and thus provide the clearest articulation of an interactive, positive and universal definition of disability, which contrasts so strongly with the limited, negative and individual definitions of political theory.

society than political theory. As such, international practice provides a new way forward for political theorists interested in incorporating disability into their theories of justice and citizenship. I conclude by arguing if political theorists are truly serious about including disability into their analysis, a reconceptualization of key concepts such as equality and freedom, as they are defined in liberal theory, will be required; and the underlying binary upon which so much of modern liberal theory rests (autonomous, rational citizens with rights defined in opposition to dependent 'irrational', 'incapable' others with needs) rejected and replaced, as international practice has demonstrated, by a principle of universal interdependence.

Disability in Modern Political Theory

As I have argued in more depth elsewhere (Arneil 2009), in early modern political particularly liberal theory, the 'citizen' requires reason in a way that premodern subjects do not, because the citizen must consent to political authority, cooperate with others and 'know the law' in order to exercise political power. Anchoring citizenship in individuals' capacity to reason, however, has profound implications for disabled people, particularly the cognitively disabled. John Locke was the first modern philosopher to articulate a political theory rooted in reason and is explicit that people with mental disabilities or illness are *not* and never will be 'freemen' governed by political power.

> If through *defects* that may happen out of the ordinary course of Nature, anyone comes not to such a degree of Reason, wherein he might be supposed incapable to know the Law... he is *never capable of being a Free Man*, he is never let loose to the disposure of his own Will... And so Lunaticks and Ideots are never set free from the Government of their Parents. (Locke 1960 [1689]: II, 60)

This binary of the autonomous rational and industrious citizen *versus* the dependent, 'irrational' and/or 'idle' other, it turns out, will become a fundamental legacy of early modern political theory with respect to the disabled. While it may originate in Locke's thought, it persisted in liberal theory and practice over the next three centuries.

In the eighteenth century, Scottish philosopher David Hume uses the disabled mind and body to delimit equality rather than political freedom and power, as Locke had done.

> Were there a species of creature intermingled with men, which, though rational, were possessed of such *inferior* strength, *both of body and mind*, that they were incapable of all resistance, and could never, upon the highest provocation, make us feel their resentment; the necessary consequence, I think is that we should

be bound by the laws of humanity to give *gentle usage* to these creatures, but should not, properly speaking, lie under any restraint of *justice* towards them. (Hume 2000: 190)

Thus, Hume's theory is rooted in 'citizens' governed by the principles of equality and cooperation defined in opposition to the disabled governed by 'gentle usage'.

John Rawls incorporates both Locke's theory of freedom and Hume's theory of equality and cooperation to construct his own 'free and equal' beings in the original position, arguing anybody with permanent and severe 'mental disorders' and *physical* disabilities ought to be excluded from the original position because they lack reason, are not 'normal' and are unable to cooperate:

Since we wish to start from the idea of society as a fair system of cooperation, we assume that persons as citizens have all the capacities that enable them to be normal and fully cooperating members of society... *For our purposes here I leave aside permanent physical disabilities and mental disorders so severe as to prevent persons from being normal and fully cooperating members of society in the usual sense.* (Rawls 2003 [1971]: 234, emphasis added)

Rawls' use of the term 'being normal' as an ostensibly neutral criterion from his perspective to exclude disabled people from the original position is deeply problematic. While the word 'normal' was neutral at its inception when it meant 'right-angled' (Latin) and even when redefined to mean 'conforming to rules' in early modern Europe, by the late nineteenth century it came to mean the *opposite* of abnormal or deviant (a definition underpinning the quotation of Rawls above), which introduces all kinds of problematic assumptions into its meaning. Sir Francis Galton (who coined the term 'eugenics' in 1883) was responsible for renaming what had been the '*error*' curve in statistical science the '*normal*' curve. He did this in order to emphasize, in the study of human beings, the 'supra-normal' and normal from the 'sub-normal'.[4] This new understanding of 'normal' was introduced into the English language by Galton the eugenicist via the normal curve to expressly constitute the disabled as negatively abnormal or 'sub-normal', as Lennard Davis has demonstrated.

[4] Davis (1997: 10) describes how the rise of statistical 'norms' and the normal curve inevitably constructs disability as deviance: 'The norm pins down that majority of the population that fall under the arch of the standard bell-shaped curve... any bell curve will always have at its extremities those characteristics that deviate from the norm. So, with the concept of the norm comes the concept of deviations or extremes. When we think of bodies, in a society where the concept of the norm is operative, then people with disabilities will be thought of as deviants.'

More recently, Anita Silvers argues 'normalcy' continued to be deployed beyond eugenics in problematic ways in the 'medical model' of disability that 'assumes that uncompromised and unimpaired physical and mental status is the standard of "normalcy" for both medical practice and social policy'. It is this medical model and its understanding of normalcy that becomes the target of disability scholars and advocates in the 1980s and 1990s, in order to shift the 'locus of disability from immutable personal shortcoming to remediable public failure liberates disabled individuals' (1996: 210). Consequently, the word 'normal' is *not* neutral either historically or etymologically, as Rawls assumes, for people with disabilities, but constitutive of eugenics thinking and then a medical model of disability – both of which oppress disabled persons.

Meanings of Disability: Old and New

Disability scholars and advocates thus challenged these definitions of disability as found in liberal theory, proposing new ones as manifested in international documents. I created a table to contrast 'old' definitions of disability in political theory with 'new' ones in international practice, breaking down the definition of disability into three sub-categories: the where, what and why of disability.

	Defining Disability			Role of Disability in Theory	
	Where *is disability?* Individual or society?	***What*** *is disability?* Negative or positive?	***Why*** *is there disability?*	*Kinds of disabilities and meaning:*	*Key concept delimited by disability:*
Locke	*Individual*'s mind/ body	Defects: 'Ideot' 'Lunatic' Unable to work: *negative*	God, ordinary course of nature	Mental disabilities/ illness = unable to reason/ worthy poor = unable to work	*Freedom* – disabled not free because unable to reason
Hume	*Individual*'s mind/ body	'Defective' 'Inferior': *negative*	God, nature	Mental and physical disabilities = unable to resist	*Equality* – disabled not equal because unable to resist.

(*continued*)

Table (*continued*)

	Defining Disability			Role of Disability in Theory	
	Where *is disability?* Individual or society?	***What*** *is disability?* Negative or positive?	***Why*** *is there disability?*	*Kinds of disabilities and meaning:*	*Key concept delimited by disability:*
Rawls	*Individual's* mind/ body	Not 'normal' 'Unable to cooperate': *negative*	Misfortune, bad luck	Physical disabilities & mental disorders (includes illness) = unable to cooperate	*Original position* – disabled excluded because unable to be normal/ cooperate.
Social Model	*Social/environmental barriers*	*Barriers in society: negative*	*Society's attitudes/ practices*	*Disability is like race: a category of social oppression*	*No delimitation: full citizens with equal rights*
UN/WHO Document	*Interactive location between health/ environment*	*Barriers and Human diversity: negative and neutral*	*Society's attitudes/ practices and nature*	*Disability is universal – at some point, everyone will have disability*	*No delimitation: Full citizens with equal rights*

Put simply the 'where, what and why' of disability shifts radically, from an individual, negative and tragic definition experienced by a minority of the population (old) to an interactive, deeply social definition experienced universally by all people (new). Building upon these contrasting definitions, the last two columns identify the role disability plays in each political theory compared to its role in disability scholarship and international documents. I include these columns, in addition to the 'where, what and why' of disability to underline the fact these three thinkers do not simply passively exclude people with disabilities from their key concepts but use them to constitute the boundaries of these same concepts. Locke uses lunatics and idiots to constitute the boundaries of freedom; Hume uses creatures 'inferior in mind or body' to define the boundaries of 'equality' and Rawls uses mentally disordered and physically disabled persons to define the parameters of the original position. Thus, we cannot simply add disabled people into existing theories but challenge the concepts themselves as I outline in the last section of this chapter. For the bulk of this chapter, however, I now analyze *in detail* the shift from 'old' definitions to 'new' in the where, what and why of disability.

Where is Disability?

International organizations began to address disability in an explicit way in the 1970s and 1980s and located it initially, like the three political theories described above, in the individual's mind and/or body. Thus, the World Health Organization's famous *International Classification of Impairments, Disabilities and Handicaps* (ICIDH) of 1980 defined (1) *impairments* as the loss or abnormality in an individual's structure or function; (2) *disabilities* as the resulting physical or mental restrictions or lack of ability in the individual; and (3) *handicaps* as the 'disadvantages... resulting from impairment or disability'. The United Nations, in turn, adopted all three concepts as defined in the Decade of Disabled Persons (1983–92). The assumption underlying these earlier documents is that disability is wholly located in the loss, defect and/or abnormality in the mind or body of an individual person.

Almost immediately, disability scholars and advocates argued that the location of disability needed to be fundamentally rethought. One of the first organizations to make this argument was the British Union of the Physically Impaired Against Segregation (UPIAS) who advocated, beginning in the 1970s for a 'social model' of disability whereby '*disability*' should be located not in the individual but in 'the disadvantage or restriction of activity *caused by contemporary organizations* which take no or little account of people who have physical impairments and thus exclude them from the mainstream of social activities'.[5] In other words, it is not the limitations experienced by any individual in his/her body or mind that fundamentally 'disables' a person but the barriers society itself has erected to full equality and inclusion. Similarly, in the United States, disability advocates and scholars argued against the standard medical model that 'conceptualizes the disabled as biologically inferior' in relation to a socially constructed idea of 'normalcy' and for a social model of disability to be enshrined in a Americans with Disability Act. As Anita Silvers (1996: 209–10) argues: 'The ADA codifies into law the understanding that a disabling condition is a state of society itself, not a

[5] International Disability and Human Rights Network, 'The Origins of the Social Model'. The UPIAS definition of 1976 built upon Paul Hunt's definitions first published in 1966, www.daa.org.uk/index.php?page=social-model-or-unsociable-muddle.

physical or mental state of a minority of society's members, and that it is the way society is organized rather than personal deficits which disadvantages this minority.'

Many disability scholars built upon this social model of disability in their research (Finkelstein 1980; Barnes 1991; Oliver 1990, 1996) and advocates embraced it as well for providing an avenue away from an unrelenting medical focus on prevention/cure and towards a rights-based focus on accessibility and accommodation within which society was required to remove the barriers faced by people with disabilities. Before too long, however, some disability scholars, advocates and families of children with disabilities expressed concerns that a *purely* social model in which disability was *only* located in the societal realm effaced the specificity of the limitations and challenges experienced by individuals and their families/caregivers. But those defending the social model were determined, particularly in Britain, to fight any attempt to water down their stance in order to keep the focus on the social oppression experienced by the disabled.

As Shakespeare and Watson (1997: 11) argue, by the late 1990s the social model was almost untouchable in certain circles, a 'sacred cow' that 'could not easily be challenged'. Some advocates and scholars did challenge it, particularly feminist disability scholars who argued a purely social model led people with disabilities 'to deny the experience of our own bodies, insisting that our own physical differences and restrictions are entirely socially created' (Morris 2001: 10; see also Wendell 1996; French 1993; Crow 1996; O'Brien 2005) This debate over the 'where' of disability was so intense that many advocacy groups simply refused to define disability at all. Thus, Disabled Peoples' International (DPI) stated on their website: 'For many years, DPI along with many of the other major international non-governmental organizations (INGO) have not adopted a definition of disability'(DPI Position Paper on the Definition of Disability). This extraordinary statement suggests something unique about disability and its definition, for one would be hard-pressed to think of any other international organization lobbying for an issue that it steadfastly refused to define over many years. DPI and other organizations wanted to act in solidarity with those who sought to reject the medical or individual model but did not want to ignore disability advocates and family members who argued the limitations experienced by people with disabilities in their own bodies and minds must also be incorporated into defining disability.

By the turn of the twenty-first century, there was a push from both disability advocates and international organizations to try and find a 'middle ground' through which the 'social model' might 'integrate the personal experience of the impaired body afresh' rather than deny differences altogether in the interests of *focusing* on only social structures (Handley 2001: 114). Thus, not only disability groups but also the World Health Organization sought to incorporate social aspects of disability into their definitions without losing the connection to health issues through an interactive understanding of disability that included both the individual's health conditions and his/her environment.

These two trajectories (within the disability movement and international organizations) bore fruit in the early 2000s, as the WHO reviewed and substantively revised the original medical model of disability in the ICIDH to directly respond to disability advocates and scholars and find some middle ground. The *International Classification of Functioning, Disability and Health* (ICF) replaced the ICIDH in 2001 and a new definition of disability was born that included both individual health conditions and environmental barriers to inclusion. The European Commission concludes the ICF alters the definition of disability in two key ways:

> At the heart of the ICF's conception of disability... is a major paradigm shift... captured by two propositions: 1) Disability is a universal phenomenon, not the mark of a discrete social group... 2) Disability is the outcome of an interaction between the person's health condition... [and] features of the person's physical, social and attitudinal environment. (Measuring Health and Disability: Supporting Policy Development (MHADIE))

The DPI now uses this definition as the basis for their own definition of disability, as of 2005 to be 'the outcome of the interaction between a person with an impairment and the environmental and attitudinal barriers he/she may face'. The UN Convention on the Rights of Persons with Disabilities (UNCRPD) followed suit in 2006 with another altered definition of disability that located it not so much in the 'outcome' as the interaction itself – disability should be thought of as a process rather than a product: '[disability] is the *interaction* between persons with impairments and attitudinal and environmental barriers that hinders their full and effective participation in society on an equal basis with others' (Preamble (e)). Finally, the *World Report on Disability* (WHO 2011) adopted a definition of disability as a *dynamic* process, pointing to its universal nature: the '*dynamic* interaction between health conditions and contextual factors, both personal and environmental'. Despite a growing consensus around the location of disability as interactive, all three documents also refer to the revisable nature of their definitions.

While the definition may remain contingent, what is clear is that the long-assumed location of disability, reflected in both Western political theory and earlier international documents, as something wholly within the individual mind and/or body, is no longer tenable. Thus, I would argue that international *practice*, rooted in disability advocacy and scholarship, is far ahead of political *theory*. Indeed, given the interactive definition of disability described above, the most important question for political theorists might be whether theory itself is part of the disabling linguistic environment faced by people with disabilities, through the use of negative language (defects) and ascribed causes to disability (bad luck, misfortune)? Is political theory itself one dimension of disability, properly understood as the interaction between the disabled and the environment they have to negotiate on a daily basis? In order to answer this question, I turn from the 'where' of disability to consider changes to its 'what' and 'why'.

What is Disability?

If one considers the terms used to describe people with disabilities in the past (crippled, afflicted, deficient, inferior, defective, disordered, handicapped, feeble-minded, idiot, imbecile, moron, lame, retard, spaz) one is struck by a uniformly and overwhelmingly negative language. And while the advocacy of people with disabilities has led to a shift toward increasingly neutral or, in some cases, positive language of diversity to describe disabilities, deeply negative connotations remain with us in Western society generally and political theory specifically. Thus, while the 'where' of disability has shifted dramatically as described above, the 'what' of disability has not done so to the same degree, which is why language remains central for disability scholars, as Jenny Morris (2001: 2) observes: 'the *foundation* of disability studies must begin with the recognition that the language we use [is] central to the way we interpret our experiences.'

Thus, notwithstanding the elimination of many of the terms listed above from everyday language today, negative connotations remain that, because of their ubiquity, are nearly invisible. Two important examples of such ubiquitous but invisible language are: (1) the deep, persistent and nearly complete association of disability with 'defect' and (2) the profoundly negative etymological origins of the prefix 'dys/dis' that demarcates the word 'disability' from 'ability'. Let us consider each in turn and the implications such language has for both political theory and practice.

Defect or incapacity has long been used to define disability in political theory, as manifested in the theories described above: 'incapable to know the law' (Locke); 'inability to resist' (Hume); 'incapacity to cooperate'

(Rawls). It also undergirds the 1980 ICIDH's definitions of 'impairments' and 'disabilities' (loss, abnormality, disadvantages). Beyond the negative language itself, including the assumption that disability is wholly located within a 'defective' mind or body there are at least three additional implications in political theory and practice of constituting disability as 'defect', namely such defects ought to be prevented, rehabilitated and/or compensated. Let us examine each of these implications (prevention, rehabilitation and compensation) in turn, in both theory and practice.

Seeing disability as an individual defect leads almost inevitably to a focus on 'prevention'. At hospitals and doctors' offices, newly born or yet to be born children with disabilities are almost always described as 'suffering from' 'birth *defects*', 'congenital abnormalities', 'deformations', 'disorders' or 'syndromes', but few doctors and even fewer parents stop to think of the historical origins of such terms, or whether a child 'with Down's syndrome', for example, should be described as 'defective' as opposed to simply different: one dimension of human diversity. Davis (2002: 20) argues that the term 'defect', like 'normal', is a product of eugenics: 'The model involved in the idea of the birth "defect" comes to us direct and unaltered from a eugenic model of the human body', as eugenicists used 'defect' along with abnormal to demarcate bodies and minds that should be prevented from reproducing via forced sterilization or institutionalization. While prevention as a goal may have been initiated by the eugenicists at the turn of the twentieth century, new reproductive technologies now make the goal of 'ridding' the human race of such 'defects' ever more viable. Indeed, 90 percent of fetuses 'with Down's syndrome' are now aborted in Europe and North America with little discussion in mainstream theory about the ethics or politics of this near universal practice (Mansfield et al. 1999). The eugenicists at the turn of the century could only dream of such 'success' with respect to the 'prevention' of 'defects'.

Disability scholar Susan Wendell (1996: 82) argues if disability were seen not as defect but simply one aspect of human difference, like gender or race, the ethics of the termination of pregnancies would become a very different calculus: 'To people who value disabilities as differences, attempts to prevent disability by preventing the birth of people with disabilities can seem analogous to attempts to guarantee the birth of male babies because they are more highly valued, or to wipe out colour differences by genetic technologies.' Thus, if people 'with Down's syndrome' were viewed as part of the full spectrum of human diversity (albeit with specific kinds of challenges) rather than defective, more fetuses would be brought to term and live among us. In raising this question, I am not challenging the right of women and their partners to choose; rather I am challenging the linguistic environment within which they make those choices. If fetuses with disabilities are invariably constituted as 'defective', it should not surprise us that women and their partners make the choices that they do, with the resulting outcomes.[6]

The second implication of defining disability as *defect* is the assumed overarching need to 'cure' or 'rehabilitate' people with disabilities and transform them back to 'normalcy' as far as possible. The language of rehabilitation emerged out of the First World War, as disabled soldiers returned from war and sought to reintegrate into society. Questioning rehabilitation as an overarching frame for understanding disability does not challenge the utility of all kinds of physical, therapeutic and occupational rehabilitation as critically important tools through which people with disabilities can regain certain capacities and functions lost through war, accident or disease. Thus, 'rehabilitation' as a term is not problematic when understood as a tool to support and facilitate the disabled in their daily lives, but becomes so when it is the sole paradigm by which disability is governed. For example, in the United States from 1920 until 1990 people with disabilities were governed under successive rehabilitation acts (1920 Civilian Rehabilitation Act, 1954 Vocational Rehabilitation Act and 1973 Rehabilitation Act).

As Henri Stiker argues in *History of Disability*, this was not unique to America: rehabilitation was the overarching paradigm governing disability in the twentieth century throughout industrialized countries in the same way that Christian 'charity' was the governing paradigm in the seventeenth and eighteenth centuries. Rehabilitation as a paradigm fundamentally constructs the disabled as 'potential' or postulated rather than full beings, always living in a 'situation that existed for the able but... only postulated for the others' (Stiker 2000: 122). This conceptualization of people with disabilities as potential beings needing to be made whole and returned to 'normalcy' animates such scholars' theories as Harvard professor and Rawlsian theorist Norman Daniels (1987: 273; 1990: 290), who concludes that a 'just society' gives priority in health services to whatever will 'restore [the disabled] to normal functioning',

[6] The general ethical issue of 'prevention' of disability through reproductive technologies and science has been addressed at the international level through the Universal Declaration on the Human Genome and Human Rights, adopted by the UN General Assembly in 1998, www.unesco.org/new/en/social-and-human-sciences/themes/bioethics/human-genome-and-human-rights. Again, largely motivated by disability advocates and scholars, this document seeks to recognize and preserve genetic diversity and human dignity in the context of a new science of genetics. Its application, however, is very limited given the statistics quoted above with respect to fetuses 'with Down's syndrome'.

and Charles Taylor (1994: 65) who describes the 'handicapped' as 'incapable of realizing their potential in the normal way'.

The limitations of 'rehabilitation' as a paradigm by which to govern people with disabilities is perhaps best demonstrated by the paradigm that replaced it. In 1990, the Americans with Disabilities Act (1990) replaced all previous rehabilitation acts, up to and including the Rehabilitation Act (1973). The ADA, for the first time in American political practice, fundamentally reconceived people with disabilities as citizens with rights rather than potential persons or 'patients' to be 'cured' or rehabilitated. Similarly, at the international level, the rehabilitative paradigm of the defective person in the ICIDH was replaced by human rights in the ICF, the UNCRPD and the WRD.

The third and final implication in both political theory and practice of viewing disability as 'defect' is that it deserves compensation. This is related to the assumed cause of disability as bad luck since it is argued, by luck egalitarians in particular, that the disabled individual should be recompensed for his/her 'bad luck'. Thus, Ronald Dworkin (2005: 192) uses disability as his key example of unfortunate outcomes due to nature rather than choice that ought to be compensated via a hypothetical insurance scheme: 'In my view, people are entitled to receive some form of compensation when they are handicapped or lack marketable talent.'

The principle of compensation becomes translated, in practice, as higher benefits for the disabled in liberal welfare states, with its earliest roots in Locke's *Essay on the Poor Laws* that distinguishes between people *unwilling* to labor (the unworthy poor) who should be given nothing and those *unable* to labor (the worthy poor), whose needs should be taken care of by others, as discussed earlier. Such a division is foundational to industrialized welfare states in the twentieth century, as sociologist Theda Skocpol (1992: 149) notes of the United States: 'Institutional and cultural oppositions between the morally "deserving" and the less deserving run like fault lines through the entire history of American social provision', with the former receiving higher benefits/compensation from the state because of their 'unfortunate circumstances'.

This division between charity and compensation for the worthy poor and punitive measures for the unworthy poor ultimately leads to the principle in theory and practice that people with disabilities should receive such additional compensation if they are defined as 'unable to work'.[7]

[7] The US Social Security Administration is succinct: 'Disability under Social Security is based on your inability to work' (www.ssa.gov/dibplan/dqualify4.htm). Similarly Human Resources and Skills Development Canada notes: 'Canada Pension Plan Disability (CPPD) provides financial assistance to CPP contributors who are unable to work because of a severe and prolonged disability.'

This requirement, however, traps disabled people in a dilemma caused by the foundational binary underpinning liberal theory – *either* they have defects and are 'charity' cases so get higher levels of compensation because they are *un*employable and dependent, or they have no 'defects', are *employable* and assumed to be 'autonomous'. But should a disabled person take a job, they risk losing his/her higher benefits because they will no longer be defined as unemployable and therefore worthy of compensation, which creates a perverse disincentive to work, particularly if one has a cyclical form of disability or where supports/accommodations are weak at best. This is a profound problem in liberal welfare states that disability organizations have worked long and hard to alter in order to recognize the interdependent and interactive nature of disability and employment, but with limited success because of the fundamental binary in liberal theory discussed above and attenuated by the principle of compensation for defect (OECD 2003; Barnes 2003).

As shall be discussed in more depth shortly, inherent in the definition of compensation for the worthy poor is a particular 'why' of disability, namely the cause of disability is understood by definition to be tragedy, misfortune or bad luck that occurs in 'nature'. Thus, '*luck* egalitarian' Dworkin argues that persons with disabilities are not responsible for their 'bad luck', as opposed to those who make bad choices. This leads him to develop his famous insurance scheme against 'natural misfortunes', which provides us with the essence of equality in his theory:

> People [should] be made equal, so far as this is possible, in their opportunity to insure or provide against bad luck before it has occurred, or, if that is not possible, that people be awarded the compensation it is likely they would have insured to have if they had had that opportunity. (Dworkin 2005: 191)

Like liberal theorists, disability is defined as something that occurs wholly within an individual's mind/body as the result of bad luck and, like Hume's theory, disabled people are the boundaries of Dworkin's concept of equality since they are the quintessential example of those who are unequal because of bad luck.

Jeffrey Kirby (2004) ultimately concludes that the influential political theories of both Norman Daniels (who emphasizes rehabilitation) and Ronald Dworkin (who emphasizes compensation) rooted in Rawls' original position have led states to view the disabled almost entirely through a framework of redistributive charity for the minority of defective and needy. Kirby defines compensation as a 'monetarized' fix for the defect in these kinds of justice theories:

> Most liberal theorists and mainstream bioethicists… advocate resource redistribution as the primary mechanism for handling justice issues related to health

care and disability. Distributive models such as those advocated by Daniels which call for the allocation of resources for the 'fixing' of disabilities and the restoring of individuals to normal species functioning, and that advocated by Ronald Dworkin, which offers insurance-type compensation for those with disabilities, have provided a theoretical basis for taxation-related redistribution of public resources to the disabled. (Kirby 2004: 230)

The problem for disability advocates of such theories is twofold: disability remains an individual defect brought on by bad luck (rather than constituted in part or whole by barriers/lack of accommodations in society) and the disabled are defined as dependent welfare *clients* or healthcare *patients* with needs rather than citizens with rights.

Anita Silvers, philosopher and disability advocate/scholar concludes the liberal redistributive model and luck egalitarianism creates the conditions it seeks to solve:

Schemes to allocate extraordinary resources to the class of the disabled... cannot help but construct the class's members as being uniformly needy... To so construct disability nourishes the exclusionary practices that isolate people into the very state of neediness purported to have warranted the initial construction of their neediness... For these reasons, I do not agree with treating people with disabilities justly consists in extraordinary distributions made in virtue of disability. (Silvers 1993: 35)

By challenging compensation as an overarching concept, I am not challenging the utility of financial supports (such as rehabilitation) as important tools for people with disabilities to live their lives. But compensation, like rehabilitation, is problematic when it is not just a tool of support but becomes the governing paradigm by which liberal thinkers and states understand the disabled rooted in a binary between the autonomous and dependent, the worthy and unworthy poor, the whole and the defective. Compensation along with rehabilitation thus fundamentally constitutes the disabled as 'charity' cases, patients in the healthcare system or clients of the welfare system, rather than citizens with rights.

While the language of 'defects' remains with us in modern medicine and welfare state policies with all of the real-world implications I have described above (prevention, rehabilitation and compensation), there is, again, some movement internationally, as a result of disability scholarship and advocacy to constitute disability not as defects of the few but universal to all. Thus, the ICF and WRD challenge the assumption (of luck egalitarians) that it is only a minority of people who experience disability, compared to a 'normal' population. The language of 'health conditions' instead leads to viewing disability as universal to all. The ICF puts the notions of 'health' and 'disability' in a new light. It acknowledges that every human being can experience a decrement in health and thereby experience some degree of disability. Disability is not something that only happens to a minority of humanity. The ICF thus 'mainstreams' the experience of disability and recognizes it as a universal human experience.

Seeing disability in this way not only undermines traditional models of disability as a defect in a minority population but also challenges disability advocates who view disability as entirely analogous to race, where minority groups overcome the oppression exercised by the majority over the few. Seeing disability as something universal has not infiltrated liberal democratic society, in particular hospitals or doctors' offices, nor has it been incorporated into liberal theory, which continues to define disability in terms of 'defect', deficit and compensation.

A second example of negative language, beyond defects, is found in the word disability itself, or more precisely the prefix 'dis'. While advocates, scholars and international documents all employ 'disability' as a word preferable to previous terms such as 'handicapped', 'mentally deficient' or 'crippled', the etymological root of the prefix 'dis' raises questions of its own. The ancient Greek prefix 'dys' can be translated as bad and/or malfunctioning/impaired – hence something that is either evil and/or does not work. Thus, in ancient Roman mythology, 'dis' is used as a name for hell or the devil: thus, in Virgil's sixth book of *Aeneid*, *Dispater* is the father of the underworld and *Dis* is hell as described below:

> Right before the entrance, in the very jaws of Orcus,
> Grief and vengeful Care have made their beds,
> and pallid Sickness lives there, and sad Old Age,
> and Fear, and persuasive Hunger, and vile Need,
> forms terrible to look on, and Death and Pain:
> then Death's brother Sleep, and Evil Pleasure of the mind,
> and, on the threshold opposite, death-dealing War,
> and the steel chambers of the Furies, and mad Discord,
> her snaky hair entwined with blood-wet ribbons.[8]

Based on this description, Dante also adopted *Dis* in the *Divine Comedy* as the name of the city that occupied the sixth to ninth circles of Hell in Cantos 8–10 of the Inferno.

It should not surprise us, based on this etymology, that so many words in English with 'dys' or 'dis' as a prefix are associated with deeply negative feelings and/or situations: dysfunctional, dysentery, disturb, distress, distort, distraught, disappoint, which raises a serious question as to whether the word 'disability', with all of the negative linguistic baggage attached

[8] Virgil, *The Aeneid*, Book VI (264–94), www.poetryintranslation.com/PITBR/Latin/VirgilAeneidVI.htm.

to its prefix is the best word to use to describe people with physical or cognitive limitations. Indeed, this etymological analysis sheds light on why the UPIAS, Michael Oliver and other disability scholars wanted to apply 'disability' to the oppressive nature of society rather than any limitations experienced by individuals in their minds and/or bodies. The pure social model of disability, in essence, directs all the negative associations of the prefix 'dis' away from individuals and towards social oppression; this may also help to explain why civil society organizations such as the DPI found it so hard to settle on *any* definition of disability because it seems almost impossible to escape the profoundly negative connotations associated with 'dis' while trying to embrace the positive connotations of 'disability' over other negative terms.

The question becomes whether it is possible to escape these etymological associations and use it as a neutral or even positive term in theory and practice as most disability scholars/advocates and international documents would argue or whether, despite its ubiquity, its profound negative baggage might suggest that it ought to be abandoned? Some disability advocates suggest alternative terms to 'disability' including 'differently abled', 'extraordinary' or 'special needs', but as Susan Wendell argues, there are perils in such attempts:

> The introduction of new... euphemistic expressions for disabilities [such as] 'differently abled'... suggest that there is nothing wrong with being the way people with disabilities are, just different... Yet to call someone 'differently-abled' is much like calling her 'differently-coloured' or 'differently-gendered'. It says: 'This person is not the norm or paradigm of humanity.' If anything, it increases the Otherness of people with disabilities [and] suggests a... disregard of the special difficulties, struggles and suffering people with disabilities face. We are *dis-abled*. We live with particular social and physical struggles that are partly consequences of our bodies and/or minds and partly consequences of the structures and expectations of our societies, but they are struggles that only people with bodies and /or minds like ours experience. (Wendell 1996: 80)

Wendell argues that in the real lives of people with disabilities, there are good reasons to continue to use the word 'disability' exactly because it carries with it the idea of difficulty or struggle. This is a critically important point and reminds us that disabilities can be painful, difficult and very negative for the person living with them as well as their caregivers and families in and of themselves and not only because of a hostile environment.[9]

The issue raised by Wendell of how negatively we should view, in particular, the limitations experienced by the disabled opens up a profound

[9] I am grateful to Maxine Eichner, Professor of Law at University of North Carolina School of Law for drawing my attention to this issue in such a clear and compelling way.

set of questions with no simple answers as to what language we should use or *not* use. It is the question at the heart of the debate between Martha Nussbaum and Eva Kittay over whether disability or certain kinds of disability are inherently 'tragic'. Nussbaum in earlier versions of her analysis of disability wrote of its tragic nature and Kittay responded that one must be careful not to assume from a non-disabled perspective that the life of a person with a disability is necessarily tragic as opposed to simply different. As important as Kittay's observation that a 'tragic' narrative so ubiquitous to Western practice and theory should not be the only or even dominant understanding of what it is to live with disability, it is equally important to recognize, as Wendell and Nussbaum argue, that disabilities *can* be painful and even tragic.

I would add to this debate over the 'tragic' or painful nature of *some* disabilities, the specific and universal sense of sadness and loss experienced by individuals and their families with the onset of increasing physical and/or mental limitations at the end of life. This universal dimension of disability is particularly germane if one accepts the definition articulated in both the ICF and WRD as something that occurs to us all at some point in our lives. My own experience when my father became increasingly 'disabled' both mentally and physically before he died was a deep sense of sadness and loss as he struggled, at a rapid rate, with a daily set of rapidly increasing limitations on his mind and body. This loss of function due to terminal illness or old age is universal, indeed it is exactly because this is the case that the sadness and sense of tragedy associated with end-of-life limitations should not overwhelm the experience of many people living with disabilities throughout their lives who see themselves as neither unfortunate nor tragic but simply different from others and one manifestation of human diversity to be preserved and protected rather than prevented or cured.

Ultimately, disabilities ought to be viewed as having both positive and negative dimensions rather than being unrelentingly negative or even tragic, particularly if such images of disability are projected onto the disabled from a non-disabled perspective. The challenge for political theory is to find a language strong enough to replace the long-held view that disability as defect is inherently and relentlessly negative or tragic (which, in turn, creates enormous linguistic and social barriers to people with disabilities who wish to see themselves as simply one dimension of human diversity) while simultaneously acknowledging that disability can be profoundly negative and even tragic in the lived experience of some individuals and their families either at certain points in their lives or over the whole course of a life when one lives with particular kinds of disability.

Accepting that disability is universal over the lifespan does not change the centrality of the principle 'nothing for us without us', meaning those people with disabilities at any particular moment must continue to be the advocates that articulate the meaning of disability and the paradigms and language by which they are governed.

Which is why, while this analysis of the prefix 'dys/dis' seems to suggest that 'disability' may not be a perfect term given the negative etymological baggage described above, it is the word chosen by disability advocates and scholars themselves to anchor their work and the ICF, the UNCRPD and the WRD in turn. As such, as long as it remains the preferred language of the disabled, it must also be the language used by everybody else. And as Wendell argues, even its negative connotations may be useful to remind us that there are indeed challenges and difficulties living with certain kinds of disabilities, the term itself as a replacement to 'handicapped' or 'crippled/retarded' reflects a larger political process on the part of the disabled of transcending negative language. Thus, like queer studies recaptured and redefined 'queer' in ways that were positive and neutral rather than simply negative, people with disabilities have redefined and redeployed disability (including its prefix) to reflect their realities, be they positive, neutral and/or negative – an important form of politics in and of itself.

The Why of Disability? Changing Causes

Column three of the table speaks to the 'causes' of disability and is, of course, closely linked to both the 'where' and 'what' of disability in Western political theory and practice. The perceived causes of disability have changed over the modern era, a point manifested in the changes in political theory from one century to the next in the three authors described above. In the seventeenth and eighteenth centuries, disability was viewed as something caused by nature but ultimately the result of God's will. As such, while the disabled were viewed as defective, so too were all human beings in relation to the perfection of God who had created all humans in his image, and helps to explain why the overarching principle towards disability at this time was one of charity manifested in both Locke's and Hume's political theories, as discussed.

In the nineteenth century, under the influence of science and the emerging biological theories of evolution and statistics, nature or, more specifically, natural selection was thought to cause human variation, including disability. With nature and natural selection replacing God as the cause of disability, the disabled moved from being the *same* as other human beings but different *in degree* (all being imperfect relative to God) to becoming the *opposite* of, and hence different *in kind* from, 'normal' human beings, that is abnormal or defective. Science, particularly Galton's statistical science, thus measured the degree of defect on a 'normal curve', which as discussed earlier, manifested itself in contemporary theory in Rawls' use of the term 'normal' to define the parameters of the original position.

After the First World War, the cause of disability shifted again to human action and choices rather than 'God's will' or 'natural selection'. And as has already been discussed under the 'what' of disability, this change in the cause of disability led to rehabilitation becoming the principle governing the disabled for much of the twentieth century. The cause shifted in the second half of the twentieth century with the advent of the word 'handicapped'. The cause of disability became bad luck or misfortune (the word 'handicap' is taken from a game of luck, known as 'hand in cap'). Leading contemporary theorists, including Dworkin, as discussed above, and Charles Taylor use the term 'handicapped' in their theories because of this principle of both 'bad luck' and burden. Taylor thus claims the handicapped are the victims of 'circumstances that have befallen them' (Taylor 1994; Arneil 2009). Put simply, as the cause of disability shifts from God to nature to human action to bad luck, the overarching principle by which the disabled are governed likewise changes from charity to institutionalization to rehabilitation to compensation for the handicapped.

Disability scholars and advocates have challenged the 'whys' of disability, linked necessarily to the redefining of the 'where' and 'what' of disability as described above. It follows that if the 'where' of disability involves environmental barriers, it cannot be God, nature, bad luck or misfortune that caused these barriers, but society itself. International documents like the ICF and WRD not only claim the causes of disability must include 'social' or environmental factors but also go so far as to argue that the interactive nature of disability ultimately means it is not as important to identify the exact *cause*s of disability as it is to identify the *impacts*, specifically the degree to which full equality and inclusion are supported and facilitated in relation to *both* health conditions and environmental barriers. 'The ICF… by shifting the focus from cause to impact… places all health conditions on an equal footing allowing them to be compared using a common metric – the rule of health and disability.' It is worth noting that Statistics Canada has followed the ICF example and changed its definition of disability to 'impacts and limits on participation' in their 2001 Participation and Activity Limitations Survey (PALS), instead of measuring individual limitations and their causes in the 1991 Health and Activity Limitations Survey (HALS).[10] Ultimately, it is not simply that the 'causes' of disability have changed through recent international documents but the question is raised as to whether identifying such causes actually matters, compared to ascertaining its impact.

New Definitions of Disability: Implications for Political Theory

It is clear from the preceding analysis that the three dimensions of modern liberal theory's definitions of disability ('where', 'what' and 'why') as used by Locke, Hume and Rawls are untenable in contemporary political theory when viewed in light of the emergence of new definitions constituted by people with disabilities themselves manifested in disability scholarship/advocacy and through recently negotiated international documents. The challenge posed by these new definitions is not simply to include them and therefore people with disabilities into existing concepts (freedom, equality/cooperation and justice), the concepts themselves must be rethought since each one is explicitly constituted in opposition to disabled minds and/or bodies as described earlier. At the heart of this problem is the underlying binary upon which all of these old definitions are founded: autonomous, 'normal', rational citizens with rights constituted in opposition to a minority of dependent, defective people with needs. What is clear from the preceding analysis is that the new 'where, what and why' of disability, as described above must be fully incorporated. In this last section I hope to outline what I see to be some basic elements of a political theory of citizenship that incorporates these new definitions of disability into its understanding of equality and freedom.

Given that the new 'where' of disability is understood now as an interactive process of health conditions and environmental barriers rather than simply an individual defect, political theory needs to remove the linguistic barriers to full inclusion within its own language as described above. From there, it needs to theorize the accommodations necessary to ensure the full citizenship of all. As such, a substantive and more robust definition of equality would be needed than the one articulated in liberal theory. As discussed earlier, Hume and Rawls deploy a *formal*, procedural definition of equality only by defining disabled people outside the ambit of justice (being unable to resist or cooperate). If disability is located not only in the individual but in the environment, a *substantive* definition of

[10] Stats Canada 'A New Approach to Disability Data', 2001, www.statcan.gc.ca/pub/89-578-x/89-578-x2002001-eng.pdf, p. 17.

equality is necessary to ensure barriers are removed and accommodations provided as necessary to the real equality of the disabled.

As a factum by the Council of Canadians with Disabilities argued in a 2011 case (*B.C. v Moore*) before the Supreme Court of Canada,[11] 'substantive equality' means society has a *positive* duty to accommodate people with disabilities rather a *passive* duty not to discriminate against them or to 'treat them the same as all others'. If the court embraces formal equality and the liberal principle of 'same treatment' for all within any 'duty to accommodate', equality rights become meaningless for people with disabilities. Thus, the new 'where' of disability requires the state to go beyond charity, rehabilitation, compensation and non-discrimination through a substantive redefinition of equality to proactively address barriers, accommodations and supports.

The new 'what' and 'why' of disability also requires political theory to purge itself of the universally negative language of 'inferiority', 'defect', 'incapacity', bad luck and misfortune within its own texts and embrace the idea of human diversity (even as it retains the recognition of difficulties and challenges associated with various kinds of disabilities). Just as multicultural theorists (Kymlicka, Taylor) brought critical attention to theorizing citizenship in ways that accommodate ethnic diversity (by challenging the assumed universality and cultural neutrality of classical liberal democracy), so too disability theorists require political theorists to reconceptualize a seemingly neutral able-bodied world as one actually shaped by ableist assumptions. It follows in both cases, that states have a duty to protect and preserve cultural differences and human diversity (including disability) rather than allowing such cultures or disabilities to be pathologized and eliminated through an ostensibly neutral frame that is, in reality, hostile to difference.

The unrelenting focus on the prevention of 'defects' in the medical realm in particular requires a theory that, at the very least, redraws the terrain of choice by including neutral and positive dimensions of disability. If disability were theorized as a dimension of human diversity rather than negative defect as is currently done, 'birth defects' detected through new reproductive technologies will become something different both in language and in substance. While the human rights protocol around the human genome is a good starting point for developing a political theory that supports disability as human diversity, these insights need to be expanded through the state and fully disseminated in the public healthcare systems so that whatever choices women and their partners

[11] *British Columbia (Ministry of Education) v Moore* (2010 BCAA 478). CCD Factum in the *Moore* case can be found at www.ccdonline.ca/en/humanrights/litigation/moore-factum.

make on continuing a pregnancy are done in light of both the specific medical downsides of certain disabilities *as well as the* human benefits to themselves and society of protecting and preserving human diversity in its various forms.

The new 'what and why' of disability at the international level also requires political theory to incorporate disability as something experienced universally as part of the human experience as opposed to Locke, Hume, Rawls and Dworkin, who invariably define disability as something that occurs to a minority of persons who have defects because of misfortune. The new universal definition of disability challenges not only traditional liberal theories but also disability advocates who define disability as *only* a minority group issue similar to other minorities subject to oppression (the UK social model) and/or civil rights/equality/anti-discrimination (the US/Canada civil rights model). While it is important to recognize the universality of disability over the entire lifespan of all human beings, it is also important to recognize that at any given time only a minority of people experience disabilities, including some who are disabled their entire lives. Given the history of non-disabled people misrecognizing people with disabilities as described above, the central principle, 'nothing about us without us', used by disability advocates and scholars should not be diluted by the recognition of universality. Instead, what I am arguing is that the new 'what and why' of disability requires political theory to theorize disability as simultaneously something that is *particular to a specific group at a given point in time* (and thus nothing about us without us is key) *and universal to us all across the lifespan* (and thus something we all see as central to our own identity).

Finally, freedom or autonomy as defined in most liberal theory as the antonym to dependence needs to be replaced by some other understanding. It is important to note that autonomy or 'independent living' has been an important principle for many people with disabilities, so it is not that this concept of autonomy is meaningless (as some care theorists argue), but rather the binary between freedom and dependence needs to be replaced with something else. That something else is *interdependence*, which I believe would be the underlying guiding principle of a political theory inclusive of disability. Thus, just as the 'where' of disability leads us to a substantive rather than formal definition of equality, the new 'what' and why of disability leads us to replace the binary of autonomy/rights versus dependency/needs of liberal theory with a principle of interdependence.

Interdependence means dependency would not be an *antonym* to autonomy or freedom, as liberal theory assumes, but its precondition and correlate. As disability scholar Michael Davidson (2007: i–ii) observes: "A number of disability activists... see dependence not as a relinquishing of agency to the care of others but as a constellation of interrelations, whose ultimate trajectory is independence." Dependence, understood in this way, becomes intertwined with independence as a goal for most human beings and shifts our lens as political theorists from disability as a site of 'dependency' and the non-disabled as a site of autonomy to ask ourselves what set of social relations might be necessary to support both dependence and facilitate independence simultaneously for all, including disabled people?

If interdependency, along with a substantive definition of equality, were to replace the binary undergirding the traditional 'where, what and why' of disability upon which so much liberal theory rests with an alternative gradient scale in which we are all, in various ways and to different degrees, both dependent on others and independent, depending on the particular stage we are at in the lifecycle as well as the degree to which the world is structured to respond to some variations better than others, political theory will have gone a long way toward the full inclusion of people with disabilities into its own understanding of citizenship through a redefinition of the key concepts of equality and freedom.

2 The Ableist Contract: Intellectual Disability and the Limits of Justice in Kant's Political Thought

*Lucas G. Pinheiro**

Introduction

As Carole Pateman (1988: ix) rightly noted in the preface to *The Sexual Contract*: "There has been a major revival of interest in contract theory since the early 1970s that shows no immediate signs of abating." Since Pateman penned these words in the late 1980s, scholarly interest in the social contract has, as she surmised, far from abated.[1] Following the "contractarian renaissance" that ensued from John Rawls' *A Theory of Justice* in 1971, the social contract reinstituted its standing in the Anglo-American academy as "a recurrent feature of contemporary political philosophy" (Boucher and Kelly 1994: 1). For well over four decades, political theorists have incessantly elicited the social contract as a model for ideal theory, a device for normative approaches to justice, and a subject of disputed historical inquiry.[2]

While the origins of the social contract can be traced to classical antiquity when Glaucon defined justice as the product of a compact among men in Plato's *Republic*, the social contract of modern political thought begins in 1651 with Thomas Hobbes, whose *Leviathan* is widely recognized as a key intellectual reference for some of the most influential European political ideas of the seventeenth and eighteenth centuries

* I would like to thank Christopher Brooke, Nancy Hirschmann, Barbara Arneil, and the anonymous reviewers from Cambridge University Press for their insightful feedback on earlier drafts of this chapter. I first presented this essay at the 2013 American Political Science Association Annual Meeting, and I am grateful for the comments I received from those present that day, including the editors and many of the contributors to this volume. I would also like to express my gratitude for the Department of Political Science at the University of Chicago and the members of my dissertation committee – Patchen Markell, Jennifer Pitts, and Sankar Muthu – for their support.

[1] The three central figures in the contractarian revival of the 1970s and 1980s were John Rawls (2003 [1971]), Robert Nozick (1974), and David Gauthier (1986).

[2] For contractarian reconstructions, see Jean Hampton (1999) and Gregory Kavka, (1999). For applications of contractarian arguments to global justice, see Thomas Pogge (2002b) and Charles Beitz (2005). For historical analyses, see Harro Höpfl and Martyn Thompson (1979) and Deborah Baumgold (2010).

(Kymlicka 1993).[3] In more ways than one, the contractual character of modern theories of justice stems from Hobbes' original framework. Indeed, the legacy of the social contract as an ideal and universal theory for a just, free, and equal political society has fundamentally influenced the course of Western political ideas for over three centuries.

Shortly after its Rawlsian revival, however, social contract theory was authoritatively questioned as its claim to universality came under rigorous feminist scrutiny. While Susan Moller Okin's (1979) *Women in Western Political Thought* is often credited as the pioneering feminist critique of the Rawlsian renaissance, Carole Pateman and Teresa Brennan's (1979: 198) "Mere Auxiliaries to the Commonwealth" remains one of the most trenchant early critiques of the patriarchal foundations of modern political thought.[4] By arguing that women's subjection voided the premise of natural freedom and equality in Hobbes and Locke, Pateman and Brennan introduced a novel and unrelenting challenge to the social contract tradition (Pateman 2007: 214). This challenge – brought forth in the political problem of marriage – is a pivotal motif in Pateman's (1988) classic revision of contractarian theory in *The Sexual Contract*, where she exposes patriarchal marginalization as an endemic and pervasive feature of the social contract tradition that permeates the core of its theoretical and political edifice.

In *The Sexual Contract*, Pateman famously decried the very idea of a "social contract," whose avowal of universal freedom and justice was a mere artifice: a fictitious veneer for masculine exclusivity premised upon the subjection of women (1988: 1–18). Within the "sexual contract," Pateman argued, contractarian notions of political right are properly stripped of their universal character and reduced to a patriarchal maneuver deployed to mask the reality of "sex-right"; that is, women's lack of right (1988: 1–3, 105–6). From this vantage, then, contract, the act whence political society originates, transforms natural, equal freedom "into civil mastery and subordination" for women (1988: 76). Whereas the social contract recounts a story of justice, freedom, and equality among men, the sexual contract disinters – from centuries-old patriarchal formulations of man as the rightful universal subject of

[3] As Höpfl and Thompson (1979: 920–5) contend, the intellectual origins of classical contract theory remain largely contested. For a classical forerunner of the social contract in Book II of *The Republic*, see: Plato (1991: 36–7): "[I]t seems profitable – to those who are not able to escape the one [injustice] and choose the other [justice] – to set down a compact among themselves neither to do injustice nor to suffer it. And from there they began to set down their own laws and compacts and to name what the law commands lawful and just. And this, then, is the genesis and being of justice." For Hobbes' canonical formulation of contract and covenant, see: Hobbes (1985: chapter 14, especially 192–4).

[4] See also Coole (1994: 193).

justice – a history of subjugation and marginality for women (1988: 2–10). Stemming from Pateman's critique, Charles W. Mills (1997) argued nearly a decade later in *The Racial Contract*, that white supremacy was for the "Racial Contract" what patriarchy represented in the "sexual contract": a suppressed normative framework premised upon the moral and political exclusion of non-white subjects from formulations of personhood and citizenship alike.[5] In exposing the tradition's exclusionary structure veiled by an illusory universalism, Pateman and Mills crafted a significant and lasting challenge to the Rawlsian-propelled "contractarian renaissance."

In this chapter, I build on the critiques advanced by Pateman and Mills in an attempt to extend their political projects to the realm of intellectual disability. My aim is therefore to outline a preliminary model for revealing a third case of contractarian exclusion through what I call the "ableist contract." The ableist contract mirrors its sexual and racial progenitors in one vital respect. While the classical social contract broaches a conjectural theory of universal freedom and inclusion, the sexual, racial, and ableist contracts disclose veiled historical realities of targeted subjection – that is, earmarked practices of marginalization intended to exclude politicized identities whose perceived singularities threatened the homogeneity of the social contract's claim to universality.[6] Wherever Pateman speaks of patriarchy and Mills of racism as normative structures responsible for the political and moral estrangement of women and non-white populations, I employ the concept of "ableism," which I define – for the purposes of this argument – as modalities, mechanisms, and techniques of marginalization and oppression specifically directed at disabled persons due to their disabilities. As I argue below, this moral and political form of targeted subjection takes place in specific and intricate ways throughout Immanuel Kant's treatment of justice, which encompasses his formulations of rights, duties, the public and private sphere, freedom, civil society, citizenship, personhood, and the human species.

This chapter is part of a broader project on the question of disability in the history of modern political thought from Hobbes to Rawls, going through Locke, Rousseau, and Nietzsche (Pinheiro 2012a, 2012b, 2012c, 2014, 2015a, 2015b). My primary goal in introducing

[5] Mills (1997: 9–13) makes a semantic distinction in his work between the Racial Contract and the "Racial Contract."

[6] The central difference between Mills' approach and Pateman's is her conception of contract as *necessarily* oppressive. In Mills' work, domination within the social contract is more contingent than it is for Pateman who remains hostile to the project of retrieving the social contract for positive ends. Mills, however, advocates retrieving Rawls' contractarian framework for racial justice, a theoretical move he has recently called the "liberalization of illiberal liberalism" (Mills 1997: 136n9, 137; 2007: 79–80, 104–5; 2012).

the "ableist contract" as a foil to the social contract is to foreground the latent capacity-laden modes of exclusion in social contract theory while, at the same time, assessing how these forms of marginalization affect some of the most canonic modern ideas of justice in the history of Western political thought. While I recognize the question of capacity as a defining element in explaining the social contract's antagonistic relationship to disability, I find it insufficient as a means of conveying the scope and sophistication of the contract's structural indisposition to enfranchising the disabled. As I argue elsewhere, social contract theorists, such as Locke and Rousseau, exclude both the intellectually *and* physically disabled from many of the fundamental political concessions of their theories (Pinheiro 2012b, 2012c, 2015b). As much for Locke as for Rousseau, mind and body exist in a state of continual flux, at once inalienable and interdependent. On these materialist accounts of personhood, the cognitive development of rationality in the mind is contingent upon, and necessarily preceded by, the physical development of an able and healthy body, such that reason is not simply related to the body in some vague and contingent way. Rather, the able mind is strictly *dependent* on an able body. Locke and Rousseau therefore justify excluding the physically disabled from the social contract because their "deformed," "crippled," or "improper" bodies, in lying outside the able-bodied somatic norm, do not yield the physical competences necessary for the development of rational thought in the mind.

In recent years, scholars have begun to interrogate social contract theory from a critical disability perspective. These critiques have been largely based on the problem of rational capacity, outlining the ways in which the contract's threshold of reason represents an insurmountable barrier to entry for the severely intellectually disabled, who are, as a result, excluded from the contract's realm of justice. In my view, however, critiques of the social contract premised exclusively upon the problem of capacity – important, necessary, and forceful though they are – do not go far enough in renouncing the discriminatory ableism at the core of the tradition.[7] While these interpretations bring forth a theoretical failure in the contractarian framework, they often overlook the empirical depiction of disability offered by modern thinkers who, as I argue below regarding Kant, explicitly single out disability by constructing the disabled as embodied antagonists of their political theories. The disabled are therefore excluded from the social contract not only in light of the contract's threshold for rational capacity but also in spite of it; that is, the disabled are deliberately and

[7] For critiques of disability from the perspectives of capabilities and capacity, respectively, see: Martha Nussbaum (2004, 2006, 2009) and Stacy Clifford (2014).

exclusively characterized as non-subjects of justice – outside the bounds of personhood, citizenship, and at times the human species – independently of the social contract's capacity-laden barriers to entry.

Moreover, if both the physically and intellectually disabled are selectively excluded from the classical contract, it follows that the discerning factor barring disabled subjects from these theories is not merely the disabled's alleged incapacity to do so, but additionally the ableist renderings of disability by social contract theorists as "deviant," "deformed," "lacking," "abject," and altogether "inferior," regardless of whether the disabled are deemed capable of reason. To be clear if a rational yet physically disabled person can be excluded from social contract theories, as in Locke and Rousseau, then this exclusion is premised on an ableist formulation of disability as the mark of an exceptional and irreconcilable political and moral inferiority, rather than on the disabled subject's capacity for rational thought alone. Thus, the idea of "ableism," as I define it above, is an indispensable condition of the social contract's political relationship to disability that is not entirely captured in the question of rational capacity.

With these theoretical considerations in mind, this chapter probes the political and moral spaces occupied by intellectually disabled subjects in the political, ethical, and moral thought of Immanuel Kant. To this end, I place particular emphasis on the ways in which Kant's "empirical" observations on disability fundamentally impact his political formulations of justice, freedom, citizenship, personhood, and the human species. My approach to interpreting intellectual disability in Kant's theory of justice begins with a close reading of his practical definitions of disability in lesser-known works on anthropology, physical geography, and natural history. I then deploy this reading as a source for contextualizing his political ideas and thus uncovering the meaning and political significance of his exclusionary terminology in the *Metaphysics of Morals* as it pertains to the treatment of intellectually disabled subjects in his theory of justice. It is important to note that, in the context of Kant's political and moral philosophy, I use the term "contract" figuratively, since my argument applies broadly to contractarian ideas of rights, freedom, civil society, and justice in the history of modern political thought as a whole. So, with respect to Kant, "contract" operates as a placeholder for the totality of his political constituency which is composed by his moral laws, doctrines of rights and duties (private and public), theory of the state, scale of progress, and formulation of civil society.

To be sure, Kant's political ideas – including his definitions of justice, personhood, freedom, rights, duties, citizenship, and the state – are not limited to the *Metaphysics of Morals*, just as they are not exclusive to his writings on practical and transcendental philosophy. Much the contrary, in fact, Kant articulates his political theory through an expansive and eclectic array of sources, scattered across an impressively diverse range of fields and genres well beyond his strictly political writings and moral philosophy.[8] Although perhaps unfamiliar to a contemporary political theory audience, Kant's empirical works encompass a detailed, rich, and intricate sociopolitical system, whose relevance to his political ideas I attempt to recover by interpreting his onomasiology of intellectual disability. Indeed, as I will argue, Kant's understanding of disability affects and informs his theory of justice in such constitutive ways that its continual neglect has resulted in an insufficiently critical and accurate interpretation of Kant's political thought writ large. From a broader perspective, my interpretation of disability in Kant seeks to recast the political thrust of Kant's theory by rearticulating its relationship to other strains of the Kantian corpus that, while less accepted, less philosophical, and undoubtedly less agreeable, are, on my account, no less politically and philosophically significant to his thought than the "strictly" political and philosophical works.

As of late, a host of scholars in disability studies have vocally contested Kant's moral theory of personhood. This burgeoning literature on Kant and disability is largely composed of critical responses to the works of Jeff McMahan (1995, 1996, 2002, 2005, 2009) and Peter Singer (1994, 2009), both of whom vindicate non-human moral standing by grounding the corporeal existence of animals within an ethically defensible, intra-species moral realm, akin to that of Kant's person. In his work, McMahan (2009: 583–4) invokes cognitive disability as the premise of a *reductio* argument that figures the severely intellectually disabled as a rhetorical device tasked with exposing the logical contradiction of theories that grant moral status to the severely mentally disabled while denying it to non-human animals with commensurate cognitive capacities. Singer likewise argues that, since many non-human animals possess cognitive capacities that are often on a par with or superior to, those of severely intellectually disabled humans, it is altogether groundless and unjustifiable – that is, "speciesist" – to deny the former group (animals) moral standing while extending it to the latter (the disabled) (1994, 2009: 567–8).

In building their philosophical arguments for intra-species moral standing, both Singer (2009: 573–4) and McMahan (2002: 245–6, 252–5)

[8] For a collection of key texts in Kant's political thought, see Pauline Kleingeld's edited volume titled, Toward Perpetual Peace *and Other Writings on Politics, Peace, and History* (Kant 2006b) and *Practical Philosophy*, edited by Mary J. Gregor (Kant 1996).

rely prominently on Kant's personhood–animality split as a means to support their formulations of extra-corporeal moral status, grounded on intellectual predispositions and cognitive capacities. Yet, both philosophers part ways with Kant insofar as they believe human animality and species membership should play no role as criteria for determining moral life (Singer 2009: 572–3; McMahan 2002: 148, 209–17).[9] McMahan's (2009: 604) idea that "differences of moral status are grounded in differences of psychological capacity" prefigures Singer's (2009: 575) suggestion to "abandon the idea of the equal value of all humans" and replace it with a "graduated view in which moral status depends on some aspects of cognitive ability." As a result, both Singer and McMahan advocate integrating non-human animals to a moral community of "persons" at the expense of denying personhood to humans who fall below a Kantian moral threshold rooted entirely in cognitive capacity as opposed to human animality.

Unsurprisingly, Singer and McMahan have received ample criticism from scholars seeking to include or maintain the cognitively disabled within the bounds of our moral community of persons. As I see it, the central and most politically salient aspect of these critiques resides in the Kantian discourse Singer and McMahan mobilize in support of their projects. Pushing back against rationalist conceptions of moral status, philosopher Eva Kittay (2001, 2005a, 2005b, 2009a, 2009b) has argued that species membership alone should suffice as a criterion for equal moral status among human beings. Licia Carlson (2009, 2010), who furthers Kittay's critique of reason-centric moral theories, questions the political discourse through which these conceptions of personhood have been articulated. She recalls, for example, that viewing humans as animals "is precisely the basis on which the most horrific atrocities are justified" (2010: 160). Carlson also outlines important ways in which critiques of speciesism, such as Singer's, "rely on ableist assumptions and arguments" (2010: 157). Although Kittay and Carlson do not comment directly on Kant's specific formulation of moral personhood, they effectively highlight how and why elevating cognitive capacity to the role of arbiter for moral life, as is the case with Kant's theory of personhood, has deeply problematic repercussions for the intellectually disabled.[10]

[9] Singer (2009: 568–70) lists the cognitive capacities of non-human animals he deems at worst on a par with, at best superior to those of cognitively disabled subjects. See McMahan's (2002: 148) critique of the "species norm," as well as his comments on human species membership (2002: 209–17).

[10] Carlson (2010: 2) traces the problem of personhood and disability to Kant's moral theory.

Other scholars writing on disability and political theory have also expressed profound skepticism toward rationalist formulations of moral personhood rooted in Kant's categorical imperative.[11] One notable critic of Kantian personhood from the standpoint of disability is Barbara Arneil (2009), whose key charge against Kant's moral theory is his crowning of rational autonomy as the foundation for human dignity (2009: 224). In its quest to "protect human dignity through the mutual recognition of others as rational self-legislating 'persons,'" Arneil remarks, Kant's moral theory consequently figures the "irrational" as "not 'autonomous' and strictly speaking not 'persons' and therefore not due the dignity accorded to 'rational beings'" (2009: 224–5).[12] Moreover, Arneil exposes how Kant's formulation of personhood has pervasively found its way to the backdrop of influential political theories of justice by the likes of John Rawls and Charles Taylor. Because Kant locates personhood in the human ability to reason, Arneil argues that contemporary authors who draw on Kant (such as Taylor) are consequently "forced to define those incapable of 'rationality' as outside the 'normal' meaning of personhood," as possessing an unrealizable *potential* to become human (2009: 225, 228). Together, these works by critical disability scholars illustrate how Kant's moral philosophy has sustained a political discourse that categorically exempts the disabled from the remits of justice.

Overall, three important conclusions can be drawn from the literature on Kant and disability. First, scholars working on intellectual disability and political theory have provided convincing arguments as to how Kantian conceptions of personhood misrecognize the inherent humanity of the intellectually disabled. Second, these scholars have compellingly identified why, from a political standpoint of justice, liberty, and equality, it is desirable to move away from such reason-centric formulations of moral status that privilege the able-minded over the intellectually disabled. Third, many of these commentators have conclusively outlined how Kant's moral philosophy is conceptually, albeit indirectly, implicated in the political marginalization of the disabled persons.

Notwithstanding the merits of their projects, the authors in question have limited their critiques of Kant's political thought to his moral and practical philosophies, or what is colloquially known as the "pure" segment of his work. Take Tobin Siebers' (2011: 89) following claim for

[11] For commentators who have critiqued the rationalist normativity in Kant's theory of moral personhood from the perspective of disability, see Buchanan (1990: 235–41); Stark (2009: 377–8); Becker (2005); Silvers and Francis (2009); and Hirschmann (2009: 157–60).

[12] Arneil (2009: 240n22) also argues that reason in Kant, "Refers every maxim of the will, regarding it as legislating universal to every other will and also to every action towards oneself."

instance: "Theories of rationality [...] configure rationality itself in terms of the objective properties and identifying characteristics of those agents whom Kant called rational beings, and these characteristics do not allow for the inclusion of people with disabilities." Siebers' point here illustrates a general trend in critiques of Kant's moral philosophy from the perspective of disability in which Kant's empirical views on the disabled are persistently overlooked. Because of this oversight, discussions of Kant and disability are limited to speculative arguments that hinge on the impenetrability of Kant's moral theory by the intellectually disabled. As such, Kant's extensive definitions of cognitive disability and lively figurations of disabled subjects have yet to be weighed against the political arguments of his moral and practical philosophy in an effort to assess how these views may effectively, rather than merely potentially, impact the meaning of his ideas about justice and thus sway their political and theoretical significance. As I argue throughout this chapter, Kant's empirical writings on disability are critical to this scholarly debate for two reasons. First, it is in these texts that Kant entertains political questions concerning the civil and moral standing of intellectually disabled subjects. Second, Kant's empirical works are essential to our understanding of his transcendental philosophy and political system, especially regarding the categorical imperative, because it is here – in his construction of the intellectually disabled – that Kant outlines the identity of those exceptional, irrational beings barred from the political concessions of justice.

By turning my attention to how, where, and why Kant's approach to justice fails with respect to the intellectually disabled, I intend to cast light on what I consider to be the margins of his moral philosophy and, as a result, delineate the limits of his political theory of justice. This marginal space wherein the intellectually disabled are enclosed exemplifies what Uday Mehta (1999) describes as the explicit exclusion of the unfamiliar, along with the erasure of their "sentiments, feelings, sense of location, and forms of life" (1999: 20–1). Such occult "spaces" of exception are, in Mehta's words, "places that when identified by the grid of Enlightenment rationality [become] only spots on a map or past points on the scale of civilizational progress, but not *dwellings* in which peoples lived and had deeply invested identities" (1999: 21).[13] To the extent that it moves toward recasting the meaning of his theory of justice, my interpretation of disability in Kant endeavors to reaffirm the political and conceptual significance of disability to the history of political thought and contemporary politicized identity. Read as such, I intend for the

[13] Mehta (1999: 21) notes: "These are the places that Frantz Fanon [1967: 182–3] with evocative simplicity called 'the zone of occult instability where people dwell.'"

reach of my argument to stretch beyond interpretations of Kant. By demonstrating just how problematic Kant's conception of justice is with regards to intellectual disability, this chapter consequently interrogates contemporary political theories whose ambit of justice, in being bound by reason, effectively forecloses the intellectually disabled from freedom, citizenship, and personhood.

The chapter is organized in three parts. I open by proposing two reasons why Kant's empirical writings are indispensable in determining the place intellectually disabled subjects occupy in his political constituency. I then probe Kant's empirical ethics – scattered across his work on anthropology, philosophy of history, physical geography, and applied moral philosophy – in order to engage his views on intellectual disability. At this juncture, I argue that Kant's distinction between what he defines as natural and social mental "deficiencies" informs the government of intellectually disabled persons in his empirical works. That is, while he constructs *socially* incurred cognitive "ailments" as curable and therefore not a cause for the suspension of civil union, he argues that *natural* intellectual "ills," such as "imbecility," "idiocy," and "madness," incur not merely pity but private confinement outside civil society. I pursue this argument in order to make sense of how Kant's empirical stances concerning disability affect the political and theoretical positions regarding justice he advances in his writings on moral and practical philosophy.

I conclude the chapter by engaging Martha Nussbaum's *Frontiers of Justice*, one of the first works to systematically address the question of intellectual disability and justice in the social contract tradition. By building on my reading of intellectual disability in Kant, I offer a corrective to Nussbaum's claim that disabled subjects are "omitted," rather than deliberately excluded, from classical social contract theories. For Nussbaum, a central problem regarding the place of the disabled in social contract theories is their exclusion from the initial position where the terms of the contract, including its threshold for membership, are first drafted. By focusing on omission, Nussbaum construes the relationship between contract and disability as a contingent and incidental problem. So, rather than attributing the problem of exclusion to the ideas of social contract thinkers, Nussbaum holds the social contract itself – its mechanisms and procedures – accountable for failing to accommodate and enfranchise disabled persons in light of the procedural approach to justice at the center of the tradition. By contrast, I argue that, unlike John Rawls' procedural contract theory, modern political thinkers – Locke, Rousseau, and Kant among them – explicitly elicit disabled identities in order to concretely illustrate natural life forms void of reason, autonomy, moral agency, and freedom. For Kant, disability is *not*, as it is in Rawls, left to the procedural mechanisms of his theory. Instead, Kant explicitly outlines, at specific moments in his empirical works, the political and moral standing of intellectually disabled subjects in his theory.

The Politics of Kant's Empirical Ethics

Kant's division between empirical and pure knowledge is a recurring conceptual distinction in his work, not only in regards to philosophical inquiry in general, but also with respect to the act of thinking in particular. "All cognitions," he discerns, "are either empirical, insofar as they presuppose sensations, or pure cognitions, insofar as they have no sensation as their ground" (Kant 2005: 103, 3956n). Whereas the latter form of cognition, which Kant calls "*conceptus intellectus puri* [pure concepts of the understanding]," originate in the understanding, the former arise in the senses (2005: 98, 3930n; 1997: 13, §400). In other words, because "pure concepts" are theoretical and abstract in nature, Kant treats them, for the most part, in his transcendental philosophy. "Impure concepts," on the other hand, being by nature empirical and concrete, are predominantly kept aside in his empirical works.

Building on Kant's distinction, Robert Louden (2000: 5) has suggested that to assess Kant's moral philosophy without recourse to its empirical constituency; that is, Kant's "impure ethics," amounts to a selective misrepresentation of his thought. In order to reassess the philosophical merits and shortcomings of Kant's writings on ethics as a whole, Louden pursues a systematic reinterpretation of Kant's philosophy by reintroducing impure ethics "into its rightful place within [Kant's] practical philosophy" (2000: viii, Chapter 1). In doing so, Louden sheds light on the important, though overwhelmingly neglected, relationship between Kant's empirical, transcendental, and political works.

My aim in drawing on Louden's work here is twofold. First, I hope to ground my analysis of Kant's views concerning intellectual disability on the conceptual thread woven through his impure and pure works as distinct yet mutually constitutive sides of Kant's political thought. Second, I will underscore how fragments of a system of political exclusion in Kant's philosophy only become salient and consequential to his political theory once his empirical arguments are properly considered.[14]

[14] For critiques concerning gender, see Sedgwick (1997) and Kleingeld (1993). For critiques concerning race, see Mills (2005b) and Eze (1995).

While in his pure ethics, Kant sets out to "locate and justify the fundamental a priori principles of morality," it is in his impure ethics that he takes on the task of empirically determining "how, when, and where to apply his *a priori* principles to human beings in order to make morality more efficacious in human life" (Louden 2000: 180). Louden makes clear the necessity of Kant's empirical ethics to the overarching system of his thought, while also revealing Kant's own sympathy for the integration of ethical theory and empirical knowledge of human nature as a means to make ethics more instrumentally useful to humans (Louden 2000: 170).[15]

Echoing Louden, Thomas McCarthy (2010: 47) argues that Kant's ethical thought can only illuminate human life once "the pure rays emanating from ideas of practical reason [...] are refracted through the denser medium of human nature, culture, and history" (2010: 47). McCarthy adds that, since the denser medium through which Kant's pure philosophical claims are refracted is tainted by prejudice, the philosophical positions coming out on the other side of the empirical spectrum were rife with political exclusions.

Even in his applied ethics, Kant probed human morality at the species, rather than the individual, level in an effort to understand the human being in terms of the *a priori* assumptions of his pure, moral theory (Louden 2000: 176). Kant's most "energetic and prevalent remarks," Louden suggests, "concern the moral destiny of the human species *as a whole*," ideas that, in being "driven by a strong teleological assumption," compose what is "a priori and non-empirical in his thought – "pure rather than impure" (2000: 176). Kant's empirical work is therefore grounded on pure philosophical axioms, rather than the other way around, revealing an order of development in his ethical thought, whereby moral axioms herald and delineate his empirical observations. On this account, Kant's philosophy is best described as an empirically informed, rather than an empirically determined, system.

By focusing exclusively on the impenetrability of Kant's categorical imperative scholars working on Kant and disability have largely overlooked his empirical views on the disabled mind, including the political purchase these positions may have on his practical philosophy. This oversight is part of a widespread interpretive tendency to bracket Kant's empirical judgments as though an "analytic cavity" divided his corpus in two allegedly disconnected folds: one "impure," irrelevant, minor, and empirical; the other "pure," relevant, important, and philosophical.

[15] For a complementary position see Wood (1999: 10–11, Chapter 6, 193–225).

By contrast, my focus on the connection between Kant's empirical ethics and practical philosophy places Kant's moral and political theories under the scrutiny of his empirical verdict on human nature, such that his taxonomy of disability becomes legible as an empirical projection of his moral theory and the latter a theoretical articulation of the former. To this end, I will pair Kant's institutional formulations of human nature with an exegetical analysis of his empirical positions on intellectual disability in order to lay bare the ways in which the rationality threshold of his categorical imperative corroborates his empirical construals of disability as politically and philosophically significant exceptions to his formulations of personhood, citizenship, and the human species.

In essence, Kant's overall conception of human nature is grounded in the subject's transition from a crude to a moral state through socialization. In his impure ethics, Kant recognizes the dependence of human moral development on communal relationships (Louden 2000: 173). Yet, Kant's institutional provisions for moral development also operate as instruments for political exclusion. That is, the process of socialization and community in Kant are emancipatory instruments of progress only to those human subjects whose potential for civic development in the public sphere is properly expressed by their use of reason. Since Kant designates the irrational as an exception to moral development, his institutions of socialization become institutions of sequestration for the intellectually disabled whose disability disbars them from the apparatuses tasked with moralizing humanity's crude nature. The main reason why Louden considers an empirically informed theory as a "more *useful* ethical theory" is because it reveals a specific moral human subject behind the abstract rational being of the categorical imperative (Louden 2000: 171).

The indispensable prerequisites for inclusion in Kant's moral theory are membership in the human species, followed by inclusion in institutions of socialization. Without the *a priori* requirement of human species membership, it is impossible to transition from the natural to the moral realm. In Louden's account, Kant's pure ethics applies to rational creatures in general and his impure ethics to human beings in particular. As such, Kant's (1997) oft-cited claim that every person is an end in himself features prominently in his pure philosophy, whose subject is the rational being. However, once Kant qualifies the rational subject of his theory as "human," he consequently brings to life the "species-specific features of human beings" that, in turn, "call into play the multiple roles of educational, civic, legal, artistic, scientific, and religious institutions in forming and shaping human moral character" (1997: 36, §428). So, *pace* Louden, I argue that Kant's transformation of his subject of justice from the rational to the human being in his empirical writings has the effect of narrowing down the scope of his theory in light of the limitations of Kant's definition of human beings. Yet on his final assessment of the role played by institutions in Kant's theory of progress, Louden denies that Kant's empirical views on race, gender, and ethnicity affect his ethical and moral theory in a philosophically meaningful.

According to Charles W. Mills (2005b: 175–9) and Pauline Kleingeld (1993: 142–3), the respective racialization and gendering of Kant's human subject in his empirical works cast serious doubt on the universality of his moral philosophy. McCarthy (2010: 47) aptly expresses this tension by noting that Kant's empirical positions on human nature are "'impure' in more than one sense." Louden (2000: 81), on the other hand, classifies Kant's treatment of race and gender, which he tenderly derides as "hard to swallow," into a lower epistemic order in the Kantian system, ultimately dismissing them as contingent and philosophically inconsequential (2000: 177–8). Yet, as Mills and Kleingeld make plain, Kant's empirical definition of the human being offers a concrete corrective to the illusive universalism of his practical philosophy. Siding with Mills, Kleingeld, and McCarthy, I argue that the exclusionary thrust of Kant's thought can only be revealed by taking heed of how his marginalization of women, non-whites, and the disabled in his empirical texts sustain the political arguments of his practical philosophy.

Nature, Society, and Disability in Kant

In his 1764 "Essay on the Maladies of the Head," Kant (2007 [1764a]: 69) sets up an empirical lexicon of derangement where he identifies two possible manifestations of "mental frailty": the social, which incurs contempt, and the natural, which incurs pity. The degree to which these conditions are said to abrade the mind informs Kant's judgment as to whether an ailment is private or public. In other words, his natural–social spectrum concerning origin and cause map onto his private–public split concerning cure and rehabilitation. According to Kant, natural mental derangements that incur pity are grounds for the suspension of civil community and confinement in the private realm. So, while scorned socially incurred frailties (such as "folly" and "foolishness") "do not suspend civil community," pitied and natural maladies are grounds for "official care provision" (2007 [1764a]: 69); that is, private confinement in "lunatic asylums" (2007 [1798]: 288, 320) and "madhouses" (2007 [1798]: 309) outside the public sphere. In other words, what sets natural mental maladies apart from social frailties is the need they engender for external (psychiatric and medical) intervention and extradition from the realm of politics in the form of coerced institutionalization. Kant reserves this medicalized private space for those he designates as naturally unfit to participate in civil society.

Although both the "mentally disturbed" and the "imbecile" bear mental illnesses that "suspend civil community," only imbecility is incurable. Therefore, the distinct types of "official care provision" extended to each group serve opposite ends. Whereas the disturbed and deranged receive medical treatment under the general guise of rehabilitation, imbeciles receive "care" in the form of permanent detention (Kant 2007 [1764a]: 69). Kant's classification of cognitive disability as either social or natural hinges on, among other things, an underlying distinction between acquired and congenital ailments, which is consistent in his portrayals of sensory, physical, and intellectual disabilities. Kant defines congenital intellectual deficiencies as an incurable product of nature that marks the impossibility of political society *par excellence*. This definition conforms with a fundamental tenet of his theory of progress, the idea that any rational human being is "destined by his reason to live in a society with human beings and in it to *cultivate* himself, to *civilize* himself, and to *moralize* himself by means of the arts and sciences" (2007 [1798]: 420).

In his depiction of deafness in the *Anthropology*, Kant develops the distinction between inborn and acquired disabilities by asking, "Which lack or loss of sense is more serious, that of hearing or sight?" To which he responds, "When it is *inborn*, the first [deafness] is the least replaceable of all the senses" (2007 [1798]: 271, emphasis added). At the dinner table, for instance, Kant describes a deaf person as generally "annoyed, distrustful, and dissatisfied, [...] condemned to solitude" (2007 [1798]: 420). Kant's representation of deafness is consonant with his understanding of congenital, inborn, and natural disabilities as an impediment to socialization. In fact, the similarities between Kant's definitions of deafness and idiocy illustrate how his selective naturalization of certain disabilities – as irremediable biological defects – operates as a pathological lever that discerns which types of disability occasion the suspension of civil community. Hereditary, innate, and inborn cognitive disabilities cannot, according to Kant, exist in the civil realm, for those who bear them are interminably condemned to their ill natures and confined to a private life.

For Kant (2007 [1764a]), natural man's animalistic instinct is a shelter that precludes him from socially incurred mental ailments: because he "never has cause to venture far in his judgment," no dementia can ever befall him and insanity is "wholly and entirely beyond his capacity." The simple demands of nature are thus reciprocated by the simplicity of man's crude understanding. Since very little wit finds its way to the natural mind, men are in nature "well secured against every craziness" (2007 [1764a]: 75). By contrast, mental maladies such as folly and dementia can only derange the more intrinsic and developed understanding of the citizen. They are for this reason, socially incurred intellectual deficiencies.

These aliments can, unlike their natural equivalents, be cured in the civil state: in Kant's words, "[They] "permit hope of a fortunate recovery, if only they are not hereditary" (2007 [1764a]: 77). Again, as in the case of deafness, Kant distinguishes inborn from acquired derangements by ascribing natural and social foundations to each, respectively. In fact, in his definitions of mental disturbances, Kant describes socially incurred frailties as a special strain of mental illnesses that can be medically treated, "if not to put an end to their ill, at least still to ease it" (2007 [1764a]: 76).

Kant's empirical conclusion is that, although civil society aggravates and sustains the process of mental disturbance, its origin is genetic. Cognitive illnesses, he notes, originate in a germ that develops unnoticed in the body followed by an "ambiguous reversedness [...] which does not yet give suspicion of a disturbance of the mind" (2007 [1764a]: 76). It is only as time elapses that "the malady breaks out and gives occasion to locate its ground in the immediately preceding state of the mind" (2007 [1764a]: 76–7). The only mental "abnormalities" that are, in Kant's account, entirely natural are also incurable: madness, idiocy, and imbecility.

Kant's natural–social separation of mental deficiency, which in the civil state translates into his reason-laden, public–private split, is rooted in the idea that mental ailments intrinsic to the state of nature must be at once hereditary and congenital; that is, "natural" rather than gradually developed in civil society. Among these, we find "madness" and "idiocy" which resemble "imbecility" to the extent they denote a lack in understanding. With the exception of these three natural and innate conditions (madness, imbecility, and idiocy), Kant traces all other mental maladies to political society as an expression of the deranged public reason of citizens. "The human being in the state of nature," he argues, "can only be subject to a few follies and hardly any foolishness," for "the disturbance of the mind can occur only seldom in this state of simplicity" (2007 [1764a]: 75).

If natural man, Kant suggests, is "ill in the head, he will be either idiotic or mad" (2007 [1764a]: 75). Much like imbecility, idiocy and madness are natural barriers to Kant's (1996 [1793]) "politico-civil state." In their capacity as non-political subjects, the imbecile, mad, and idiot must be physically removed from the public realm and taken back to a state of "external (brutish) freedom," for if they express no prospect of ever being guided by their own reason, they cannot, by their very nature, ever be autonomous and free (1996 [1793]: 132).

Imbecility, Immaturity, and Progress

Another important distinction Kant (2007 [1764a]: 69) draws in his medico-psychological lexicon pertains to the definitions of "impotency [*Ohnmacht*]" and "reversal [*Verkehrtheit*]." The former comes under the "general appellation of *imbecility* [*Blödsinnigkeit*]," the latter "under the name of the *disturbed mind* [*Gemüt*]." Importantly, imbecility describes a "great impotency of memory, reason, and generally even of sensations"; it is a condition of mental paralysis caused by the expiration of organs in the understanding – a weakness that "never allows the unfortunate person to leave the state of childhood" (2007 [1764a]: 70). The imbecile's confinement in a state of perpetual infancy has wider implications for Kant's theory of progress.[16] As Wood (1999: 292–3) argues, nature in Kant "can *never* serve as the guide for *human* beings, for to be fully human is to have attained the condition of maturity or enlightenment."

Kant returns to the question of imbecility in his *Anthropology* as a means to introduce an exceptional case of immaturity that is both natural and permanent. He warns that a man may "relapse into civil immaturity by reasons of state if, after his legal entry into full age, he shows a weakness of understanding with respect to the administration of his estate, which portrays him as a child or an imbecile" (2007 [1798]: 316). In order to convey the difference between civil and natural immaturity, Kant elicits the images of woman and child, respectively. While women are, "regardless of age, [...] declared to be immature in civil matters" (2007 [1798]: 315, 399), children are only temporarily immature until they attain the age of reason.[17] In being distinct from women and children, Kant's imbecile illustrates a third instance of immaturity at once natural and permanent. In sum, if woman represents *civil* immaturity *at all ages* and the child natural immaturity *up to a certain age*, the imbecile embodies *natural* immaturity at *all ages*.

Although the equation of imbecility (as well as idiocy) with perpetual infancy precedes Kant, his formulation of intellectual disability as the personification of permanent and natural immaturity, conveys an exceptional stage in his scale of development best described as natural stagnation, an anomaly forcefully relayed in his rendering of the

[16] The theme of human progress expressed as a transition from a crude to a perfect state features prominently in two of Kant's empirical works: "Idea for a Universal History with a Cosmopolitan Aim" (2007 [1784]) and his "Lectures on Pedagogy" (2007 [1803]).

[17] In his famous essay, "Observations on the Feeling of the Beautiful and the Sublime," Kant (2007 [1764b]: 41) goes as far to suggest that women have "just as much understanding as the male."

imbecile, whose mental weakness "never allows [him] to leave the state of childhood" (2007 [1764a]: 70). [18] According to Kant's (2007 [1786]) theory of progress, human history is "nothing other than the transition from the crudity of a merely animal creature into humanity, from the go-cart [*Gänglewagen*] of instinct to the guidance of reason – in a word, from the guardianship [*Unmündigkeit*] of nature into the condition of freedom" (2007 [1786]: 168).[19] In the context of this schema, Kant's imbecile symbolizes an exceptional curb in the wheels of progress moving history from the "epoch of nature" to the "epoch of freedom."[20]

Madness and Citizenship

In his treatment of the relationship between cognitive development and civil community, Kant introduces the concept of madness as a congenital defect that, much like idiocy and imbecility, frustrates any hope of cure and socialization. "The germ of madness," he claims, "develops at the same time with the germ of reproduction, so that this too is hereditary" (2007 [1978]: 322). Because "the accidental causes of this illness," are unknown to man it would be a mistake to define it "not as hereditary but rather as acquired, as if the misfortunate one himself were to blame for it" (2007 [1978]: 310). As such, madness is the "most profound degradation of humanity" that, though idiopathic, is unequivocally "attributable to *nature*" (2007 [1978]: 320, emphasis added). This profound degradation of humanity is only borne by the "mad [*toll*]," for whom "the word *deranged* is only a euphemistic expression" (2007 [1978]: 319). Madness is thus an "incurable disorder" that renders any and all prospect of cure entirely fruitless (2007 [1978]: 320). Yet, despite originating in nature, Kant sets madness apart from idiocy and imbecility inasmuch the madman does not, like the idiot, lack a soul. So, while madness degrades humanity it is not, unlike idiocy, an impediment to membership in the human species.

[18] Although the equation of intellectual disability to infancy was familiar in the nineteenth century (when Édouard Séguin's "physiological system for educating idiots" was widely adopted in France, Britain, and the United States), Rousseau also used it in the eighteenth century. Licia Carlson (2010: 28–33) discusses this question with reference to Séguin, Rousseau (1979: 61), Foucault (2008: 207–9), and others.

[19] Wood explains his translation of *Gänglewagen* as a "two-wheeled cart that was used in the eighteenth century to teach a child to walk by giving it support, the way training wheels are used on a bicycle." He also explains *Unmündigkeit* as the "'incapacity to make use of one's understanding without the guidance of another;' [Kant] defines 'enlightenment' (*Aufklärung*) as 'emergence from self-incurred guardianship,' and considers guardianship 'self-incurred' when it is due not to a lack of understanding but "to a lack of courage and resoluteness in thinking for oneself" (Kant 2007 [1786]: 168n).

[20] For an analysis of Kant's distinction between the "epoch of nature" and the "epoch of freedom," see Wood (1999: 296).

In line with Kant's reason-laden public/private dyad concerning social and natural intellectual maladies, madness – like imbecility and idiocy – calls for the suspension of civil union through the private confinement of madmen in "cells" (2007 [1978]: 310), "madhouses" (2007 [1978]: 309), and "lunatic asylums" (2007 [1978]: 288, 320). Madmen, Kant argues, must be guided by someone else's reason, for they lack the requisite maturity required for citizenship, which necessarily exempts them from the public realm. Unlike the madmen, whose dwelling is the psychiatric institution, "mentally deficient" figures such as the "simpleton, the imprudent person, the stupid person, the coxcomb, the fool, and the buffoon," are mentally ill not merely in degree:

> But in the distinctive quality of their mental discord, and because of their ailments they do not yet belong in the madhouse; that is, a place where human beings, despite the maturity and strength of their age, must sill, with regard to the smallest matters of life, be kept orderly through someone else's reason. (2007 [1978]: 309)

Indeed, "privacy," as a mode of understanding, emerges as the defining property of madness in Kant's empirical ethics. "The only universal characteristic of madness," he discerns, "is the loss of *common sense* (*sensus communis*) and its replacement with *logical private sense* (*sensus privatus*)" (2007 [1978]: 324). Kant's definition of *sensus privatus* personifies the rogue antithesis of his conception of civil union, for it starkly contrasts with his idea of sociopolitical stratification. Insofar as it opposes *sensus communis*, *sensus privatus* defies public deliberation and political participation in the form of a contradiction to the natural flow of progress.

Building on his definition of madness, Kant notes that the deprivation of the *Sensorio communi* characteristic of the mental illness known as versania is a natural restriction to citizenship. In versania, the deranged subject departs "from the *Sensorio communi* [common sense] that is required for the unity of *life*... [and] finds itself transferred to a faraway place (hence the word 'derangement')." Versania is reason gone awry, what Kant calls "positive unreason"; it is "the sickness of a deranged reason" (2007 [1978]: 321). Among other subjects whose unconditioned minds demand seclusion, the madman of versania is "the furthest removed from raving" due to his "self-enclosed speculation," a condition of "complete self-sufficiency" and private concealment within the body (2007 [1978]: 321). In this sense, madness is as much a mental as it is a bodily manifestation of privacy, in the form of private sensation and the private sphere. Mentally, the madman's cognition is bound by his *sensus privatus*; materially, his embodied experience is never projected outwards into the world. By emphasizing the enclosure of the madman's thoughts and sense perception within the fringes of his own person as well as his physical sequestration in the psychiatric cell, Kant elicits a forceful image of madness as a paragon of privacy in two registers: the private self and the private sphere.

According to Kant, restraining our understanding "by the *understanding of others*, instead of *isolating* ourselves with our own understanding and judging *publicly* with our private representations" is indeed a "subjectively-necessary touchstone of the correctness of our judgment generally, and consequently also of the soundness of our understanding" (2007 [1978]: 324). It is for this very reason that censorship of theoretical opinions "offends humanity," by robbing it of the "greatest and most useful means of correcting [its] own thoughts, which happens [because] we advance them in public in order to see whether they also agree with the understanding of others" (2007 [1978]: 324). The madman, for whom "private sense [is] already valid apart from or even in opposition to common sense," is "abandoned to a play of thoughts in which he sees, acts, and judges, not in a common world, but rather in his own world (as in dreaming)" (2007 [1978]: 324). Private confinement is thus taken to its limit in the case of madness, which represents the natural impossibility of thinking, sensing, and acting in public, that is, the failure to experience the social world. In sum, the mad subject's cognitive restraint within *sensus privatus* along with his embodied state of "self-enclosure" and institutional confinement reflect a unique asocial condition of total privacy.[21]

Further, Kant cordons off the mad from social, political, and civic rights and duties on account of their lack of control over their understanding. Given their state of natural, permanent immaturity, Kant defines the mad as necessarily dependent on others as prosthetic sources of reason, highlighting, once over, his construal of intellectual disability as the antipode of autonomy and freedom. "The *delirious raving* (*delirium*) of a person who is awake and in a *feverish* state," Kant remarks, "is a physical illness and requires medical attention." Yet, "only the delirious person, in whom the physician perceives no such pathological occurrences, is called *mad*" (2007 [1978]: 319). So, whereas the disabilities of the imbecile and the idiot preclude them from the human species, that of the madman denies him citizenship.

[21] As Kim Hall (1997: 258) argues, Kant's notion of "*sensus Communis*" is fundamental to his aesthetic theory in the third Critique, which she argues is a "contract dictated by our very humanity."

In the *Metaphysics of Morals*, Kant (1996 [1797]) explains, in straightforward juridical terms, the political consequences of and moral-juridical grounds for excluding non-subjects from civil society. Only citizens of a state (*cives*), or "members of a society who are united for giving law (*societas civilis*)," possess rights, which Kant defines as "the attributes of a citizen, inseparable from his essence (as a citizen)" (1996 [1797]: 457).[22] The juridical and political affordances of Kant's rule of justice, from which the mad are excluded, include "lawful *freedom*," "civil *equality*," and "civil *independence*" (1996 [1797]: 457–8). Civil independence is particularly important for Kant as the source of civil personality, which imparts the citizen with the "attribute of not needing to be represented by another where rights are concerned" (1996 [1797]: 458). As Nussbaum (2006: 127–40) observes, Kant's threshold for citizenship is expressed by his juxtaposition between the active and passive citizen.[23] Passive citizens, "whose preservation in existence ([their] being fed and protected) depends not on [their] management... but on arrangements made by another" (Kant 1996 [1797]: 458). For this reason Kant (1996 [1797]: 458) designates these non-subjects as "underlings [*Handlanger*] of the commonwealth". While passive citizens do not possess civil personality, their dependence and inequality as non-citizens, Kant (1996 [1797]: 458) exclaims, is "in no way opposed to their freedom and equality as *human beings*, who together make up a people".

From this vantage, it is clear that civic passivity, insofar as it engulfs Kant's category of the intellectually disabled, is exclusive to those disabilities whose political expression is the suspension of civil community. That is, Kant's formulation of passive citizenship cannot, by definition, encompass idiots whose disability, as I suggest below, excludes them from the human species altogether, a process that precedes Kant's distinction of private and active citizenship. Consequently, three discrete gradations of civic destitution become salient in Kant's political constituency, all of which are determined by the degree of cognitive development and the origin of mental derangement he ascribes to each disabled identity in his empirical work. The first level of marginalization ensues from Kant's differentiation between non-humans and non-citizens. Out of all the classifications in Kant's onomasiology of unreason, only idiocy

[22] Kant (1996 [1797]: 484) also defines citizens as "co-legislating members of a state (not merely as means, but also as ends in themselves), and must therefore give their free assent, through their representatives."

[23] For an informative analysis of Kant's construction of women as passive citizens and their consequent exclusion from his civic realm, see Kleingeld (1993: 138–9).

absolves membership in the human species. In other words, no other subject besides those who lack a soul are dubbed non-humans. Idiots are therefore below Kant's class of "passive citizens."[24]

The second echelon of destitution in Kant emerges from a nuance *within* his definition of passive citizenship, one that maps onto the natural/social divide in his taxonomy of cognitive deficiency. As Kant (1996 [1797]: 458–9) argues, passive citizens are endowed with natural freedom and equality, which their humanity has bequeathed them. This natural anthropological minimum means "anyone can work his way up from this passive condition to an active one" (1996 [1797]: 459). While Kant refers here to passive citizens such as "the woodcutter," "the blacksmith in India," and the "tenant farmer," his comment also applies to passive citizens whose civic immaturity, insofar as it is attributable to a curable mental malady may be rescinded. In contrast, however, madmen are, in light of their incurable natural disability, unable to progress from civic passivity to civic activity. On the other hand, those who bear a curable mental malady find themselves in a surmountable state of passivity spanning the duration of their mental illness.[25] Finally, once we consider how Kant's views on intellectual disability intersect with his spectrum of citizenship, we can appreciate the ways in which his passivity-activity binary carries a more profound and intricate relationship to his treatment of intellectually disabled subjects than previously believed (Nussbaum 2006: 52). In fact, the significance of this relationship resides in the discrete degrees of natural and political abjection it reveals, and in how Kant's specific distinctions of intellectually disabled identities inform the particular forms of exclusion in his politics.

Idiocy and Species Membership

Toward the end of his 1764 "Essay on the Maladies of the Head," Kant (2007 [1764a]) proposes a final and crucial empirical observation setting natural intellectual disabilities apart from socially incurred mental illnesses: the absolute and perfect absence of reason. Kant develops

[24] Kant also discusses the juridical status of the lowest rank of non-citizens, the "bondsman [*Leibeigener*] (*servus in sensu strictu*)." As Kant (1996 [1797]: 471–2) writes: "No human being in a state can be without any dignity, since he at least has the dignity of a citizen. The exception is someone who has lost it by his own *crime*, because of which, though he is kept alive, he is made a mere tool of another's choice (either of the state or of another citizen)." However, as I have argued, the bondsman is not the only exception to the inherent dignity in human beings.

[25] This contradicts Kant's (1996 [1797]: 478) idea of citizens by birth: "A *country* (*territorium*) whose inhabitants are citizens of it simply by its constitution, without their having to perform any special act to establish the right (and so are citizens by birth), is called their *native land*. A country of which they are not citizens apart from this condition is called a foreign *country*."

this idea in his construction of "idiocy [*Dummköpfigkeit*]" as the most exceptional of all mental conditions in his taxonomy. While the "*dull head* [*der stumpfe Kopf*]," for instance, "lacks wit; the *idiot* [*Dummkopf*]," Kant notes, "lacks understanding" (2007 [1764a]: 66). In his 1775–6 *Lectures on Anthropology*, Kant (2012: 94) defines idiocy with respect to the idiot's self-referential existence and unawareness of his being in the world: "The one who does not perceive his state in the world is idiotic." In his lectures of 1784–5, Kant (2012: 415) defines idiocy once again with respect to the idiot's inability to ground his existence in the public sphere by relating to others in a social context. "Idiocy and simplemindedness," he writes, "are a lack of understanding"; that is, the inability of checking "one's judgment against others," of seeing "whether one's beliefs are equal to the touchstone." In both lectures, Kant carefully distinguishes the idiot from other disabled or deranged figures by identifying idiocy as a "mental frailty." While the disturbed person "acts against the rule," Kant discerns, his condition "does not concern the lack of the mental powers, but [their] incorrect use" (2012: 415). The idiot, on the other hand, "is crippled in the mind; he can hardly use his mental powers; he has an innate stupidity" (2012: 415). In contrast to psychological and cognitive frailties that arise in a state of reason, Kant defines idiocy as a natural accident whose formation in the mind precedes and precludes reason. Finally, by 1798 Kant had built on the natural aspect of idiocy with astounding resolve in the *Anthropology*.

In this work, Kant (2007 [1798]) revisits his earlier formulations of idiocy from 1764, 1775–6, and 1784–5. To this end, his new definition imparts strong animalistic imagery to convey, in a negative vein, the abstract idea of embodied soullessness:

> Complete mental deficiency, which either does not suffice even for animal use of the vital force (as among the *Cretins* of Valais), or which is just sufficient for a mechanical imitation of external actions that are possible through animals (sawing, digging, and so on), is called *idiocy*. It cannot really be called sickness of soul; it is rather absence of soul. (Kant 2007 [1978]: 317)

Kant's definition of idiocy here describes less a cognitive condition or state than an embodied disabled identity; it is categorically distinct from intellectual disabilities that "arise with reason" and can therefore not exist in a state of natural unreason, which is precisely where Kant locates idiocy (Kant 2012: 94). Further, Kant's new definition of idiocy as the embodiment of unreason is descriptive of a "non-identity" insofar as it concretely illustrates the abstract ideas of a soulless body and a subject void of subjectivity, as an amoral, merely physical natural creature.

Unlike all other categories of psychological and cognitive illnesses in Kant's onomasiology, idiocy is the only one he does not characterize as a deranged state of the understanding, for the idiot has no soul to be corrupted.[26] The distinction between derangement and reversal introduced by imbecility is no longer applicable as a marker of idiocy, because idiocy is neither a reversal nor a derangement of reason, but its abyss: the human mind as bottomless gulf. Idiocy is to reason what "savagery" is to Western civilization: "the negative antipode against which civilized (white) humanity [defines] itself" (Mills 2005b: 190). For Mills, "interlocking conceptual relationships," such as non-white savagery and civilized white humanity, delineate Kant's idea of civilization, that is, *who* shall "rise above nature" and *what* shall not (2005b: 190). In the case of Kant's ascribed weight to reason as a marker of civilizational progress and human development, his construal of idiocy as mental nullity illustrates what we could only intimate from the categorical imperative, that any being who lacks reason cannot be considered part of the human species.

For Kant, human character is as much physical as it is moral.[27] "On the one hand," he proposes, "it is said that a certain human being has *this* or that (physical) character; on the other hand that he simply has *a* character (a moral character), which can only be one, or nothing at all" (Kant 2007 [1798]: 384). Kant makes it clear that only the rational, autonomous and free by nature, possesses the physical and moral character of humanity. While physical character is the "distinguishing mark of the human being as a sensible or natural being," moral character represents the "distinguishing mark of the human being as a rational being endowed with freedom" (2007 [1798]: 384).[28]

As such, Kant's threshold for membership in the human species is unattainable to those he defines as idiots. While they are unequivocally natural and physical beings, their existence is not "sensible" in a way that would significantly distinguish them from the physical sensibility of non-human animals. If anything, the idiot's physical character, as per his conceptual propinquity to animality, evokes the brutish corporeal existence of bestial life. Insofar as moral character is concerned, Kant's verdict is clear: the idiot has neither soul nor moral character. That is, out of the two distinguishing marks

[26] Kant (2007 [1798]) identifies two strains of mental illness: melancholia (hypochondria) and mental derangement (mania), both of which are characterized by error in, instead of complete lack of, reason: "The defects of the cognitive faculty are either *mental deficiencies* or *mental illnesses*" (2007 [1798]: 309).

[27] For an analytically rigorous interpretation of Kant's division between moral and physical character in human beings see Eze (1995: 105, 107, 113).

[28] For interpretations on the ways reason and freedom intersect in Kant's definition of human nature, see Allison (1990: 85–99) and Guyer (2000: 129–71). For a feminist interpretation of Kant's theory of freedom, see Hirschmann (2008: 195–207).

of human morality – reason and freedom – he possesses neither.[29] Kant's move here corroborates his formulation of innate rights in the *Metaphysics*, where he conceives freedom as "the only original right belonging to every man by virtue of his humanity" (Kant 1996 [1798]: 393). Natural freedom, it should be clear, is a critical aspect of Kant's moral philosophy, as he recalls in one of his 1784 lectures on ethics, "One may dispose of things that have no freedom, but not of a being that itself has free choice" (1997: 127).

Moreover, Kant defines the human being with recourse to the same descriptive devices he used to define idiocy. As he writes in the *Critique of the Power of Judgment*:

> An organized being is thus not a mere machine, for that has only a *motive* power, while the organized being possesses in itself a *formative* power, and indeed one that it communicates to the matter, which does not have it (it organizes the latter): thus [an organized being] has a self-propagating formative power, which cannot be explained through the capacity for movement alone (that is, mechanism). (Kant 2000 [1790]: 246)

Kant deploys an analogous set of terms in order to place the "human" within the "human being" category as he does to place the idiot outside of it. "The idiot" is capable of nothing other than the "*mechanical* imitation of *external actions* that are possible through animals" (Kant 2007 [1798]: 317, emphasis added). The "capacity for movement alone" is not a formative power, but a mechanism, akin to the idiot's exclusive capacity for "mechanical imitation."[30]

The idiot's exclusively physical character has deeper implications for Kant's political theory at large, particularly in regards to his principles of duties to oneself and others. Kant (1996 [1797]: 546–59) divides his notion of one's duties to oneself in two parts: "Man's duty to himself as an animal" and "the human being's duty to himself merely as a moral being" (1996 [1797]: 552–9). Thus, we have duties in two fronts: animality and morality, be it our own or that of others. Further, the "subject that is bound, as well as the subject that binds, is always the *human being only*" (1996 [1797]: 544).[31] Although we may think of body and soul as conceptually distinct, we may not think of them, according to Kant, as "different substances

[29] Kant (2007 [1798]: 369) also describes natural freedom as "the most violent inclination of all," an abstract conception present even in a newborn infant. For Kant (2005: 187, 4759n), a "being that has understanding" is "affected by sensibility [...] in communion with others," and "transcendentally free."

[30] Since I am making a claim about similarity in language, I resorted to a second translation, by Louden (2011: xviii), which confirms my interpretation.

[31] Kant (1997: 140) reminds us in one of his lectures on moral philosophy from 1784 that, "The health of the soul in a healthy body is among the self-regarding duties. So far as the perfections of our mental powers are bound up with the essential ends of humanity, it is one of our self-regarding duties to promote them."

putting [the human being] under obligation, so as to justify a division of duties to the *body* and duties to the *soul*" (1996 [1797]: 544). From this, Kant deems it is "inconceivable that [the human being] should have a duty to a *body* (as a subject imposing obligation), even to a human body" (1996 [1797]: 544). So, even if we take the idiot's body to be human it would still impose no obligation on a human subject.

Building on Kant's understanding of our private and public duties, "idiots" owe no duties to themselves, nor do others owe any duties to them, for they are merely physical beings. This formulation is consistent with two tenets of Kant's moral theory. First, that the human being is the only subject who binds and is bound. In the context of Kant's moral theory, humans have no duties toward non-human idiots who in turn have no duties whatsoever. Second, the opposition between humanity and idiocy confirms Kant's view on one's duties to self-perfection, which confers the human being "a duty to raise himself from the crude state of his nature, from his animality (*quoad actum*), more and more toward humanity, by which he alone is capable of setting himself ends" (1996 [1797]: 518). Constructing the idiot outside the bounds of humanity carries wider implications for Kant's theory of human progress, as expressed in his 1784 essay, "Idea for a Universal History with a Cosmopolitan Aim," whose opening proposition asserts Kant's endorsement of a teleological doctrine of nature, "*All natural predispositions of a creature are determined sometime to develop themselves completely and purposively*" (2007 [1784]: 109).

Not only does the distinction between natural/congenital versus social/acquired intellectual disabilities persist in Kant's formulation of idiocy, but this definition is transformed by his differentiations of lack and error. Because he lacks a soul, the idiot's existence is at once apolitical, asocial, and amoral. Bereft of all cognitive power and equipped only with an animalistic instinct for mechanical imitation, the idiot is perfectly dehumanized, lowered to the rank of subhuman animality. As such, intellectually disabled subjects in Kant are consequently demoted to a natural and crude state, perpetually confined to an amoral and apolitical existence where they will never require the very understanding they lack.

Disability and Contract: Rethinking Nussbaum's *Frontiers of Justice*

In *Frontiers of Justice*, Martha Nussbaum (2006: 11) describes the social contract tradition as a "vivid, rigorous, and illuminating way of thinking about justice among equal persons." Despite her praise for the legacy of this tradition, Nussbaum is critical of the social contract in many respects, including its treatment of the disabled. For Nussbaum, these are problems that demand solutions, for, as she puts it, "correcting the *oversight* of previous theories [should not be] a matter of simply applying the same old theories to a new problem," but of "getting the theoretical structure right" (2006: 14, emphasis added).[32] Unlike Pateman, who renounces the social contract as a model of justice based on its intransigently oppressive structure, Nussbaum sets out to mitigate the contract's structural failures through a sophisticated theoretical reconstruction of the classical model rooted in her "capabilities approach" to justice.

Nussbaum's work is an impressive and invaluable contribution to the literature. I applaud her foresight and emphatically endorse her rigorous interrogation of the social contract's exclusion of disability as a fundamental problem of justice. Notwithstanding the significant merits of her book, my foregoing reading of disability in Kant calls to question two of Nussbaum's contentions. First, she reduces what I argue to be a deliberate exclusion of disabled subjects to a form of "oversight" and "omission." Second, she attributes the "oversight" in the exclusions of disabled persons to the social contract's procedural approach to justice. These problems cannot be easily dismissed as they consequently impact the political tenor of her critique to the extent they reduce the social contract's problem of exclusion, *qua* categorical marginalization, to a matter of historical contingency.

Exclusion versus Omission

Nussbaum (2006: 4) begins by noting that classical contract theorists "assumed that their contracting agents were men who were roughly equal in capacity, and capable of productive economic activity." This initial assumption, she continues, meant that those cast as unproductive due to their physical and mental difference were consequently omitted from the bargaining position (2006: 33). On this account, the fact that the disabled were not parties to "the group of those by whom basic political principles are chosen" explains their exclusion from the original contracting position (2006: 14–16). Nussbaum contends, moreover, that even if we were to "assume that those *omissions* [were] not a serious problem for the theories," the disabled are nonetheless "absent from the contracting group," and consequently "absent from the group

[32] Whether or not Nussbaum's alternative solution actually achieves this goal is another question altogether. For critical analyses of her capabilities approach from a disabilities perspective, see Silvers and Francis (2009) and Bérubé (2009). While both articles take issue with Nussbaum's conclusion and prescription, they do not critique her procedure or methodology.

of citizens for whom the principles of justice are framed" (2006: 33, emphasis added).

As a result, Nussbaum treats contractarian exclusion as an "omission from the situation of choice"; that is, an initial stage in which principles of justice – rights, duties, freedom, equality, and so forth – are said to be primarily chosen and allocated to citizens (2006: 15). In interpreting exclusion as omission, Nussbaum ultimately understates how crucial intellectually disabled identities in fact were to contractarian accounts of justice. Her analysis overlooks the ways in which the dominant subjects of social contract theories are brought to life in figurations of the disabled as non-citizens, non-persons, and non-humans who never transcend their own crude nature. As such, Nussbaum's reading does not attend to the social contract's fundamental dependence on disabled identities as a means to concretely demarcate the limits of justice. Insofar as Kant's formulation of madness, imbecility, and idiocy, for instance, portray the "irrational other" against which his rational citizen and moral person are constructed as political, civil, and human subjects, Kant's notion of disability consequently sketches the scope of justice in his political theory, identifying – to a striking degree of detail – those who do and do not qualify as contracting subjects.

What Nussbaum discerns as "the *omission* of people with impairments and disabilities from the contract situation," becomes ever more damaging, she avers, "once we take account of a striking *structural feature* of all social contract theories": the conflation of two distinct questions: "by whom are society's basic principles designed" and "for whom are society's basic principles designed" (2006: 15–16, emphasis added). Put differently, since white, able-minded, able-bodied men presumably devised the social contract, Nussbaum concludes, they consequently envisaged themselves and those with whom they assimilated as the contract's primary subjects of justice. As a result, the argument goes, intellectually disabled persons, along with other marginalized subjects incapable of meeting the contract's de facto threshold for membership, were inevitably *omitted*. Since the parameters of classical contract theory, including its principles of justice, are delineated by and for its primary subjects of justice, the tradition's insistence on "certain abilities (rationality, language, roughly equal physical and mental capacity) as prerequisites for participation in the procedure that chooses principles" will ineluctably have "large consequences for the treatment of people with impairments and disabilities as recipients or subjects of justice in the resulting society" (Nussbaum 2006: 16, emphasis added). Nussbaum states, at last, that the "*omission* of people with disabilities from the initial choice of basic political principles has large consequences for their equal citizenship…

through the structure that is characteristic of social contract theories" (2006: 17–18, emphasis added). In essence, Nussbaum (2004) traces the contract's disregard for the disabled to their omission from the group for whom and by whom the theory's principles of justice were designed. This first omission, she maintains, is a consequence of the historical invisibility of persons with disability in early modern Europe – because they were historically excluded from society, they were inevitably omitted from the group charged with designing the contract's principles of justice. Nussbaum thus frames the question of disability in the social contract as a flaw in design rather than a matter of explicit discrimination or, as I suggest, the result of a system of exclusionary strategies directed at disabled bodies and minds who, in case of Kant's political thought, are empirically profiled.[33]

According to Nussbaum, the disabled are never explicitly constructed by social contract theorists as non-citizens, non-persons, and non-humans; they are instead denied entry as a result of the contract's *a priori* capacity threshold for membership. By contrast, I take the dominant subject of justice to be delineated and demarcated *qua* citizen, person, and human in large part as a result of the explicit and *a priori* construction of the intellectually disabled *qua* non-citizen, non-person, and non-human – what Mills (1997: 43) calls "the characterization of oneself by reference to what one is not."[34] Modern political thinkers, such as Kant, explicitly define the intellectually disabled subject through their permanent and innate *lack* of reason, soul, freedom, and autonomy. It is the intellectually disabled person's natural inadequacy that, in turn, reifies the social contract's abstract threshold of normalcy and the rational requisite for citizenship, personhood, and, more importantly, the human species. Rather than simply omitting disability from his principles of justice, Kant evokes intellectually disabled identities, as the embodiment of perfect political destitution (pertaining to the public and civic spheres of citizenship) and amoral, non-human life (in regards to the private realm

[33] Anita Silvers (2005) has taken issue with Nussbaum's interpretation of the social contract's treatment of disability as an "outlier problem." Nussbaum argues that, since those best served by the social contract are those who designed its principles of justice, the social contract's disregard for the disabled is a product of their historical exclusion from society at the time when contractarian theories of justice were conceived in seventeenth- and eighteenth-century Europe. That is, because they were historically *omitted* from society (i.e., invisible), the disabled were consequently *omitted* form the contract's design, and are for this reason not able to benefit from the contract's principles of justice (Silvers 2005: 50–2). Yet, as Kant's writings on disability aver, the disabled were as much visible in modern European societies as they were present in the works of key European political thinkers such as Hobbes, Locke, and Rousseau.

[34] Mills is drawing on Hayden White's (1972: 5) analysis of the wild man represented as the "technique of ostensive self-definition by negation."

of personhood). Thus, Kant's political theory of justice is firmly rooted in what Uday Mehta (1990) has called "strategies of exclusion." In short, if we agree that the disabled are indeed marginalized in Kant's political thought, his construal of disabled identities in his empirical ethics demonstrates that this is not merely incidental, or a structural shortcoming of a procedural approach to justice, as Nussbaum suggests.

Indeed, the social contract's procedural approach to justice, which Nussbaum traces back to Kant, accounts for much of her explanation as to why these theories fail to enfranchise the disabled (Nussbaum 2006: 270, 276). The problem of omission for Nussbaum derives in large part from "proceduralism," the idea that justice proceeds from a contractarian apparatus composed of the necessary principles required to achieve a just outcome. On this account, "proceduralism" is a fundamental mechanism of the social contract model; it is a core characteristic of the structure and framework which Nussbaum (2006: 4) attempts to reconstruct in order to render the theory permeable by those groups it originally omitted. The question of whether the end result of this procedure will be universally applicable to all humans depends, according to Nussbaum, on whether those who designed the contract's mechanisms of justice include subjects whose identities and abilities differ from the founding parties of the social contract.

Procedural Justice and the Social Contract

Broadly, Nussbaum's emphasis on omission, as a product of either oversight or proceduralism, veils the discriminatory intentions in the social contract's strategies of exclusion. "People with mental impairments," she argues, "are not among those for whom and in reciprocity with whom society's basic institutions are structured" (2006: 98). Put differently, contract theorists set out to demonstrate the natural condition of moral, physical, and cognitive equality between human beings in order to render any one person's domination over another arbitrary and thus unjustifiable.[35] From this it follows that if classical contractarian arguments made in the name of freedom and justice, rooted in natural equality, included beings who were naturally unequal to able-bodied, able-minded white men as the physically and cognitively disabled, then the anti-absolutist logic of the social contract would be compromised. In light of this, Nussbaum concludes that the "equality assumption" of social contract thinkers "requires [them] to put some important issues of justice on

[35] Pateman (1988: 39) makes a similar claim with respect to sexual difference.

hold. In particular, justice for people with severe mental impairments" (2006: 31–2).[36]

Contrary to Nussbaum's claim, my analysis of Kant's empirical writings shows that disabled identities are not only explicitly invoked in his text, but that they are in addition singled out for a specific purpose, which is altogether indispensable to his political theory, namely his formulation of the subjects of justice. Nussbaum's contention that Kant "does not explicitly mention this category [the disabled]," but speaks of "generally anyone who must depend for his support [...] on arrangements by others" is therefore insufficiently accurate (2006: 420, 37n). Rather than relying on the assumption that disabled identities are omitted by Kant, or that their exclusion proceeds from the rationalist threshold in his moral theory, I argue that Kant's specific views on intellectual disability earmark exactly where and how disabled persons – as opposed to disability as an abstract category – are excluded from his political constituency.

Moreover, my foregoing textual interpretation of Kant's empirical works reveals that his uses of disability as subcategories of citizenship and the human species in his anthropology are fundamentally related to the active–passive and public–private dyads in his transcendental philosophy. According to Nussbaum, Kant's distinction between active and passive citizens ensues from his view that dependent non-contractors lack civil personality (2006: 52). She reads Kant's definition of a natural, pre-social form of rough equality as the foundation for his two-tiered model of citizenship, which she interprets as a binary between active and passive binary rather than a gradual scale. While active citizens, Nussbaum has it, are figured as both the framers and subjects of Kant's political theory, passive non-citizens are omitted from the political, civic, and economic domains of public life.

While some passive non-citizens can exit their private status, Nussbaum writes, "women and people with disabilities are permanently in the passive category" (2006: 52). As her language suggests, Nussbaum can only infer that Kant's category of passive citizenship pertains to the disabled, since her reading of his theory of justice is predominantly based on the *Metaphysics*. To this end, Nussbaum overlooks the significant consortium between Kant's philosophical prescriptions and empirical reflections. Only by reading Kant's empirical work as a constituent of his moral and political theory, can we come to terms with how his articulations of passive and active citizenship at once reflect and corroborate his distinctions

[36] Building on the work of C. B. Macpherson, Pateman and Brennan (1979: 52) offer an alternative interpretation of the contractarian equality assumption. They explain why social contract theorists relied on the "equality assumption" with recourse to the "emergence of the capitalist, market economy, and the liberal constitutional state."

between natural, congenital, permanent, social, acquired, and curable "frailties of the head" in his empirical ethics.

Interpreting Kant's exclusion of passive non-citizens from the civic, public, and political realms against the backdrop of his empirical views on human nature is a way to contextualize his understanding of "passive citizenship" according to the types of identities he deems naturally and permanently passive as a matter of empirical observation. On my account, Kant's category of passivity was more than a heuristic trope meant to convey the exclusion of an abstract and loosely defined irrational subject. Rather, Kant's formulation of the imbecile's natural and permanent passivity is a political strategy of exclusion leveled against specific disabled identities. According to Kant's taxonomy, the naturally disabled subject cannot be cured or rehabilitated so that his condition is one of total, permanent passivity and private confinement. Yet, whenever a cognitive disability is not inborn but developed in civil society, as a consequence of social relations, the disabled subject may, once cured, transcend his passive state.

Kant's understanding of passivity was so intricate and expansive that even within his formulation of permanent passivity, we find a system of nuanced gradations of marginalization whose political significance is brought forth in his onomastic of intellectual disabilities. While madness, for instance, justifies exclusion from the public realm, idiocy warrants exclusion from the human species altogether. The point being that, by paying heed to Kant's empirical views on disability, we are able to devise a more accurate and compelling interpretation of key tenets in his moral and political philosophy, such as his notions of passive and active citizenship, which, as I have argued, attest to and sustain commensurate distinctions in his onomasiology of cognitive disabilities. In short, my interpretative textual approach here, characterized by a reading of Kant's transcendental philosophy and political theory against the backdrop of his empirical ethics, registers his writings on intellectual disability as a fundamental subtext of Kant's theory of justice, its margins and its limits. In a word, Kant's account of the realities of disability is a critical supplement to our understanding for whom the principles of justice in his political theory were meant. Justice in Kant begins where the amoral, soulless figure of the idiot ends. *Pace* Nussbaum, the limit of justice for Kant is not merely a consequence of the procedural structure of his theory; that is, of a threshold based on rational capacity or a product of his omission of intellectual disability. In order to unveil the margins of Kant's approach to justice, it is necessary to push critique beyond the theoretical abstractions and capacity thresholds of his theory. The procedural approach to justice in the social contract is part of what Mills

(1997: 10), has called "a purely hypothetical exercise [...] in establishing what a just 'basic structure' would be." As I argue throughout this chapter, it is important to account for Kant's empirical works when assessing his thoughts on justice so that his overt exclusion of the intellectually disabled is not misinterpreted as a contingent consequence of a purely abstract and hypothetical exercise. Indeed, it is in Kant's construction of the disabled as non-person, non-citizen, and non-human that his strategy of exclusion finds its most biting political expression as a concrete form of injustice against madmen, imbeciles, and idiots, all of whom roam the margins of his theory, somewhere in the "philosophically unimportant" pages of his ethics.

Further, by analyzing the relevance of Kant's outlook on disability we are able to re-evaluate Nussbaum's claim that Kant's rationalist formulation of personhood contradicts the central moral concession of his categorical imperative, which defines human beings as ends in themselves. As I note above, Nussbaum (2006) assumes that what is "true of animals is *bound* to be true of all beings who lack the rather complex capacity for moral and prudential reasoning" (2006: 130–1, emphasis added). Without recourse to Kant's empirical writings, Nussbaum claims that Kantian moral personhood is "deeply at odds with the central insight of his moral theory, namely, that each person is to be treated as an end, and not as a mere means to the ends of others" (2006: 220–1). Although seemingly contradictory, these two aspects of Kant's philosophy are in fact complementary: Kant's moral theory would only fall apart if he had not explicitly excluded the intellectually disabled from the category of citizens, persons, and humans in his empirical works. Put differently, a contradiction between what holds in theory (i.e., his categorical imperative) and what Kant deems as observably verifiable in practice (i.e., his empirical ethics) would only arise had Kant constructed the intellectually disabled as human beings in his empirical works.

By taking Kant's *Anthropology* as an empirical appendix to his rationalist formulation of personhood in the *Metaphysics*, we come to appreciate that his construction of idiocy, as a non-human embodiment of unreason, prevents his moral theory from colliding with the categorical imperative for the simple reason that idiots do not belong in the human species to begin with (Kant 2007 [1798]: 317). In fact, an inconsistency would have held only if Kant's theory of moral personhood had *not* been rooted in rational agency. Had this been the case, his exclusion of idiocy would have been at odds with his moral theory since no synthetic *a priori* justification for excluding idiots as ends in themselves would have existed. In fact, it is precisely because rationality operates as the supreme condition for personhood that the central axiom in Kant's categorical imperative holds. In other words, each and every person is treated as an end precisely because those who are not so treated (in light of their absolute lack of reason) are neither persons nor humans. In this sense, the problem of disability in Kant is not that his theory "run[s] into some... difficulties with mental disability" (Nussbaum 2006: 133), but that Kant himself uses disability and disabled identities as illustrations of the scope of justice in his theory. In a strictly analytical reading, Kant's theory would have run into difficulties if he had not outlined in his empirical writings the groups of people meant as human beings.

Finally, my foregoing reading of Kant's empirical ethics sought to expose a central problem in Nussbaum's prescription to ground dignity in human animality instead of rationality as a solution to Kant's dehumanization of intellectual disability. Nussbaum finds Kant's partitioning of personhood and animality to be "deeply problematic" because it "wrongly denies that animality can itself have dignity," that human dignity is "the dignity of a certain sort of animal" (2006: 132). Her solution to this problem is to ground Kantian moral dignity in human animality rather than rational capacity. While this would be a plausible solution in its own right, as a departure from Kantian moral dignity, it would not conform to Kant's philosophical system since, as I have argued, Kant also excludes the intellectually disabled from his definition of human animals. For Kant, the animality of idiots is not the same as that of humans. In light of this, a project to reformulate Kantian dignity by relocating it in human animality (instead of rationality) would not necessarily extend dignity to intellectually disabled individuals as long as their animality is considered non-human. Therefore, to the extent that one of the goals of critical disability theory is to accord dignity to the intellectually disabled by grounding dignity on species membership, then the first step would be to include the intellectually disabled in the definition of human animality at the core of the moral theory in question. In the case of Kant, extending human dignity to a notion of human animality that already excludes the disabled is not a solution for rendering Kant's moral theory more capacious.

In order to accept Nussbaum's prescription to ground dignity in human animality as a reconstructive move away from Kant's normative framework, it is necessary to both acknowledge and resolve the exclusion of disabled subjects from the category of human animals. Moreover, the animalization of idiocy is not exclusive to Kant's thought, but a recurring, structural problem in the history of Western political thought (Carlson 2010: 151–64). Locke, for instance, uses the term "changeling" to define intellectually disabled children born to rational, human parents. The changeling's absolute incapacity to reason – much like in the case of

Kant's idiot – absolves the non-human matter of his body from human animality, placing him somewhere "between Man and Beast" (Locke 1975 [1690]: 569).[37] Much like in Locke, Kant's explicit construction of the idiot's animality as non-human mass means that to ground dignity in the human animal does not necessarily grant dignity to the severely cognitively disabled whose bodies have been historically associated with non-human animality. In closing, then, even if we accept Nussbaum's prescription to address the non-human animalization of idiocy in Kant, this solution would still not resolve the dehumanization of intellectual disability as a historical and political, rather than purely conceptual or analytical, problem in Western political thought.

Through the course of this chapter, I have argued that intellectually disabled identities occupy a unique place of political and moral destitution in Kant's thought. Kant's invocation of intellectually disabled identities brings the limits of civil and moral existence to the fore of his theory of justice. In failing to meet the rationality threshold for citizenship and personhood, on top of being explicitly constructed as naturally and permanently irrational as well as an amoral, non-human being, the intellectually disabled – the madman, the imbecile, and the idiot – are excluded, by their nature, from the most liberating and dignifying concessions in Kant's political theory.

As I outlined at the outset, my argument builds directly upon Pateman's and Mills' critiques of contractarian universality, in an attempt to introduce their respective projects to the realm of intellectual disability. From its inception, my analysis was underpinned by the sexual and racial contracts, which have in turn provided the critical conceptual framework through which I remitted my textual interpretation of disability in Kant. From framing my project as a reaction to, and continuation of, Pateman's and Mills' works, I argued that a third category of exclusion engendered a third contract of marginality premised upon the latent oppression of disabled subjects, what I have termed the "ableist contract." As such, the ableist contract retains the sexual contract's pestering of the civil–natural binary sketched by modern political theorists, while continuing, at the same time, the racial contract's unmasking of the classical contract's fictitious claim to universal moral personhood, freedom, and justice for all human beings.

My reading of Kant accentuated the distinct and particular abjection of cognitively disabled subjects, which he elaborates at the margins of

[37] For accounts of the animalization of idiocy in the history of political thought, see Goodey and Stainton (2001: 234–7) and Goodey (1994).

his thought. Kant's strategies of identifying and marginalizing disabled persons underscore the direct and explicit means by which he discharges intellectual disability from his designations of personhood, citizenship, and the human species. The ableist contract is only able to sustain the social contract's illusive mandate of universal justice by denying disabled persons the "universal" political rights and freedom extended to the subjects of justice as rational, active, moral, and human citizens of civil society. Thus, the political theory that ensues beneath the project of civil society is a system of targeted subjection that betrays the veiled exclusion of disabled persons, by virtue of their intellectual disabilities, from politics, freedom, and justice.

3 Disavowals of Disability in Rawls' Theory of Justice and his Critics

*Stacy Clifford Simplican**

Disability studies scholars suggest that the anxiety underwriting disability is primarily one of *contracting* disability: the fear that "we" (the non-disabled) will become disabled (McRuer 2006) or, likewise, that "we" (the disabled) will become *more* disabled (Kafer 2013). Political theorists who take up issues of disability agree. Nancy Hirschmann argues that disability undermines the liberal sovereign self, explaining: "The apprehension of disability forces individuals to come to grips with the way the body changes and can change further without warning, betraying the self's conception of who and what it is" (2012: 400). Although these insights are important, I argue that theoretical diagnoses of ableism that center on the fear of *being* disabled overlook equally palpable anxieties that stem from living in a world *with* the disabled. To uncover this latter type of anxiety, I turn to John Rawls' removal of disability from his theory of justice. Rawls' revival of social contract theory discloses a series of *capacity contracts*, the terms of which foreclose political membership to people with significant disabilities. If the anxiety of *contracting disability* reveals the unpredictability and vulnerability of human subjects, then Rawls' capacity contracts aim to restore rationality's (fictional) control over oneself and the world.[1]

Returning to Rawls' take on disability may prompt a sense of feminist déjà vu – or even a distinct form of Rawlsian fatigue. Indeed, feminist philosophers intent on including all or most people with disabilities have turned to Rawls' work to redefine equality (Kittay 1999), trust (Silvers and Francis 2005), citizenship (Wong 2009), cooperation (Hartley 2011), and freedom (Hirschmann 2013b). While these feminist critiques are essential, they may prove insufficient. Because many disability scholars and feminist theorists *begin* with Rawls' disavowal of disability in *Political Liberalism*, they neglect how disability already saturates the foundation of his social contract theory.

* I dedicate this chapter to my mother, Peggy Clifford, who passed away very suddenly from inflammatory breast cancer on November 8, 2016.

[1] I thank Barbara Arneil for pointing out this double meaning of contract.

In the first half of this chapter, I show three versions of the capacity contract that Rawls developed before his publication of *A Theory of Justice* in 1971. These capacity contracts reveal how Rawls used disability to define key concepts even as later iterations of these contracts disavow the role disability actually played. In the second half of the chapter, I turn to the work of critical race, feminist, and disability studies scholars to show how they, too, marginalize people with cognitive disabilities. More specifically, diverse philosophical accounts ranging from liberal to feminist idealize the human capacity for knowledge as a keystone to democratic progress and thus cement the devaluation of intellectual disability.

John Rawls and the Disavowal of Disability

Rawls' work offers a fruitful starting place, in part because many philosophical accounts of disability use his work as a springboard, but also because his theory has two foundational features that should be well suited for promoting the full inclusion of all persons. First, Rawls insists that a theory of justice must accord "each member of society... an inviolability founded on justice, which even the welfare of everyone else cannot override" (1999 [1967]: 131). This fundamental commitment should protect people with disabilities. Second, Rawls' construction of the original position as an imaginative device used to destabilize our thinking potentially offers a way to challenge ableist norms. These two foundational elements in Rawls' corpus – his substantive commitment to universal equality and his methodological tool to disrupt prejudice – seem *crafted* for a project on disability. What goes wrong?

Readers familiar with Rawls' work will recall that he "put aside" people with severe and mental disabilities in *Political Liberalism* because they are unable to cooperate in society and are inessential to the main questions of justice (2005: 20). When Rawls uses the language of *putting aside disability* and *waiting until the case can be examined*, he suggests that disability plays no part in his theory of justice (2005: 21). Yet, disability saturates Rawls' enterprise as his early work draws upon disability to define key conceptions and narrow his normative field. Rawls' reliance on ideal theory – in which he conceptualizes key themes without recourse to studying systematic patterns of injustice – obscures the way in which disability *functions* throughout his work.

In ideal theory, conceptions of the person and justice are seemingly formed without recourse to studying systematic patterns of injustice. The ideal dimension of Rawls' social contract theory forces him to enact a *double disavowal* of disability. By double disavowal, I refer to the ways in which Rawls' treatment of disability has two stages.[2] At the first stage, Rawls draws on cognitive disability to define key conceptions, including personhood, the original position, and the principle of redress. This stage stigmatizes disability, marking disabled people as pitiful abnormalities who threaten to drain limited national resources. Rawls' reliance on disability, however, is only one part of the problem. At the second stage, Rawls explicitly removes disability from theoretical consideration. For instance, in *Political Liberalism*, he removes people with significant disabilities from the scope of citizenship and healthcare concerns. This explicit removal disavows the role disability actually already played. The two-stage aspect of disavowal – that first uses disability to define key conceptions and then disavows disability's prior theoretical role – is evident in Rawls' original position, his subcontract of advantage, and his discussion of redress. Significantly, we can think of each of these three instances as capacity contracts: each proscribes rules of fairness while also normalizing threshold levels of *compulsory capacity*.

Compulsory capacity draws heavily on the work of disability studies scholars who link liberal promises of human perfectibility with the stigmatization of people with disabilities. For Robert McRuer (2006: 10), the "problem" of disability is the "inevitable impossibility, even as it is made compulsory, of an able-bodied identity." Political philosophers since Aristotle have defined man by his cognitive capacities, but Rawls' location in the twentieth century positioned him at a time when ideal capacities collapsed into normal capacities. This replacement of "the ideal" with "normal" naturalizes a fictional account of compulsory capacity. For disability theorist Lennard Davis, the twentieth century fostered a "new ideal of ranked order [that] is powered by the imperative of the norm, and then is supplemented by the notion of progress, human perfectibility, and the elimination of deviance, to create a dominating, hegemonic vision of what the human body should be" (1995: 8). David Mitchell and Sharon Snyder (2003: 861) describe a "uniquely modern utopian fantasy of a future world uncontaminated by defective bodies." Rawls' capacity contracts, which share in this modern utopian fantasy, evolved over the course of his career, often developed prior to the publication of his seminal work *A Theory of Justice* in 1971. Most of my interventions into Rawls' work begin not with his explicit exclusion of disability in *Political Liberalism*, but his work between 1951 and 1971 as we see him develop and then obscure his commitment to compulsory capacity.

[2] Other treatments of disability and political theory also take up the theme of disavowal. See Knight (2014) and Kafer (2013).

Defining the Normal Range of Capacity

We see Rawls' two stages of disavowal in his original position: he relies on disability to define moral agents' range of normal functioning, while simultaneously excluding issues surrounding disability from consideration. In the original position, agents are unaware of their exact intelligence, but they know their cognitive capacities fall within a "normal range" (Rawls 2001: 18, 21). Rawls (2001: 272) specifies the normal range as follows: "since the fundamental problem of justice concerns the relations among those who are full and active participants in society, [...] it is reasonable to assume that everyone has physical needs and psychological capacities within some normal range." This explanation, however, fails to convey what constitutes the normal range; rather, Rawls assumes that he and his reader already know and share the same conception of what it means to be "full and active participants in society."

Although Rawls fails to specify the normal range, he offers us some guidance in an article he published in 1951 in which he draws on intelligence tests to define the normal range of moral reasoning. Rawls (1999 [1951]: 2) argues that moral insight demands "a certain requisite degree of intelligence, which may be thought of as that ability which intelligence tests are designed to measure." By suggesting that we can discern "normal" functioning from intelligence tests, Rawls taps into the normative legitimacy of statistical tests that fostered the creation and new idealization of normal. As Davis describes, American psychologists promoted IQ tests as a way to rank humans from the most intelligent (and superior in birth) to the mentally deficient. Intelligence tests transformed normal into a new ideal and created a subnormal category of existence – often symbolized by people with cognitive disabilities. Professionals used IQ tests to prove the inferiority of people with disabilities, African Americans, and immigrants (McWhorter 2009). Hence, intelligence tests are not an innocent measure of human capacity, but rather draw upon raced, gendered, class, and ableist constructions of citizenship that animated early twentieth-century North America.

For Davis, accompanying the ideal of a ranked order is the desire to eliminate deviance and we see this in Rawls' removal of disability from the original position. In describing the "mentally defective," Rawls argues: "Besides prematurely introducing difficult questions that may take us beyond the theory of justice, the consideration of these hard cases can distract our moral perception by leading us to think of people distant from us whose fate arouses pity and anxiety" (1999 [1967]: 259; 2003 [1971]: 84). Several troubling assumptions pervade this statement. First, Rawls suggests that moral agents' perception will function poorly if contaminated by anxiety and pity. Rawls makes compulsory both the level of reason and its emotional detachment. It's not disability that Rawls worries his moral agents will contract, but rather the anxiety surrounding it. Reason and anxiety thus oppose one another and Rawls feels compelled to sanitize the original position – removing both disability and anxiety – to safeguard judgment.

Additionally, according to the dictates of ideal theory, moral agents in the original position are ignorant of the societal situation of people with cognitive disabilities in the non-ideal world. Hence, they are unaware of societal prejudice, built barriers, failures in long-term care, and the spatial segregation of people with disability. Thus, the anxiety and pity that moral agents may experience if confronted with the mentally defective is driven entirely by the bare facts of disability, whatever those might be in a decontextualized world.

By describing the "mentally defective" as "distant from us," Rawls naturalizes human difference as insurmountable, as if disability is so abnormal as to be unimaginable, rather than a predictable aspect of human functioning across the lifespan. Rawls' description of "hard cases" as already "beyond" his theory of justice imports a false permanency of health and vitality into his description of "normal" functioning, thus making "normal" compulsory for belonging. Rawls adds, "the problem of justice concerns the relations among those who in the everyday course of things are full and active participants in society" (2003 [1971]: 84). Like the language of normal and basic, Rawls' construction of the "everyday course of things" assumes that confrontations with disabled people infrequently occur, if at all, and thus depoliticizes the twentieth century's forced segregation of people with disabilities.

Finally, what does Rawls mean when he argues that the mentally defective *distract* us from the main questions of justice? Issues such as healthcare, education, and accessibility fall squarely within the purview of politics, so why would these considerations take us far beyond a theory of justice? I argue that it is not the *content* of the political questions, but rather the anxiety-producing effect that Rawls finds too distracting.

By depicting moral agents in the original position as *normal*, while also emphasizing the *main* and *basic* questions of justice, Rawls constructs people with cognitive disabilities as peripheral to matters of justice and abnormal to human functioning. His oscillation between describing agents as ideal and normal intensifies compulsory capacity as both fictive and mandatory. While Rawls' exclusion of disability from the original position is likely the most familiar – as feminists have made it central to their critique – it is not the only instantiation of compulsory capacity. Indeed, there are other capacity contracts lurking.

A Contract with the Least Able

Unlike the original position that is designed to conceal differences in capacity, Rawls offers multiple iterations of a subcontract forged between the most and least advantaged – a subcontract moment in which individuals involved "do know their talents and abilities" (1999 [1963]: 81). Indeed, both this section and the next take up Rawls' attempt to determine how institutions can divide resources justly between people with diverse capacities. In this way, these early iterations of capacity contracts show that Rawls was not a pure resourcist who disregarded "natural diversity" altogether (see Pogge 2002a for a resourcist approach to Rawls). Instead, Rawls' first iteration of the subcontract between the most and the least able is concerned *precisely* with differential capacities. The contract of advantage first appears in a 1963 article "Constitutional Liberty and the Concept of Justice," then in a 1968 article "Distributive Justice: Some Addenda," then in *A Theory of Justice*, and finally, in *Justice as Fairness: A Restatement.* Because Rawls returns repeatedly to this subcontract moment over a span of almost 40 years, we can presume it is significant to his broader project. The evolution of this capacity contract discloses another instantiation of Rawls' double disavowal of disability in which he designs the initial contract by proscribing different levels of capacity to moral agents as the key element of the contract, but then over time, gradually obscures the role that differences in human capacity play in his contract.

When Rawls first formulates the contract between the most and least advantaged, he fails to circumscribe agents' range of human capacities. In the contract of advantage of 1963, Rawls instructs us to "fix attention on two representative men, one for the upper and one for the lower ranges of ability" (1999 [1963]: 82). Based on this description, people with intellectual disabilities should occupy the least advantaged class. Indeed, Rawls conjures differences in ability when he describes the two men as the "more" and "less able" (1999 [1963]: 82). In this subcontract moment, each man must choose between a caste society or a society ordered by Rawls' difference principle.

The difference principle is part of one of the two principles of justice that together form the main thrust of Rawls' theory. In the original position, moral agents choose these two principles to guide the formation of politics. The first principle, which is given priority over the second principle, gives all members of society the same share of "basic liberty," including liberties such as freedom of speech, religion, and assembly. The second principle aims to ensure that social and economic inequalities are fair – that all people have an equal opportunity to positions and offices, and second, that all inequalities are to benefit the least advantaged in society. This second component is the difference principle.

Consequently, economic inequalities are fair if they benefit the least advantaged. The subcontract of advantage helps Rawls defend the fairness of the difference principle. Importantly, it is the least talented man who determines the subcontract's legitimacy. The most talented man will always choose the society ordered by the difference principle. With his reliable toolkit of talent and ability, the most able man can assume his success in a society marked by (some measure of) social and economic inequality. In contrast, the caste society symbolizes for the most talented man the risk of subordination. If he is born into a lower class, his superior ability is meaningless.

From the standpoint of the least able man, the choice appears quite different. Because he is on the "lower range of ability," he knows he will be the least advantaged in Rawls' merit-informed economy. While he will have the same share of basic rights and liberties as the most able man, he will most likely have less money and less prestige. In contrast, the caste society offers him the possibility of advantage: his potential birth into the upper class can secure what his lackluster abilities cannot. Rawls argues, however, that the less able man is better off in the society of the two principles of justice because any advantages that accrue to the most advantaged must also improve the lives of the least talented. We assume quite the opposite in the caste society: the most advantaged have no incentive to improve the lives of the less fortunate. Thus, the least able man will avoid risking the slim possibility of social and economic privilege and will instead opt for the guarantee of equal liberty and the resignation to economic and social inequality.

Rawls' subcontract discloses disturbing assumptions about the naturalization of inequality, but it also offers us a way to judge the distribution of privilege. On the one hand, we see in Rawls' "original" subcontract certain disabling assumptions already at work, most importantly of which is that the least advantaged class perfectly maps on to the least able. Rawls fixes disabled and abled categories to different socioeconomic conditions and he naturalizes the "worse off" as an obvious outcome of impairment. This understanding reflects the medical model of disability that depicts disability as an individual defect, and thus ignores how bodies, environments, and stigma interact to produce disability. On the other hand, because the subcontract ensures that any benefit to the most advantaged will equally improve the lives of people on the "lower range of ability," the subcontract has the potential to raise important questions about societal relationships between the disabled and abled. For instance, how do we design a world that every advantage of the abled similarly enhances the lives of the disabled? The subcontract gives us a way to think about human interdependency in a way that the original position does not. In theorizing the relationship between the most and least able, Rawls' subcontract engineers engagement and, in the process, reveals ableist anxiety and the barriers it helps sustain.

But this engagement evaporates as Rawls revises the terms of the subcontract and gradually idealizes the class of "least advantaged." In "Distributive Justice: Some Addenda" published in 1968, Rawls contends, "the least advantaged are represented by the typical unskilled worker" (1999 [1968]: 163). By 1971, with the publication of *A Theory of Justice*, Rawls circumscribes the least advantaged to the "unskilled worker" or those whose income is comparable to the least skilled (2003 [1971]: 84). Rawls acknowledges that these inequalities may be the result of "natural characteristics," such as sex, race, or culture, and moreover, that this kind of inequality is "seldom, if ever, to the advantage of the less favored" (2003 [1971]: 85). But he no longer mentions capacity. Indeed, Rawls eliminates any descriptions of the least advantaged as the "less able" on "the lower ranges of ability." He seems to have intentionally (and quietly) displaced the role of capacity or ability as a characteristic of a dis/advantage that is morally arbitrary. Yet, the earlier subcontract haunts the newer instantiation, shadowing the unskilled worker with the assumption that he is an unskilled worker *because* of his lesser capacity.

By removing differences in capacity, Rawls also alters the terms of the agreement for the most talented. Because the most able man assumes that he will be the most economically privileged, with *whom* he contracts is significant. According to the difference principle, he must consent to redistribute some of his wealth to maintain fairness. The terms of redistribution will change according to the range of capacities present. For example, Amartya Sen shows that people with disabilities may need a larger share of resources to convert into the same level of capabilities as non-disabled citizens. For some people with disabilities, the cost of freedom of mobility and equal participation is higher (Sen 1983 1990). Thus, if we take into account a wide range of human diversity, then we will need a more robust redistribution of wealth. By removing radical differences in capacity from the subcontract, Rawls limits the most able man's agreement to redistribute economic and social inequalities among some members of society only. By excluding disability, economic redistributions to disabled people are depoliticized and made the purview of charity or virtue. Disability is thus out of sight, out of mind, and out of politics.

Perhaps one reason to remove disability from the subcontract of advantage is that it naturalizes the vertical relationship between the most and least advantaged. This is an argument that Thomas Pogge takes up in his critique of the capabilities approach and his defense of a Rawlsian resourcist view of justice. For Pogge (2002a: 204–5), the capabilities approach is problematic because it regards "human natural diversity in *vertical* terms and human beings as better or worse endowed." Rawls' *original* subcontract of advantage hinges on the ability of the least able man to understand himself as vertically inferior to the most able man. Instead of this vertical positioning, Pogge argues, a horizontal understanding of difference will "see persons as different – in regard to the color of their eyes, for instance – without believing that having green eyes is either better or worse than having brown eyes" (2002a: 205). In changing the terms from the "least able" to the "least advantaged," Rawls' subcontract is more align with Pogge's horizontal understanding of difference, as advantage is decoupled from ability.

Yet, in surveying the evolution of Rawls' subcontract, the double disavowal of disability is clear: we see him define disadvantage in relation to capacity, but then remove the least able from political consideration. Rawls' subcontract is potentially a tool to think about disability: to understand how societal structures generate disadvantage. Instead, Rawls' subcontract's evolution renders differences in capacity irrelevant. We also see why setting aside disability is so troublesome: because individuals consent to distribute advantage only among those who possess a threshold level of capacity, widening the range of capacity alters drastically the terms of agreement. Hence, this capacity contract illustrates the importance of thinking theoretically about living in a society with people who have a wide range of capacities – and for pushing back against Pogge's emphasis on horizontal rather than vertical diversity. The subcontract's terms will differ whether forged between people with different eye color or abilities. By circumscribing the range of human capacities, Rawls constructs an artificial society in which differences in capacities are meaningful and yet invisible.

Redress and the Defective

Like the original position and the contract of advantage, Rawls' discussion of redress – first in 1968 and then again in 1971 – offers us a radical way to envision the demands of equality for people with intellectual disabilities. Indeed, Rawls uses differences in human capacity to explain and legitimize redress, as any society intent on ensuring equality should be concerned with how inequalities of capacity threaten to map onto political inequalities. Careful examination, however, suggests no such radicalization. Instead, only individuals with a narrow range of human capacities fall under the purview of redress for Rawls, thereby depoliticizing societal responsibilities toward people with disabilities.

For Rawls, redress requires political interventions to remedy human inequalities and he argues that redress is essential to any theory of justice. Intellectual disability seemingly qualifies for considerations of redress "since inequalities of birth and natural endowment are undeserved," for Rawls, and that "these inequalities are to be somehow compensated for." Rawls continues:

> in order to treat all persons equally, society must give more attention to those with fewer native assets and to those born into the less favorable social positions. [...] In pursuit of this principle greater resources might be spent on the education of the less rather than the more intelligent, at least over a certain time of life, say the earlier years of school. (Rawls 2003 [1971]: 86)

Rawls continues, arguing that levels of intelligence are "simply natural facts. What is just and unjust is the way that institutions deal with these facts" (2003 [1971]: 87). Rawls' descriptions suggest both limitations and possibilities for a disability politic.

On the one hand, there are problems with Rawls' description of people with "fewer native assets" and their differences in capacity as "simply natural facts." Both descriptions conform to a medical model of disability that understands disability as arising naturally out of the body, rather than as a cultural phenomenon created through patterns of inequality and discrimination that stigmatize some bodies over others. As earlier described by disability studies scholar Lennard Davis, norms of intelligence and the means of measuring intelligence are highly contested. Indeed, what are "native assets"? Rawls seems to suggest that we can easily disentangle biological abilities from the social realities that produce these abilities.[3]

On the other hand, by focusing on how "institutions deal with these facts," Rawls shifts the significance of differences in capacity to societal relationships. Momentarily, how we design institutions and respond to human differences in ability comprise the basic problem of justice. Although Rawls follows a medical model of disability, his focus on institutions invites readers to adopt a social model of disability that focuses on the disabling consequences of institutions and systematic prejudice.

But what does Rawls have in mind when he refers to "those with fewer native assets"? I suggest that we can piece together more of Rawls' outlook on disability by analyzing his footnotes in the section on redress. When Rawls states, "undeserved inequalities call for redress" he chooses

[3] On criticisms of biological determinism, see Moore (2007) and Lerner (2007).

for evidence two articles in which authors use people with disabilities to modify the meaning and obligations associated with redress. Because Rawls seldom cites work in footnotes and because these citations recur as he is refining his argument over time, we can infer that Rawls accorded these references considerable importance. These include a 1944 article, "A Defense of Human Equality," by Herbert Spiegelberg and a 1950 article "Justice and Liberty" by D. D. Raphael. Raphael and Spiegelberg disagree regarding the treatment of disabled people: Raphael accords them unequal treatment to ensure their well-being, whereas Spiegelberg worries that equalizing handicaps threatens to dull the talents of the most privileged. These authors help us piece together more fully a picture of disability: both authors divide the defective from the normal and presume an overriding assumption about the misery of disability.

Rawls cites Raphael in his 1968 and 1971 discussion of redress, immediately after he states, "undeserved inequalities call for redress" (2003 [1971]: 86). According to Raphael,

> We think it right to make special provision for those affected by special needs, through natural disability, such as mental or physical weakness... We attempt to remedy, so far as we can, the inequality of nature... the inequality of treatment is an attempt to reduce the existing inequality, to bring the needy person up to the same level of advantages as the normal. (Raphael 1950: 187–8)

Repeatedly, Raphael distinguishes between the "needy" and the "normal." While "we" (the non-disabled/normal) cannot make "them" (the disabled/needy) equal, Raphael argues that "we" are obligated to care for "them" (1950: 189). Raphael depicts disabled people as outside his readership – passive subjects only – whose lives are pitiful. Accordingly, "Our recognition of 'special' needs is a recognition that some persons, by reasons of nature or accident, fall below the normal level of satisfactions, below the level which most people enjoy and which we regard as essential for decent living" (1950: 189). Raphael's take on disability seems aligned with Rawls' depiction of the mentally defective as arousing pity for moral agents. Raphael uses disability to expand the reach of redress, but under these conditions: that disabled people can never be "us" and that their lives must always be miserable. These are difficult terms to accept.

In contrast, Spiegelberg uses disability to delimit redress and, importantly, Rawls agrees: "we are to weigh [redress] against the principle to improve the average standard of life, or to advance the common good" (2003 [1971]: 86; 1999 [1968]: 166). Rawls restates this passage – first in 1968 and again in 1971 – and, both times, he adds a footnote to Spiegelberg. In the passages cited, Spiegelberg addresses the risks posed by redress. If taken too far, redress threatens to disadvantage the most privileged. For Spiegelberg (1944: 120), "it should be considered that the destruction of native advantages may easily constitute a cruel injustice against the better equipped individual." Disability helps Spiegelberg explain this form of cruel injustice: "In the case of the mentally handicapped this would amount to inflicting upon him an extra dose of training, obviously with a very dubious chance of success and in all probability even against his definite desire" (1944: 119; see also Pogge 2002a: 193). Improving the lives of people with disabilities, for Spiegelberg, threatens the common good as it wastes an inordinate amount of resources to enhance the well-being of disabled people – a goal with minimal success at best. Rawls seems to agree, arguing that the difference principle "does not require society to try to even out handicaps as if all were expected to compete on a fair basis in the same race" (2003 [1971]: 86). Rawls fails to clarify which handicaps are under societal domain and which are provinces of nature. Rawls' capacity contracts, which narrow the range of human abilities under political consideration, seem to depoliticize human incapacity in proportion to the impairment's severity. If Raphael helps us understand Rawls' assumption that disability arouses pity, then Spiegelberg suggests why Rawls might have considered disability so anxiety-inducing: disabled people threaten to drain scarce resources and stifle the development of the most talented.

In concluding his section on redress, Rawls states that he "shall not consider questions of eugenics," and yet familiarity with the logic of eugenics shows that Rawls did not escape from eugenic thinking. Immediately after he suggests that he will not consider eugenics, Rawls ties the promise of liberal equality to the improvement of human capacities. According to Rawls, "over time a society is to take steps at least to preserve the general level of natural abilities and to prevent the diffusion of serious defects." Consequently, "it is possible to adopt eugenic policies, more or less explicit" because it is "in the interest of each to have greater natural assets" (2003 [1971]: 92). Rawls fails to question how his own theory of justice privileges some people by, first, treating their abilities as biologically given and, second, by limiting their responsibility to people with impairments. Rawls continues: "We might conjecture that in the long run, if there is an upper bound on ability, we would eventually reach a society with the greatest equal liberty the members of which enjoy the greatest equal talent" (2003 [1971]: 92–3). Rawls clearly equates compulsory capacity with greater liberty, thereby marking disability as an essential threat to liberal progress.

Using the work of Spiegelberg and Raphael to reconstruct the image of the mentally defective reveals another instance of double disavowal in Rawls' discussion of redress. Again, we see Rawls conjure differences in human capacity to help legitimize redress, but then exclude some forms of human difference from political consideration. The work of Spiegelberg and Raphael also helps us understand the potent and diffuse anxiety that threatens Rawls' moral agents in the original position. It is not really an anxiety of whether or not agents have or will acquire a disability. Indeed, Rawls has already assuaged moral agents of this fear because they know their capacities fall within a "normal" range. It is instead a more diffuse anxiety that threatens moral agents: the anxiety of existing in a world *with* the disabled. For each theorist, disability is an abnormal failure of human functioning that erodes the well-being of non-disabled individuals and liberal society.

Feminist and Critical Capacity Contracts

Although critical and feminist theorists criticize Rawls' exclusion of disability, they too revert to an idealized cognitive subject to anchor democratic progress, thus becoming inadvertent signatories to Rawls' capacity contract. These critical capacity contracts continue to disavow disability, either by failing to comprehend fully the function of disability in Rawls' work or by relying on citizens' cognitive capacities to remedy the consequences of deeply embedded theoretical exclusions. My purpose is not to mark these theorists as hypocritical, but rather to show the deeply troubled and yet sticky commitment to compulsory capacity in political theory.

Adding Disability into the Contract

Theorists who take up issues of disability in Rawls sometimes assume that the problem is about exclusion and thereby overlook how disability already saturates Rawls' theory of justice. For instance, when Martha Nussbaum criticizes Rawls' treatment of disability, she assumes that social contract theorists have omitted disability from their theories. "These problems," as she describes in relation to disability, "cannot be ignored or postponed on the grounds that they affect only a small number of people" (2006: 100). Her depiction of the problem in Rawls as a mere postponement fails to grasp the depths to which disability permeates his normative framework. This move only concedes the second stage of disavowal and thus misses the important defining work that occurs at the first stage.

As Nussbaum's discussion suggests, this kind of approach assumes that disability is absent from social contract theory. Christie Hartley (2011) and Licia Carlson and Eva Kittay (2009) similarly refer to the total absence or marginal existence of people with intellectual disabilities from political thought. While I agree that people with intellectual disabilities appear only recently in political theory as an oppressed category, it is erroneous to assume that they never appear in the canon of political theory. Critical disability scholars argue that disabled people surface often as narrative tropes, used to symbolize death, foreboding, or malevolent natures in literature (Mitchell and Snyder 2000). Likewise, I expect that if we investigate the history of political thought more broadly, we will find disability performing important theoretical work (Arneil 2009; Clifford 2014).

Making the Contract and Capacities More Capacious

Other philosophers – such as Sophia Wong, Christie Hartley, Thomas Pogge, and Anita Silvers and Leslie Pickering Francis – aim to restore the promise of Rawls' egalitarianism by working within his framework to include all or most people with disabilities. These interventions aim to correct Rawls' exclusion, but many share Rawls' resignation that justice cannot encompass people with the most severe disabilities. As such, these capacity contracts fail to dislodge Rawls' ranked order of capacities and thus fail to wrestle fully with underlying ableist prejudice.

Wong (2009) argues that we should understand Rawls' two moral powers of citizenship as potential capacities that require certain enabling conditions, such as education, relationships, and human interaction. Because we cannot identify which human beings will develop these capacities, we need to ensure the full set of enabling conditions for all individuals. Wong uses as evidence people with intellectual disabilities abandoned in institutions who later gained important cognitive skills, making them capable of Rawls' moral powers. Although Wong offers us essential insight into the history of people with intellectual disabilities, I worry that her approach concedes too much to Rawls' conception of citizens. By retaining the two moral powers of citizenship, Wong neglects how persons with profound intellectual impairments may be able to contribute to society even if they lack the requisite abilities. Moreover, returning to Davis' idea of a ranked order, Wong's maintenance of Rawls' moral powers leaves intact ableist norms that rank individuals by their capacities.

Hartley reinterprets Rawls' social contract theory to include most people with intellectual disabilities, arguing that anyone "who can make a *cooperative* contribution to a society based on mutual respect should be viewed as members of society entitled to justice" (2009: 28, original emphasis). Even if some people with intellectual disabilities lack Rawls' two moral powers, many of them may still participate in the labor market, "engage in mutually supportive relationships," and help others develop important human values, such as humility and kindness (2009: 28–9). Hartley thus offers us a capacity contract with minimal capacities required. Hartley's cooperation, however, hinges on non-disabled people's willingness to engage with the disabled – to form mutually supportive relationships with them or to learn important lessons of kindness from them. Psychological research into ableist attitudes, however, unsettles this assumption (Ostapczuk and Musch 2011). Faced with ableist prejudice, people with severe intellectual disabilities may find few people willing to engage with them who can thus prove their cooperative potential. In addition, Hartley admits that some people with severe disabilities will be unable to cooperate, but like Rawls, she suggests that other principles outside of justice will preside over these rare cases (2009: 30–1).

Accordingly, the approaches of Hartley and Wong may be insufficient to undermine the exclusionary force of Rawls' capacity contracts, a point they share with Nussbaum's capabilities approach. While attempting to dismantle ableist assumptions within social contract theory, Nussbaum (2006: 181) concludes that the condition of "a permanent *vegetative* state of a (former) human being... is not a human life at all, in any meaningful way." In her insistence that "the social goal should be understood in terms of getting citizens above this capability threshold," Nussbaum enforces compulsory capacity at the foundation of her approach.

Pogge introduces an alternative approach to getting more people with disabilities into a Rawlsian resourcist framework. As mentioned, Pogge rejects a capabilities approach because it forces institutions to measure individuals' capacities, which reinforces ableist stigma. Instead, Pogge argues that all people deserve an equal share of resources and only people whose disability is *socially caused* have a claim to additional resources through compensation. He suggests that this approach will encompass most people with disabilities. People with disabilities that arise from genetic variation, bad choices, or bad luck do not merit additional resources under the purview of justice, and therefore will require alternative principles, such as charity or human solidarity, to ensure that their basic needs are met (Pogge 2002a: 188). But as Linda Barclay (2010: 159) argues, this response is not only counterintuitive to our ideas about fairness, but it is also at odds with Pogge's critique of the vertical evaluation of natural diversity. For Barclay (2010: 165): "It would apparently not insult me to offer me additional resources as compensation for my loss of hearing caused by a lack of occupational safety in my previous workplace, but it would insult me to offer me additional resources beyond the standard package for the genetic disorder that causes my hearing loss." Barclay's response illustrates that Pogge's resourcist view cannot evade vertical terms of evaluating capacities, but rather leaves some people with disabilities no recourse for compensation in the sphere of justice.

Silvers and Francis' revision of social contract theory to be "more like a project for engendering trust than a bargaining session" seems the most promising intervention (2005: 43). They argue that most people with intellectual disabilities can give or withhold trust. For those who cannot, their societal presence and treatment can bolster trust for all participants. "For people's trust in whether a society really understands and is committed to justice is influenced by whether inferior treatment of the disabled and other 'outliers' is prohibited or permitted" (2005: 74). While Silvers and Francis dislodge individual capacity as a requirement of social contract theory, they seem to presume that non-disabled people possess a high level of concern for the quality of treatment shown to people with severe disabilities – an assumption again weakened by entrenched ableist prejudice.

Each of these approaches foregrounds the capacities of citizens as the starting point for political evaluation. Moreover, they provide us with a narrow set of theoretical options within social contract theory. Hartley's typology between contractualism and contractarianism, for instance, neglects a third option of critical contract theory propelled especially by Charles Mills, which seems best equipped to unravel the domination of compulsory capacity.

Developing Capacities – and Disavowal

Charles Mills' treatment of race and social contract theory offers fruitful inroads for a project on disability as Mills targets specifically Rawls' depoliticized construction of rational capacity. For Mills (2009: 162), Rawls' reliance on ideal theory sustains the "systematic omission" and "evasion" of racial oppression. Mills argues that ideal theory idealizes cognitive capacities:

> The human agents as visualized in the theory will also often have completely unrealistic capacities attributed to them – unrealistic even for the privileged minority, let alone those subordinated in different ways, who would not have had an equal opportunity for their natural capacities to develop, and who would in fact typically be disabled in crucial respects. (Mills 2005b: 169)

Ideal theory promotes two distinct fictions in relation to idealized capacities: it neglects inequalities in cognitive capacities – whether these inequalities are caused by injustice or impairment – and it exaggerates the abilities of the privileged, constituting a class of not just able-bodied but super-bodied agents. Disabled capacities, however, are an outcome of systematic injustice for Mills and he avoids addressing how Rawls excludes people with disabilities.

Mills (1997: 18) argues that racism causes an epistemology of ignorance in which "cognitive dysfunctions" leave whites "unable to understand" because they live in a "cognitive model that precludes self-transparency." Mills describes the racial contract as promoting an epistemology of ignorance among (most) whites in which white people are ignorant of their own complicity with racism. In many ways, we can import Mills' description of the effects of the racial contract onto Rawls' treatment of disability. For example, for Mills the "cultivation of patterns of affect and empathy... are only weakly, if at all, influenced by nonwhite [disabled] suffering" (1997: 95). Moreover, in the racial contract "[e]vasion and self-deception thus become the epistemic norm" as certain non-white/disabled "realities were made invisible" (1997: 97, 92).

If the problem is ignorance for Mills, then the answer is to become more cognizant, both for whites and non-whites. If whites live in a "racial fairyland," non-whites must launch a cognitive voyage to overturn racism (1997: 97). "One has to learn to trust one's own cognitive powers, to develop one's own concepts, insights, modes of explanation, overarching theories, and to oppose the epistemic hegemony of conceptual frameworks designed in part to thwart and suppress the exploration of such matters; one has to think *against the grain*" (1997: 119, emphasis in original). Similarly, Licia Carlson (2009) refers to an epistemology of ignorance among philosophers around disability, suggesting that if we knew more about people with disabilities and their histories, we could craft better theories.

Mills is not the first to propose cognitive self-consciousness-raising as a first step to emancipatory politics, but judged from the lens of cognitive disability, this familiar route to empowerment is troublesome. Mills straddles a strange divide: he critiques Rawls' construction of ideal cognitive capacities as a source of inequality, but then calls upon the production of heightened cognitive skills to combat inequality.

While an epistemology of ignorance captures many components of domination, the language of ignorance seems ill-advised for an emancipatory project around intellectual disability, namely because of the ways in which the familiar Enlightenment category of ignorant/cognizant maps onto morally wrong/right. For Mills, ignorance shrouds the morally inferior while the cognitively superior are also morally superior. Better politics demands smarter people.

Another critical approach to Rawls is offered by Iris Young, which integrates queer theory to show how Rawls' conception of personhood normalizes one particular kind of identity by rendering deviant alternative ways of being in the world. For Young (2006: 95), the "situation of people with disabilities illustrates the problems of normalization most starkly." She criticizes philosophers' assumption "that lacking specific bodily or mental functionings automatically makes a person less competent than those that have them" (2006: 95). Offering the example of a person in a wheelchair, Young argues that readdressing architectural barriers alters the contribution-potential of disabled populations to the public. With inclusive attitudes and accessible spaces, disability disappears.

Although essential, Young's critique is incomplete. She recognizes how normalization affects people with disabilities, but her own example of wheelchair users threatens to reinforce the precariousness of people with intellectual disabilities. With physical obstacles removed, the wheelchair user can now achieve Rawls' construction of human behavior in the "usual sense" by contributing to society. Although Young is drawing our attention to the ways in which society creates disability, she also reaffirms that the *usual* way of being interdependent through relationships of productivity and mobility, thereby sustaining the stigma against people with profound disabilities.

Another reason to discard the language of ignorance is the different kinds of oppression at work behind ableism and racism. Ignorance promotes invisibility. As Mills' (2009) critique of Rawls reveals, issues of race seldom surface. White privilege sustains philosophers' evasion of race (Mills 2005a). In contrast, disavowal exceeds disappearance. Young understands this in her description of the paradoxical quality of normalization: deviant groups are both invisible *and* hyper-visible. We see this in the political thought of Rawls in which, unlike race, the threat of disability circulates *all the time*. Disability is present and yet forgotten, palpable and yet invisible, recurring but aberrant. Psychological insight into the multilayered account of bias helps us understand disability's complex position in philosophy: whether we explicitly aim to exclude or include it, implicit negative assumptions about disability persist.

These critical and feminist approaches thus reveal how we continue to disavow the severity of some disabilities, as if convincing ourselves that by engineering societal structures, revealing entrenched prejudice, or increasing knowledge we can eradicate intellectual disabilities entirely. In these multiple ways, critical interventions into mainstream philosophy's treatment of disability heighten the ideal of compulsory capacity and minimize cognitive difference as soon as it glimpses its possibility.

In making claims about ignorance and knowledge, critics of Rawls have more in common with his epistemology than they suspect. Both the original position and an epistemology of ignorance offer us intellectual agendas that promise knowable political transformations. Whether we are to choose political principles from behind the veil of ignorance or launch onto a course of rigorous education to overturn prejudice, these directions encase intellectuals in a purposeful and righteous agenda. In this we glimpse again that always confident cognitively ideal self: she grasps the problem, she knows the solution. If political transformation fails to occur as her epistemology promised, then the fault falls upon the ignorant who are unaware of or uncommitted to an emancipatory politic. In contrast, an epistemology of disavowal upsets our cognitively ideal fantasyland. Even if we increase our knowledge about disability, our biases may continue operating implicitly. Indeed, people with more education and higher incomes are more likely to prefer death over disability (White 2008). In a profession defined by cognitive demands, academics may harbor deep anxieties about cognitive incapacity that likely seep into our theoretical norms.

Conclusion: An Epistemology of Disavowal

Why focus so much attention on anxiety amid all the political obstacles facing people with disabilities, such as poverty, unemployment, abuse, and inequality? Why not focus on changing systems rather than implicit attitudes? Most scholars emphasize this structural change when they detail the benefits of architectural ramps, how ramps increase accessibility for all people, and how ramps offer a way to radically upend what it means to be able-bodied and disabled. Ramps, once in place, promote everyone's accessibility and require little to no behavioral modifications for people who rely on their feet for mobility needs. Confronting the problem of anxiety, however, forces us to rethink the ways in which we engage (or fail to engage) across radical differences in capacities.

Just as ignorance is the flip-side of knowledge, then countering disavowal requires confrontations with and engagement *amid* anxiety. Researchers repeatedly find that contact with disabled people is the most reliable predictor of positive attitudes toward people with intellectual disabilities. Contact is effective, I believe, because it makes disavowal untenable as it reveals to us our own implicit bias and we can no longer disavow our negative attitudes. Interpersonal contact also requires us to rethink our modes of interaction, asking how cognitive privilege enforces norms that penalize and exclude others. Insofar as our philosophical work captures this democratic mode of contact, we may better accomplish inclusion. Both Eva Feder Kittay and Sophia Isako Wong, for example, offer us examples of philosophically engineered contact as they enfold their philosophies in narratives, histories, and photographs of people with intellectual disabilities.

Additionally, feminist philosophers such as Kittay and Carlson upend the philosophical project from one of knowing to unknowing. For example, Kittay (2009b) issues two new rules for philosophers: epistemic responsibility and epistemic modesty. First, if philosophers are going to consider the issue of disability, then they are responsible for examining and knowing the actual lives of disabled people. If they refuse to do so, then they must acknowledge their own epistemic modesty, or as Kittay says, "know what you don't know" (2009b: 617). Kittay inverts philosophers' relationship to intellectual disability by emphasizing philosophers' limited cognitive capacities. Similarly, Carlson (2009: 563) argues, "the complexity of intellectual disability as a lived experience suggests that some barriers to knowledge for those who are not defined as intellectually disabled may be insurmountable, either temporarily or perhaps permanently." Here, Carlson and Kittay argue that acknowledging the *limits* of knowledge is necessary for expanding justice for people with disabilities.

Perhaps this is another reason why philosophy is so resistant to the full inclusion of people with intellectual disabilities: because the physical spaces we inhabit to pursue philosophical thought discriminate on the basis of cognitive capacity and that our philosophical solutions to democracy hinge on their further exclusion. As we consider our complicity with the exclusionary landscape of academe, we might at least glimpse one facet of transformation that needs to occur: the weakening border between the cognitively non-disabled and the intellectually disabled, both in our conceptual and physical worlds. Confronted with radical cognitive differences, we may begin to consider how we repeatedly tighten our identities, our places, and our futures to compulsory capacity. When we presume we can dismantle our anxiety about disability with knowledge, we reassert the fantasyland of the cognitively ideal world. That we have control over our minds; that we can decide to choose the way we think and, on demand, recalibrate the way we feel. This fantasy disavows disability all over again as it sustains once again the familiar and fantastic cognitively ideal self – always troublesome, always seductive.

4 Disabling Barriers, Enabling Freedom

Nancy J. Hirschmann

As all disability scholars know (but many political theorists may not), there are two "models" for understanding disability. The "medical model of disability" has been the dominant view since at least the Enlightenment, when advances in science and medicine created the realization that humans can intervene in the body to overcome disease (Stiker 2000).[1] In this model, disability is seen as an individual condition arising from a flawed body, which presents a "problem" that must be "fixed" or "cured." The problem is intrinsic to the body, which must adapt to the pre-existing environment. Disability is viewed as a loss, even a tragedy, that the person must want to escape, the appropriate response to which is pity; the less appropriate but more common response being repulsion. This view has dominated popular and official understandings of disability, affecting laws, policies, and institutions as well as customs, practices, and attitudes. Indeed, it has affected political theorists as well, as other essays in this volume attest.

The "social model of disability," by contrast, maintains that disability does not stem intrinsically from bodily difference but rather is brought about by social context, including the way the physical environment is built, as well as laws concerning, beliefs about, and attitudes towards persons with "different" bodies. On this latter view, the fact that I have difficulty walking and use a wheelchair does not in itself constitute a "disability": rather, the fact that most buildings have stairs rather than ramps, and lack elevators and automatic doors, "disables" my body from gaining access to various buildings. On this model, disability is a social construction in the most overt sense: because of the ways that social

[1] Although obviously it dates much earlier, to ancient times when "deformed" infants were abandoned to die from exposure because they could not be "cured" or "fixed," I am concerned in this chapter with the modern conception of freedom and thus the new ways in which the body was seen by Enlightenment science is worth noting. Whereas one could argue that in ancient times, neither the body nor the environment were seen as within the realm of human intervention, in the modern era the body is seen as one such changeable arena.

relations, the built environment, laws, and practices are structured and organized, certain bodies are hindered and made to be disabled, while other bodies are supported and facilitated.

Most disability scholars today recognize that a correct understanding of disability must draw from both of these models, despite the historical damage that the medical model may have caused (Shakespeare 2013). Overemphasis on the medical model has throughout history caused great injury to disabled persons who have been institutionalized, sterilized, and ostracized (Schweik 2009; Burch and Joyner 2015), forced to undergo torturous "curing" treatments (see Hirschmann and Smith, this volume), and excluded from political participation and the workplace (O'Brien 2001). The social model presented an important advance in a political and epistemological strategy to remedy such treatment by drawing attention to the ways that such an approach *produced* the very outcomes it assumed, and showing how small changes (like temporary barriers around manhole covers: tenBroek 1966b) would vastly increase the life prospects of disabled persons. Whereas disability is considered on the medical model as a "defect" that makes the person less valuable and constrained in her abilities and options, on the social model it is considered a "difference" that is *turned into* a disadvantage by hostile material, social, economic, and legal forces.[2]

But when the social model is carried to the extreme – that disability is *only* and *always* a product of discriminatory treatment – the body, and certain aspects of bodily experience, such as pain, ironically became decentralized and even ignored (Wendell 2001; Siebers 2001). Many realize that disability is produced by the interaction of specific body types and specific kinds of physical or material spaces, social practices, attitudes, assumptions, beliefs, and biases.

Nevertheless, the social model, while not telling a complete story of disability, tells a vital part of the story that is particularly relevant to freedom. Following claims of feminists, for instance, who have rejected historical claims that women are naturally unable to be lawyers, doctors, philosophers, boxers, or firefighters, and instead have pointed out that they have been *prevented and restrained* from engaging in these professions by norms, laws, practices, customs, and regulations that "disable" their minds and bodies from achieving whatever they otherwise could, disability scholars have helped us adjust our perspective. For instance, when a person using a wheelchair cannot enter a building because doing so requires one to climb stairs, the architecture of the building can be seen

[2] I say "material forces" here rather than "physical forces" to avoid the possibility that the reader may think I am discussing the body rather than, say, stairs.

as a barrier to that person's freedom. Forces that disabled bodies face daily – social arrangements, attitudes, built environments – all of which seem unproblematic from a non-disabled perspective, can and often do present barriers and constraints to disabled persons' living their lives as they wish. Many persons with disabilities do not want to change their bodies, they want to change these barriers, they want the able-bodied to see these facets of the world *as* barriers and not as inevitable or natural.

Thus, although I do not hold onto an extreme notion of the social model that ignores some physical limitations created by certain impairments, in this chapter I seek to draw on the social model's basic epistemological framework of situating bodies within specific kinds of physical and social spaces to critically engage the relation between desire, ability, will, and action: the basic components of freedom. The social model importantly keeps us from forgetting that things that are invisible to non-disabled persons, that seem like "normal background conditions," look very different from a disability perspective, and there is in many cases no logical reason why those conditions cannot be changed.

But what do I mean by "freedom"? Certainly, the late twentieth and early twenty-first centuries have seen a wide variety of theories of freedom, ranging from Hayek's (1978) and Friedman's (1962) strongly individualist conceptions to recent arguments about freedom as non-domination (Pettit 2001) and the expression of capabilities (Sen 1999). Much of the debate since the mid-twentieth century followed from Isaiah Berlin's "Two Concepts of Liberty" (Berlin 1971), which established a notion of "negative" liberty as the absence of external obstacles, and "positive" liberty that includes internal obstacles, providing positive resources to help people take advantage of negative liberties, and even evaluation of our preferences and desires as more or less important to us (Hirschmann 2003). But across these differences there are three primary characteristics of "mainstream" freedom theory: our definition of what counts as a "barrier" to freedom; the relationship between freedom and ability; and the nature of desire and the will. All of these involve in different ways the social construction of the choosing subject, and they involve different aspects of the relationship between the social and medical models of disability, although with increasing complexity. I will consider each of them in turn in the sections that follow.

Disabling Barriers

A key element of all Western conceptions of freedom concerns the notion of what counts as a "barrier" to freedom. The most common assumption found in dominant or mainstream freedom theories is that barriers to freedom, to be such, must come from outside the self, following

Isaiah Berlin's concept of "negative liberty" wherein freedom entails not being restricted by others from doing what you want to do (Berlin 1971; Hirschmann 2003). Starting at least with Hobbes, the notion of barrier as external to the self is key to the meaning of freedom. Hence he says:

> By *liberty*, is understood, according to the proper signification of the word, the *absence of external impediments*: which impediments, may oft take away part of man's power to do what he would... Liberty, or freedom, signifieth (properly) the *absence of Opposition*; (by Opposition, I mean external Impediments of motion). (Hobbes 1985: 189, 261)

For Hobbes, as for many theorists who followed him, obstacles must lie outside the self, they are "external." For instance, many would accept as unproblematic that if you locked me in a room, the locked door would be a barrier to my freedom to exit. Yet the matter is not always so straightforward: what if I had a key? Or what if there was another easy exit from the room? In such cases, the status of the locked door as a barrier becomes at least complicated; some could argue that it is still a barrier, but an inessential one, others could suggest that there is no barrier at all. But the barrier's "externality" becomes complicated as well: what if, instead of a key, I have a lock-pick set and know how to use it? Not everyone knows how to pick a lock, so having the set in itself would not constitute a way around the locked door, it would depend on my internal abilities to know how to use the set and to be able to actually use it (e.g., my hands don't shake uncontrollably).

In this sense, the application of freedom to the social model of disability seems to follow Isaiah Berlin's concept of "negative liberty" fairly straightforwardly; it simply challenges the way "external barriers" are defined and enlarges our conception of what counts as a barrier. As I have already suggested, the social model enables us to see that aspects of the built environment, social life, and law that we take for granted can be seen as external barriers to disabled persons' freedom.

But in other accounts of freedom, psychological states can also count as barriers to freedom and complicate the notion of what counts as an "external impediment" as Hobbes put it: what if the door is only closed, not locked, but my husband has threatened me if I leave the room? Unless I leave the room, I won't know whether he will act on that threat or not; sometimes he does, sometimes he doesn't, but when he does, I get beaten extremely badly. So I am understandably afraid: does my fear count as a barrier? Again, Hobbes says no; fear only gives me a reason to make one choice rather than another, such as when I face death on the battlefield and instead "consent" to the authority of a new sovereign and to my new role as servant of the soldier who spared my life. But many other people believe that when a thief holds a gun to your head and says "your money or your life," you are being coerced, not persuaded, into turning over your wallet and jewelry (Feinberg 1986).

These examples too, however, emblemize important insights of the social model, which pertain to the connection between the options that are available to us and the desires and preferences we form: if social relations are structured to make it impossible to ever attain X, the status of the desire for X changes dramatically. For instance, if I cannot enter a building because an earthquake caused structural damage, we would not say that my freedom is impeded; but if I cannot enter because someone locked the door to keep me out, we would so argue. So it is not that we cannot desire the impossible, but that in order to be seen as restrained in my freedom to realize a desire, the impossibility has to be seen as coming from an identifiable source that can be changed. To be unfree, on this view, someone – an agent – must prevent me from doing what I want (or force me to do what I do not want), and this agent must be acting with purpose and intent. If that purposive and intentional restraint is missing, then we cannot say I am "unfree," because freedom falls out of the picture. Thus, if a tree in my yard is hit by lightning and dies, I cannot say that my freedom to maintain my property as I wish has been restricted. By contrast, if my neighbor used poisonous chemicals on her lawn, which washed directly onto my yard and killed the tree, the story would be rather different and we would hold her responsible for interfering with my freedom to maintain my property. Barriers, restraints, or interference have to come from elsewhere on this negative liberty view, but they also have to be purposive and intentional (Benn 1988, Flathman 1984, Gray 1980; see Hirschmann 2003: 3–30 for a review of this literature).

But again, psychological factors complicate this notion: if my desires come from unfounded fears based on hallucinations, for instance, we would not say that barriers come from outside the self, but from inside. For instance, returning to the example of the locked door, suppose that instead of being locked, there is a large red X on the door, and I have a fear of red Xs. Berlin and other negative libertarians discount such fears in terms of their being barriers to freedom; they are exceptions that get set aside, and freedom in a sense steps around them. Disability scholarship complicates this further, however, for a wide range of cognitive abilities, from autism to what used to be called mental retardation, are often not seen as a barrier at all, but only defines the person's set of abilities that he or she should be free to develop and pursue (Nussbaum 2006).

Dis/Ability and Freedom

This last point leads to the second feature of most dominant theories of freedom, namely the relationship between freedom and ability. In much mainstream freedom theory, it is a commonly accepted truism that *freedom presupposes ability*: as Richard Flathman puts it, it is silly to say that I am not able "to jump, unaided, twenty-five feet straight up from the surface of the earth, to develop gills instead of or in addition to lungs" (1984: 139). What humans are *able* to do sets the context for freedom, for even thinking about freedom. Similarly (and less fantastically), Christine Swanton says that if I desire to *be* a millionaire, we could not label my lack of money as a "barrier" to my freedom, but if I were prevented from working hard in order to *try to become* a millionaire, then my freedom would be restricted (Swanton 1992: 48). Many other contemporary freedom theorists such as Raz (1986), Miller (1983), Gray (1980), Feinberg (1986), and Benn (1988) all include this assumption in their theories: I cannot be said to be unfree to do something that I am incapable of doing. Freedom presupposes ability.

Indeed, Berlin himself articulated this view in his famous essay "Two Concepts of Liberty":

> If I say that I am unable to jump more than ten feet in the air, or cannot read because I am blind, or cannot understand the darker pages of Hegel, it would be eccentric to say that I am to that degree enslaved or coerced. Coercion implies the deliberate interference of other human beings within the area in which I could otherwise act. (Berlin 1971: 122)

In a related vein, in "From Hope and Fear Set Free" he notes:

> If I am ignorant of my rights, or too neurotic (or too poor) to benefit by them, that makes them useless to me; but it does not make them non-existent; a door is closed to a path that leads to other, open doors. To destroy or lack a condition for freedom (knowledge, money) is not to destroy that freedom itself; for its essence does not lie in its accessibility, though its value may do so. The more avenues men can enter... the freer they are. (Berlin 1979: 192).

A number of things are notable about these passages from a disability perspective. First is his following the "medical model" in his conceptualization of blindness; although he may not have anticipated the variety of adaptive devices currently available to vision-impaired persons today, certainly Braille was available long before Berlin wrote this essay; and of course his reductive notion of blindness as the complete absence of vision collapses the considerable differences among persons with vision impairments (Kleege 1999). Second is his equation of psychological or cognitive disabilities with ignorance and poverty. On the one hand, all three are socially produced, one could argue: scholars have argued that poverty is both a construction of specific economic forms and a barrier to freedom, and indeed others have argued that poverty breeds ignorance and vice versa, as education has been identified as the single most important factor influencing wealth and poverty (Cohen 1979; Sen 1999). But on the other hand, whereas the goal would be to eliminate poverty and ignorance, with their elimination being essential to freedom, disability scholars advocate not the elimination of various cognitive disabilities but rather the acceptance and accommodation of the differences that cognitively disabled persons bring to social life. Thus, from the start, Berlin's account does not seem promising for disability, completely circumventing the thinking found in the social model.

A third notable quality is the imagery of the open door itself, which has particular significance for wheelchair users; after all, even if a door is open, if the doorframe is too narrow – as most doorframes are that have not been built with accessibility in mind – I cannot go through the door. The question then is whether the narrow doorframe is a *barrier* to my freedom – since the door is open, after all – or whether it just constitutes a "fact" about the environment that my body must figure out how to negotiate, much as gravity is a fact that I have to figure out how to overcome in order to jump higher. For indeed, Berlin asserts that an avenue's being "inaccessible" affects only the "value," not the "essence," of liberty, much like Rawls' distinction between "liberty" and the "worth of liberty" (Rawls 2003 [1971]: 204). But if freedom is defined by the number of "avenues men can enter" – with the crucial "can" encompassing the standard notion that freedom presupposes ability – there would seem to be a contradiction; if an avenue is inaccessible, then it is contradictory to say I "can" enter it. This distinction between an avenue's being "open" and "accessible" reveals a deeper, more disturbing assumption of Berlin's perspective; that is, this is consistent only from the perspective of those who do have access to the avenue – in the specific example I have invoked, from the perspective of the able-bodied walker.

Obviously, since Berlin's essay long predates the creation of the social model of disability, as well as widespread disability awareness, we might forgive him for these specific lacks. But his conceptualization of freedom is part and parcel of the modern history of the concept of freedom, and Berlin's essay has had considerable influence on contemporary theory. In particular, the distinction between being "unfree" and "unable" sits at the heart of contemporary theorists' consideration of what counts as a "barrier" or "restraint," which by definition are things that limit my freedom, whereas "inability" is seen as something that is intrinsic to myself or the world, part of nature or natural causes. Berlin wants to maintain a distinct division between those two, and he conceptualizes freedom with that in mind.

Again, this distinction can be seen to go back to Thomas Hobbes. In defining "the proper signification of liberty," Hobbes notes that "A free-man is he, that in those things, which by his strength and wit he is able to do, is not hindered to do what he has a will to" (1985: 262). Although most contemporary theorists who write on Hobbes focus on the "hindrances" or restraints caused by "external impediments of motion," as previously discussed, an equally important dimension of Hobbes' definition is ability: that "which by his strength and wit he is able to do." This latter aspect of his definition is more of a challenge for disability, for it has become such an important assumption of contemporary freedom theory as to merit hardly any notice.

For Hobbes, this criterion of ability is central to freedom; thus "a stone [that] lyeth still" is no more unfree than "a man... fastned to his bed by sicknesse," because both simply lack the ability to move; it is as much the property of stones not to be able to move under their own force as it is for someone with a bad case of flu – or in the late stages of cancer, or some version of paralysis – to be unable to rise from her bed. What prevents them from motion lies within themselves, and freedom concerns the absence or presence of strictly external obstacles (Hobbes 1985: 262). The comparison of the disabled or ill person to a "stone" might strike the disability theorist as ironic, given the ways in which disabled persons have been likened to animals and other non-human things throughout history.[3]

But the implications of this passage for the freedom of disabled persons are my primary focus, and the way in which disability is offered as the limiting condition of freedom is theoretically significant. In establishing that ability is the starting point for freedom – that we cannot be said to be hindered from something that we are otherwise unable to do – Hobbes sets in motion a liberal common sense view that dominates contemporary liberal theory. It is true that "sicknesse" could be construed as "external Impediments of motion," as when we think of a virus attacking the body (Hobbes 1985: 189, 261);[4] indeed, since Hobbes experienced a life-threatening and seriously disabling illness in 1647, causing him to suspend work on *Leviathan* – the culminating work, according to

[3] Twenty-first-century scholars will also note my collapsing of the two categories of illness and disability together, a move that I believe is justified by the seventeenth century's profound lack of knowledge about the variety of specific disorders that produce disability. See Stiker (2000).

[4] Thanks to Quentin Skinner for pointing out to me the possibility that illness could be construed as an external obstacle in Hobbes' view.

Quentin Skinner, of Hobbes' theory of liberty (Skinner 1996: 122) – for six months, one might think that he could be very sympathetic to such a view. Obviously, this would require a fuller understanding of Hobbes' view of illness, which we do not have, but such a view would make the comparison of the sick man to the stone serve no purpose. It also might be suggested that what the sick man and stone lack is not ability, but will; the man may be so ill as not to wish to arise, and the stone has no will at all. However, Hobbes' particular construal of the will runs against this. First, we have no control over what we will, only over how we act; the will is assimilated to desire, and my "will" is the final desire I have, the one that leads me to action. If the sick man does not want to get up, then he is doing what he wants to do when he lies there. But if he is so weak and tired that he is unable to get up no matter how hard he tries, it is the lack of ability that prevents him. But that does not mean, for Hobbes, that his body is thwarting his will; it means that the desire to lay where he is outweighs the desire to get up, and that is therefore his will because that is the desire that prevails. That is what leads me to conclude that in his comparison with the stone, Hobbes is talking about ability, not will. For as Hobbes notes, "One can, in truth, be free to *act*; one cannot, however, be free to *desire*" (1991: ch. 11, sect. 3, 46).

Moreover, the important point to be gained from Hobbes' analogy is that in his strictly descriptive account, if freedom presupposes ability, disabled persons are not made unfree by their conditions. Instead, those conditions define the limiting condition of their freedom. That is, an entire range of issues concerning freedom are simply swept off the table because if I am unable to do X, Y, or Z, then the question of my being free to do those things becomes completely irrelevant: freedom is beside the point. In Hobbes' logic, if I have lost the use of my legs, I am physically unable to walk across the room, and therefore my desire to do so is not properly thought of as relevant to liberty, much like Flathman's example of "growing gills." I might drag myself across the room, but one might think that, because such effort is more difficult, perhaps even dangerous, than the act of walking across the room is for an ambulatory person, the latter is intrinsically freer than the former; but Hobbes would disagree. If getting across the room is so difficult and tiring that I decide it is not worth the effort to drag myself, then, Hobbes says, that shows that I just don't want to do it. My decision to sit where I am, therefore, is a free one.

This relationship between freedom and ability pertains to cognitive abilities as well, and Hobbes' concept of "Madnesse" is interesting to consider in this light, because madness often prevents me from thinking clearly about what I really want. Madness is an overabundance of passion, which can be temporary (as in rage) or longer lasting (leading to distraction). But it is a condition to which all men are subject, and indeed one could argue that it was the main cause of the English Civil War. Curbing this madness, this overabundance of passion, is the purpose of men's giving up natural liberty to an absolute monarch in Hobbes' account of the social contract, because they are unable to regulate themselves.

Clearly, Hobbes believes that following appetites is the only possible meaning of freedom; but because such freedom can get us into trouble, and specifically threatening our lives, it needs to be reined in. Passions often interfere with our ability to choose what is in our best interest. This indeed is why "Children, Fooles, and Madmen that have no use of Reason, may be Personated by Guardians, or Curators" (Hobbes 1985: 219), a philosophy that guides Hobbes' thinking on the social contract. If we are rational, thinking about our survival, we will consent to establish a sovereign power with absolute authority to create law and punish those, including ourselves, who break the law. Since this is the only rational choice that we can possibly make in the state of nature, those who fail to consent to the social contract must in fact have intended to consent to it whether they realize it or not; for anyone who chooses to violate his own interests "is not to be understood as if he meant it" (Hobbes 1985: 192).[5] This would certainly be the case for those with passions so strong as to overcome the rational desire for self-preservation; vainglory ("I'm not going to consent to someone else's authority; I should be the sovereign!"), rage ("I can't believe the majority chose him, that's an outrage, there's no way I'll consent to that!") and so forth can be seen as instances of madness, and would justify others to speak on behalf of persons acting on those passions. Thus, all are obligated to the contract regardless of whether they (think they) want to consent or not, for "as well he that *Voted for it*, as he that *Voted against it*, shall *Authorize* all the Actions and Judgements, of that Man, or Assembly of men, in the same manner, as if they were his own" (Hobbes 1985: 229). Given the ease with which any of us can be mad temporarily, such as when we are in a jealous rage, or in a frenzy of "vainglory," or "blind lust," Hobbes might be taken to be saying that we are all – or at least most of us – disabled, which is why we need the authoritative absolute sovereign to protect us from ourselves.

This distinction between freedom and ability – and the claim that freedom presupposes ability, such that an inability to do X eliminates X from the consideration of freedom altogether – is a building block of many modern theories of freedom up through the contemporary age, particularly among liberal theorists who value the individualism at the heart of

[5] See also Skinner (1996: 136), on the relationship between fear, will, and freedom.

negative liberty: I have already offered some examples (e.g., Flathman, Swanton), but Kristján Kristjánsson (1992: 297) offers the most relevant example directly related to disability, of someone who must use a wheelchair due to a broken leg, saying baldly that I am "*free*" to run but "*unable*" to do so. That is, no one is preventing him from running, he simply lacks the ability.

The apparent paradox of saying that someone with a broken leg is "free" to run, however – a usage of the word that only those of us used to analytical philosophy could understand – is deepened when we consider a student with cerebral palsy who uses a wheelchair but who cannot attend my class because my building lacks an elevator: on the mainstream view of freedom illustrated by Kristjánsson, she, too, is "free" to attend my lecture, but she is "unable" to do so. Nobody interferes with her freedom on this view. After all, the stairs were not built with the intention of keeping out people who use wheelchairs, and the university administration does not ban disabled students from admission. In the dominant view, her disability is not relevant to freedom at all, for the problem is with her body.

This is precisely the view that disability theory's "social model" challenges. Kristjánsson's approach, like much of mainstream political theory and philosophy, at least tacitly if not explicitly employs the medical model of disability: his inability is specific to him, caused by the natural limits of his body. The problem is not seen to be the built environment, but his defective – even "broken" – body. This is a commonly shared view. Consider the fact, for instance, that many people – including many philosophers – often describe such a person as "confined to a wheelchair," rather than the more neutral "using a wheelchair." The chair is construed as a thing that is restricting her, rather than as the means for her freedom of movement; and since she is seen to be "confined" to the chair by the limitations of her body rather than limited in her *use* of the chair by built-environmental features like stairs or narrow doorways or curbs, her unfreedom is located in her body, not in those environmental barriers. The conceptual language that is commonly used to describe wheelchair users heavily deploys this medical model of thinking about freedom that Kristjánsson illustrates.

Moreover, in Kristjánsson's specific example, when he conjures a broken leg rather than a permanent impairment, he unconsciously shifts the reader's sympathies to agree with his argument: the broken leg is, we think, an inconvenience that many people experience but it is a temporary one and so it would be unreasonable to expect large-scale architectural or social changes, or vast expenditures. He should just be patient. There is a certain common-sense smugness to these arguments;

by positing desires such as growing gills or jumping 25 feet in the air or running with a broken leg – things nobody can do – philosophers set up ridiculous hypotheticals that can be easily batted away, leaving our ableist intuitions comfortably intact. But thinking about this scene from the perspective of the disabled student can shift our view.

In the first place, the student is prevented from not simply a particular act like running – or, in this case, getting into a building and attending my lecture. Rather, attending class is tied up with an entire "plan of life" to borrow from Rawls (2003 [1971]: 92, 406–17) – going to college, fulfilling the requirements of her preferred major, getting a degree, starting a career, earning a living. Attending class is a component part, but it in itself is only a part of the larger life plan that she is being prevented from pursuing. Moreover, this student's life plan is not one that is eccentric or difficult to fulfill but rather is one that vast numbers of other people pursue every day. Certainly, not all life plans can be attained because we lack, as Rawls points out, relevant "natural talents." So for instance, if someone who cannot sing very well dreamed of being a famous operatic singer, does society have the obligation to help make that happen? The fact that we generally reject such a claim on the basis of the person's inability to sing is the kind of thinking that leads to the rejection of disability claims. But the context for the example – singing opera – is already limited to a very small number of people who sing unusually well, so focusing on the person who is a very poor singer helps us forget that.[6]

Yet admittedly, the obstacle this student faces is not a universal one, like gravity is to jumping 25 feet into the air; it is only certain kinds of bodies that stairs obstruct, much as only certain kinds of bodies, with certain configurations of vocal chords, can achieve operatic greatness. So doesn't that show that the medical model is right – that the barrier is located in the student's body, not the stairs? That would have to depend

[6] Although in fact Florence Foster Jenkins, a wealthy and "tone-deaf" woman, was famous *for* being a terrible singer and even held a sold-out concert at Carnegie Hall a month before she died. She apparently was not bothered by the fact that her audience would laugh raucously at her performances (MacIntyre 2004). Now famous to current generations, thanks to the recently released movie about her starring Meryl Streep, I first learned of her thanks to an NPR radio show in 2009; an audio clip of her attempting to sing the "Queen of Night Aria" from *The Magic Flute* can be found at www.npr.org/templates/story/story.php?storyId=114075281. This may be a concrete example of Swanton's would-be millionaire; Jenkins was not barred from renting Carnegie Hall, but her lack of a good singing voice could not count as an inhibition to her liberty to *try* to be a celebrated diva. One infers from Swanton's account that persons with disabilities would similarly not be seen as unfree by virtue of those disabilities, but only if they were prevented by others from trying to achieve their goals. However, given the notion promoted by the social model that the built environment does itself pose barriers to such efforts, one cannot determine from her argument what society's responsibility would be to create the conditions to enable persons to pursue their goals.

on several incorrect assumptions that lie at the heart of the standard approach to freedom theory and which a disability perspective can help reveal. The first incorrect assumption is that "the world as we know it" is conceived as "natural," not a product of agency and choice. For instance, it was not natural or inevitable that stairs should be the dominant mode of movement between floors in buildings; buildings could have been built with ramps around their perimeters, for instance. But the dominant view assumes that stairs were a part of the "natural evolution" of the human practice of building, we might say. We therefore assume that humans should not be held responsible for building stairs before wheelchairs were so common; although cost is the primary justification for exempting many inaccessible older buildings from retrofitting today, the tacit *moral* argument underlying that justification is that nobody *intended* to harm or obstruct disabled people via such architectural design. That is why so many freedom theorists follow Berlin in claiming that barriers, to be such, must be erected intentionally and purposely. For instance, when it was discovered that tobacco companies apparently *did* intend to harm consumers, or at least knew about the harm and didn't care, that fact made them morally culpable, and so they had to pay large amounts of money. Intention is relevant when cost might seem otherwise prohibitive. But nobody builds a building with the *intention* of keeping wheelchair users out, we tend to think. In most cases, the wheelchair user doesn't even enter the builder's mind.

But that is precisely the problem from a disability perspective: just as sexual harassment had to be identified and named for us to understand that making unwanted sexual advances toward your secretary is not flattering but oppressive, so do disability scholars seek to change the way people think about and look at the built environment from the perspective of disability. Bodies are different, but some kinds of differences have been the subject of social preference. White bodies are preferred over bodies of color; male bodies are preferred over female bodies; bodies that can walk, see, have two upper limbs of a particular proportion and appearance are preferred over bodies that do not fit those descriptions. Disability is much like race and gender in these ways, and the barriers persons with those bodies face to participation in social life – like obtaining a university education – are arbitrary and discriminatory. They thus can be said to restrict freedom. Like feminism, disability theory can help reinforce our understanding that so much of our social world is socially constructed in the crudest sense: it is manufactured and produced through a series of human choices and actions that have reflected the experiences, perspectives, and interests of a particular subset population of the human species. They have literally "constructed" this world in a way that serves their *particular* needs rather than universal needs, even if they did not consciously decide to exclude certain kinds of people in their designs.

Disability, Desire, and Will

Disability thus challenges both of these basic assumptions of mainstream freedom theory. The relation between ability and freedom becomes linked to the notion of external barriers to both expand on what we count as a barrier – including aspects of the social and material landscape that are generally seen as "normal" – and to complicate and blur the line between inner and outer barriers. But this, in turn, leads to the third aspect of freedom theory, namely the place and meaning of desire and will. In *The Subject of Liberty* I argued that gender is a foundational if often hidden subtext for the way that modern freedom theory is structured, and particularly for who the "free subject" is, and I here make a similar case for disability. Just as feminism recognizes the ways in which patriarchy shapes women's desires, suggesting that the contrast between internal and external barriers itself is false, a disability theory of freedom must attend to how the interaction of the impaired body with the external environment creates the choosing subject.

In considering questions of subjectivity, it is important politically and epistemologically to hold onto the insights of the social model, for disabled persons still have to fight assumptions held by able-bodied persons that disabled persons do not value their lives, that they must want to die, even that they are incapable of having "normal" desires. The collapsing of intellectual and physical disabilities has moreover led to assumptions about the lack of rationality in all disabled persons. At the same time, the intellectual abilities of cognitively disabled persons to form desires and preferences and to imagine a life plan for themselves is often severely underestimated (Clifford 2012). All of these ableist assumptions have implications for a disability theory of freedom, and the social model has revealed them to disability scholars.

Yet even for disability scholars who reject the more radical social model and share a more complex view that disability is a result of the interaction of specific bodies and their impairments with a particular physical environment, a distinction between the body and the social also retains an epistemological and political importance. The social and the medical models, even if related, are distinct, and it is important to maintain a critical framework that allows us to argue that a wheelchair user confronting stairs has been made unfree not by her wheelchair but by the stairs or the lack of accommodating structures such as a ramp or elevator, even as we recognize that certain activities – such as taking a shower and getting dressed – are simply more difficult and time-consuming than they are for persons without mobility impairments. While we do not want to return to the old medical model per se and its long history of the mistreatment and dehumanization of disabled persons, the bodily aspects of disability must be recognized. We may need another term to account for these aspects in order to avoid the negative associations with "medical model" terminology.

For understanding how disability socially constructs desire encounters certain paradoxes that can be made apparent by comparing critical discourses of disability to previous parallel discourses in gender. For instance, whereas the history of feminism has significantly entailed the battling of patriarchal forces that constitute "women" as beings who must want certain things (like marriage, children, and sex with men) and cannot possibly want other things (such as education, careers, or sexual relations with women), the history of disability has significantly involved a struggle for recognition that what disabled persons want is for the most part not very different from what non-disabled persons want – and that often means to fit precisely into normalized gender categories that feminists have struggled to problematize. For instance, disabled males are sometimes seen as "feminine" because disability is imagined to produce "weakness" and "dependency," and some may thereby desire to prove their masculinity by becoming "supercrips" who perform daredevil stunts with prosthetic limbs, or become skilled players of "murderball" (Emens 2012: 230; *Murderball* 2005). Some disabled women, ironically, seen as unfeminine because of "distorted" bodies, or because they are seen as unfit to reproduce or incapable of raising their children, may thereby develop strong desires to fill traditional feminine norms.

But beyond those gendered categories is something more basic: Jacobus tenBroek's notion of "a right to live in the world" articulated the ways in which persons with disabilities just want to be able to live their lives, earn a living, go on vacation, have families, go shopping, ride the bus, and other quotidian activities. Indeed, much of the disability rights movement has entailed the fight simply to secure subsistence income, to remain alive (tenBroek 1966b; also tenBroek 1966a). The reluctance to engage "the social construction of desire" is thus understandable; it risks casting into doubt the aspirations of disabled persons to be treated just like everybody else, to be "normal."

The desire to lead a "normal" life is, on the one hand, understandable and apparently innocent: we all need to have economic support, for instance, and earning a salary is the primary way in which most people accomplish that, despite feminist and other leftist critiques of capitalism, and even of the ADA as a "welfare reform bill" that facilitated neoconservative social policy (Bagenstos 2003: 954; Hirschmann 2016). Privacy is important to most people, and having our own homes is an important facilitator. But the stress on "normality" has its own colonizing effects, as Foucault (1988) maintained. For desire is shaped and produced for disabled subjects no less than non-disabled ones, albeit in different ways.

In the examples I have just mentioned, the "difference" of disability is both something to escape and the marker of achievement; and the "internal" realm of will and desire is always informed simultaneously by the body and by the "external" realm of social context and environment. Freedom is not just about the ability to act on our will and our desires, it is also about forming and having desires and will in the first place, as feminists have shown (Hirschmann 2003; Cornell 1998). But disability helps us remember something that is true of everybody, not just people with disabilities, which is that desire and will are shaped by the particularities of the body. The way that we think about the body must always shape how we think about freedom: not just what it is possible to want to do, to think of being free to do, but how the concept of freedom itself is conceptualized.

What we might call the "ableism" of modern freedom theory is problematic not just for the discriminatory implications it has for the practical rights, entitlements, and liberties of disabled persons. It is also conceptually problematic because the body – or rather, the way we understand the body – is central to our understanding of freedom. In the modern canon, particularly once we enter the eighteenth century, we tend to think of freedom as a property of the mind and will; the body is merely notable by its absence, or at best as the instrument of enacting the will and freedom. Kant is often thought of as the main proponent of such a view, devaluing the freedom of action as belonging to the "phenomenal" realm, in contrast to the more valuable "noumenal" realm where the will resides. Although Kant acknowledges that we are sensible creatures, we are also intelligible ones, and to be free we must strive to reside in the noumenal realm as much as possible. Freedom is defined by rational *a priori* reasoning to the categorical imperative, and lies in the will and intention, "let the consequences be what they may." Women, of course, are not appropriate subjects of liberty because of their lack of rational thought; limited by their sensuality and physicality, they can occupy only the phenomenal world – although whether this is because of nature or social design is a matter of some debate.[7]

[7] In Hirschmann (2008), I argue that there is a tension in Kant's texts between claims that women are naturally incapable of rationality, and that they are capable but *should not* develop their rational capacities.

Rousseau, despite his infamous attention to sexuality and sensuality, similarly defines the highest freedom as "moral liberty," which consists in obedience to laws we prescribe to ourselves (Rousseau 1991: bk. 1, ch. 7), a freedom he contrasts to "the impulse of appetite," which he considers "slavery."[8] The body must be contained and controlled by the will, which lies in the mind. Rousseau particularly (and repeatedly) describes himself as "enslaved" by the passion he feels for women, and proclaims that passion is opposed to liberty (Rousseau 1953, 1997a).[9] Indeed, it is because of the fact that women stimulate the passions that they must be restrained in the private sphere in order to enable men to pursue the moral freedom of the general will in the public sphere. Women, Rousseau argues throughout *Emile*, are defined primarily by their bodies rather than their minds; and even though they are shrewd calculators who are skilled at manipulating men to do what they wish them to do, such actions never amount to freedom but rather are the instruments of men's enslavement. Because women are always sexual, and always desirous of sex, their bodies define them much more profoundly than is the case for men. Men, by contrast, can exercise will and reason to achieve the highest freedom, moral freedom. Although women can contribute to this project by being virtuous – a virtuous wife being an essential accouterment of the virtuous citizen – the struggle between desire and will, the body and the mind or soul, is often worked out through the public/private split and the division of the genders into primary association with two distinct realms.

Feminists have sorely criticized Kant and Rousseau for these understandings of freedom and their systematic denial of freedom to women by restricting them to bodily existence and the private realm (Schott 1997; Lange 2002). But even liberals like Mill and Locke tend to reject the body as a reliable source of desire; Mill distinguishes between the mental and physical pleasures in his hierarchy of utility, suggesting that pursuit of the higher (intellectual) pleasures enhances an individual's freedom. Locke, too, by emphasizing the role of rationality, suggests that freedom requires more than making one's own choices: it requires that one make the right choices, which may often involve eschewal of sensual pleasures and gaining command of the body, as he particularly demonstrates in

[8] Augustine similarly believed that bodily lust was opposed to the will, in that lust produced unhappiness and nobody "chose" to be unhappy; but he also believed that such people "chose" to give in to their lusts and thus paradoxically chose their own unhappiness. Rousseau thus provides a clearer account of the bifurcation I am describing; and at any rate I am concerned with specifically modern conceptualizations. See Augustine (1964), esp. Book I.

[9] See Hirschmann (2008), Wingrove (2000), and Zerilli (1994) for discussions of this aspect of Rousseau's theory.

Thoughts Concerning Education. There, following the principle (as Kant later did in his own education treatise) of "sound mind in a sound body," he dedicates almost two-thirds of his essay to the physical training and health of children with prescriptions for diet, exercise, regularity and constipation, and the positive health effects of letting children run around with cold, wet feet. The purpose of such bodily centered early education, however, is to control the child's will, and enable the parents to mold and shape it so that the child will want the things that he or she should want by the dictates of right reason. The body is seen as a potential thwarter of the will, of rationality, and of freedom. It is only in the last third of the essay that he turns to the subjects of traditional educational instruction, as these are necessary for the deployment and application of right reason, but the point of Locke's work is that the body must be subordinated to the will of another – the parent – if the child is to learn how to subordinate the body to his own will.[10]

And yet the body is actually central to many modernist conceptions of freedom, even if it is not generally recognized, or seen as subordinated to the will. For instance, despite the importance of rationality to freedom for Locke, freedom does not lie solely in the mind in his theory. Rather, freedom becomes a relevant issue insofar as the body can or cannot act on its preferences. Locke says that "Liberty is not an Idea belonging to Volition," for willing is different from acting on the will. Thus when "a Palsie" prevents my legs from moving me across the room when I want to move, "there is want of freedom" (Locke 1975 [1690]: 2.21.8); my own legs can prevent me from enacting my will. Although will may be a necessary condition for freedom to exist, it is not a sufficient condition. Indeed, Locke says that "Liberty cannot be, where there is no Thought, no Volition, no Will; but there may be Thought, there may be Will, there may be Volition, where there is no Liberty" (1975 [1690]: 2.21.8). Accordingly, "there is want of Freedom, though the sitting still even of a Paralytick, whilst he prefers it to a removal, is truly voluntary" (1975 [1690]: 2.21.11). The body is the locus of freedom. Even in the *Education*, the fact that most of the essay is dedicated to controlling the body, while on the one hand suggesting that the body is, should be, and must be subordinate to the mind and the will, on the other reveals that the body nevertheless plays a crucial role; in Kantian

[10] I use the male pronoun because of the ambiguous relationship of girls and women to reason in this essay and in the rest of Locke's work. Locke explicitly notes that his essay is primarily concerned with how to turn a boy into a "gentleman" and his precepts "will not so perfectly suit the Education of *Daughters*" (Locke, *Education*, 117). But see Mehta (1992) for a chilling account of the place of female bodies in the *Education*. Also see Hirschmann (2008: ch. 2).

terms, although we may strive to live in the noumenal realm, we are inescapably phenomenal creatures.

Hobbes might be considered the most obvious political philosopher for appreciating the place of the body in freedom, for as I have already noted, freedom for him is about the body's ability to move in a desired motion. Will and desire were relevant to motivating the body to move; will is what moves the body, being not "an act of Deliberation" itself but rather the outcome of deliberation, "the last Appetite, or Aversion, immediately adhaering to the action, or to the omission thereof" (Hobbes 1985: 127). Thus, as Locke was to later argue, the will is not an appropriate locus of freedom; according to Hobbes, we are driven by appetites and aversions, and these are things that lie outside our control – it is only within our control how to react to them. Thus, Hobbes says:

> No man can determine his own will. For the will is appetite; nor can a man more determine his will than any other appetite, that is, more than he can determine when he shall be hungry and when not. When a man is hungry, it is in his choice to eat or not eat; this is the liberty of the man. But to be hungry or not hungry, which is that which I hold to proceed from necessity, is not in his choice. (Hobbes 1999: 72)

Will is the function of desire, and desire simply comes to us, it is not something that we choose. I choose only whether and how to fulfill (or deny) my desires, not whether to have them; "One can, in truth, be free to *act*; one cannot, however, be free to *desire*" (Hobbes 1991: 11.3). This means that freedom cannot be at odds with my will; whatever my body ends up doing, whatever choice I make, reflects my will, or my last deliberation. Freedom therefore would seem to lie in the body, not in the will. Yet the will is far more directly connected to the body for Hobbes than it is for the other theorists mentioned here; Hobbes' lengthy description of the body as a machine includes the mind as part of that machine, part of that body.

The perspective of disability follows more closely on Hobbes' and Locke's approach than that of Kant and Rousseau, for it challenges the latter's subordination of the body to will. But even Hobbes and Locke rely on a bifurcation of body and will that affects their conceptions of freedom, and particularly rely on images of disability, as illustrated above. And certainly Locke separates will from freedom, locating the former in a mind that may be thwarted by the body, similar to Rousseau's portrayal of the body as posing a constant threat of betrayal of the will. Even if a disability perspective wishes to maintain a distinction between desire and will, contra Hobbes, it nevertheless wants to push further on the notion that Hobbes particularly seems to endorse of the will being intimately connected to the body, if not located in it altogether.

Rethinking the Will Through the Body

To communicate this idea, let me offer an example not unique to disability. Imagine that you are at a conference. It's after lunch, we've been drinking lots of coffee all day to stay awake, and water to stay hydrated, and those fluids are building up. You have needed to go to the bathroom for some time now; you had earlier decided to wait so as not to miss the exciting and stimulating discussion of the panel you are attending. In fact, two luminaries have been dancing around their differences for some time now, and it's about to explode into one of those moments that will go down in academic history, and you don't want to miss it. But you've reached a critical point, and you need to go. Now.

In this case, what is your "desire": to go to the bathroom, or to postpone further, for just one more interesting question and colloquy? In other words, who is the "you" that is doing the wanting and willing? The typical way of conceptualizing this dilemma is: does the free subject lie in the body or in the mind? In political theory, the conflict is often seen as a struggle between the mind and the body, with the desire of the mind (staying and listening to the panel discussion) being valued as superior to the desire of the body (to eliminate waste), and so your body expresses a desire at odds with your will. In Rousseau's terms, "you" are your mind, and the body is enslaving you, forcing you to do something against your will. For Kant, the will is the only way in which freedom is possible; indeed, the phenomenal realm, the world of the body and desire, "determines" us.

But disability theory turns that around, and suggests that the body has a will that runs contrary to desire – you really *want* to stay, after all, that is your preference: but if you don't leave this minute you're going to have an "accident." The body will assert its preferences despite what "you" want; and in this sense it could be said to have a will that overrides desire. Indeed, recent research in neuroscience argues that the will resides totally in the body, that the idea that "we" have "free choice" is an illusion, because approximately seven seconds before we are conscious of making a choice, our "brains have already decided… Consciousness of a decision may be a mere biochemical afterthought, with no influence whatsoever on a person's actions" (Smith 2011: 24).

Even if this new neuroscience research oversimplifies the philosophy of free will (as I think it does), it suggests at least that the will and desire are much more intimately connected with the body than many political theorists have allowed. Certainly, at a minimum, the brain is a bodily organ that directs and even controls other parts of the body; it is not a separate entity, and it is certainly not a simple duality of body/desire, mind/will. So disability theory at least enables us to say that, regardless of how unpleasant the body's demands are, no matter how at odds with particular desires, it is part of "you," and therefore of your "will."

Disability offers many examples of this sort, ranging from the "tics" of Tourette syndrome to an epileptic seizure to a diabetic low blood sugar. These are moments when the body forces its needs on the brain, on consciousness, and directs the mind to take a particular action. The body and mind are more than complementary, they are part of the same thing, and the bifurcation we have imposed on them through philosophy has distorted our understanding of their relationship. Feminists have, of course, long critiqued the mind/body duality, but I'm suggesting that disability carries this further.

But what purpose does it serve to say the will is located in the body? Doesn't it unnecessarily confuse an important distinction between the demands a body makes on us and how we respond to those demands? Isn't it important to recognize that we do have the capacity to resist at least some of the body's demands? My point is not to deny the capacity of humans to make choices and act on them. Nor is it to engage a technical discussion in neuroscience about how neurons travel through the body and how the brain operates, or to collapse rational deliberation into autonomic response. Rather what I'm suggesting is that how we in theory and philosophy talk and think about the will should attend to the insights of disability scholarship as discussed above, which can deepen and extend the feminist insight that our choices must be and always are made within the constraints of the body, that the body shapes and even at times dictates our choices, that to dismiss such dictation by a simple demotion to "desire" that can be controlled by the superior "will" is to distort what choice entails. We have to remember that the very *idea* of the will is a construction of human understanding; it is a concept that humans have created and defined over the course of centuries and millennia. So what I am arguing for here is just a different way of understanding and thinking about the idea of the will, about how we conceive of the will.

After all, in my hypothetical scenario here, the expression of this bodily function of elimination is not "just" or "purely" biological or autonomic: it is socially constructed. Imagine, for instance, that we lived in a culture that did not communicate shame about urination and defecation; perhaps even a culture where "I have to go to the bathroom" is greeted with smiles and well wishes to "have a good one." In such a society, perhaps instead of toilets and urinals being hidden away in special rooms, they are integrated into living spaces (like conference rooms) and you won't miss a single minute of the panel. Indeed, in ancient Ephesus (in Turkey), public toilets were constructed in just such a way as part of the Scholastic Baths so that men could discuss matters of the day as they moved their bowels.[11] The fact that we find elimination distasteful and shameful is a cultural product, it is not necessarily natural, any more than stairs rather than ramps are natural. So how we treat and shape and think about elimination is socially constructed through discourse, not a natural function of the body. As Susan Bordo maintains, "The body… is a medium of culture" (1993: 165). This affects our choices, our desires, and how we see the will in relation to these bodily impulses. In *Bodies that Matter*, Butler notes that even if there are

> "materialities" that pertain to the body, that which is signified by the domains of biology, anatomy, physiology, hormonal and chemical composition, illness, age, weight, metabolism, life, death… the undeniability of these "materialities" in no way implies what it means to affirm them… The linguistic categories that are understood to "denote" the materiality of the body are themselves troubled by a referent that is never fully or permanently resolved or contained by any given signified. (Butler 1993: 66–7)

Rather than materiality (in this case, physical bodies) and discourse being opposed, or even in tension, they are mutually constitutive: materiality could not have meaning without language, and language produces material reality: "it is not that one cannot get outside of language in order to grasp materiality in and of itself; rather, every effort to refer to materiality takes place through a signifying process which, in its phenomenality, is always already material" (Butler 1993: 68). Thus, "what constitutes the fixity of the body, its contours, its movements, will be fully material, but materiality will be rethought as the effect of power, as power's most productive affect" (Butler 1993: 2). The body may or may not exist outside of language, but we can never know such "outside" because the very attempt to "know" or "apprehend" or "understand" or even "experience" the body engages us in discourse. As Sara Ahmed (2008) maintains, this hardly means that the body disappears into language, or that materiality doesn't "matter." The body "as such" can never exist in some pure unmediated form but is always constituted by how we think about and treat it.

Recognition of this social construction of the body and its needs and impulses, in my view, helps complicate our standard bifurcation of body

[11] Thanks to Barbara Arneil for making me aware of this; see www.ephesus.ws/ephesus-latrines-public-toilets.html for photos of these public toilets' ruins.

and will within theories of freedom. It helps us see the will as located, at least partly, *in* the body itself. As Arthur Frank puts it, we are often "at the will of the body": he argues that when one becomes ill or experiences a change through impairment, "the body forces the question upon the mind... what's happening to me?" (1991: 8). He documents the ways in which pain caused by testicular cancer forced him to see a doctor, how it disrupted his sleep patterns, creating an "incoherence" in his life that he struggled to understand. His body made demands on him, forcing action and decisions that his conscious mind preferred not to make, imposing its will – his will – on his mind. Although we may be tempted to view this situation, once again, as bodily needs being "alien" to the "true self" that resides in the mind, Frank rejects that, for the body is the source of will in his view, it is the entity through which we live and we have to "acknowledg[e] its control." Rather than seeing the body as the extension of "I," the "essential me-ness" that resides in the mind, we should see the "mind is an extension of my body" (Frank 1991: 59).

Frank does not deny the place of consciousness, and what is traditionally understood as the will. We often make choices, after all, about how to respond to the body's demands: "I am a bodily process, but I am also a consciousness," he notes. But "the bodily process and the consciousness do not oppose each other." Indeed:

> what illness teaches is their unity. The mind gives meaning to what happens in the body, but the mind also thinks through the body it is a part of. The mind does not simply contemplate itself in a body with cancer. As cancer reshapes that body, the mind changes in response to the disease's effects. Pain taught me the body's power to shape thinking. But my thinking was shaping the pain even as it was being shaped by that pain – the circle is unbroken...We cannot fight cancer or tumors. We can only trust the body's will and get as much medical help as we can. We form the body's will through years of conscious acts, but in the end what finally happens just happens. (Frank 1991: 87–8)

This notion of "the body's will" is not so foreign to mainstream political theory and philosophy, although we may not often recognize that. After all, Descartes himself noted that "the mind depends so much on the temperament and disposition of the bodily organs," and Duncan maintains that for Descartes, "pain serves as evidence for his overall thesis of mind and body as conjoint, but different, substances" (Duncan 2000: 489). So on Duncan's reading, even for the philosopher sometimes credited as a key promoter of the mind/body dualism, the mind and the body are so integrated that perhaps the location of the will in the body itself is not such an odd idea.

Feminists have offered similar examples pertaining to reproduction in particular, such as menstruation, lactation, and parturition, all of which "dictate" in the same way that Frank discusses. Taking a disability perspective, however, allows us to engage a more pointed confrontation with political theory. For whereas women's bodily experiences can be simultaneously recognized and dismissed insofar as philosophy and political theory have been dominated by men, who by definition will not share in these experiences, any philosopher, male or female, can experience disability. That is something that most people fear; the common sentiment that "I'd rather be dead" than, for instance, blind or paralyzed expresses a very commonly held belief that disability is a lack, a loss, a tragedy. We therefore do not want to think about our becoming disabled, although it could happen to us at any moment (see Silvers 1995: 35–6; Libel et al. 2003; Hirschmann 2013c). Yet many disabled individuals welcome their bodily differences or disabilities and do not experience them as alien or hostile. Instead of seeing these events as alien attacks by the body on the self, moments of loss of self-control, from a disability perspective the body is communicating its needs and "the self" cannot be conceptualized apart from them. If we try to separate them, and ignore the claims of the body, the body will assert itself with a vengeance. A theory of freedom that attends to the lessons of both feminism and disability can help incorporate this primary role of the body in defining will and desire; it will be a theory that more accurately captures the human experience and aspiration of freedom.

5 Wollstonecraft, Hobbes, and the Rationality of Women's Anxiety

Eileen Hunt Botting

Women's anxiety is a hard case to assess within both disability studies and feminist political theory, because of two countervailing trends in the way it is conceptualized in law and medicine in the twenty-first century. On the one hand, clinical anxiety – understood as a range of anxiety, mutism, phobia, and panic disorders – is conceptualized in universal terms as a mental illness in psychiatry and as a mental disability in law.[1] Clinical anxiety often impairs people's ability to function well in society, and therefore is disabling to them. A paradigmatic example would be an adult whose agoraphobia is so severe that s/he cannot leave the house to work, or even buy groceries for food. Because clinical anxiety causes serious impairments in physical, cognitive, emotional, and social functioning, the 1990 Americans with Disabilities Act (updated in 2009) requires that people with clinical anxiety have the right to formal accommodation for the disabilities that result from their condition, by guaranteeing freedom from disability-based discrimination in employment, public transportation, public accommodation, and telecommunications. Under this ADA paradigm, clinical anxiety ought to be treated in the same way as any other disability: with legally guaranteed rights and accommodations that enable people, regardless of class, race, gender, further disabilities, or other status, to function well in society with their disability or disabilities.[2]

[1] The American Psychiatric Association (APA)'s *Diagnostic and Statistical Manual of Mental Disorders* (DSM-5) provides the medical definition of nine clinical anxiety disorders: (1) separation anxiety, (2) selective mutism, (3) specific phobia, (4) social phobia, (5) panic disorder, (6) agoraphobia, (7) generalized anxiety disorder, (8) substance-induced or medication-induced anxiety disorder, and (9) anxiety disorder due to a general medical condition (APA 2013: 189–90). For the legal definition of a mental disability as "a mental impairment that substantially limits one or more major life activities," or "the record of such an impairment," or "being regarded as having such an impairment," see the Americans with Disabilities Act (ADA 2009: Sec. 12102).

[2] The Key Bridge Foundation, under a contract from the Department of Justice, helps to enforce the ADA by enabling mediations of claims outside of court. In 2006, they reported a successful mediation in which a Virginia dentist was compelled to cease discriminatory pricing practices against a girl with Asperger's Syndrome and an anxiety disorder, and repay the parent for past excessive charges (US Department of Justice, Civil

On the other hand, it is often repeated that clinical anxiety has become an "epidemic" among girls and women today (Angell 2011; *Scientific American Mind* 2013). In twenty-first-century psychiatry, it is taught that women are twice as likely as men to present symptoms of panic attacks, generalized anxiety disorder, agoraphobia, and specific phobias (Hollander and Simeon 2008). Thus, anxiety is widely understood as a gender-specific mental disability that predominantly affects women. Among some medical practitioners and health-policymakers, there is a concern with overdiagnosis of the condition, especially among adolescent girls (Abrams 2012; APA 2013: 224). Since the beginnings of psychiatry in the nineteenth century, most famously in the work of Sigmund Freud, the medical profession has tended to negatively associate anxiety with women and attribute it to their female physiology (Showalter 1987: 160, 200). While contemporary psychiatry has moved beyond Freudian psychoanalytic theory and many of its gender stereotypes, it has not overcome the longstanding problem of sexual discrimination toward women in regard to their mental health and medical care (Busfield 1989; Rowley 2013).

These two countervailing trends in the legal and medical understandings of clinical anxiety, one universalistic and the other gender-specific, raise a series of interrelated questions for both disability studies and feminist political theory. If clinical anxiety may be treated as a bona fide disability under the ADA, then are all forms of anxiety potentially disabling? If anxiety is not necessarily disabling, then how are we to understand the relationship of non-disabling anxiety to disabling anxiety? If women are twice as likely to be clinically anxious than men, what accounts for the prevalence of this mental disability among women? Is it female physiology or gender discrimination against women that stands at the root of this remarkable difference in human epidemiology? Lastly, should women be treated differently than men on the basis of this tendency toward anxiety, whatever its ultimate cause?

In order to bring the insights of feminist political theory and disability studies to bear on these questions, I must lay down a few key terms and definitions. Although "female anxiety" is the common term for the aforesaid range of mental disorders diagnosed in girls and women, I will avoid it due to its sexist and essentialist implications. I only use the term "female anxiety" when I am speaking of the common ways in which the

Rights Division, Disability Rights Section 2006: 9). In a case that went to court, a veteran successfully appealed to the US District Court for the District of Utah for his right under the ADA to have a service dog in his condominium complex, due to his depression and anxiety disorder. He was awarded $20,000 in monetary relief for past disability-based discrimination (US Department of Justice, Civil Rights Division 2012).

aforesaid range of women's mental disorders are discussed in both science and popular media; the point of this chapter is to make a moral and political case for moving past such linguistic usage. When I use the term "female" or the term "women" it is as synonyms for "girls and women"; likewise, I use the term "male" synonymously with "men" and "boys and men." Hence, "women's anxiety" means girls' and women's diverse experiences of anxiety across the lifespan. Likewise, I use the broader concept of "mental disability" to describe a variety of cognitive and/or affective disabilities. I understand clinical anxiety disorders as kinds of mental disabilities that involve both cognitive and affective capacities, especially reason and fear. Following the feminist philosopher and disability theorist Eva Kittay, I do not assume that mental disability necessarily "results from a physiological impairment" or is purely "a consequence of an environment built to accommodate certain capacities but not others" (Kittay 2002: 264–5). Rather, I conceptualize anxiety as a kind of mental disability that may have either physiological or social bases, and is most likely a combination of both. Finally, I distinguish between clinical and less severe forms of anxiety, but do not treat the former to the exclusion of the latter, but rather see both kinds of anxiety as part of a continuum of fearful and often rational responses to the social environment. Whether or not anxiety is clinically diagnosed, it may be (but is not necessarily) disabling to a person in a given social context. If disabling, anxiety may entail formal accommodation to enable the person to function well in that context.[3]

Political theory has long concerned itself with questions of psychology, including the definition and significance of anxiety within human communities. Although Freud and Søren Kierkegaard are more typically cited, Thomas Hobbes (1588–1679) may be the most important philosopher of anxiety, because of his general premise that fear is a primary motivator of human behavior, and his specific treatment of the

[3] Disabling anxiety would, in the vast majority of cases, need to be clinically diagnosed in order to be legally recognized under the ADA, since the law specifies that current or historic evidence of the disability is sufficient for gaining rights under its auspices. If a person with disabling anxiety can show that s/he has been discriminated against on the basis of "being regarded as having such an impairment," then it might not be initially necessary to have a medical diagnosis, but it probably would be necessary in the long run to win a discrimination case (See note 1; ADA 2009, Sec. 12102). In the disability discrimination cases cited in footnote 2, however, the legal definition of anxiety as a mental disability mirrored the medical definition of clinical anxiety disorders, suggesting that clinical diagnosis was necessary for legal recognition as a person with disabling anxiety. The recent revision of the fifth edition of the DSM to streamline the list of clinical anxiety disorders from 12 (in 2000) to 9 (in 2013) indicates that people with disabling anxiety may be subject to multiple revisions of the medical and legal definitions of their condition (See note 1; APA 2013: 189–90).

experience of anxiety in his theory of human nature.[4] Hobbes viewed anxiety as a basic human cognitive and affective ability that can blend both reason and fearful feelings into a kind of forward-looking and life-affirming problem-solving skill.[5] Engaging Hobbes' political thought indirectly through her careful reading of John Locke and especially Jean-Jacques Rousseau, Mary Wollstonecraft (1759–97) used a similar concept of anxiety to address explicitly feminist political concerns, such as women's capacity to use their rational feelings of anxiety to develop solutions to the social problems posed to them by patriarchy.[6]

Political theorists such as Wollstonecraft, and Hobbes before her, have long argued that women's unequal social condition relative to men is primarily a product of society and law, not rooted in biological sexual difference. Disability theorists have made a similar case with regard to physical disabilities in particular. The paradigmatic example is a person in a wheelchair whose access to a building is blocked by the lack of a ramp (Kittay 2002: 264–5). While the person has a serious physical impairment, her disability is not caused by the impairment but rather by society's lack of accommodation for her handicap. In both the case of the woman and the wheelchair user, society could rectify their experience of unjust inequality by assuring the equal rights of all citizens, without discrimination of sex and/or disability. Bringing together these two schools of thought on the social construction of inequality, I argue that anxiety (clinical or not) is partly socially constructed by a broader system of gender inequality. This does not mean that anxiety is not real or is only imagined by the women and other people who experience it, or that anxiety cannot be a bona fide disability. Rather, anxiety can be a disability for anyone, regardless of sex, but it has predominantly affected women due to broader conditions of gender-based injustice.

[4] Søren Kierkegaard, *The Concept of Anxiety* (1844); Sigmund Freud, "Fear and Anxiety," *A General Introduction to Psychoanalysis*, part III, section 25 (1920). The applicability of each of these theories of anxiety to a secular feminist social and political theory of anxiety is limited by 1) Kierkegaard's focus on a Christian concept of original sin as the source of anxiety and 2) Freud's sexist prejudices against women, which contributed to the common view of anxiety as a "female malady".

[5] Throughout, I build on Nancy Hirschmann's point that Hobbes built a concept of "ability" into his definition of freedom. One is free when one is able to act on one's desires, due to the absence of external obstacles to achieving one's desires. This definition of freedom has some surprisingly positive implications for disability studies, for it allows us to diversely conceptualize the experience of human freedom and the abilities that enable it (Hirschmann 2013a: 170–5).

[6] Wollstonecraft makes what appears to be an indirect critical reference to Hobbes and other materialists in a footnote to *A Vindication of the Rights of Woman* (1792) (Wollstonecraft 1989h: 185). Although she never directly references Hobbes, her careful reading of Rousseau and Locke means that she was undoubtedly aware of the varied tributaries of the "Hobbist" school of thought.

The social basis for anxiety means that it can and should be revaluated by women and society at large, rather than construed as a permanent feature of female biology that is somehow immune to social criticism and transformation. Since women often feel anxiety as a valid response to unfavorable social conditions, they may learn to understand and employ anxiety as a means for anticipating, critically assessing, and navigating the gender-inflected difficulties of life. For example, girls with severe anxiety about their appearance that leads them to feel social phobia to the extent of missing school might be taught that this so-called "weakness" or "vulnerability" in their self-image is actually a potential strength of their psyches. Girls who are aware of the problems with sexist representations of female beauty have used their reason to gain a critical perspective on their social environment. This critical perspective can aid them in learning ways to navigate the problems posed by this environment, rather than being limited by them. As the social worker Brene Brown has argued, vulnerability properly understood is actually a form of strength, because it conditions people to be familiar with "uncertainty, risk, and emotional exposure" (Brown 2012: 33). Such vulnerability enables women to learn to be courageous in the face of their deepest fears, and, I will add, use their anxiety as a means for responding rationally and positively to challenges in everyday life. I aim to show how the political theories of Hobbes and Wollstonecraft can assist us in such a positive reconceptualization of women's anxiety for the benefit of those women disabled by it and for society at large today.

Using Wollstonecraft and Hobbes to Build a Social Model of Women's Anxiety

Because of their groundbreaking philosophical attention to the social construction of gender inequality and their similar psychological accounts of the cooperative relationship between reason and emotion in the human experience of anxiety, Hobbes and Wollstonecraft can serve as inspirations for a new social model of women's anxiety that emphasizes the ways that the experience of anxiety is constructed or shaped within particular social contexts. Hobbes and Wollstonecraft are particularly important resources for reconceptualizing women's anxiety because they both insisted upon theorizing the rough equality of the sexes in terms of their shared and defining human impulses, faculties, and abilities, such as reason, desire, love, freedom, and self-preservation. According to this feminist reading of Hobbes and Wollstonecraft, anxiety is neither an entrenched gender-specific "feminine" mental disability nor an essential female tendency toward irrationality. Rather, people (female and male) can learn to experience anxiety as an emotional and rational *skillful ability* to confront and solve their current or anticipated problems within broader circumstances of socially constructed domination. On this account, the reason for the prevalence of anxiety among women is the fact that they are far more subjected to domination and other forms of arbitrary sexual discrimination than men.

Following Hobbes and Wollstonecraft, I underscore that women's adaptation to suboptimal social conditions, although often detrimental or even deadly to them, can also be reflective of their strong capability for employing reason and emotion to navigate the obstacles to their (and their dependents') well-being. Linking the insights of Hobbes and Wollstonecraft to contemporary theories of disability, I emphasize how humans exercise their rational and emotional abilities in a way that is circumscribed by their dependency on people. Other people provide the social stimulation and relationships that enable the development of those abilities for emotion and reason in the first place. In the spirit of the work of Eva Kittay, this account of dependency as integral to the human condition opens the door to an ethical and political revaluation of disability (Kittay 2002: 257–76). Because humans are fundamentally dependent on others yet at the same time enabled in their development and well-being by this dependency, one can view their mental capabilities (such as reason and emotion) in a similar way to their disabilities (such as clinical anxiety disorders). Both mental capabilities and mental disabilities have as their common source the human experience of dependency and development within a particular (historically situated) community.

By developing a social model of women's anxiety, I strive to move past the prejudicial binaries that typically have been built into medical definitions of anxiety. The medical model frames anxiety in particular and disability in general in terms of curing the patient of it, or at least minimizing the impairment it causes for the patient. By contrast, the social model frames anxiety in particular and disability in general as broader, socially constructed phenomena that include, but cannot be reduced to, disabled persons' and doctors' experience of treating disability in these medical senses. Taking a critical normative perspective on disability, the social model "posits that people with disabilities are primarily oppressed by the structural barriers in society that handicap them" not by their physical or mental impairments (Malhotra 2006: 72).

Anxiety has been a broad, and therefore controversial, diagnostic category in several fields of human science and medicine. Building on the American Psychiatric Association's *Diagnostic and Statistical Manual*, a 2008 article in the *Clinical Journal of Oncology Nursing* succinctly defined anxiety as "an emotional or physiologic response to known or unknown causes that may range from a normal reaction to extreme dysfunction (indicative of an anxiety disorder), impact decision-making, impact adherence to treatment, and impair functioning or impact quality of life" (Sheldon et al. 2008). However simple and clear, this definition of anxiety is predicated upon several problematic binaries: the divide between feeling a physiological response and how one responds to it; the idea that emotions get in the way of decision-making rather than enhancing them; the assumption of an inverse relationship between impairment and quality of life; and the overarching opposition between dysfunction and normalcy. Against such prejudicial binaries, Michael Bérubé and Eva Kittay have set forth two influential revaluations of the abilities of the mentally disabled (Bérubé 1996: 179–80; Kittay 1999, 2002: 265–8). Critical disability theorists have exposed the moral and political problems with such binaries, since they reinforce stereotypes associated with disabilities rather than assess the social forces that contribute to their stigmatization in the first place.[7]

The ethical implications of such binaries are, on the whole, bad for people, and especially women with anxiety. When combined with the highly publicized statistic that women are twice as likely as men to be clinically diagnosed with anxiety disorders, these symbolic binaries contribute to pernicious gender stereotypes. In particular, the longstanding stereotype of anxiety as a "female malady" compounds the general stereotype of women (and especially those who panic, fear, or worry) as more emotional than rational, less capable of self-control and decision-making, and worst, rendered impaired and dysfunctional by apprehension to the point of deep unhappiness (Showalter 1987: 160, 200). Consequently, not only is anxiety cast as a disability regardless of whether it is actually disabling, but women with other disabilities are cast as more anxious. These intersecting gender and disability stereotypes negatively affect men as well, insofar as boys and men who have anxiety are stigmatized with a "feminized" disorder.

My goal is not to renounce the medical model of anxiety, because anxiety can create life-threatening problems for women (and other humans) that may need medical intervention. Rather, my goal is to pose a complementary social model that can reorient women and the broader society to see the potentially empowering dimensions of the

[7] Disability theorists often use the terms "stigmatized" and "stereotyped" interchangeably in describing how disabilities take on negative associations in society that become generalized in culture in a way that is harmful to the well-being of disabled persons (Brown 2013: 152; Frazee et al. 2006). In addition to deconstructing the binaries that produce the stereotypes that harm disabled women, the latter critical disability theorists note that disabled women are generally stereotyped as anxious (Frazee et al. 2006: 227).

anxiety spectrum, from worry to generalized anxiety disorder. Such a complementary social model of women's anxiety can work alongside science and medicine to help girls and women in the here and now, while simultaneously contributing to the slower social work of changing the way that girls and women are treated by society. For it is only by changing the social treatment of women that women will experience less psychologically and physically harmful anxiety in response to the disfavored status of their gender in society. More importantly, such broad-scale changes in the treatment of women are the only sure path to eradicating deeper structures of sexism and patriarchy that led to women's disadvantaged status in the first place.

This feminist theory of women's anxiety articulates in philosophical terms the broader cultural trend toward reclaiming disabilities as skillful and "different" abilities for personal and communal empowerment. My theory reflects and aims for solidarity with other women's attempts to use reason to rethink anxiety for the benefit of women and humanity as a whole. As the social worker and blogger "Anxiety Girl" has put it with poignant wit, she is (as all women with anxiety are) "striving for super hero courage in the face of fear" (Kristin: 2015). With not only Hobbes and Wollstonecraft as inspirations but also the stories of many college-age women with anxiety whom I teach and advise, I write this philosophical revaluation of female anxiety not to dismiss or minimize the seriousness of clinical anxiety disorders but rather to show my solidarity with all women who deal with different kinds of anxiety (whether clinically diagnosed or not), and to promote a broader culture of self-care and personal empowerment among us. Thus, the spirit of this chapter is the same as the contemporary "Mad Pride" movement, which seeks to reclaim the term "mad" from its pejorative social connotations in order to empower the people who deal with a variety of stereotyped mental illnesses to "come out" and represent their perspectives in the public sphere (Lewis 2013: 115–31). While anxiety is not always stereotyped as "madness," it could benefit from a similar public movement to rethink its meaning. Without denying that anxiety is often a serious disability for women, which is insidiously shaped by social forces largely beyond their control, I argue that anxiety can and should be revalued by women as a cognitive and affective ability to rationally and emotionally adapt to circumstances of injustice in a way that is potentially empowering and transformative for themselves and other people. The psychological and political paradox at the heart of this argument can be simply put but requires philosophical reflection to be fully understood: although anxiety is a disability for many women that is indicative of their oppression as women, this "different ability" or "(dis)ability" can empower women to work to overcome the conditions of patriarchal oppression that harm them as a whole (Hirschmann 2013a).

Rethinking Anxiety with Hobbes and Wollstonecraft: Understanding the Cooperative Relationship between Reason and Emotion

To offer a philosophical, yet politically useful, rethinking of women's anxiety, I return to Hobbes and Wollstonecraft for their innovative views on the cooperative relationship between reason and emotion. Because anxiety is a complex psychological phenomenon that involves both cognitive and affective capabilities, it cannot be defined philosophically without considering the broader relationship between reason and emotion (especially fear). For Hobbes, Wollstonecraft, and other Western European philosophers of the seventeenth and eighteenth centuries, the emotions or feelings were typically categorized as passions. In Chapter 6 of *Leviathan* (1651), Hobbes defined the "passions" that drive human behavior as falling under two categories, appetite and aversion. Aversive passions led to "TROUBLE OF MIND" and "more or less Displeasure or Offence." The simple passion of aversion provoked the more complex passion of "feare," as an anticipation of "hurt from the object" (Hobbes 2010a: 35–6). He went on in Chapter 12 to define "anxiety" as a kind of fear of the unknown or invisible. Anxiety, for Hobbes, was not solely an emotion or feeling, but could also be a rational response to one's unfavorable circumstances, especially unknown yet probable threats or harms. In a similar vein, Wollstonecraft did not conceptualize anxiety as a necessarily irrational emotion, but rather as a potentially rational feeling that humans, including women, could use to strategically navigate the difficulties of their social circumstances.

For Hobbes and Wollstonecraft, reason and emotion are not necessarily opposed or incompatible. This is the case abstractly (in the logic of their theories of the human being) and concretely (in their empirical observations on how human beings actually behave). In Chapter 8 of *Leviathan*, Hobbes argues that the passions, if "unguided" by reason, are "for the most part meere Madnesse" (2010a: 49). Reason must guide passion in order for humans to avoid merely passion-driven, or even mentally ill, behavior (Gert 2001: 244–5). Here, Hobbes employs a binary between reason and madness, but it does not presuppose a fundamental opposition between reason and emotion. His reliance on the reason/madness binary is problematic for its implication that people with bona fide mental illnesses are on the whole devoid of reason. However, Hobbes refrains from advancing a stronger claim about the incompatibility of reason with passion in human nature. In addition, his theory of human nature posits the passions, categorized into appetites and aversions, as the primary drivers behind deliberation, will, and behavior. The primacy of the passions in his theory of human nature allows him to conceptualize reason as a "guide" for the passions, and even imply that the guiding relationship between reason and passion holds irrespective of the particular disabilities or abilities of a person. Therefore, even a person with "Madnesse" might be guided by reason into social behavior, just as a people convulsed by civil war might be guided to choose an absolute sovereign capable of producing peace among them (Hirschmann 2013a: 174). Bolstering this point, Hobbes distinguishes between the "madness" of the theological "Schoole-men," who reasoned from false premises about incomprehensible subjects, and "Idiots," who merely lack education of their rational capacities (Hobbes 2010a: 51). Neither one is a lost cause, for both the mad schoolman and the mere idiot can be educated to use reason as a guide for the passions. Hobbes' metaphor of the "guide" suggests the image of reason walking alongside passion, pointing the way to rational decision-making. Yet this rational outcome is not lacking passion, but rather is driven by it. Passion takes the more active role, and reason the more passive yet still potent role, in this cooperative relationship. Hobbesian reason is the "scout" who points the way while letting the passions do the driving (Hobbes 2010a: 47).

As the philosopher Bernard Gert demonstrated, this conception of reason as a guide for the passions "cannot possibly be instrumental reason, for instrumental reason does not set any limits to the ends of the passions, all that it does is choose to act in that way that best satisfies a person's overall system of ends" (Gert 2001: 245). Hobbes' conception of reason is not solely instrumental but also normative: he posits better and worse outcomes for people based on whether reason has been a satisfactory guide to the passions that drive them. Gert's example to illustrate this point is helpful for developing a critical disability studies perspective on anxiety and other clinically defined mental health issues. According to Gert, Hobbes never concludes that suicide would be a rational outcome for a mentally disabled person to pursue, even if it would fully satisfy their preferences within their given "system of ends" or present set of desires. Rather, Hobbes' normative theory of the cooperative relationship between reason and passion entails that total submission to passion ought not to be endorsed for the good of any human being.[8]

[8] In addition to dismantling the view of Hobbes as a defender of a purely formal (and, specifically, instrumental) account of reason without regard for the content of the ends satisfied by the use of reason, Gert (2001: 244) also makes the related point that Hobbes is not a psychological egoist who posits that adult humans are solely driven by self-interest.

Wollstonecraft generally shared a view similar to Hobbes on the cooperative relationship between reason and passion. She likewise rejects a purely formal or merely instrumental account of reason in favor of a normative account of reason's role in realizing a circumscribed set of human goods rather than any given set of desires, regardless of content. In her first political treatise, *A Vindication of the Rights of Men* (1790), Wollstonecraft theorized that "self-preservation is, literally speaking, the first law of nature;... the care necessary to support and guard the body is the first step to unfold the mind... The passions are necessary auxiliaries of reason; a present impulse pushes us forward, and when we discover that the game did not deserve the chase, we find that we have gone over much ground, and not only gained many new ideas, but a habit of thinking" (Wollstonecraft 1989: vol. 5, 16).[9] Similarly to Chapter 14 of *Leviathan*, Wollstonecraft posits self-preservation as the "first law of nature" (Hobbes 2010a: 80). Hobbes had called this basic "impulse" to self-preservation "the right of nature." He subsequently derived the two parts of "the first law of nature" (or the first law of human morality) from this assumption: (1) "to seek peace, and follow it" and (2) "by all means we can, defend ourselves". Hobbes explicitly identified the second part of "the first law of nature" as the "right of nature" (2010a: 80). So Wollstonecraft's use of the term "first law of nature" to describe what Hobbes called the "right of nature" on one level makes explicit in language what logically follows from Hobbes' foundational claims about human nature: the fundamental right to self-preservation is the justificatory premise for the first law of human morality, to seek peace with others insofar as it preserves your life.

While Wollstonecraft's rational dissenting Christian theological commitments make her sound more like Locke than Hobbes at times, the above passage from the *Rights of Men* indicates that she thought the law of self-preservation was fundamental to the human condition. Like Hobbes and Rousseau, but unlike Locke, she posited self-preservation as an inherent right of humans, not a specific and perfect duty to God (Botting 2016). Like Locke, however, she framed all rights as derivative of duties, and all duties as directives of God's rational moral law. For Wollstonecraft, to follow the first law of nature was to *indirectly* follow God's law. One could say the same of Hobbes, in the sense that the laws of nature were for him practical and rationally deducible maxims for the promotion of peace, which at best approximated the laws of

[9] Susan Khin Zaw pointed out that this passage likely reflects Wollstonecraft's devoted reading of Rousseau, especially *On the Social Contract* (1762) (Zaw 1998: 98–9). It is also illuminating to note the Hobbesian background for both Rousseau's and Wollstonecraft's accounts of the relationship between reason and passion.

God that stood fundamentally beyond human comprehension (Hobbes 2010a: 79–98).

In the passage cited above from the *Rights of Men*, Wollstonecraft went on to describe the passions (including, first and foremost, self-preservation) as the "necessary auxiliaries of reason." "Auxiliaries," in the eighteenth-century English lexicon, were helpers or assistants (sometimes referring to military assistance, but originally referring to intellectual relationships, such as the productive role of mathematics for physics).[10] The passions, especially the primary "impulse" to self-preservation, were thus the helpers or assistants for the proper development of human reason (Wollstonecraft 1989: vol. 5, 16). For Wollstonecraft, as for Hobbes, the development of human reason was not open-ended or morally neutral, but rather aimed toward the realization of a circumscribed set of human goods. The passions assisted reason's development such that adult humans came to understand the value of their rational "struggle" with passion as constitutive of the goods that defined their lives as ones worth living and preserving (Wollstonecraft 1989: vol. 5, 180). Even if it was difficult to negotiate what she called the "game" of life – partly because of the impulses of passion – a person could rationally grasp the most important (and often unexpected) moral lessons from the process of playing the game (Wollstonecraft 1989: vol. 5, 16).

As the philosopher Susan Khin Zaw indicated, it was Wollstonecraft's personal experience of severe class- and gender-based oppression that led her to see the potentially liberating power of reason for people exposed to injustice. Reason could work with passion to effectively critique the system that dealt them a bad hand. Hobbes, on the other hand, faced a similar predicament to Wollstonecraft. With an impending civil war driving his concern with both self-preservation and peace, Hobbes theorized the liberating power of reason and the passions when they worked in tandem to solve the problems that undercut the endurance of human life itself (Gert 2001: 243).

There is an important difference between Hobbes and Wollstonecraft on the nature of the passions, however. Chapter 6 of *Leviathan* argued that the passions derived from basic appetites (for pleasure and life) and aversions (to pain and death). These passions were refined into "manners," or peaceful behaviors, through education, religion, economics, and other systems of social habituation – most importantly, those imposed by the state. Wollstonecraft, in contrast, drew a stronger moral distinction between appetite and passion. Wollstonecraft construed the passions as a product of the complementary interaction of reason and emotion.

[10] "Auxiliary, adj. and noun," *Oxford English Dictionary* online, www.oed.com.

Reason helped to constitute or build the passions, and substantively distinguish them from mere appetite. As Zaw (1998: 100) perceptively put it, Wollstonecraft understood reason as strengthening the passions and preventing their devolution into the appetites from which they originally sprung. This account of the passions as deeply shaped by reason is a productive variant on Hobbesian logic, for it allows Wollstonecraft to theorize emotions such as anxiety as potentially rational feelings that cannot be reduced to non-rational or irrational expressions of fixed and distinct physiological appetites.

Theorizing Anxiety as a Rational Feeling with Wollstonecraft and Hobbes

For both Hobbes and Wollstonecraft, anxiety is a fearful emotion that may be rationally felt. In Chapter 11 of *Leviathan*, Hobbes explains that "Anxiety for the future time, disposeth men to enquire into the causes of things: because the knowledge of them, maketh men the better able to order the present to their better advantage" (2010a: 65). As the political theorist Philip Pettit puts it, this capacity for anxiety, combined with speech and reason, enables people "to take precautionary action against various dangers. It primes them to worry about the range of future possibilities" (2009: 149). Such anxiety can ultimately lead to either self-preservation or self-destruction, depending on the extent to which people cooperate to achieve the end of peace. However, feeling anxiety about an unknown future is fundamentally rational because the unknown may pose a threat to one's life or felicity. For Hobbes, this rational feeling of anxiety also promotes rational thought: anxious people strive to use their rational faculties to uncover the causes of things so as to better predict the outcomes produced by such causes. Better predictions enable better judgment about choices to promote one's well-being.

Wollstonecraft provides a parallel use of the term "anxiety" in her first novel, *Mary, a Fiction* (1788). It is the tale of a young woman who is arranged to be married to a man she loathes, and seeks refuge from the relationship by traveling to Portugal to care for a sick friend. The eponymous (and partly autobiographical) heroine of *Mary* experiences anxiety, first, as a rational feeling and, second, as a motive for further rational thought. When her best friend Ann was dying, "She worked up her mind to such a degree of anxiety, that she determined, once more, to seek medical aid" (Wollstonecraft 1989: vol. 1, 31). Mary's anxiety concerning Ann's illness is rational because her death is an as yet unknown, yet highly probable, bad outcome of her current medical condition and care. Her rational feeling of anxiety also spurs rational, problem-solving thought. Mary strives to understand the causes of Ann's pain in order to relieve her friend's suffering and prevent her untimely death.

Not all feelings of anxiety are rational, however. Anxiety is the impetus to discover causes for the unknown, but the outcome of this conjunction of reason and passion may be irrational. As we have seen, for Hobbes anxiety may be felt rationally in the face of uncertainty about the future, because the unknown may pose a threat to our self-preservation or well-being. As a negative corollary of this thesis, he posits that anxiety may be felt irrationally if a person fearfully seeks to know what is absolutely unknowable. His classic example of such irrational anxiety is found in Chapter 12 of *Leviathan*, "Of Religion." He remarks that when people cannot be assured of the "true causes of things," they "suppose" causes according to personal "fancy" or the external "Authority of other men" (Hobbes 2010a: 66–7). These suppositions are mere conjectures, as they lack evidence for their claims about the unknowable first causes of things (i.e., the cause of the world itself). As indefensible conjectures, these suppositions promote a backward-looking, myth-making thought process rather than a forward-looking, problem-solving thought process. That Hobbes thinks religion is the most obvious result of such irrational anxiety is made clear through his wit (Hirschmann and Wright 2013: 22). He dryly observes how religions appear "ridiculous" to each other and yet people do not rationally assess the assertions about absolutely unknowable "Invisible Powers" at the root of their own faiths (Hobbes 2010a: 69).[11] An example of this folly was religious people who identified cases of demonic possession; in Hobbes' sober view, the possessed were actually "Lunatiques" whose passions had overridden reason to the point that their experience of "Madnesse" was more severe than it was for most people who suffered it only temporarily. Hobbesian "Lunatiques" may lose the ability to govern themselves or even live in peace with others, and therefore offer a hard case of the deleterious effects of the passions if unguided by reason. On the other hand, bona fide "Lunatiques" are rare for Hobbes, but religious people making "ridiculous" claims of "Invisible Powers" are common. To his credit, he directs his scathing criticism to the latter category of religious people driven by irrational anxiety. From a critical disability studies standpoint, he may even be read as showing sympathy for those people persecuted as "Lunatiques" because they were taken to be possessed by demons in the view of irrational religious people. It is not too much of a stretch to infer that Hobbes had sympathy for both the lunatics' internal struggle with the passions and their external

[11] Despite its harsh sarcasm, Hobbes' skepticism about knowledge of first causes does not necessarily entail a philosophical atheism on his (or anyone's) part.

struggle with the dangerous stereotypes that seventeenth-century religion imposed upon them (Hobbes 2010a: 243).[12]

In her early educational writings, Wollstonecraft similarly complicates her view of anxiety by showing how it can be hurtful to people who feel it. In her first book, *Thoughts on the Education of Daughters* (1787), she warns that if anxiety of any sort is "concealed" rather than revealed, it may "impair" the constitution of girls (Wollstonecraft 1989: vol. 4, 25). This practical concern of her educational theory suggests that it is physiologically best for girls to express or communicate their anxiety rather than to repress or hide it. For example, girls might healthfully share feelings of anxiety by working through the answers to their common moral problems together, as modeled in her 1788 children's book *Original Stories*. The latter work also stated that anxiety may cause "unsound" sleep and other health problems in girls (Wollstonecraft 1989: vol. 4, 385). Both of these examples of the physiological pathologies of "concealed" and "unsound" experiences of anxiety imply the dangers of repressing it. Girls repress anxiety because they are told it is a bad, shameful, or irrational passion, but the repression of anxiety prevents them from tapping into its positive capability for rational problem-solving. Such repression is in fact irrational and bad for one's health, whereas the rational and open expression of anxiety may promote at least physical (if not moral) health.

These observations suggest that Wollstonecraft thought that bad practices of education made girls particularly subject to irrational feelings of anxiety, which were detrimental to their self-development as humans. In her broader political theory, and especially in *A Vindication of the Rights of Woman*, she located the cause of this trend in the contingent and largely pernicious gender and class norms of her eighteenth-century society. Girls must be taught to feel anxiety in a rational way, not because they are naturally incapable of it, but because society had encouraged norms for women that obstructed their free and full development of the basic human ability for rationality. For the perpetuation of such stultifying gender norms, she partly blamed women's own "anxiety" to inculcate the superficial manners of society in their children: "the anxiety expressed by most mothers, on the score of manners… stifle, in their birth, the virtues of man" (Wollstonecraft 1989: vol. 5, 230). This anxiety is irrational because it in fact harms the people it seeks to serve, by stifling the growth of universal, rational moral "virtues" in favor of artificial, gender- and class-based "manners" in the rising generation.

[12] From the fifteenth century, the persecution of witches was tied to the Catholic Church's "charges of demonic possession" (Levack 2013: 307, note 66).

Understanding the difference between irrational anxiety and rational anxiety was key for restructuring the educational process such that it precipitated what Wollstonecraft called a "revolution in female manners," or more egalitarian gender norms (Wollstonecraft 1989: vol. 5, 114). Irrational anxiety was self-destructive because it did not aim to solve potential or actual problems, but merely allowed those problems to grow in the mind of the girl by feeding on her fearful emotions. Rational anxiety was life enhancing because it enabled girls and women to think through their social predicaments and puzzle out a way toward greater physical or even moral health for themselves and others. For example, Mary's "anxiety" about Ann's cough "led her to practice physic" (Wollstonecraft 1989: vol. 1, 22). This medical knowledge enabled her to alleviate the pain of her dying friend, and consequently increase her own sense of usefulness to others beyond the meager gender roles allotted to women of her time and class. Although Ann dies, Mary lives with a recalibrated sense of moral and social purpose. Egalitarian reform of education on a broader scale would enable many more women to rationally recalibrate their sense of being useful to others and humanity as a whole.

Both Hobbes and Wollstonecraft acknowledge the rational and irrational feelings of anxiety that tend to preoccupy people, male and female. Yet they also contend that anxiety, (1) if rationally felt, can (2) generate a rational response to one's fears. Under these twin conditions, anxiety can function as a kind of skillful ability for using reason and emotion (1) in tandem and (2) appropriately within a given set of circumstances. By both accounts, anxiety is skillful if it contributes to the individual's capability for rational assessment of internal and external circumstances that are actually or potentially harmful to her well-being.[13] This is a radically egalitarian capability according to Hobbes, as he hypothesizes that all human beings (regardless of sex or other attributes) in a state of nature have an "equality of ability" for prudential (or rational, life-affirming) thinking (2010a: 76). Wollstonecraft's heroine Mary exercised such a skillful ability when she realized her beau Henry, whom she met in Portugal while caring for her friend Ann, would likely die of pneumonia: "With eager anxiety she cried, 'What shall I do?' This day will kill thee, and I shall not die with thee" (Wollstonecraft 1989: vol. 1, 66). Although on one level this is a dark – borderline suicidal – thought, in which she contemplates the bleakness and undesirability of a life without her beloved, Mary resists following any self-destructive urge and

[13] Well-being for Hobbes (an anti-Aristotelian materialist) could be merely physical, whereas for Wollstonecraft (a religious feminist with a Christianized account of the Aristotelian virtues) it ideally has a moral and a physical component.

instead rationally confronts the fact of Henry's imminent death and the deep emotional loss it entails for her. Her "eager anxiety" initially steers her toward the thought of suicide but she refuses this escape from life's tragedies. The eagerness of her anxiety leads her to affirm the value of her own life without him, but not in a way that denies the bitter realities of their mortality. We thus see in Wollstonecraft's first novel a reason for revaluing not only anxiety but rationality itself within both feminist theory and critical disability studies. While Western philosophy has often conceptualized reason as male or masculine, or treated it as an essential property of the able-minded, these patriarchal and ableist prejudices are historically contingent and therefore culturally surmountable. Building on Hobbes' fundamentally humanistic and egalitarian conception of anxiety, Wollstonecraft's *Mary* breaks away from the tropes of many a sentimental novel of its time. This autobiographical, and therefore realistic, fiction suggests to its readers that anxiety, understood and practiced as a rational feeling, enables women and other disabled people to handle the challenges dealt them by the broader social and political system.

For Hobbes and Wollstonecraft, anxiety is successfully strategic if it empowers a person to solve, in at least the short term, the problems posed to her by her circumstances. Hobbes' state of nature explains how successfully strategic anxiety works on the formal, or abstractly rational, level. In Chapter 13 of *Leviathan*, he sets up the state of nature as a hypothetical conception of human life outside of positive law and government. This hypothetical scenario raises the questions: what if humans lived in this way? How would they interact with each other, if at all? Hobbes' answers show not only the rationality but also the successful strategy of worrying about the parity of abilities across people in such anarchic circumstances. In theory, everyone has the power to steal away the conditions of each other's well-being. If equally faced with such a threat, people would rationally choose to seek peace with one another by transferring their collective power to an absolute sovereign capable of ruling them all, rather than risk the loss of life that a projected "warre of every man against every man" would entail (Hobbes 2010a: 79). This outcome is not only strategic (it exchanges perfect freedom for total peace under an absolute ruler) but also successful (it preserves life for all through the contractual exchange of freedom for peace).

On a personal level, Wollstonecraft expressed a similar logic of survival and peace in her *Letters Written during a Short Residence in Sweden, Norway, and Denmark* (1796). In this emotionally raw yet seriously literary collection of letters originally written to her adulterous common-law husband Gilbert Imlay, she confronted, contemplated, and eventually came to terms with the break-up of their marriage. As she moved closer to psychological acceptance of the bleak fact that their once blissful relationship is over, she wrote, "I shall wait with some degree of anxiety till I am informed how your affairs terminate" (Wollstonecraft 1989: vol. 6, 425). This forward-looking concern with the presently unknown outcome of his (and therefore her) business affairs in Scandinavia was colored by "some degree of anxiety," but she calmly reasoned (to him, but most of all, to herself) that this feeling would likely be resolved once she returned home to England to see him. By anticipating the final resolution of their marital and business affairs, she hints at the possibility of peace, if not between them, then with herself.

According to the moral and psychological theories of Hobbes and Wollstonecraft, male and female humans may exercise their skillful ability for anxiety toward the end of rational, problem-solving analysis of their particular predicaments. For Wollstonecraft, however, this capability is even more salient for girls and women in society due to the circumstances of injustice that they face as a result of arbitrary, man-made norms of gender and sex discrimination. Wollstonecraft's view of women as artificially degraded does not proceed from a hypothetical original condition, such as a Hobbesian state of nature, but rather from her historical observations on the "oppressed state of her sex" (1989: vol. 6, 269). With this empirical approach, she contrasts the moral and physical corruption of the typical upper-class women of her time with a few recent examples of "wild girls" who were primarily raised in a free, outdoor environment, often by accident or abandonment (Wollstonecraft 1989: vol. 5, 112). Formulating a forward-looking conditional, she wonders if girls were generally raised with freedom akin to these wild children, would they then develop the strength of mind and body necessary to develop the full range and degree of human virtues previously associated only with men? Since they are not raised with freedom, girls and women must deal with suboptimal conditions for the development of their capabilities as humans. Women's anxious awareness of this socially constructed predicament is the first step toward their rational assessment of adaptive solutions to it. The women of Wollstonecraft's society could tap into the power of anxiety for their strategic advantage, perhaps especially if they pooled their "care and anxiety" for other people into problem-solving endeavors for the benefit of their "sisters" (Wollstonecraft 1989: vol. 5, 200). As Wollstonecraft reflected in her *Short Residence in Sweden, Norway, and Denmark*, the experience of "care and anxiety" for her daughter Fanny helped to propel her sense of solidarity with womankind's struggles as a whole: "I feel more than a mother's fondness and anxiety when I reflect on the dependent and oppressed state of her sex" (1989: vol. 6, 269). Instances of familial care could build outward toward global concerns for women's (and human) well-being, both on the individual and group levels. It was in her final work, *Maria, or the Wrongs of Woman* (1798), that Wollstonecraft theorized how such a chain of "fond anxiety" could, in turn, link together women through their rational feelings of care for the dependent and vulnerable (1989: vol. 1, 123). Women's anxieties might then become widespread and powerful motives for rational, cooperative, peaceful, woman-friendly social reforms.

In *Maria*, Wollstonecraft used the literary form of the political novel to develop a theory of emancipation for women and by women. The novel's Gothic setting in an asylum is a visionary metaphor for the social construction of women's mental disabilities. The protagonist Maria is imprisoned in the asylum against her will by her abusive husband, not because she is incapable of caring for herself or their infant daughter, but because she resisted his attempt to sell her into prostitution. From a critical disability studies perspective, what is striking about the novel is its political prescription of solidarity among women as a step toward realizing justice for and by women. Alone and afraid, women can do little to affect change for themselves or others. But when they band together, as Maria does with her jailor Jemima by bonding over their personal experiences of patriarchal oppression, they are able to feel "fond anxiety" for each other's plights, unlock the door, and escape the asylum of patriarchy together.

Hobbes thought that all people have reason to feel anxiety, because the unknown may pose threats to our lives and well-being. Wollstonecraft applied this general thesis with greater specificity to girls and women, who have good reason to feel anxiety, given their particular gender-based problems as produced by a patriarchal society. The realization that such anxiety is rational not irrational is the first step in a therapeutic moral psychology of self-care (Ure 2008: 67). If empowered with the idea that anxiety may be a skillful ability for navigating obstacles to their personal and communal happiness, girls and women will not see this psychological disposition as absolutely disabling, essentially female, or necessarily irrational.

Toward a Political Theory of the Rationality of Women's Anxiety

The political implications of this theory of the rationality of women's anxiety are twofold, negative and positive. First, the theory ironically runs the risk of reinforcing conditions of patriarchal domination by way of valorizing individual female capabilities for short-term rational navigation of the obstacles posed by the social system. As long as "exemplary" women (like Wollstonecraft herself) manage to escape the snares of oppression through their smarts, it is easier to dismiss her overarching theory that the social, economic, and political system actually disfavors women's advancement on the whole even when some women seemingly succeed. But this objection lacks depth from the standpoint of both feminist political theory and disability studies. Just because some people overcome obstacles, like Wollstonecraft did in her own difficult life, not everyone will demonstrate that same capability. The exception does not prove the rule. Moreover, a woman like Wollstonecraft (or her characters Jemima and Maria) who uses her rational command of anxiety to puzzle a way out of the asylum of patriarchy is acting in response to an extant sexist social system. She is learning to use rational anxiety to her advantage precisely because she and all other women are systematically disadvantaged in comparison to men.

On the positive side, the aforesaid risk of reinforcing conditions of patriarchal domination might be effectively minimized by emphasizing the value of this normative model of the rationality of women's anxiety for the healthcare community – both patients and practitioners alike. If female patients and their caregivers were indeed encouraged to think of anxiety as a strategic capability and rational adaptive response to unfavorable social predicaments, then the practical possibility of a population-wide "gestalt switch" on the issue would be real (Kuhn 1996: 111–35).[14] Women's anxiety would no longer be seen as an "epidemic" to be cured but rather a potential strength of women born of their historic vulnerability in society. The instantiation of a positive conception of women's anxiety within medical care could in turn shape the views of wide swathes of the human population, across the generations. Several gender and disability stereotypes could be cast aside as a result. Maternal anxiety might not be negatively associated with the older notion of female anxiety as irrational and essential to woman's nature (Showalter 1987: 70). What Wollstonecraft called "fond anxiety" for children might not be predominantly associated with women in particular, but rather with humane people as a whole (Kittay 1999: 162–81; Held 2006: 16).

Such a medical, cultural, and psychological "paradigm shift" would have spillover effects among other groups, such as encouraging anxious boys' and men's, and non-anxious people's, recognition of the situational and strategic value of rational anxiety (Kuhn 1996: 111–35). Over time, entrenched patriarchal values could be countered with a revaluation of

[14] Like many other humanists, I borrow Kuhn's concept of the "gestalt switch" or "paradigm shift" in worldviews and apply it to a normative domain outside of the hard sciences.

women's anxiety in the face of male domination. Careful practice of "fond anxiety" for self and other across a broad section of the human population could lead to the successful treatment of the root cause of the problem (a patriarchal system that devalues women's lives and caring work), rather than mere triage of the symptoms (individual females' struggles with worry, exploitation, and unhappiness).

While Hobbes and Wollstonecraft agree that it is rational to have anxiety about the unknown, they think it irrational to posit explanations or causes for the unknowable. Religion is Hobbes' standard example of such an irrational attempt to explain the unknowable (e.g., the view that the Book of Genesis literally chronicles the origin of the world) (Hobbes 2010a: 67). Patriarchy is Wollstonecraft's standard example of a phenomenon with unknown origins for which people irrationally posit conjectural causes (e.g., the view that Eve was made from Adam's rib, therefore woman is subordinate to man) (Wollstonecraft 1989: vol. 5, 95).

Such backward-looking explanations of the unknowable are irrational, but it is rational to attempt forward-looking analyses of potential harms to oneself (and others for whom one cares). According to both Hobbes and Wollstonecraft, it is rational to seek power (a "present means, to obtain some future apparent good") to avoid as yet unknown but probable harms (Hobbes 2010a: 53). Forward-looking, problem-solving anxiety is one such kind of power, whereas backward-looking anxiety is a kind of myth-making, problem-feeding thought process. When reconceptualized according to the political theories of Hobbes and Wollstonecraft, women's anxiety is better understood as a potentially problem-solving skill that combines intuitive emotion and prognostic reason than as an essentially disabling tendency toward irrationality. From this moral vantage, the contemporary "epidemic" of female anxiety need not be alarming, but if people do care enough to worry about these women, it may be, paradoxically, a good sign for the future empowerment of humanity as a whole. Indeed, the paradox of women's anxiety is ultimately a political one: the more we are aware of anxiety as a (dis)ability that has predominantly affected women yet is potentially empowering to all people, the more prepared we are to take on the challenges of overcoming structural inequality for the benefit of all.

6 Dyslexia Manifesto

Kathy E. Ferguson

Elan looks solemnly at me from his side of my kitchen table as I assemble my materials. He is waiting for his lesson to begin. He tells me about his weekend as I get out cards, papers, pencils, magnets, and books. He eyes this accumulation hopefully, looking for the colorful cubes or objects that could signal a fun activity – a treasure hunt or a story – but he is willing to do any task I set for him, even if it is difficult or repetitive. Elan wants to learn how to read and write.

Elan has trouble with sequencing. The requirements of linear order evade him. He has difficulty putting sounds or words in a row and keeping them there. His many talents – his curiosity, sense of humor, and deep thinking – allow him to soar in verbal exchanges, but in order to read and write, he has to be able to relate sounds to symbols in an orderly, step-by-step fashion, not leaving any needed letters out, not putting any extra ones in, not substituting one for another. While skilled reading is not limited to a linear process – it requires interactive feedback loops, parallel processes, and reactivations – there is nonetheless a basic aspect of reading that requires step-by-step movement through the parts of the text. Words and sentences have two parts, as far as Elan is concerned – the first part and the rest. The first word in *Cats like to drink milk* is *cats*, he readily acknowledges, but the rest is a jumble. The first syllable of *magnify* is *mag*, but the order of the other two syllables is a mystery. The other kids make fun of him for not apprehending the order that seems obvious to them: "Sometimes I get things backwards," he tells me. For Elan, everything is either the first thing, or not the first thing. But reading and writing don't work like that. Without clear sequence, the word *bold* easily becomes *blood*; *drip* becomes *dirt*; *fern* becomes *friend*. Accurate sequence is critical to literacy.

On a different day, at the same kitchen table, Karen readies herself for our lesson to begin. Karen is able to put letters and numbers in order; sequencing is not her main problem. At least, it is not immediately evident as a problem. In our very first lesson, she read a lengthy passage aloud from a children's story with few errors of decoding (reading individual words). To my amazement, she read as smoothly when the text was upside down as she did when it was right side up. Yet, when she looked up from the page, she retained nothing at all of the content. She did not recall the most basic elements of the story – that it was about two children, that there was a mysterious man in a cape, that the children were in a woods – nothing. Her eyes filled with tears and she gave a hopeless little shrug. "I have trouble..." she said in a small voice.

In the language of Orton-Gillingham analysis, Elan has problems with phonological awareness, while Karen lags in reading comprehension. Both these children are dyslexic. They have a great deal of trouble functioning in the world of written signs. When tutoring commenced, Elan had just finished kindergarten, while Karen was half way through fifth grade. Orton-Gillingham (O-G) is the name of the language therapy most effective in teaching dyslexic people to read, write, and spell. Named after neuroscientist Samuel Orton and educator Anna Gillingham, O-G is the foundation of multisensory, structured language education. For nearly 20 years I have been using O-G to tutor dyslexic children and adults, starting with my own sons.[1] Without O-G instruction, I am certain that neither of my sons would have learned to read or write well. If effective O-G instruction were widely available in schools, it is a virtual certainty that the huge proportion of fourth graders who cannot read with adequate fluency and comprehension – now estimated at 38 percent nationwide – would be substantially reduced (Moats 2010: 6; Wolf 2007: 135).

Reflecting on this experience, not as the panicked parent of struggling children but as a political theorist attentive to the politics of language, leads me to think about O-G as a kind of biopolitics, an apparatus for managing difference through a cascade of orchestrated techniques. Through a tight series of visual and auditory drills, structured multisensory repetition, detailed analysis of errors, thorough attention to patterns and exceptions, and calculated practice, O-G brings a strict order to language's unruly assemblages. We teach the child to see the word, the whole word, and nothing but the word. It works – we can teach most people to understand the relations between sounds, symbols, and meaning, to both apprehend and produce them in the proper order. We can teach most people to read and write. Yet most schools do not use this approach to reading and writing, despite its availability for close to a century, and despite the high costs of failure for dyslexic individuals, their families,

[1] My thanks to Ron Yoshimoto and Sue Voit, Fellows of the Orton Gillingham Society of Educators and Practitioners, for teaching me.

and society as a whole. This chapter investigates the biopolitics of dyslexia and of Orton-Gillingham interventions into dyslexia, as well as the political implications of current and alternative approaches to literacy.

The Biopolitics of Dyslexia

Only a few scholars (Philpott 1998; Connolly 2002; Campbell 2011) outside of neuroscience and education have found dyslexia interesting. Those who look at its political aspects tend to focus on the rights of people with learning disabilities to acquire remediation or accommodation in schools or workplaces. While those questions are important, I come at them through another line of inquiry – I examine O-G training as a kind of neuropolitics, an intervention in the circuits of bodies, brains, and cultures that has implications for how we think together and live together. William Connolly (2002: xiii) defines neuropolitics as "the politics through which cultural life mixes into the composition of body/brain processes." Examining how we successfully teach a dyslexic learner to read and write provides further insight into Connolly's (2002: xiii) explorations of "the layered character of thinking" and "the critical significance of *technique* in thinking, ethics and politics."

The term *dyslexia* drives from the Greek combining forms *dys* (difficulty) and *lex* (words). Difficulty with words. Dyslexia is not one thing, but rather a constellation of traits; it occurs on a sliding scale from mild to severe. The International Dyslexia Association (2002) and the National Institutes of Health have adopted the following definition:

> Dyslexia is a specific learning disability that is neurological in origin. It is characterized by difficulties with accurate and/or fluent word recognition and by poor spelling and decoding abilities. These difficulties typically result from a deficit in the phonological component of language that is often unexpected in relation to other cognitive abilities and the provision of effective classroom instruction. Secondary consequences may include problems in reading comprehension and reduced reading experience that can impede growth of vocabulary and background knowledge.

Dyslexia has many names: specific learning disability, language learning disability, developmental reading disorder, visual and/or auditory-perceptual handicap, strephosymbolia, mirror reading, minimal brain dysfunction, special learning disability, and perceptual-motor handicap (Rome and Osman 2000: 1). English researchers who identified and named dyslexia in the late nineteenth century called it, picturesquely, congenital word blindness. It is not a malfunction of the eyes or ears, but rather a "glitch" in the brain's processing of visual and auditory information (Shaywitz 2003: 82). It often runs in families; frequently, dyslexic adults first come to understand their own troubled academic history when they seek help for their struggling children.

Within disability communities, dyslexia is a bit odd. It is not a disease. It does not have a cure. It does not "hurt" in the conventional sense of that term. It is not caused by a trauma to the mind or body. It is not visible. It is variable, "kicking in" at some times more than others (Ryan 1994: 7). More obviously than most other disabilities, it is socially constructed in the strong sense that it does not exist in societies without written language. It is often accompanied by talents in arenas requiring enhanced spatial awareness and the ability to think in pictures rather than words, including art, sports, engineering, architecture, speech, computers, games, mechanics, and acting. Dyslexics can often "pass" and may become adept at disguising or compensating for their difficulties. Yet passing causes its own problems: teachers and parents see a bright, otherwise capable child who is unaccountably inept at reading, writing, and spelling, and often conclude that the child is not trying. The child knows that s/he is in fact trying, often much harder than other children, but flounders in a sea of random sounds and marks. S/he cannot crack the code. The order that others seem to find effortlessly eludes the dyslexic student. As one dyslexic child wailed, "I can't find the words. I can't make the book talk" (Lavoi 2003). Being urged to try harder only exacerbates the child's growing conviction that s/he is stupid. Dyslexic children grow up to be dyslexic adults, often carrying the legacy of school failure – depression, anxiety, anger, and shame, along with functional illiteracy – into higher education, workplaces, marriages, and parenting.

Matthew Philpott (1998), then a philosophy graduate student at Warwick University, gives a uniquely insightful picture of his own dyslexia, using insights from Merleau-Ponty's phenomenology to conceptualize "the perpetual unfolding of the reciprocal relationship *between* the world and ourselves" (Philpott 1998: 2, emphasis in original). His philosophical resources allow him to explore struggles with written texts that younger, less sophisticated dyslexic learners share but often do not understand. Like Elan, Philpott (1998: 3) has trouble with putting sounds, syllables, and words in order: "The slowness of my work clearly has its roots in the constant stopping, re-sequencing, and starting again of my tasks, and my awareness of this linguistic deficit only heightens the external pressure of trying to keep up with other students." Dyslexic children are often flummoxed when their teacher urges them to "sound out" the parts of words, because, as Maryanne Wolf (2007: 174) explains, they "do not perceive, segment, or manipulate individual syllables and phonemes in the same way as average-reading children do." These children need to be directly taught the relations between sounds and symbols. Philpott's academic success, despite his challenges, suggests that he has been taught or has somehow designed for himself a system to catch his sequencing problems and get around them, but it is not a cost-free adjustment. While going back to the beginning of the word or sentence is often necessary for the dyslexic reader to take in all the parts, continually restarting the process is distracting. It slows the reader down, interrupts the flow of the text, and invests the reader's efforts in decoding (reading individual words) rather than comprehension.

Also like Elan, Philpott omits sounds and syllables as he reads. He "jumps ahead" rather than reading the whole word or sentence. He calls it "slippage through over-anticipation":

> I often feel that when I am reading a sentence I seem to be rushing through the words, and at times seem to jump ahead of myself. This jumping ahead is not simply trying to anticipate the general direction of where the sentence is taking me; rather I seem to jump well ahead of myself, over-anticipating what the sentence actually means. Instead of reading the sentence as a whole, and deriving my meaning from an overall interpretation, I desperately look for a single word that will give me an initial access as to the sentence's meaning. (Philpott 1998: 18)

Skilled readers also look ahead as they read. Wolf (2007: 148) explains, "our eyes continually make small movements called saccades," followed by very brief pauses (called fixations) and sometimes by returns to previous text to pick up past information. Wolf continues:

> One brilliant design feature of our eyes allows us to see "ahead" into a parafoveal region and still farther along the line of text into the peripheral region. We now know that when we read in English, we actually see about fourteen or fifteen letters to the right of our fixed focus, and we see the same number of letters to the left if we read in Hebrew. (Wolf 2007: 148)

Skilled readers make good use of these previews because their minds rapidly process the visual information, determine whether the letters form recognizable words, and decide whether they can make sense of what they see or need to go back and look for clues in prior text. My hunch is that Elan and Matthew Philpott, at their very different levels of language use, are both looking for orthographic patterns they recognize and having trouble finding them.

Like both Elan and Karen, Philpott's working memory – the ability to hold onto information long enough to do something with it – is limited. Philpott (1998: 17) calls it "slippage through loss of reflection." Wolf explains this slippage as a temporal faltering, a brief but critical loss of time needed to think and feel. Philpott (1998: 17–18) says, "the meaningfulness of the text" suddenly diminishes, and "the rhythm of my reading falls flat":

> I can be reading a line of text in a sentence, and although I am perfectly comfortable with the vocabulary I am dealing with, I am suddenly alerted to the fact that the last few words I have read made little impact on me, and in fact I have stopped reading... it seems that at certain points in my reading process, the capacity to reflect on the meaning of the words that have come only a number of seconds ago is diminished. Because of this loss of capacity to reflect, the meaning of the words that I am currently reading is quickly diminished, and the unity of meaning conveyed by the sentence as a whole becomes confused. (Philpott 1998: 18)

Philpott's self-analysis helps us understand Karen's difficulty as well: she too loses "the capacity to reflect on the meaning of the words" because she has to invest a disproportionate amount of time and effort in decoding. In Elan's case, his labored and often inaccurate decoding makes this obvious. But Karen's decoding is relatively smooth and accurate, leading a listener to falsely conclude that she is reading effectively. However, her decoding lacks the needed automaticity "to allocate time for comprehension" (Wolf 2007: 177). It takes a skilled reader one-half of a second to read nearly any word. During that half second, a great deal happens: "the almost instantaneous fusion of cognitive, linguistic, and affective processes; multiple brain regions; and billions of neurons that are the sum of all that goes into reading" (Wolf 2007: 145). Without "the secret gift of time to think" that emerges in a skillfully reading brain, readers may decode words on a page but they do not readily develop the capacity to think beyond those words (Wolf 2007: 221).

The Biopolitics of Orton-Gillingham

The children, teenagers, and adults who seek out the services of an Orton-Gillingham tutor are, usually, highly motivated to improve their reading and writing, while (unless they are very young) scarred by previous failure to do so. They come to me, or someone like me, to change their brains (Richards and Berninger 2008). People who are, in Wolf's felicitous phrase, "average-reading" generally pick up on the workings of English after modest exposure to its elements; they do not need to be directly and systematically taught the patterns and exceptions. Dyslexic learners are generally not able to intuit the patterns on their own. Despite repeated exposure, they encounter a baffling variety of sounds and marks with no inherent logic to their relations. O-G intervenes in the layered network of culture/body/brain dynamics to orchestrate a new set of responses, to normalize and interiorize the brain's processing of language.

In *The Flesh of Words*, Jacques Rancière (2004: 3) writes for the non-dyslexic reader: "Since Plato and the *Cratylus* it has been understood that words do not resemble what they say. That is the price of thought. Any resemblance must be resisted." For the laboring dyslexic reader, there is no solid prior resemblance of symbols to sounds that could then be resisted. The resistance comes first. Rancière (2004: 3) evokes the potential of creative movement of ideas: "The problem is not that the resemblance is unfaithful, but that it is too faithful, still attached to what has been said when already it should be elsewhere, near where the meaning of what has been said must speak." But for dyslexic readers, there is no firm prior anchor of words to "what has been said." The dyslexic readers have been "elsewhere" from the get-go. They struggle to achieve the confinement that Rancière bemoans, to pin down words around the already-said.[2]

Could we, as teachers, as parents, as employers, as a culture... could we free them from this struggle? Could they free themselves? Could we encourage them to take advantage of their initial "luck" at sidestepping the confinements of the logos? At the very least, this would require us to accept a riot of undisciplined spelling, grammar, punctuation, letter formation, spacing of words, capitalization, sentence structure, and organization of ideas. The 26 letters in the English language combine to make about 44 phonemes (sound units) that are represented in writing by many hundreds of graphemes (written letters and letter combinations) (Moats 2010: 30). The sound /ā/, for example, can be spelled eight different ways: *ai, ay, a*-consonant-*e*, *a* in an open syllable, *eigh, ea, ei*, and *ey*. Learning to differentiate them, for those who do not intuit the patterns in the material, requires precise explanations of the rules governing each grapheme's construction, placement, and frequency. The sound of /ā/ at the end of a word, for example, is spelled *ay*; in the beginning or middle of the word or syllable, it is *ai*. Yet the /ā/ in *a*-consonant-*e* is also in the middle – so why, students quickly complain, is the same sound and placement written one way in *Jane* and a different way in *rain*? At this point there are no solid generalizations to describe the patterns, so we resort to grouping the words together within each pattern and creating familiarity through repeated association. It takes often takes many, many repetitions before the dyslexic learner can say, "It just looks right," because that seemingly innocuous observation is built upon sustained multisensory practice. Literature, Rancière (2004: 5) remarks, "lives only by evading

[2] Few philosophers of language consider dyslexia. One who has approached the life world of dyslexic learners is Jean-Paul Sartre (1981) in his book on Flaubert. I discuss Sartre's analysis briefly in Ferguson (2008b). I am grateful to my colleague Michael J. Shapiro (1988) for his discussion of Flaubert in this book and in many conversations.

the incarnation that it incessantly puts into play." But for dyslexic readers, the incarnation is evading the reader already. Allowing, much less celebrating, this evasion before the prior order has been put into play in the first place is an unsettling thought.

In the last section of this chapter, I will consider the potential politics of a rebellion against the confinements of representation and the educational disenfranchisement of dyslexic learners. But first I want to explore the biopolitical techniques of O-G. Rancière (2004: 3) offers this provocative simile: "The written letter is like a silent painting that retains on its body the movements that animate the logos and bring it to its destination." Here Rancière has supplied a remarkable opportunity to think of O-G as a highly disciplined form of art appreciation. Letters have their uses and their patterns written on them, for those who know how to "see," in their order, their gatherings with other letters, their placement in words and sentences, their size, and their proximity to punctuation. To learn to read, O-G teaches the dyslexic learner to interpret the "silent painting," to detect its animating movement and follow it where it is going. To learn to write, O-G teaches the student to create her/his own silent paintings, reproducing the needed animations so that other readers may follow. Completing the example, above, of spellings of the sound /ā/: *eigh* is usually followed by *t* (as in *eight)*; *a* in an open syllable (as in *baby)* is always at the end of the syllable, with no subsequent consonant to close the syllable and make the vowel short; *ei* (as in *vein)* and *ea* (as in *break*) are always in the middle of the word, while *ey* (as in *prey*) is always at the end. The last three are sufficiently rare that they can be memorized. Each silent painting must be painstakingly analyzed, explained, and practiced. Both reading and writing require the dyslexic student to learn to visualize the words in the mind's eye so that the silent paintings can be interpreted and reproduced.

The first principle of O-G instruction is that it must be multisensory.[3] All the pathways to learning – visual, auditory, kinesthetic, and tactile – are coordinated to reinforce one another. O-G teachers directly address what Connolly (2002: 1) calls the compositional dimension of thinking: "the way in which thinking helps to shape and consolidate brain connections, corporeal dispositions, habits and sensibilities." We teach to the students' intelligence, using their cognitive abilities to directly explain and enact language processes and patterns. The power of simultaneously bringing all available senses to bear on reading and writing creates new

[3] The full list of essential elements in O-G teaching: multisensory; alphabetic-phonetic; synthetic-analytic; structured; sequential; cumulative; repetitive; cognitive; diagnostic; prescriptive (Rome and Osman 2000: 9).

brain connections and new embodied language habits. O-G intervenes in the complex, layered, neurocultural activity of thinking, activating new relays and feedback loops, teaching the brain to change itself. As Connolly (2002: 2) notes, "thinking itself can sometimes modify the microcomposition of body/brain processes, as a new pattern of thinking becomes infused" into them. The new patterns of thinking O-G fosters bring language to order by painstakingly teaching the sounds, syllables, rules, generalizations, and exceptions that govern the language. Where dyslexic students used to meet a maze of random sounds and symbols, we teach them to find and use regularities. The purpose of all this order-making is to make language "make sense" to learners who initially see no meaningful patterns. Ultimately, we hope that work on the compositional dimension of thinking will feed into the creative dimensions as well, furthering what Connolly (2002: 1) calls "the opaque process by which new ideas, concepts and judgments bubble into being."

We do all this by choreographing a cumulative series of techniques of the self, involving images, sounds, gestures, and sensations. With regard to images: dyslexic learners tend to have weak visual imagery – their ability to process visual images in the brain after the eye has received them (not their ability to see) is impaired. Early researchers aptly named the extreme of weak visual imagery "word blindness," which is the opposite end of the spectrum of visual processing from eidetic (photographic) memory. Most people are somewhere in the middle. With regard to sounds, dyslexic learners tend to have weak auditory processing ability (not poor hearing, but impaired ability to process sound impulses in the brain once the ears receive them). At the extreme, they are "word deaf," which is the opposite end of the spectrum from the excellent auditory memory, perception, sequencing, and retention that Rome and Osman (2000: 4) call "tape recorder" memory. Again, most people are somewhere in the middle. Among dyslexics, about 60 percent of individuals with visual processing problems also have difficulties with auditory processing (Rome and Osman 2000: 4). With regard to gestures: there is a distribution of kinesthetic/tactile abilities in the human population, ranging from extreme lack of coordination (dyspraxia) to very superior coordination. Again, most people are somewhere between the two extremes. People with impaired fine motor skills may have trouble producing legible script or sustaining the task of writing (dysgraphia). For individuals with difficulty in processing visual and auditory information, the tactile and kinesthetic pathways are crucial: the movements of hands and arms, of lips, tongue, and throat, and of fingertips on surfaces are necessary learning sources. None of these pathways stands alone – they are not isolated channels but fertile processes that intermix to create more pathways. They must be taught to "pay close attention to one another" (Rome and Osman 2000: 13).

O-G coordinates the resources of seeing, hearing, touching, and feeling to crack the code of written language. An O-G lesson begins with two drills: first visual, then auditory, each with two sections. In the visual drill, the student sees the written sound and says it (also giving any relevant rules regarding its use), then sees words containing that sound and pronounces them. This is the see-and-say drill. In the auditory drill, the student hears the sound, then repeats and writes it, then hears words using that sound, and repeats and writes the words, sounding out the elements as s/he writes. This is the hear-and-write drill. The first drill moves from sight to sound, the second from sound to sight. For example, I show three cards on which are written *-ck, -dge,* and *–tch* (one on each card). Elan looks at the cards and says the corresponding sounds: /k/, /ğ/, and /ch/. He tells me they are found at the end of a one-syllable word after a short vowel. I then show him a list of words containing the sounds – *speck, witch, dodge* – and he decodes (reads) each. Then we reverse the direction: I say the sounds and he repeats and writes them. I dictate words using those sounds (not the same words), and he repeats, writes, and then reads each word.

A complicated system for correcting errors brings in strong tactile and kinesthetic dimensions. In the visual drill, Karen traces difficult sounds with her pointer finger and middle finger of her writing hand on a rough surface (heavily grained wood, felt, carpeting, or sand, for example) while saying the sound, watching her hand trace the sound, feeling her throat, teeth, lips, and tongue articulate the sound, feeling her arm move to produce the needed motion, hearing her voice uttering the sound. Tracing is a powerful tool that makes the student's fingers into a writing instrument and taps phonological memories and muscle memories.[4] In the auditory drill, Karen fingerspells problematic words: she places her non-writing hand on the table, her fingers curled as though she were playing a piano; beginning with the finger on the far left (so that she moves from left to right, as written text does in English), she taps out each sound in the word, saying the sounds, feeling her mouth shape the sounds, hearing herself say the sounds, and feeling her fingers hit the surface, one for each sound in the word. (For longer words, her fingers count off syllables rather than sounds.) Fingerspelling is a powerful tool for segmenting words into their constituent sounds and retraining the brain to hear each

[4] My thanks to Cindy Carson for this and other insights into Orton-Gillingham procedures.

sound. Since dyslexic learners often hear words as a single blast of sound rather than as component parts, fingerspelling reinforces hearing, seeing, and writing each element of the word. Adjustments are made in the drills to accommodate the age and needs of the students, but the basic integration of the senses remains fundamental.

The Dyslexic Sensorium

O-G's techniques draw the sensory pathways together, treating them not as discrete channels but as overlapping, mutually influencing processes.

Hearing

Auditory processing is "what happens when your brain recognizes and interprets the sounds around you" (Tridas 2007: 43). The brain processes spoken sounds and words, including vocabulary, syntax (the order of words in a sentence), narrative order, figures of speech, tone of voice, volume, and meaning (Tridas 2007: 5). Walter Ong (1982: 8) calls sound "the natural habitat of language" in the sense that language is "nested in sound" from the beginning. Nonetheless, in a writing culture, Ong (1982: 11) argues, most readers are uneasy with total dependence on verbalization because sound is "so little thing-like." Sound leaves no trace, Ong (1982: 32) argues; "there is no way to stop sound and have sound." Since "there is no equivalent of a still shot for sound," in oral cultures words are events rather than things (Ong 1982: 32). Ong (1982: 59–60) argues that writing fosters "the sense of individual words as significantly discrete items." For many dyslexics, it is more the opposite: comprehending words and parts of words as discrete items is a necessary step to foster writing.

Vowels are particularly critical and problematic sounds, especially for dyslexic learners. First, vowels have more than one sound, whereas most consonants have only one sound.[5] Second, their soft sounds are quite similar, making it easy to confuse /ĭ/ with /ĕ/ or /ă/ with /ŏ/. Third, their pronunciation varies by region. Fourth, they combine with *r* to form distinct sounds, called *r-controlled* sounds. Fifth, they can combine with each other or with *w* and *y* to make unique sounds, such as *oy*, *oa*, or *aw*. Sixth, they can mutate into the dreaded schwa, that indistinct /ŭ/ sound

[5] Four consonants have multiple sounds: *c* and *g* have both a hard sound (as in *cat*, *goat*) and a soft sound (*cell*, *gym*); *s* can say both /s/ and /z/; *y* can say /yh/ as a consonant but /ē/, /ī/, and / ĭ/ when it is a vowel. The changes in consonants are largely controlled by vowels: *c* and *g* become soft when followed by *e*, *i*, or *y*; *s* says /z/ between two vowels.

(written as an upside down, backwards *e*) that can be spelled with any vowel letter. Seventh, they are essential to every word and every syllable; the definition of a syllable is a chunk of a word with a talking vowel. Small wonder that Ong finds the invention of vowels to be a turning point in human development. The original Semitic alphabet consisted of consonants and "semi-vowels," but vowels enabled "a new level of abstract analytic, visual coding of the elusive world of sound" (Ong 1982: 28). While on the phylogenic level, vowels were an advance, on the ontogenic level, dyslexics often stumble on the written vowels' sliding relationships with their sounds.

Seeing

With regard to reading and writing, Rome and Osman (2000: 3) claim primacy for visual processing: "The visual pathway is the most important pathway involved with the acquisition of written language skills." Tridas agrees:

> Visual processing interprets space, patterns, and shapes. It is what allows a person to understand maps and symbols, see visual patterns (e.g., roots of words) or shapes, perform mental math computation, and understand geometric concepts. The visual system is instrumental in the automatic recognition of words that allows a person to become a fluent reader. It is an essential element in writing and other subjects, such as mathematics. In addition, it helps the brain develop a sense of the organization of space. (Tridas 2007: 5–6)

Learners must associate the visual symbol of letters with the letter's name and the letter's sound(s). Yet dyslexic learners cannot rely on their visual memory. Because they do not intuit the patterns that allow them to generalize about relations between sounds and symbols, they do not develop the shortcuts that the rest of us use to decode (read) and encode (write) unfamiliar words. Dyslexic learners often memorize each word as though it were a unique entity, a strategy that can work in the beginning but fails by around third grade, when students are expected to have finished learning to read so that they can now read to learn.

In a writing culture, Ong (1982: 11) explains, words appear to most people as things, because "we can see and touch such inscribed 'words' in texts and books." When literate people are asked to think about a word, they generally imagine a written thing. It's hard for them to think of a word without "adverting to any lettering but *only* to the sound" (Ong 1982: 12, emphasis in original). While average-reading people tend to naturalize visual memory, many dyslexics are hampered in their ability to visualize words.

Touching and Feeling

Attending to the movements of the speech musculature helps dyslexic students "to produce speech sounds and to sequence these sounds for spelling" (Rome and Osman 2000: 17). Hand gestures, as Connolly (2002: xiii–xiv) indicates, do not simply accompany speech; they help to produce it. The movements of the writing hand and arm reinforce the sounds the mouth is making and the ears are hearing. Tracing is a powerful tool precisely because it can tap motor memories and trigger connections between sounds and symbols that have not become automatic, but are available for recall. In her study of George Herbert Mead's social psychology, Ruth Leys (1993: 302) concludes that our hands make "internal representations" possible. In a 1907 article in *Psychological Review*, Mead (1907: 389) wrote, "The great importance of the human hand for perception lies in the fact that it is essentially mediatory within the organic as out of which the physiological process of life is made up." Mead emphasizes our hands as mediating links with physical nature; O-G shows hands to also mediate between people and the realm of the symbolic. My students often become conscious of the differences between sounds, and the relations of sounds to written signs, with their hands.

Ong points out that speech leaves no trace, nothing to "look up." Spoken words are "occurrences, events," while written words are things, "'out there' on a flat surface" (Ong 1982: 31, 32). Fingerspelling makes written words more like events than objects because the non-writing hand acts out the written word. Tapping out sounds with one's fingers makes the word stretch out over time as well as space. Ong (1982: 73) attributes "thing-like repose" to the written word, but O-G disrupts writing's settledness by calling out the individual sounds and marking them with touch.

To simplify my material and make it manageable, I have separated sight, hearing, and touch as though they were autonomous channels through which information flowed to waiting brains. Yet the simultaneity of the sensory practices in O-G suggests otherwise: the tracing fingers "hear" and "see" the word; the tapping fingers "touch" the sounds.[6] Most people can recognize from their ordinary experience that the senses of smell and taste are connected; we know that if we can't smell our food then it's difficult to taste it. But the links among seeing, hearing, and touching are less intuitively obvious, since they appear to be the products of distinct

[6] My thanks to Davide Panagia (2009) for helping me to understand sensoria as a rich and layered interpolation of senses rather than a series of discrete channels.

organs lacking connective passageways. However, O-G's success suggests otherwise: the simultaneous orchestration of seeing, hearing and touching is not simply adding together discrete information channels, but is intermixing the organs, the senses, and the sensed material. For example, Elan was working to spell the word *flick*, which requires a great deal of a struggling writer. He needs to understand the difference between a phoneme and a blend: a phoneme is a sound unit, which can be composed of more than one letter, while a blend is a close connection of two discrete sounds. The *ck* in *flick* is a phoneme because the *c* and the *k* cannot be pronounced separately, then blended. The *fl* in the same word is a blend, because the speaker pronounces and can hear both the *f* and the *l*; the letters are blended together for ease of pronunciation, but still detectable. This distinction matters for Elan because he struggles to hear each sound in the word in its proper order, and to reproduce that sequence of sounds when he decodes (reads) or encodes (writes) the word. If he misses the components of the initial blend, he is likely to say and write *fick*. If he forgets the rule governing the final /k/ sound (at the end of a one-syllable word, following a single short vowel, /k/ is written *ck*), he might write *flik* or he might insert a letter and write *flink*. If he confuses his vowel sounds, he might write *fleck*. If he does all three at the same time, he's likely to write *fek*. A teacher untrained in O-G might well throw up her hands in despair at this point, because the word he wrote bears little resemblance to the word he was trying to write. His errors, however, are not random, but can be analyzed and addressed, one by one.

It helps Elan enormously to have multiple strategies to externalize the sounds and see them in action. Fingerspelling, explained above, is one such method. So is a process of pulling sound tiles, which goes like this: I assemble a group of small, magnetized tiles, each carrying a phoneme, in this case one tile each with the letters *f, l, i* and *ck*. I place them along the top of my magnetic board. Elan says each sound as he pulls the tile down to the middle of the board, assembling the word, sound by sound. I initially did not understand the full force of the pulling gesture, and I asked him merely to touch each tile. The tiles are flat and smooth on top, with no distinguishing texture or shape, so touching each tile was an unimpressive tactile experience. But pulling each tile down in a firm, slightly sweeping motion, as he pronounced the sound, looked at the written letter, felt his hand pull the sound toward himself, felt his mouth form the sound, heard his voice say the sound – this combination was mind-altering. It was as though his hand was scooping up that sound and bringing it into him, making it his. I heard a quiet little "oh" from Elan, as he saw/heard/felt what was happening. The relation of the *f* and the *l*, the sound of the *i*, the role of the *ck* – they became his. Elan's small epiphany defies neat sorting into separate sensory channels: does he see and hear with his hands? Does he look with his ears, or listen with his eyes? O-G teaches his senses to pay close attention to one another, as Rome and Osman explain, in the process blurring the distinctions among them.

Dyslexia as a Political Problem

While my first line of inquiry has followed Elan, Karen, and other dyslexic learners into the world where their brains are on O-G, my second set of queries looks at these non-conforming learners within the school system that, with a few exceptions, serves them so poorly now. We know how to teach these students successfully, and we know the high financial and personal costs of not doing so. We know how to identify children most at risk for reading failure, and we know how to intervene to prevent or mitigate the devastating consequences of early failure in school (Wolf 2007: 167). We also know that our prisons and juvenile facilities are full of dyslexic learners who did not receive the education they needed and were subsequently scarred by corrosive histories of academic failure. While 10–15 percent of the general population is dyslexic, half of children and teenagers in the US with serious drug and alcohol problems also have significant reading problems (Lyon 2003: 17). Dyslexic teenagers are more likely than their non-dyslexic peers to drop out of school, withdraw from social relationships, and attempt suicide (Gorman 2003: 55). Approximately 30 percent of young people in the juvenile correction system have a learning disability, with dyslexia being the most common (National Council on Disability 2003; Raskind 2005).[7] Yet our schools continue, for the most part, to do a dismal job of educating dyslexic kids. Why? Certainly schools' resources are limited, teachers often overtaxed and poorly prepared, bureaucracies in state departments of education and in universities' schools of education are sluggish and resistant. Yet, these are not explanations, merely descriptions of the malign neglect of education in our society. Within that impoverished institutional horizon, according to G. Reid Lyon (2004), former Chief of the Child Development and Behavior Branch at the National Institutes of Health, the two biggest causes of reading failure in the US are poverty and (unremediated) dyslexia. We know that O-G instruction helps struggling readers who are not dyslexic as well as those who are. So, we know

[7] For an overview of this information, see Ferguson (2008a: 16, *passim*). This small book is available upon request at no cost. While some of the information is specific to Hawai'i, much of it is relevant to dyslexic persons, their families, and their teachers anywhere. Contact the Hawai'i Branch of the International Dyslexia Association (HIDA) at www.interdys.org to request a copy.

how to solve this problem, but we do not solve it, which leads a political theorist who is paying attention to wonder if perhaps we have a stake in the problem itself. I speculate that for many literate people, and for the larger society where authority is implicitly imbricated in literacy, dyslexics are a needed Other. They are the extremes on the bell curve, the abnormals who enable the norm. They are primitive, stuck in orality; we are advanced, literate, better. They could be like us if they just tried harder, so they must be either lazy or stupid. Their failure in school, their high rates of unemployment and incarceration, even their quirky disproportionate talents, are a satisfying marker of our normality. While it is not news to suggest that capitalism both produces and requires poor people, it is somewhat more startling, or at least less familiar, to suggest that our school system produces and requires learning disabilities. If my suspicion is even partly correct, then, in order for the lives of dyslexic learners to change, the lives of the rest of us need to change as well.

What Is To Be Done?

We need to change the way that we approach literacy. This manifesto calls for denaturalizing our approach to literacy, acknowledging literacy's downsides, learning to value neurodiversity, and instituting different kinds of schools as well as different approaches to teaching in existing schools. Before I sketch these changes, I need to recognize several potential difficulties with my project.

First, there is danger in taking yet again the well-trodden path of Otherness to come to terms with another out-group in our society. Disability theorist Ellen Jean Samuels (2002: 63) cautions us to avoid taking "the physically deviant body as a trope, rather than a body in its own right." She encourages us to bypass the lure of constitutive otherness and encounter disability in its "real complexity" (Samuels 2002: 73). Yet the "real" in real complexity is itself a problem. Serving as both metaphor and model for the not-normal, as dyslexics have done since the late nineteenth century, is part of the reality of dyslexic lives. I agree with Samuels that we should not reduce persons with disabilities to their disabilities, or to their society's interpretation of the disabilities. Those are not the whole of the person or the community, but they are part of it, and it does not serve the effort to respect "real complexity" to overlook the discursive and material constructions of the outsider.

Second, there are the contentious debates surrounding the status of neuroscience and its political engagements. Due to the recent explosion of fMRI-based research into the ways we use our brains when we read, information on the science of dyslexia and O-G is growing rapidly. Current neuroscientific research suggests that the body-brain-language connections of dyslexic people are distinct from those of non-dyslexic people (Temple et al. 2001). The brightly colored blotches captured by fMRI machines measure differential uses of oxygen, showing which regions of different learners' brains are more active during particular tasks. But what kind of evidence is this for political analysis? Some critics scorn "blobology" for its heedless popularization of neuroscience because the scans cannot tell us what the activations mean to the person whose brain is being monitored or to the rest of us (Satel and Lilienfield 2013). Others anticipate that "cognitive and developmental neuroscience research has great potential but is still at a very formative stage" (Hruby and Hind 2006: 550).[8] Jan De Vos goes further, questioning not just the current utility but the larger epistemological and political frame of neuroscientific research. He takes Connolly to task for, in De Vos' view, mistakenly taking neuroscience "to be a neutral and straightforward source for political theory" (De Vos 2013: 4). Yet I think De Vos miscalculates the status of neuroscientific research in Connolly's work. Contrary to De Vos' charge, one does not have to be a *"believer"* to make use of neurology; one only has to consider it as one among other possible sources of information (De Vos 2013: 5, emphasis in original). The analysis of O-G that I offer here does not rest on a claim to transcendental knowledge; it rests on observation of teaching strategies that work or do not work for dyslexic learners. Neuroscientific research into the body-brain-culture systems that produce or inhibit literacy has largely supported the remarkable insights of Samuel Orton and the pedagogic inventions of Anna Gillingham and her colleagues in the 1920s and 1930s. The fMRI studies are not an unquestioned authority, but they do provide strong support for successful pedagogies that predate them by nearly a century. The status of neuroscience, like that of personal narratives and educational outcomes, is not Truth with a capital T, but threads that we can gather to offer an account.

Third, there is the prickly political problem of my own authority in this matter. I am not dyslexic. I glimpse that world, which varies for different participants and is subject to many possible interpretations, but I am free to leave, while Elan and Karen are not. My sons are not. Further, I enter their world as a tutor bent on changing them, reorganizing their ways of processing information so they can function better in the world of written signs. My scholarly interventions into Elan's and Karen's treacherous journeys toward literacy are intended to honor the specificity and variety

[8] While Hruby and Hind (2006: 550) usefully remind us that "models of the reading mind are basically visualized descriptive analogies," their dismissive review of Shaywitz's important book is unwarranted.

of their lived experience as well as to use their stories, multiplied many thousand-fold, to understand unconventional thinking more fully and to challenge the educational status quo.

Recognizing those potential limitations, I believe the following changes are essential.

Denaturalize Literacy

Those of us who took readily to the world of written signs are likely to have forgotten that we ever learned it. Those memories probably reside at the virtual level, below the range of explicit recollection. We have interiorized reading and writing, perhaps we even believe they are "natural." Anyone should be able to do it. People who cannot read and write, then, seem incomprehensible, nothing like us. Connolly quotes Bergson to good effect: "the lesson once learned bears upon it no mark which betrays it origin and classes it in the past; it is part of my present, exactly like my habit of walking or of writing; it is live and acted, rather than represented: I might believe it innate" (Bergson 1911: 91, quoted in Connolly 2002: 28). To denaturalize literacy is to give one's literate present a history, so that we can understand how it came to be rather than assuming that it was somehow always there.

Recognize Literacy's Limitations

We need to recognize literacy as an ambiguous achievement. It is close to heresy within O-G circles to question the value of reading and writing. Yet others have done so before us, so it is not impossible.[9] Connolly (2008: 301) developed the tension-filled concept of *ambiguous achievement* in order to think about the production of the modern self as a subject, one who is capable of democratic self-governance while at the same time subjected to a particular regime of power and knowledge capable of producing such individuals. Reflecting on Flaubert, Shapiro (2012: 200) encourages us to see "language competence (fluency) as an ambiguous achievement," recognizing that it enhances communication but can also "stymie critical thinking." Shapiro (2012: 200) is building upon Sartre's recognition that Flaubert's creative genius was enabled by "com[ing] late into language." Flaubert did not learn to read until after his ninth birthday. Shapiro (2012: 200) concludes, "as a result, he was not deprived early on of his innate poetic ability."

[9] Debates rage over the status and desirability of literacy within other fields. See, for example, Luke (1994).

Indigenous educators have a substantial history of critically evaluating the costs of literacy. For example, Native Hawaiian educator Noelani Goodyear-Ka'ōpua (2013: 54) calls for "a multitude of literacies" to express the valued practices of indigenous education: "a range of critically engaged observational, interpretive, and expressive skills that encompass but are not limited to human linguistic and social practices." James Scott (2009: 229) argues that the peoples of upland Southeast Asia often evade literacy that "could as easily be an avenue for disempowerment as for empowerment" because it often serves the interests of states and conquerors. If we position reading and writing as ambiguous achievements rather than unqualified goods, we take a step toward recognizing and perhaps even cherishing other kinds of communicative practices carrying their own forms of creativity and excellence.

Value Neurodiversity

We need to recognize our (literate) interdependency with (non- or not-yet-literate) others. They are not lesser versions of us; they know and do things we don't know and do as well. Dyslexia's considerable gifts are the flip-side of its difficulties: the abilities of some people with dyslexia, for example, to think in pictures rather than words, to manifest highly developed spatial imaginations, to possess creativity in arts, crafts, and technologies, to speak persuasively and lead effectively, and more, are not separate aspects of those people. Efforts to "cure" dyslexia by gene therapy are dangerous because dyslexia's strengths and weaknesses are bound together. Dyslexics are often not impressed by the long list of successful people with dyslexia that we tutors produce to encourage struggling learners: Thomas Edison, Woodrow Wilson, Nelson Rockefeller, Gustave Flaubert, Bruce Jenner, Erin Brockovich, Agatha Christie, Emma Goldman, John De Lancie, Tom Cruise, Whoopi Goldberg, Cher. The list goes on, but people with dyslexia generally have a hard time identifying with these famous names (although their parents may find the list reassuring). Dyslexic learners' uncertainty about their capacity to read and write is far deeper, more written into their virtual memories, than any exhortations about talented dyslexics can touch. But the rest of us could pay attention, learn to value neurodiversity that dyslexic learners embody, take steps to empower children to advocate on behalf of themselves. Dyslexia is not a disaster; it can be a gift.[10] It is our school system that is a disaster.

[10] For a good critique of the narrative of tragedy and disaster with regard to disabilities, see Arneil (2009).

Educate Differently

I can imagine three options for challenging this disaster. The first rebels against the prevailing governing of language; the second creates a radically different kind of school; the third brings O-G into existing educational systems. They are not mutually exclusive; in fact, they can be combined in many ways.

Dis-governing language, as I am imagining it, would entail backing away from the demands of order in proper English, bending and expanding the guidelines for spelling, grammar, syntax, etc. that are expected of effective written communication. Because language is continuously changing, the standardization of grammar and sentence structure is always to some degree contested. Digital media encourage us along these lines by employing now-familiar condensations of spelling and writing: for example, email often dispenses with the formal salutations and closings expected of conventional letters; Twitter utilizes condensed spellings (*4* for *for*, *u* for *you*, etc.) to accommodate the 144 character limit in tweets. And so on. Our society might follow those leads, loosening the hand of order in the production of respectable written text.

Lovers of the English language are likely to cringe at these assaults on treasured conventions of language. Those requiring unambiguous recording and communication of information, including scientists, bankers, and armies, would decry such an orthographic nightmare. Many whom Wolf calls "average-reading" language users just want to be able to communicate and would resist the extra labor required to make sense of non-standardized spelling and writing. Yet it is not impossible to imagine dyslexic learners engaging in a Great Refusal, insisting on spelling the words and constructing the sentences "like they sound" with little regard for the rules of proper English. Perhaps it would catch on, especially in informal settings, especially among the young. But my hunch is that it is too late to de-govern sound/symbol relations. Dyslexic learners would pay a high price for that rebellion; many doors would be slammed shut in a culture that implicitly, consistently confuses illiteracy and stupidity. There are, I think, other sites of rebellion more available, other places to put pressure on educational expectations and practices to make greater room for dyslexia's confoundments.

Creating radically different schools is an option that, while challenging, has the advantage of having already been done, so models are available for adaptation. The Modern Schools created by anarchists in the first half of the twentieth century are a compelling example. While different in important ways, contemporary Hawaiian-language charter schools are also powerful models.[11] Mental and manual learning are combined and equally valued. Students' curiosities and commitments, and the shared projects those inspire, lead the curriculum. Noise is welcome. Bodies move about. The built environment and the natural environment overlap. Teachers and students collaborate, and authority, in the sense of being the author of the classroom, is shared.

In standard schools, dyslexic students fail early and often because the skills they have trouble developing are precisely the ones that are demanded in the first few grades, while the things they are good at often make a belated appearance (if at all). If there were more balance in the curriculum, if art, music, woodworking, machine building and repair, sewing, cooking, dance, theater, and sports were as important as reading and writing in elementary school; if handling animals skillfully, speaking eloquently, thinking deeply, growing food well, and interacting effectively with others were recognized and rewarded; if the conceptual side of mathematics came before the paper-and-pencil requirements of arithmetic: then dyslexic students would be more likely to find their talents before the consequences of their weaknesses have done substantial harm. If students could show what they know orally and manually as well as in written form; if we didn't expect students to read-to-learn until later, and we let children come to reading and writing at their own pace; if we taught everyone in ways that work for them: most dyslexic students, in fact, most students, would not fail.

Even in classrooms as they are now, there are productive avenues to pursue. If every teacher is taught the skills of O-G, so that they have an expanded toolbox from which to draw pedagogical strategies, many students would never end up in "special education" and those who do might actually get the sort of instruction that could help them. If we conduct the right kind of assessment – brief, frequent, non-invasive snapshots of a child's learning, to let his/her teachers know where s/he may be floundering, rather than elaborate high-stakes testing – teachers would have useful information with which to assist children (Burns 2010). If we minimize timed tests, and give extended time on tests as needed, students like Karen, who need to read everything twice – the first time for decoding, the second time for comprehension – could show what they know. Other accommodations can make a difference: using a laptop to take notes can be important, since listening while typing is often more do-able for a dyslexic student than listening while writing. Finding help with writing and editing, often through school writing labs, can make a contribution

[11] My thanks to Lianne Charlie in Polsci 610 (Fall 2014) for pointing out the similarities between anarchist and indigenous education.

to struggling writers. Being able to show what they know verbally, rather than having all the assignments depend on writing, can be crucial. I am not suggesting that teachers and professors should expect less of students with dyslexia than they do of other students: I am asking that all students' learning be structured so that they can succeed.

My experiences as an O-G tutor convince me that Connolly is right when he argues that interventions into neurocultural circuits can create new possibilities. O-G can cultivate a new identity (as a literate person) or "thought-imbued disposition" (eager rather than fearful or indifferent to reading) or a new capacity (literacy) (Connolly 2002: 1). After a year of tutoring, Elan no longer stutters. After his second year of tutoring, he won an award for being the best reader in his class. Karen now comprehends at grade level, providing she has time to read the text twice. Now an adolescent, she readily accepts her need to read assignments twice because she knows it works for her. In Connolly's (2002: 97) words, O-G orchestrates the compositional arrangements of thinking "by new pathways mapped into the body and brain as new thinking becomes habituated." As a tutor, I tend to think of my actions as "doing" O-G, but my students are also "doing" O-G; they are not just responding to me, they are working on themselves and in the end both of us are changed. Connolly (2002: 104) continues: "To think is to move something. And to modify a pattern of body/brain connections helps to draw a habit, a disposition to judgment, or a capacity of action into being." The capacity of action could be the ability to hear and write the sequence of *f* and *l* in *flick* or to accurately identify the vowel or to recognize the proper way to write /k/ after a short vowel in a short word. The new habit could be to embrace the need to read twice, once for decoding, the second time for meaning. The new disposition to judgment could be the alleviation of the constant self-judging voice in one's head – "Why am I so stupid?" – replaced by a more confident and forgiving self-assessment.

The last demand in my manifesto has to do, perhaps unexpectedly, with cautions directed toward enthusiastic O-G advocates such as myself. When I tutor, I change the configuration of my students' brains. More accurately, I teach them to change their brains, and they are generally eager to comply. But what might those brains have accomplished, had we left them alone? Changing the compositional dimension of body-brain-culture practices also effects the creative side, where, again in Connolly's (2002: 75) words, "New thoughts bubble, flow, or surge into being from a virtual register hard at work below the threshold of feeling and intellectual attention." O-G interferes with that virtual register, orchestrating a different set of responses in order to normalize that brain's processing of written and spoken signs. If Wolf is correct, then that interference can lead to the "gift of time" in which creativity can happen. But, what happens to the creativity that might have been? There is no way to know, and there is no "untouched" brain with which to compare those that have been worked on by O-G; a "hands-off" policy on the brain is not an option. Wolf (2007: 229) argues persuasively that skilled reading produces its own creativity by providing "the mysterious, invisible gift of time to think beyond." She calls it "the reading brain's greatest achievement" (Wolf 2007: 229). I see this creativity in my students and am encouraged by it. Yet, the elaborate organization of tasks and stringent repetition in O-G lessons sometimes feels like an educational version of a time-and-motion study. Frederick Winslow Taylor would recognize the technologies in an instant, although he put them to different uses. I think, and my students think (and certainly their parents think) that the consequences of their impaired literacy are worse than the consequences of O-G itself. Still, it should give us pause to imagine what we might lose.

This mandate to reflect becomes more pressing when we think about the unsavory history of our society's reception of dyslexia. Tom Campbell (2011: 452) makes a persuasive case that dyslexia came to the notice of governments, educators, and doctors in the nineteenth century when states were developing statistical techniques for "rendering the population in numerical terms." Norms could be articulated around the ubiquitous bell curve, allowing learners to be measured against classifications that became visible only through the statistical modeling process. Campbell (2011: 452) writes: "The norm is a technology of power that only operated in assemblage with other mechanisms. It often served as an amplifier, allowing power to flow deeper into the body of an individual or the population." States and employers needed literate populations. Dyslexic individuals could be "rescued" from the larger population of illiterate persons: by recognizing their gifts as well as their academic deficits, and establishing that dyslexia was not the "fault" of the learner, early researchers were able to distinguish "word blindness" from "feeble-mindedness" and present dyslexia as "a deserving defect" (Campbell 2011: 460).

I speculate that state and corporate interests in dyslexia have taken a different turn in the twentieth and twenty-first centuries. States, corporations, and schools still claim to find illiteracy problematic and literacy beneficial. Public pronouncements on the subject are unanimous, often pious: our children's future is endangered. No child should be left behind. But we continue to do more of what we were doing before, rather than change our ways of teaching, even though we know what to do. Could it be that it is convenient for the powers-that-be that 38 percent of fourth graders can't read or write well? Could those children's disempowerment – seen in high dropout rates, unemployment, drug use, and incarceration – be a service to state and corporate power? Could their educational enablement be a threat? In our society, today, illiteracy disempowers. Literacy might empower. It is not far-fetched to imagine a dyslexic civil rights movement, overcoming failure and shame with both remedial interventions and cultural rethinkings of literacy and neurodiversity. I will continue to periodically worry about my role in normalizing my students' brains, and to argue for radical transformations of schools, but I will also continue to use O-G's highly focused biopolitical techniques to teach my students to read and write.

7 Rethinking Membership and Participation in an Inclusive Democracy: Cognitive Disability, Children, Animals

*Sue Donaldson and Will Kymlicka**

One of the most important citizenship struggles in recent decades has focused on people with cognitive disabilities (henceforth CD). Advocates have challenged exclusionary conceptions of citizenship that relegate people with CD to a kind of second-class citizenship or wardship, accorded at best certain paternalistic protection from harms and provision for objectively defined basic needs. Advocates (including self-advocates) have insisted that society must also recognize and support the agency of people with CD, enabling, insofar as possible, their ability to participate in key decisions affecting their lives, and to be co-creators of the societies we share. Society must, in short, acknowledge and enable their citizenship.

Much remains to be done to instantiate this new vision of inclusive citizenship, but it has already shaped laws and policies around the world, including the UN Convention on the Rights of People with Disabilities (2006), which calls for 'full and effective participation and inclusion in society'. This convention affirms that people with CD are entitled to the full recognition of their human rights, and emphasizes their agency and their right to participate in individual and collective self-determination.[1]

* Versions of this paper have been presented at the 'Domesticity and Beyond' conference (Queen's University, Kingston), the CREUM Workshop on Animal Citizenship (University of Montreal), Dartmouth College, the Kenan Institute for Ethics at Duke University, Cal State Fresno, KU Leuven, European University Institute, University of Amsterdam, Johns Hopkins University, and the Minding Animals International conference in Delhi. Thank you to the organizers for inviting us, and to the participants for their questions. Special thanks to Barbara Arneil, Nancy Hirschmann, Kristin Voigt and Dinesh Wadiwel for detailed and helpful comments on an earlier draft.

[1] The UN Committee that monitors the Convention has recently elaborated the meaning of these rights in a helpful document (UN Committee on the Rights of Persons with Disabilities, *General Comment on Article 12: Equal Recognition Before the Law* (Eleventh session, March 30–April 11, 2014, CRPD/C/11/4). This Comment makes clear that insofar as people with CD are unable on their own to make certain decisions, the alternative is not 'substitute decision-making' (using an objective best-interests standard) but rather 'supported decision-making, which respects the person's autonomy, will, and preferences' (paragraph 22). For discussion of this Convention, see Arneil's chapter in this volume.

With this new emphasis on participation we see a conscious reorientation of the disability rights movement around 'citizenship as the central organizing principle and benchmark' (Prince 2009: 3; cf. Carey 2009).

We believe that the new practices of citizenship emerging within the disability movement are of profound significance, and not just for citizens with CD. They require us to expand our understanding of the very meaning and purpose of citizenship, and to rethink its fundamental practices, and the spaces and places where these practices occur. They require us to rethink citizenship theory, and indeed democratic theory, from the ground up.

In this chapter, we want to draw out these broader implications of the citizenship struggles of people with CD by connecting them to two other challenges of inclusive citizenship: children (particularly young children) and animals (particularly the domesticated animals whom we have brought into our society). We will argue that developments around CD shed light on these two other cases, and vice versa. Examining these cases together can enrich our understanding of the emancipatory potential of inclusive citizenship, and also sharpen our understanding of the many challenges we face in achieving this goal.

Rethinking Citizenship

The inclusion of people with CD represents an historical shift in ideas of citizenship, not just in terms of *who* can be conceived as a full citizen, but in terms of *how* we think of citizenship. In traditional political theory, the citizen has been conceived as a person with capacities for public reason or *logos* or Kantian autonomy or rational reflection and deliberation – complex language-mediated capacities which we will call (following Gary Steiner) 'linguistic agency' (Steiner 2013: 196). Linguistic agency has operated not just as an ideal, but as a threshold capacity. Those seen as lacking this capacity have been relegated to the margins of political community, situated as passive wards to whom society owes duties of care rather than as co-citizens with equal rights.

Recent citizenship struggles for people with CD offer a very different conception of the basis and purpose of citizenship – a conception based not on the possession of linguistic agency, but on rights of membership and participation in a society of equals. Citizenship isn't a select club for linguistic agents; it's a commitment to include and empower all members of society, across the whole spectrum of diversity, on their own terms.[2]

[2] 'Respect for difference and acceptance of persons with disabilities as part of human diversity and humanity… is incompatible with granting legal capacity on an assimilationist basis' (UN Committee on the Rights of Persons with Disabilities, *General Comment on Article 12: Equal Recognition Before the Law*, paragraph 29).

People with CD should be recognized, not (or not only) as vulnerable individuals with special needs for protection and provision, but as members of society involved in dense webs of trust, communication and cooperation with others. As such, they have both rights of participation to help shape social norms as well as responsibilities to comply with those social norms. Citizenship is a means of affirming these rights of membership and participation, and of obliging states to support citizens' legal and political agency.

This new conception of citizenship is not just emerging in the context of CD. We see similar ideas in the field of children's citizenship (e.g., Wall 2011; Jans 2004), inspired in part by the 1989 UN Convention on the Rights of the Child (UNCRC). The UNCRC embraces what is called a 3P model, affirming rights of participation, not just protection and provision, even for very young children who lack linguistic agency.[3]

This revised conception of citizenship has multiple benefits compared to the traditional conception tied to linguistic agency. If we say that to qualify as a citizen, it is not enough to participate in social life and be responsive to social norms, but one must also be able to rationally reflect on, evaluate and articulate propositions regarding these norms, then we quickly slide into a very exclusionary conception of citizenship. Not everyone has this capacity, and no one has it for all of their lives. Defining citizenship in this way would give all of us, at best, a fragile and conditional citizenship status.

It's not simply exclusionary, but misses the point of citizenship, which is to recognize and uphold membership in a shared society. Citizenship is a way of acknowledging who belongs here, who is a member of the people in whose name the state governs, and whose subjective good must be considered in determining the public interest and in shaping the social norms that structure our cooperative relations.[4]

Viewed this way, the fundamental basis of democratic citizenship is not linguistic agency, but rather the capacity for norm responsiveness in intersubjective relationships – the ability to moderate behaviour in accord with internalized norms when relating to other selves (Krause 2011: 299). Recent disability theorists argue that capacities for agency and citizenship are embedded in ongoing social relations among responsive, reflexive and interdependent selves, not located in a threshold individual capacity for rational reflection and public deliberation. CD

[3] The UNCRC does not affirm full legal and political rights for children (unlike the UNCRPD), but does affirm their right to freely express their views, which must be 'given due weight in accordance with the age and maturity of the child' (Article 12).

[4] For a defence of this conception of citizenship as tracking membership, see Donaldson and Kymlicka (2011: 55–61).

does not disqualify individuals from participating in, and contributing to, norm-governed and morally valuable practices (Arneil 2009, Clifford 2012, Silvers and Francis 2005).

This approach challenges not just traditional ideas about the alleged *capacities* required for citizenship, but also about the *locations* and *practices* that define citizenship. Implementing citizenship rights and responsibilities in relation to non-linguistic agents requires developing new ways of engaging the subjectivity of these co-citizens, focusing less on the ability to articulate or understand propositions, and more on attending to their 'varied modes of doing, saying and being' (Neale 2004: 15).[5] We need to create new mechanisms for the enactment of citizenship, bringing citizenship to the places and spaces where membership, participation and decision-making are meaningful to the individuals involved.

For example, if children are to be enabled 'to form and express a view' on 'all matters affecting' them – as required by the UNCRC – we need 'child-sized' spaces for citizenship (Jans 2004). Similarly, for people with CD, we need to focus not on how they deviate from some ideal of an articulate, autonomous agent engaged in public reason in the public square, but on where, how and with whom they live their lives, and how power and decision-making are negotiated in these places and spaces.

This has implications for how we think about citizenship practices. In her discussion of political rights for people with CD, Nussbaum states that without an equal capability to vote and to participate in juries, people with CD are 'disqualified from most essential functions of citizenship' (Nussbaum 2009: 347). But this is to grab the wrong end of the stick. Ideas of the 'essential functions of citizenship' are precisely what are at stake in the struggle for an inclusive citizenship. The question is not (or not only) how we can enable people with CD to participate in the practices that society has already deemed 'essential functions of citizenship'. We must also ask how people with CD can participate in *creating* norms of citizenship. Instead of fetishizing certain practices such as jury duty or voting as the hallmark of 'real' citizenship, we need to consider the new places and spaces of citizenship that are meaningful to people with CD, and that enable them to shape our shared social life. This may or may not include voting and participating on juries.[6] To find out, we

[5] On the importance of attending to physical expressions, gestures and sounds as key to understanding an individual's subjective good, and socializing them into trusting relations built around cooperative norms, see Alderson (2008) concerning children, and Francis and Silvers (2007), Wong (2009) and Kittay (2001) concerning people with CD.

[6] Vorhaus (2005) argues that people with CD are badly served by fetishizing voting at the expense of other forms of participation that would be more effective in enabling them to shape our common life. While we agree with Nussbaum that it is crucial to remove barriers to participation in traditional citizenship practices, we disagree with her claim that *not* participating in these practices means that equality is denied. Equality is denied when

need to start from those places and spaces and work from the ground up, rather than uncritically assuming that the citizenship functions created by and for neurotypical adults are the only valid ones.[7]

A lot of important work has already been done within both the disability and children's rights movements to elaborate this new vision of citizenship. In this chapter, we will argue that these developments also have implications for thinking about domesticated animals (hereafter DAs), and that bringing animals into the conversation can help clarify and enrich the challenges we face in building inclusive citizenship.

In previous work, we articulate a moral argument for extending the revised conception of citizenship to DAs (Donaldson and Kymlicka 2011: chs. 4–5). If citizenship is indeed about recognizing membership, voice and agency within socially meaningful relationships involving cooperation, trust and intersubjective recognition – rather than threshold capacities for linguistic agency – then DAs qualify. Indeed, the process of domestication is precisely about the incorporation of animals into such relations. Domestication has presupposed, and further developed, capacities for trust, cooperation and communication, in ways that lay the behavioural foundations for relationships of co-citizenship. Having incorporated them into our society, and bred them to be dependent on us (or interdependent with us), we are morally obliged to recognize the membership of DAs in society, and to enable their participation in shaping the norms that govern that shared society.[8]

Our goal in this chapter is not to repeat that moral argument, but rather to discuss what we can learn about the prospects and challenges

you are denied the opportunity to participate in and shape practices that are or could be meaningful for you.

[7] Nussbaum's account replicates a problem identified by Neale in relation to children's citizenship, namely that if people with CD and very young children are subsumed into the larger categories of 'disability' and 'children', then the key challenges and radical potential of their inclusion are missed. Neale notes that much of the literature on the UNCRC focuses on older children, whose inclusion requires relatively little change to established democratic practices, since they are assumed to be (almost) able to follow adult modes of behaviour and communication. But the Convention also applies to very young children, and taking their citizenship seriously requires re-imagining practices in order "to accommodate children's varied modes of doing, saying and being" (Neale 2004: 15). Similarly, Nussbaum's focus on removing barriers to inclusion in the pre-existing functions of citizenship makes sense in relation to people with physical disabilities or mild CD, but when she moves to the case of people with significant CD, she fails to see that a more radical reconceptualization of those functions might be required (cf. Bérubé 2009: 357).

[8] Our theory does not endorse continuing the practice of domestication (human-controlled breeding of animals to promote traits beneficial to humans). Citizens are not bred to serve the purposes of other citizens. Rather, we must take existing DAs as they are (i.e., as they have been shaped by historical processes of domestication), recognize their membership rights, and move forward on the basis of co-citizenship (not husbandry, selective breeding or domestication).

of inclusive citizenship by bringing the cases of CD, children and DAs into conversation with each other. In all three contexts, if citizenship is to be more than a symbol or a slogan, we need to give a robust account of the practices of citizenship that give it life. We hope to show that insights from citizenship struggles for people with CD can illuminate the challenges, and possibilities, of citizenship for children and DAs, and vice versa. There is much to learn, and to share, regarding the upholding of membership and participation rights for a diverse citizenry.

Rebooting the Disability Rights/Animals Rights Conversation

In exploring this shared terrain, we wish to avoid some of the past missteps in discussions connecting disability and animal rights theory. As disability scholars have noted, some animal rights theorists have engaged in a kind of 'conceptual exploitation' of disability, using people with CD as a passing (and often ill-informed) thought experiment 'to bolster the case' for animals (Carlson 2009: 552). For example, various animal rights theorists have invoked the so-called argument from marginal cases (AMC) to defend the moral status of animals. This argument assumes that so-called normal humans with capacities for linguistic agency have unquestioned moral status – they are the core case of moral status – and that insofar as both animals and people with CD lack full possession of the relevant capacities underpinning moral status, they both constitute 'marginal' cases. The burden of the AMC is to call for consistency in the way we deal with these 'marginal' cases, so that whatever moral status we accord to 'deficient' or 'unfortunate' people with CD, we should do so as well for animals with comparable cognitive capacities. (And if some animals exhibit cognitive capacities that some people with CD lack, then perhaps these animals should be seen as closer to the neurotypical norm than some humans, and hence accorded higher moral status).

This entire AMC strategy is multiply flawed – intellectually, morally and politically – and disability advocates have effectively criticized it (Carlson 2009; Kittay 2005b, 2009a). It perpetuates a deeply problematic conception of neurotypical human cognition as defining the core of moral status, and treats other forms of subjectivity as somehow deficient bases of moral status. Deviation from the norm is arrogantly conceived as misfortune, impairment or temporary embarrassment, even if neurotypicals then find ad hoc grounds for overlooking this deficiency when granting moral status to people with CD (in terms of potential capacities, former possession of capacities, membership in a group that possesses such capacities, relationship of attachment to such members, etc.). Rather than challenging this unwarranted privileging of neurotypical human adults, the AMC re-inscribes it, and indeed generates perverse comparisons – a kind of jockeying for position in a zero-sum game regarding who falls closest to the privileged norm.

As we hope is clear, our interest in comparing the citizenship struggles of people with CD and DAs has no connection to this AMC strategy for comparing the moral status of people with CD and animals.[9] For one thing, we entirely reject the premise that moral status is based on a hierarchy of cognitive capacities (like linguistic agency), or on scales of neurotypicality versus deficiency/deviance. On our view, all beings who have a subjective experience of the world are self-originating sources of moral claims, regardless of their proximity or distance from any alleged norm of human neurotypicality, and regardless of their place on any alleged scale of cognitive complexity (Donaldson and Kymlicka 2011: ch. 2). The argument for animal rights would not be touched one iota if it turned out that all humans were identical in their cognitive and linguistic abilities, so that there were no overlapping or 'marginal' cases to appeal to for consistency. Our argument is not that 'marginal cases' should be treated alike, but that there are no marginal cases, because neurotypical human adults should never have been defined as the norm from which others are measured.

It's important to emphasize that animal rights theory did not introduce the idea that people with CD (or children) are 'marginal cases' for the purposes of moral status (or citizenship). That pernicious idea arose much earlier, when humanist philosophers first defined moral status in terms of a hierarchy of cognitive capacities or ideas of normality. However, animal rights theorists have too often uncritically adopted this troubling strain of Western philosophy in the process of responding to speciesist defenders of a human right to exploit animals. A typical

[9] It should be noted that 'conceptual exploitation' operates both ways. If some animal rights theorists make instrumental use of disability in order to bolster the case for animal rights, it is equally true that some disability theorists do the reverse. Some simply stipulate that the test of an acceptable defence of the moral status of people with disabilities is that it excludes animals in order 'to close the floodgates' (Wasserman et al. 2012: 14). Others suggest that animals must be excluded from the moral community to ensure vulnerable humans are not treated the same way we treat animals. According to Grandin, 'To prevent people from morally justifying mass euthanasia of the neurologically handicapped, they have to be speciesists and value humans more than other animals' (Grandin 2011: 214). For these authors, the only way to envisage humans having a dignified moral status is by denying it to animals, as if the mark of human moral worth is the right to kill and exploit non-human animals. On both sides of the animal rights/disability rights divide, questions of moral status have been instrumentalized. We discuss the persistent tendency of social justice movements to assume that progress for subaltern human groups requires reaffirming a steep species hierarchy, and the perverse effects this often has, in Kymlicka and Donaldson (2014).

speciesist claim is that linguistic agency is a threshold capacity for full moral status or citizenship; animals lack linguistic agency; therefore animals have diminished status; therefore humans can use them for our benefit. The correct response to this argument is not to point out that many humans also lack linguistic agency, and that logical consistency requires treating like cases alike (whether by elevating some animals or lowering some humans). The correct response, rather, is to directly challenge the idea that linguistic agency is a threshold capacity for moral status or citizenship, or that there is such a thing as 'normal' human cognitive capacity against which all are measured and some are found lacking. Moreover, pointing out cognitive differences (and we are all different from one another in our cognitive capacities) is just that, a description of differences. It is not an argument for unequal treatment, or for lesser or 'marginal' status.[10]

So our reason for comparing people with CD, children and DAs in this chapter is not to figure out their relative positions on some scale of moral status that has 'normal adult' humans at the top. Rather our purpose is to think through the challenges of upholding membership and participation rights for all members of society who have been excluded from traditional theories and practices of citizenship on the basis of limited linguistic agency. We believe that advocacy for all such groups can benefit from a collaborative effort which challenges the traditional conception of citizenship and its neurotypicalist bias (Salomon 2010), and which articulates compelling alternative models of membership and participation that include the full diversity of the members of society.

In this respect, we view this chapter as contributing to the project of a new 'fellowship' between disability rights and animal rights advanced by Sunaura Taylor in her recent work (Taylor 2011, 2013, 2014). As she notes, both struggles have a shared interest in contesting ableism, since 'we understand animals as inferior and not valuable for many of the same reasons disabled people are viewed these ways – they are seen as incapable, as lacking, and as different' (Taylor 2013: 761). And this in turn creates a shared interest in 'reevaluating such loaded words as "independence", "nature", and "normalcy"' (Taylor 2011: 219), since 'limited interpretations of what is natural and normal leads to the continued

[10] Garner (2013) has recently argued that radically egalitarian animal rights theories (such as ours) *require* the AMC because it is only through the demonstration of overlapping capacities across the species line that we can extend equal recognition and membership to animals. This is a simple failure to recognize that individual animals, like individual humans, are 'self-originating sources of valid claims'. Even if speciesists were to identify a uniquely human capacity – shared by all humans and possessed by no animals – so what? The fact of difference is not an argument for unequal moral or citizenship status.

oppression of both disabled people and animals' (Taylor 2013: 761). Indeed, she concludes that 'disability studies is left in a state of contradiction if it claims to find value in differing bodies and minds, different ways of being, but then excludes nonhuman animals' (2011: 219). We believe that articulating new models of inclusive citizenship offers a particularly fruitful place for advancing this new fellowship.

The Shared Challenges of Inclusive Citizenship

For all three groups, a key challenge is to enable political voice and participation without linguistic agency. People with CD, children and DAs may have a wide array of other capacities that are highly relevant to being a participating member of sociopolitical community, including having a subjective good; being aware of, and responsive to, others; engaging in intentional action and practical reason; being capable of empathy, concern and care; and of norm sensitivity and self-regulation. These are the capacities that make a shared social life possible, and the task of citizenship is to ensure that our shared social rules are responsive to the subjective good of all members who are part of this society. However, the absence of linguistic agency can pose a serious barrier to recognizing, interpreting, and enabling this range of capacities. Linguistic agents can more readily articulate their inner worlds. Individuals lacking linguistic agency are at a disadvantage in developing, demonstrating and exercising a wide range of capacities relevant to citizenship in a political arena designed to suit neurotypical human adults.

Indeed, unless we find ways of addressing this challenge, there is a serious risk that ideas of participation, co-authorship and citizenship will simply mask ongoing relations of domination under a fig-leaf of empowerment. Children, people with CD, and DAs are all vulnerable to misinterpretation, manipulation and unjustified paternalism, and it is all too easy to set up situations that appear to give a veneer of assent to practices that in fact subordinate or dominate them. This basic asymmetry of power is unavoidable. Members of these three groups have limited capacity for exercising a right of exit, or for organized mobilization or resistance to ensure that others recognize their perspectives or interests.[11] The reality is that they are dependent on others – caregivers, trustees, guardians and advocates – to support and interpret their participation. This inevitably opens the door to bias, self-interest, projection and well-intentioned error by those charged with interpreting the subjective good of those who lack linguistic agency.

[11] Although they are capable of individual acts of contestation and resistance (Hribal 2010).

Given these enormous challenges, it might be tempting to set aside the goal of enabling agency in shaping and communicating their subjective good, and supporting their decision-making, and to focus instead on more objective measures of welfare. In the case of DAs, for example, we might develop an account of species-typical needs or characteristic behaviours, and insist that caregivers respect these generic needs, without attempting to determine whether these species-typical needs do or do not track the subjective good of individual animals. Trying to solicit individual subjectivity, one might think, is at best unreliable, given the absence of linguistic agency, and at worst would simply operate to legitimate domination through biased and self-serving projections. Governing DAs according to objective species-typical norms is clearly paternalistic, but this might be preferable to baseless or self-serving efforts to interpret non-linguistic expressions of subjective good.[12]

Similar issues have arisen in the context of CD. Some political theorists have argued that where we face serious epistemic barriers in interpreting the subjective good of people with CD, we should rely instead on objective measures of the human good and species-typical norms (Nussbaum 2006). If individuals are unable to rationally judge for themselves the soundness of political propositions, society should not seek to mimic consent through the use of trustees tasked to solicit and interpret an individual's subjective experience. Rather, we should simply acknowledge that ideas of consent are not relevant, and that while we can justify measures 'for' them, we cannot justify ourselves 'to' them (Edenberg and Friedman 2013: 358). In other words, trustees for people with CD should make their best judgement of the objective interests of the person being represented, rather than making their best effort to understand how the person with CD conceives her own interests.

Most disability theorists and activists have been deeply distrustful of such paternalistic models of trusteeship. This is understandable in a movement that has had to fight a long battle against pernicious forms of paternalism, but as Bérubé notes, rather than developing less paternalistic models of guardianship for those without linguistic agency, many disability theorists have simply avoided the issue entirely, focusing on cases where the underlying problem is 'removing barriers' to self-representation rather than cases where the challenge is constructing new forms of dependent agency:[13]

[12] See Nurse and Ryland (2013); Nussbaum (2006).

[13] It is easier 'to speak of a "barrier-free environment" when one is speaking of wheelchairs and ramps than when one is speaking of significant cognitive disabilities' (Bérubé 2009: 357).

> [D]isability studies in the United States has drastically undertheorized surrogacy and guardianship, emphasizing the self-representation of people with disabilities and overlooking the position of people with disabilities whose only substantial hope of representation lies in having their wishes (insofar as we can know their wishes) represented by another. The reasons for this undertheorization are numerous: disability studies theorists have tended subtly to emphasize physical over cognitive disabilities, particularly severe cognitive disabilities, in part because you don't find a lot of people with severe cognitive disability holding academic positions; autonomy and self-representation remain an alluring ideal even (or especially) for people with disabilities; too strong an emphasis on guardianship seems to entail the further infantilization of people with cognitive disabilities; and in my wing of the humanities, where we have been post-something for quite some time, we are still too accustomed to think in terms of the 'indignity of speaking for others,' as Gilles Deleuze put it in an oft-cited interview with Michel Foucault. (Bérubé 2009: 357–8)

In short, we seem caught between two unsatisfactory models: an anti-paternalistic model that relies entirely on an individual's self-representation of her subjective experience; and a paternalistic model that relies on third-party judgments of objective well-being. Neither model provides a plausible picture for enabling participation by those members of society without linguistic agency. They have a right as citizens that their subjective good and voice shape social norms, but can only do so in ways that are, to varying degrees, mediated, interpreted and represented by others.

To overcome this impasse, we need to rethink the 'justification for/justification to' dichotomy. If we start from the assumption that justification *to* individuals only applies if they meet demanding threshold standards of rationality and theoretical understanding, then some individuals simply fall below this threshold (Edenberg and Friedman 2013: 356, 358). On this view, first-person experience of a particular rule or practice is only relevant if it can be reflectively and linguistically articulated. But justification to individuals is not a simple yes/no on/off threshold, and there are many contexts where standards of 'assent', 'acquiescence', 'contestation' and other forms of 'justification to' are relevant even where legal thresholds of informed 'consent' are not.[14]

On this question, both disability and animal rights theorists can benefit from thinking about children's development, and what Bérubé calls "the ordinary perplexity attending any parent-child relationship" (2009: 359). In the parent–child context, we take it as obvious that both 'justification for' and 'justification to' are relevant, although the precise

[14] For the relevance of assent/acquiescence in the case of animals, see Kahn (2014: 99); in the case of CD, see Jaworska (2009).

mix changes according to context and over time. Parents intensively solicit and respond to expressions of the subjective good of young children, yet play an active role in shaping these expressions into a coherent story about the child's interests.

A few theorists have shifted towards this more nuanced model, emphasizing that people with CD, like all of us, are individuals, with unique personalities and preferences (whose interests cannot be captured by 'objective' models), and whose subjective good can be solicited and counted in shaping collective decisions (Francis and Silvers 2007). There are ways for trustees (through attentiveness, observation, trial and error and experience) to help in the construction of 'individual scripts' of the good life for people with CD, and to hold political authorities accountable to them, so that individuals with CD can exercise meaningful forms of dependent agency. On this view, autonomy is understood as a relational accomplishment, not just a capacity of individuals. The task of constructing mechanisms of dependent agency that avoid the dangers of self-serving bias and projection on the part of trustees is a daunting one, but the risks are worth it, and the dangers of a threshold framework ('justification to' if you are above the linguistic agency line; 'justification for' if you are below the line) are worse.[15]

In the rest of this chapter, we want to build upon these promising beginnings, to see how they can inform a new vision of inclusive citizenship for people with CD, children and DAs. If inclusive citizenship is to serve emancipatory goals, we need to clarify the sort of participation and agency that is morally relevant, and the safeguards and preconditions that make it possible. We will organize the discussion around three issues that arise in each context: the scope of agency; the structuring of choice; and the challenge of interpretation. In all three sections, we will argue that reflecting on similarities and differences among the citizenship of children, people with CD and DAs can clarify the prospects and challenges facing new models of inclusive and diverse citizenship.

The Scope of Agency: Macro and Micro

The scope of agency is significantly constrained, for humans and other animals. Key dimensions of our lives are fixed by our embodied species

[15] As Kittay notes, the threshold model fails not only when people with CD fall below the line and so never have the chance to 'have a say' in the matters that most affect them, but also when they fall above the line and so are denied the unique structures and relationships which would allow them to exercise meaningful agency. As she puts it, threshold models 'exclude both by ignoring the existence of those who are too far afield from the idealization and by including in problematic ways those who fall far short of the idealization' (Kittay 2009a: 219).

identity, era of existence, biological parenthood and other givens. Despite these limits, it is widely assumed that we have a wide scope for agency – for making meaningful and effective choices about how we live our lives – a scope that typically expands with age and experience, under favourable material and sociopolitical conditions. Matters such as our intimate partners, our political and religious allegiances, our work and activities, and our social networks, are seen as subject to our evolving agency.[16] We have the right and the capacity to shape many dimensions of what we might call the 'macro frame' of our lives, and exercising this capacity wherever possible and meaningful is crucial to our well-being.

As part of recent citizenship struggles, advocacy for children and people with CD has sought to broaden the scope of self-determination, affirming the potential for macro-agency. When the UNCRC says that children have the right 'to have a say' in 'all matters affecting them', these matters concern not simply day-to-day decisions within the confines of a fixed life plan (e.g., choices about food, leisure activities, how to set up their bedroom), but fundamental dimensions of their lives – for example, the kind of education they receive, whether or not they engage in paid employment, who they spend time with, where their family lives, which parent they will live with in the case of a long distance separation, or whether or not they will undergo painful life-extending medical treatment (Alderson 2008).[17] Children have a right to be consulted in these matters, and for their ideas and preferences to help shape decision-making, and not simply be drowned out by adult concerns to protect and provide for them. The scope for agency is always changing and developing, so individuals must be engaged as presumptive agents – engaged 'as if' they are agents – since this is how we discover the extent to which, in any given circumstance, they are agents, and further enable them to become agents.

As noted earlier, the UNCRC frames children's rights in terms of the 3Ps – rights to protection, provision and participation. A key challenge in

[16] By 'agency' we mean self-willed or initiated action that carries an expectation of efficacy. Krause defines agency as 'the affirmation of one's subjective existence, or identity, through concrete action in the world. To be an agent is to affect the world in ways that concretely manifest who you are, to see yourself and be seen by others in the effects you have, to recognize your deeds as being in some sense your own' (Krause 2012: 240). Agency requires not just that you can initiate action but that your action can have the results you intend. As Wehmeyer and Garner put it, "being self-determined is not a function of how much you can do for yourself, behaviourally, but instead is a function of how much you make or cause things to happen" (2003: 263). In many contexts this requires that others respond to you as an agent.

[17] A serious limitation of the UNCRC is that 'all matters affecting' children is not construed to include the public political realm.

implementing this vision is ensuring that children's participation is not unduly circumscribed out of concern for protection. Regarding mobility, for example, Alderson presents some startling statistics about the growing restriction of children's mobility rights, largely in response to fears about them being killed in traffic accidents. In the UK between 1977 and 1990 the number of children killed by vehicles fell from 1,000 to 300 – a significant reduction. At the same time 'the percentage of children aged 7–11 allowed to cross the road on their own fell from 72 to 50 percent; to walk to the park went down from 63 to 37 per cent; to ride on a bus without an adult from 48 to 15 percent' (Alderson 2008: 121). In other words, the safety of children was purchased at the cost of substantially curbing their freedom. All the evidence suggests that children themselves resent this trade-off. When they 'have a say', they ask why cars aren't restricted instead of children's mobility. And indeed, Denmark took this approach, achieving a similar reduction in accident deaths by regulating cars (creating car-free spaces to walk, cycle and play) rather than restricting children (Alderson 2008: 104).

Similar issues arise in relation to children and work. While many countries prohibit all forms of child labour in the name of protection, evidence suggests that work provides a context in which children can develop agency and competence, garner respect and income, and develop relationships which may be more positive than those at home (Oswell 2013; Gasson and Linsell 2011; Bourdillon et al. 2009). Moreover, when asked to 'have a say', children indicate that they do not want blanket restrictions on work. They want non-exploitative work conditions and labour rights (Gasson and Linsell 2011; Bourdillon et al. 2009). This balance is recognized in the UNCRC, which does not ban children from working, but stipulates that work must not be exploitative, hazardous or harmful to health, education and development (Article 32).[18] The weight of existing evidence is that children have been harmed by blanket restrictions on work, and that overemphasis on protection denies them opportunities to participate in decisions about work in ways that support rather than compromise their flourishing.

[18] The UNCRC's approach to child employment is therefore different from the 'abolitionist' approach taken by the International Labour Organization in its Convention 138 (1973), which demanded that all states adopt a minimum age below which no child 'shall be admitted to employment or work in any occupation' (Article 1). While Convention 138 remains on the books, the ILO itself has subsequently shifted focus, and adopted a new Convention 182 in 2006 that focuses on eliminating harmful forms of child labour, thus coming in line with the UNCRC. For these developments, and the debate between abolitionists and regulationists regarding child labour more generally, see Bourdillon et al. (2009).

Paternalistic restrictions on freedom can lead to self-fulfilling prophecies, in which children lack opportunities to develop skills and competence, which becomes justification for the restriction:

> If children aged four and five years are mainly confined to home, nursery, school and care, seldom allowed to learn to cope on their own, their inability to cope could be said to be imposed on them, or ascribed to them. It may then be assumed to be inevitable, part of their slow biological maturing, instead of part of social inexperience. (Alderson 2008: 73)

Children have been infantilized in Western societies, and greater and greater restrictions on their freedom have in turn have resulted in drastically reduced conceptions of their capacities (Alderson 2008; Oswell 2013).

Similar debates have arisen in relation to the macro-agency of people with CD. They too have asserted greater control over the fundamental dimensions of their lives – where and with whom they live, their employment status, their sex lives and marriage/family decisions. Many of these decisions are made in close consultation with family, caregivers and support workers, and, in the case of severe disability, the extent of the disabled person's participation might be quite limited. Nevertheless, the old model in which all of these decisions were strictly made 'on behalf of' individuals perceived as wards, not citizens, has been challenged (and, indeed, thoroughly rejected under the UNCRPD).[19] And here too, as with children, the increased emphasis on participation has put in question older assumptions about the need for blanket protections, and has revealed how restrictions can lead to self-fulfilling prophecies regarding capacities (Walker et al. 2011). When asked, people with CD do not wish to be excluded from work, but rather wish to be provided with opportunities to explore and develop their agency in these contexts, with suitable supports, social integration and appropriate protection from exploitation through robust rights protections (Flores et al. 2011; Inclusion International 2009; Reinders 2002).[20]

This commitment to discovering and expanding the scope of agency is always individualized and revisable. The boundaries of meaningful agency are variable across time and across contexts, but the possible need for paternalistic oversight or constraint in one domain at one point in time does not provide a licence for wholesale or enduring restrictions across other domains. In the disability movement, the goal of seeking the

[19] We see a clear tendency to replace older models of 'plenary guardianship' with 'tailored guardianship', and then to replace older models of tailored guardianship with assisted decision-making (Boni-Saenz 2015).

[20] This is the approach endorsed in Article 27 of the UNCRPD, regarding employment.

'least restrictive environment', as well as the emphasis on 'nothing about us without us', captures these ideals (Carey 2009).

A commitment to inclusive citizenship for children and people with CD endorses these efforts to expand macro-agency. When we turn to DAs, by contrast, the prevailing assumption is that they have no capacity or need for self-determination. The fundamental shape of their lives is assumed to be fixed by their evolutionary history and/or species nature, predetermining a life of rigid dependence on humans and human society in which humans make all of the key decisions on their behalf. DAs are born into species-defined functional roles (as food animals, experimental animals, working animals, etc.), and while we sometimes ask what duties we owe animals within these parameters, we don't question the existence or nature of those parameters. We do not acknowledge the need for, or even the possibility of, consulting individual animals regarding what sorts of lives they want to lead, what relationships they want to have (with humans or other animals), what (work or leisure) activities they find satisfying, and where they want to live.

In reality, however, there are many possible lives for DAs, and a commitment to inclusive citizenship would engage DAs as presumptive agents, exploring possible and meaningful lives for specific individuals. In some cases, these possible lives will involve less intensive interaction with humans.[21] Countless DAs have escaped human management to join feral populations either on the fringes of society or in more remote 'rewilded' communities, like mustangs on the Great Plains or camels in the Australian outback.[22] Some DAs have escaped from intensive human (mis)management and dependency to more self-determining situations. Consider a lucky pig that flees *en route* to slaughter and ends up at a farm sanctuary where she controls many more aspects of her daily life – feeding herself, or making her own decisions about shelter, activities and friendships.[23]

Given the choice, some DAs will want to spend more time with humans, partly out of dependence on humans for protection and provision, but also for reasons of sociability and companionship.[24] Indeed, one

[21] Elizabeth Marshall Thomas (1993) describes how her dog companions, given the option, chose to spend less and less time with her.

[22] Recent genetic analysis reveals that certain animal populations long thought to have been truly wild are in fact rewilded former domestics (Clutton-Brock 2012).

[23] Since Farm Sanctuary (Watkins Glen, NY) opened in 1986, the farm sanctuary movement has blossomed across North America, with dozens of shelters now in operation. We explore how these new communities are a valuable source of information concerning possible lives for DAs in Donaldson and Kymlicka (2015).

[24] Although not necessarily with the same human: Rita Mae Brown (2009) describes how her cat companion chose to go live with neighbours.

of the many perversities of our current treatment of DAs is that we've taken highly sociable animals (and domestication only works for animals capable of interspecies sociability), and then confined them in isolated settings cut off from both human contact and contact with other animals. Just as humans benefit from interspecies sociability – and the benefits to humans of animal companionship are now very well documented – so too the lives of DAs can be enriched by the endless surprises and challenges of interacting across species lines.

Here too the potential scope for agency depends on engaging DAs as presumptive agents under less and less restrictive (but carefully scaffolded) conditions.[25] The range of relevant options will vary for different species and breeds (and will alter over time as humans cease to engage in selective breeding), and the resulting choices will also vary with individual personality. DAs, like humans, are uniquely endowed individuals, with individual temperaments, talents, impulses and desires, who will therefore differ markedly in their inclinations to explore different alternatives. This process will inevitably involve a lot of trial by error and adjustment, but insofar as DAs can explore meaningful options concerning the fundamental shape of their lives, it is tyranny to deny them opportunities to do so.

Moreover, this process cannot be restricted to the realm of micro-agency, limited to the small or discrete details of a way of life that is defined by others. Many writers have extolled DA agency in this micro sense. For example, horse and dog trainers discuss how mastery of skills (e.g., agility, jumping, etc.) enlarges animals' world of possible action, a world in which they can make some of the judgments and decisions, initiate actions and engagement, and derive a sense of satisfaction from successfully accomplishing what they set out to do. This kind of agency is important, but too often it is used to rationalize a relationship in which DAs are presumed to exist (and indeed brought into existence) to serve the needs, interests and desires of humans. As trainers acknowledge, their animals' micro-agency is strictly encompassed within the pursuit of fixed goals: the explicit aim is to get animals to cooperate in the pursuit of conceptions of showmanship or mastery that humans value.[26] Trainers may disavow older forms of training that involve outright violence – 'breaking'

[25] For a fascinating account of this process, see Kerasote (2007).

[26] Despite the rhetoric of two-way communication, negotiation and partnership, 'the conversation between horse and rider in the arena takes place entirely in respect of tasks that are set by the rider' (Patton 2003: 90). As Clark notes, the focus on micro-agency gives the veneer of assent, but in fact horses have not been offered any opportunity to explore alternative relationships. Under these circumstances, the veneer of agency and consent becomes a recipe for legitimating domination (Clark 2009: 179).

horses and beating dogs into submission – but their own methods involve manipulation to achieve absolute obedience in response to human commands (Hearne 2007 [1986]: 43; Patton 2003: 90; Haraway 2008: 211). We are still talking about moulding DAs to human uses and preferences, not about enabling DAs to redefine the goals of their relations with humans.

The conception of macro-agency that underpins inclusive citizenship is incompatible with a static or fixed conception of an individual's roles or life script. All members of society should be enabled, as far as possible, to shape the fundamental relationships and activities of their lives. It is all too easy, whether in relation to DAs, children or people with CD, to ignore this macro frame, and to focus instead on fulfilling duties to provide and protect, and on fostering sufficient micro-agency to ensure a basic level of welfare and compliance. But our goal, even if it is only achievable in modest forms, should be genuine macro-agency – the ability to shape the very nature and purposes of our shared cooperative relations and activities, and the definition of community.

The Structuring of Choice

So far, we have been talking in an admittedly loose way about creating space for people with CD, children and DAs to explore alternatives, on the assumption that their response to these alternatives can inform us about their preferences. But this hides a nest of problems. Where individuals are not linguistic agents, it is difficult to explain alternatives to them, or to confirm that their response is meaningful. Perhaps behaviour prompted by exposure to alternatives is not really indicative of someone's subjective good, but simply arbitrary movement or instinctive responses to something new in the environment. One can easily imagine circumstances in which exposure to 'alternatives', if presented in a void, would be a recipe for paralysis or anguish, not agency.

Choice, to be meaningful, needs to be socially structured. It requires that individuals be socialized into particular norms and relationships that help to define the familiar and the trustworthy, and that provide a benchmark from which incremental alternatives become meaningful. This is true for all social species, humans and animals, domesticated or wild. To enable macro-agency, therefore, we must step back and think about the structuring or 'scaffolding' of meaningful choice.[27]

[27] The concept of scaffolding derives from developmental psychologists Lev Vygotsky and Jerome Bruner, but their accounts were heavily tied to linguistic agency. Our aim in this section is to think about scaffolding choice for those who are not linguistic agents.

The literature on citizenship for children and people with CD suggests two key foundations on which choice can be scaffolded. The first is basic socialization. All members of any social grouping have the right to be socialized into the rules that enable members of society to coexist. This includes norms about appropriate physical contact, sharing space, regulating noise, avoiding dangers to oneself and others, and so on. These rules make it possible for people to flourish together, without imposing undue risks or burdens on others.

Of course the particular social norms that exist at any point in time are likely to privilege some group members while disadvantaging others. This is particularly clear in the case of DAs. We tightly prohibit and regulate any animal activity that we find inconvenient or unattractive, while ignoring the many ways our activities inconvenience or discomfort DAs. Similar asymmetries arise in relation to other historically excluded or stigmatized groups, including children and people with CD. The current rules are in no sense equally committed to the mutual flourishing of all members of society, and socialization therefore involves a dimension of domination. A central task of inclusive citizenship is to enable all members of society to ultimately challenge and reshape these social norms.

Nonetheless, basic socialization is a precondition for inclusive citizenship, and a foundation for scaffolding choice. Indeed, we can say that basic socialization in this sense is a right of membership, needed to ensure the safety of the individual and others, and because successful social integration for social beings is an essential precondition of flourishing. No meaningful agency is possible without some form of basic socialization.

A second foundation of scaffolded choice discussed in the literature on children and people with CD is stable social identity. In relation to children, for example, Article 8 of the UNCRC refers to the fundamental right to an identity. Every child will have their birth registered, be given a name (which only they can change), be accorded a family status (as someone's brother/sister, child or grandchild, niece or nephew), and have a continuous biographical identity enabling the state to fulfil its obligations regarding protection, provision and participation (Alderson 2008: 82). This may seem obvious, but it represents a crucial historical change in the way societies view children. On the one hand, it reflects a commitment to the view that children are unique individuals, not fungible possessions or property of the family. But it equally reflects a commitment to the view that children have a right to secure family and community membership – a right to sufficient stability in their social world (e.g., maintaining the integrity of the family unit as much as possible, having access to coherent physical and cultural surroundings, etc.) so that they can develop a sense of identity. In other words, the right to identity contains two key elements – the right to be an identifiable unique individual, and to be the member of relevant groups such as the family, or ethnic/cultural community (Alderson 2008: 81).

It is a marker of the abject status of DAs in our society that this fundamental right to identity is not recognized. Zoo animals, laboratory animals, service animals, or companion animals are all routinely relocated with complete disregard for the 'psychological effect of disrupting a family or a social network of constructed self-identities and relationships' (Savage-Rumbaugh et al. 2007: 11; cf. Harvey 2008). Animals routinely go through the experience of having their entire lives shattered. They may be surrendered by their human 'family' to a shelter and adopted out to a new family. In the course of days, everything in their lives is upended – their home and environment, their friends and family, their food, their routines, their games. Even their names change. Protection of a basic right to stable identity must underlie any exploration of DAs' participation in society. In its absence, exposure to choice and opportunity is not just meaningless but abusive.

The scaffolding of choice, therefore, starts with socialization into a reasonably stable context for individual identity formation. From this baseline, we can then expose the individual (patiently, thoughtfully) to different opportunities, environments, activities and associates. We need to structure these opportunities so that she can make meaningful choices, and then we need to respond to those choices in ways that confirm her agency and set the stage for further opportunities and further choices. This picture of scaffolded choice underpins recent discussions of CD (e.g., Ward and Stewart 2008), and we would argue it can help inform a citizenship approach to DAs.

Some choice situations will be more complex than others. In some cases we are simply eliciting raw preferences or natural inclinations related to basic needs for food, shelter, companionship, and social structure (e.g., who to hang out with, what to eat). A more difficult case concerns activities that require learning and training. These are not activities that emerge spontaneously. Consider agility training for dogs, or advanced tracking. You can't simply take a dog to an agility course, or give him a toddler's T-shirt to sniff, and expect him to 'choose' whether or not to undertake the activity. The activity must be taught and learned.

Many animal rights abolitionists jump to the conclusion that all such forms of training are unjust, an illegitimate attempt to compel DAs to engage in unnatural acts that serve human purposes. However, this ignores a central lesson of both the children and disability rights movements: opportunities to engage in appropriately structured interaction (i.e., interactions that challenge our skills *just enough*) expand the self, and the scope for agency (Irvine 2004: 8). This is true for both humans and animals (Hillsburg 2010: 34).

Why might such activities be part of her good? A dog might be able to develop specific skills (how to gauge the Frisbee direction on a windy day, how to activate a lever to turn on the TV or generate fresh water, how to signal when a scent trail has been broken and she needs a refresher, how to take the subway, or negotiate car-filled streets), and exercising these skills might lead to pleasure, satisfaction, confidence and possibilities for greater freedom. She might develop certain kinds of knowledge (the structure of her human companion's social network or daily routines, the strange ways of cats) that enlarge her mental realm in meaningful and satisfying ways. And she might develop a range of social bonds and friendships that provide greater satisfaction than species-specific friendships. Just as humans enjoy the frisson of cross-species friendship – the strange combination of connection and mystery; the mental challenge of communication; the opportunities for surprise, respect and humour – these satisfactions may be meaningful to some DAs.[28]

This potential of interspecies activities connects to a broader point about how we should understand animal well-being. In much of the literature, the focus is overwhelmingly on the elimination of pain and suffering, without any serious attempt to understand the sources of positive well-being for animals.[29] As a result, we have not seriously considered how a mixed human–animal society can provide the preconditions for moving out into the world as a self-determining agent.

There are risks to the pursuit of such realms of freedom. Freedom can be dangerous. For example, expanded mobility and freedom for animals such as chickens, rabbits, sheep or cows may only be possible with some increase in their vulnerability to predators (Smith 2003). Greater mobility and opportunity for dogs and cats may only be possible with increased vulnerability to cars or other hazards.[30] But as Balcombe notes, a safer life isn't a better life (Balcombe 2009). In the human context we recognize the importance of self-determination in making choices regarding

[28] Cross-species interaction offers 'new information – incongruities, interruptions of expectations, challenges – in the context of familiar otherness' (Myers 1998:78; cf. Feuerstein and Terkel 2008).

[29] For a more extended discussion of this point, and how it has narrowed the vision of animal rights theories, see Donaldson and Kymlicka (2012).

[30] Thomas (1993) describes how her dog companions learned to negotiate these increased risks associated with freedom. See Donaldson and Kymlicka (2011: ch. 5) for a discussion of the challenges posed by free-roaming cats.

risk/opportunity trade-offs, and the fact that different individuals will make very different choices (Donaldson and Kymlicka 2011).

So too, we argue, with respect to DAs. Some animals will be timid and risk-averse homebodies; others will be intensely curious and adventurous. We can be guided by these differences in deciding which risks to confront, and how much effort (theirs and ours) to put into scaffolding new opportunities. And then, based on our observations, we adjust and expand the scaffold over time, introducing new, but manageable, risks. In *Merle's Door*, Ted Kerasote details the scaffolding process that allows Merle to come and go through his dog door, leading a highly self-determined life. First he has to learn the dangers of his world (like hunters and farmers with guns, charging bison, packs of coyotes), and the rules of civility (not chasing farm animals, or pestering the neighbours). With these scaffolds in place, Merle experiences an exponential leap in terms of effective agency. It is not a risk-free life, but the risks are carefully undertaken and managed (Kerasote 2007).

To sum up, we see DA agency as being structured by basic socialization, leading to incremental options that challenge 'just enough', echoing familiar themes from the disability literature. For years, people with CD and their advocates have been fighting to replace the perniciously paternalistic model (which emphasized protection and provision of basic needs according to objectively defined criteria) with models of self-determination and agency.[31] They emphasize the same issues that we have been raising here: the importance of starting from a secure social identity; moving to less restrictive environments where people with CD can explore a range of social sites and activities; scaffolding their opportunities for learning and making choices within these broadened environments, while expanding their social networks and mental worlds (Ward and Stewart 2008). Disability advocates have also explored the ways in which 'intentional communities' can be responsive to the needs of people with CD for security and stability while providing meaningful choices about friendships and work (e.g., Randell and Cumella 2009). And they also discuss many of the same ethical dilemmas regarding the trade-offs between protection and freedom.[32]

[31] Walker et al. discuss a small but telling example of a developmental centre that didn't allow residents (adults with CD) to order pizza from a delivery service. The rationale was safety – fear that the pizza would be too hot (burning risk) or too cold (contamination risk). The result was a restriction of meaningful agency. Add up a series of such instances, and the result is severe restriction in the scope for self-determination (Walker et al. 2011: 13–14).

[32] Consider reproductive freedom. Given the history of horrific abuse and forced sterilizations, the idea of (non-consensual) sterilization as a form of reproductive control for people with CD is, rightly, highly suspect. Yet in some cases, becoming pregnant (or parenting) would be dangerous or traumatic to particular individuals. And so, not infrequently, reproduction is avoided through rigorous sexual segregation (infringing association rather than bodily integrity). It is not obvious that this indirect

Indeed, theorists have created a variety of instruments and models for assessing the well-being of people with CD in various settings (Lohrmann-O'Rourke and Browder 1998; Liu et al. 2007; Flores et al. 2011). They have also developed models of social ecology that triangulate analyses of environment, agency and well-being. They can now draw on a wide range of evidence to trace the connections between expanded opportunity/access, increased agency and greater well-being for people with CD (e.g., Reinders 2002; Ward and Stewart 2008; Wehmeyer et al. 2008; Callahan et al. 2011; Walker et al. 2011).

We have less systematic evidence of the link between agency and well-being for DAs, largely because society has not committed itself to either the agency or well-being of DAs. There's plenty of evidence that animals do better in less restrictive environments – that they relish their freedom. But this is not the same as structuring opportunities for them to develop agency within society and observing how they respond to this broadening of horizons. Little research has been done on the impact on DAs of opportunities to negotiate interspecies friendships, of learning how to safely engage with different dimensions of the human-built environment, and of participating in human-facilitated work and leisure activities – in part because so few of these opportunities have ever been provided.[33]

However, let's assume, optimistically, that society will one day provide these opportunities to DA members of our society.[34] The next challenge will be to interpret the results. This will inevitably be an exploratory process as we learn to listen to what DAs tell us about their needs and preferences, to create conditions under which they can develop and communicate needs and preferences, and to respond appropriately so that they can gain some confidence in the efficacy of trying to communicate with us. This brings us to the crucial role of interpretation.

regulation of reproduction through restrictions on mobility, social bonds and sexuality is better for the individuals involved than birth control or sterilization. Here, as elsewhere, we need to better understand what matters to the individuals themselves, and how they subjectively experience different approaches. For a recent UK court decision in favour of sterilizing a man with CD in light of his relationship interests, see www.bailii.org/ew/cases/EWHC/Fam/2013/2562.html. In this case, it was possible to meaningfully consult the individual about his interests, even though it was not possible for him to meet a legal consent threshold concerning sterilization.

[33] See Savage-Rumbaugh et al. (2007) for a fascinating exception (involving captive apes, not DAs).

[34] As noted earlier, we believe that farmed animal sanctuaries can provide a preview of what these opportunities might look like. We apply the ideas discussed in this section – of scaffolding choice through secure social identity and 'just enough' challenges within intentional communities – to such sanctuaries in Donaldson and Kymlicka (2015).

Interpretation

So far, we have argued that our theories and practices of citizenship must be modified to include those members of society who are not linguistic agents – including young children, people with CD, and DAs – and that these members can and should 'have a say' regarding the terms of our shared social world – macro-agency constructed through scaffolded choice. But readers might feel that we have ignored the central problem: namely, that these forms of agency and choice are ultimately dependent on the interpretation of others, and that this negates the feasibility or desirability of a citizenship approach.

Recall that the original challenge raised by Nussbaum was that there are serious epistemic barriers to interpreting the subjective good of people who are not linguistic agents, and that where these barriers exist, we should rely instead on objective measures of the good life and on species-typical norms, rather than engaging in the speculative and potentially self-serving task of trying to understand the subjectivity of these individuals. Nussbaum (2006) applies this argument both to people with CD and to animals.

While this position has been challenged by disability advocates, it remains pervasive in relation to DAs. For DAs to enact any form of citizenship, humans must be able to 'read' animal agency, and in particular to read their agency as an expression of their subjective good. Is this realistic? As Wolch (2002: 734) asks, 'What do animals want and can we ever really know?' If we can't interpret DAs' subjective good, then the goal of human-enabled DA agency is an incoherent one.

How then can we interpret what animals tell us about their preferences and desires – their subjective good?[35] They can't, for the most part, use human language to directly tell us about their dietary preferences, their shelter and environment likes, their deepest fears and desires, their best friends, their favourite activities, whether they experience work satisfaction (e.g., from tracking lost children, visiting shut-ins, guarding sheep, pulling carts, performing cognitive tests, etc.), whether they enjoy sex, whether they want to have offspring, whether they mind giving up

[35] Our focus here is on the epistemic barriers to successful interpretation, even where humans have a good-faith intention of reading DA behaviour as an expression of their subjective good. A quite different concern is that many humans lack this good faith in the first place. To address this would require institutional checks and safeguards to ensure that trustees are indeed motivated by the well-being, interests and wishes of DAs. On both of these issues there is much to learn from the children and disability literatures, but we focus on the first.

some of their eggs, whether they are traumatized by being shorn, milked, leashed or fitted with a tracking device, and so on.[36]

How then can we hear their voices, and interpret their subjective good? At one level, this shouldn't be a mystery. Anyone who has any experience with DAs knows that they are constantly trying to communicate their preferences to us, and that they have views about how their relationship to us should be structured. In popular culture, we talk about 'dog whisperers' or 'horse whisperers' who are seen to have some sort of mystical ability to understand domesticated animals' subjective good. But this is not a mystical power: the sad truth is that many humans simply do not take the time and effort to engage with DAs and understand what they are communicating. As a result, at some point, animals give up trying to communicate.[37]

This is a familiar concern within the CD literature as well. Several studies have shown that people with CD attempt to initiate communication with caregivers and staff, but these attempts are either not recognized or ignored. And so they too eventually give up trying, leading to 'learned helplessness' in communication.[38]

We need to get away from the idea that understanding the subjective experience of animals is a mysterious power, and to think more systematically about the forms of knowledge that are available regarding how animals express their subjective good in their relations to us. And here again, we can make progress by drawing on the literatures regarding children and people with CD, particularly pre-verbal infants or people with severe CD who cannot verbally articulate their thoughts and feelings. While studies show that their attempts at communication are often ignored, it is also true that a great deal of effort and research by intimate caregivers, practitioners and scientists has been invested in understanding their subjective good.

[36] Some animals, like Alex the African Grey Parrot, can communicate using elements of human speech. Some great apes have learned sign language (and use it to communicate among themselves, as well as with humans). And the advent of computer tablets and icons has further extended the scope for communication. However, the physiology of most DAs means that human-like speech or signing aren't possible. Therefore we have to become better at reading the body language and vocalizations that they can employ.

[37] Smith suggests that this is actually a learned incompetence: as humans grow up and are taught mastery over animals, we are taught that we do not need to listen to animals, and lose our natural ability to do so. Far from being a difficult skill that needs to be nurtured, the ability to listen to animals is a natural skill that is suppressed through socialization into practices of human supremacy. Therefore, 'animals' inability to communicate with us is not a natural fact; it is an artefact of our domination over them' (Smith 2012: 124; cf. Pallotta 2008).

[38] Bray (2003) reviews several studies of this phenomenon.

These literatures suggest that there are in fact several different kinds of knowledge we can bring to bear on the task of interpreting the behaviour and preferences of those who are not linguistic agents. As a start, we could broadly distinguish three types of knowledge: expert knowledge, folk knowledge, and personal knowledge. All three are relevant, and each can help fill in the gaps left by the others (Grove et al. 1999).

Expert knowledge can tell us what to expect, in general terms, for an individual member of a particular species. For example, dogs *qua* dogs have certain predictable psychological needs in terms of sociality, play and stimulation. They have dietary requirements, health needs and susceptibilities. Moreover, experts understand enough about animals' physiology to identify objective indicators (e.g., blood cortisol or oxytocin levels; tail-biting or body postures) of elevated stress, fear, pain, excitement, love, contentment and other states relevant to subjective well-being. Experts on dogs' social world know what to expect in terms of dogs' social development, as well as how to 'read' specific dog behaviours, such as tail positions, play bows or warning growls. And there are predictable dimensions to how dogs typically interact with humans and other species. Thus expert knowledge allows us to predict the basic needs of individuals, and to assess their well-being along a range of parameters.[39]

Anyone who spends time with dogs learns some of these things, producing a kind of folk knowledge. The more time one spends with dogs, the more one starts to recognize certain behaviours and signals. Many people who encounter a dog can judge whether she will welcome an extended hand or snap at it. This does not require understanding tail and ear positions the way an expert does, or being able to articulate the knowledge in propositional form, or even knowing that one knows. One may simply respond to certain signs from the dog with an intuitive sense that the dog is friendly or fearful. This knowledge may be limited, partial and sometimes misguided, but it provides a useful frame of reference. Each time one approaches a new dog, she is not a completely unknown entity, but an instance of a type about whom one can make certain assumptions.[40]

[39] An intriguing example is a recent study on 'runner's high' (Hutchinson 2012). The study measured pre- and post-exercise levels of anandamide, a chemical that reduces pain and anxiety and promotes a sense of well-being, in humans, ferrets and dogs. Human runners increased their levels of anandamide by 2.6 times their pre-running levels, whereas ferrets had no significant increase. Dogs, however, get the biggest runner's high – their anandamide increased by 3.3 times the pre-run level. In this case, our folk knowledge that dogs running in a big field are happy is amply confirmed by objective measures of anandamide that they *are* happy.

[40] See Andrews (2011) for the role of folk knowledge as a precondition, as well as a guide, to interpreting animals' good, drawing on experience with pre-verbal human infants.

Recent research by the Family Dog Project in Budapest is demonstrating the complexity of these forms of folk knowledge. For example, as part of our co-evolutionary history, dogs have learned how to interpret a great deal of human behaviour (e.g., what we mean when we point, how emotions are indicated by our facial expressions). They have also developed a barking repertoire to communicate with humans. Humans who have spent time with dogs can listen to taped dog barks (of dogs they haven't met), and correctly identify the circumstances in which the dog is barking (e.g., 'that dog is asking to play', 'that dog is signalling an intruder or threat', 'that dog is making an urgent request to go outside, or to be fed', and so on.) This is a striking example of a kind of folk knowledge that individuals often possess without even realizing they possess it (until a scientist asks them to identify barks on a recording) (Pongrácz 2005).

Then there is personal knowledge – the knowledge of an actual individual, her personality and temperament, her idiosyncratic behaviours and habits, her likes and needs as revealed over time, her individual communication repertoire, and a shared history of interaction, social codes and systems for mutual understanding. Kittay describes how, in the case of a person with severe CD, a mere glint in the eye or a slight upturn of the lip can be interpretable signs for an intimate caregiver (Kittay 2001: 568). Parents of young infants learn to recognize their own child's repertoire of cries and other vocalizations and to attach these to specific needs and wants. Humans with dog companions learn to recognize their dog's repertoire for requesting a walk, a tummy rub or a need for time alone. Personal knowledge, like folk knowledge, is often implicit. A parent 'just knows' when her child is upset or happy or teething, without necessarily being able to articulate how or why she knows.

We can bring all of these levels of knowledge and skill to the task of interpreting subjective well-being – from personal knowledge to expert knowledge, from intuitive understanding to objective measures (Shapiro 1990). They are complementary, building on one another or serving as mutual correctives. For example, some animals tend to disguise pain (so as not to give an advantage to potential predators on one evolutionary explanation). A non-expert, lacking this knowledge, might interpret her dog's lack of whimpering or flinching to mean that he is not in pain.

In these delicate judgements, there is great room for error in our interpretation of what individuals are trying to communicate to us, and our interpretations of their well-being and interests. Animal rights abolitionists worry that this process of interpretation will be corrupted by the self-interest of humans and our desire to preserve relations of domination and exploitation.[41] But interpretation can also be distorted by powerful impulses to improve the lives of those we love. An instructive discussion of this challenge arises in Jennifer Johannesen's memoir of the life and death of her son Owen Turney (Johannesen 2011). Owen suffered multiple and severe disabilities from birth. He couldn't speak or hear, and had severely limited motor control. Therefore he couldn't sign, and, while his caregivers tried to set up pointing and trigger devices for him to express or respond to basic choices, these efforts were never successful. With such limited opportunity for outward expression, it was difficult to know very much about Owen's mental world. His family and caregivers could certainly tell when he was happy or content or distressed or miserable, and could discover various needs and desires through trial and error. But his interior world remained largely mysterious.

Johannesen's book documents the temptation to project into the unknown – to confidently assert claims about Owen's mental world without any real evidence for doing so. This was particularly problematic in some of the schools Owen attended, in which professional caregivers felt compelled to justify their role by making claims about Owen's daily experiences – his favourite songs or activities, his helpfulness or leadership qualities, learning opportunities and progress on developmental tasks. Johannesen came to realize that many of these claims were baseless projections – projections that enabled caregivers to take satisfaction in their work, or justify their efforts, either to themselves or to others, or to prompt and encourage others to keep making an effort to reach Owen, or help him to develop capacities to enlarge his world.

In all of this we have to find the right balance of 'loving ignorance' in which we 'accept what we cannot know' (Tuana 2006: 15–16) rather than filling the space with false projections, without evading responsibility by claiming that our lack of 'whisperer' skills means we can't crack the mystery of other minds, human or animal.

The literature on CD also suggests that the powerful impulse to improve the lives of others can lead to an obsessive focus on learning, normalization and development of functioning that threatens to crowd out other dimensions of existence. We lose sight of the individual's freedom to simply be who she already is, instead of who she might become. There is a danger of sacrificing well-being in the moment in the name of an elusive future in which agency might be enlarged by the right therapy, learning opportunity or activity. This relentless goal-oriented mindset

[41] Many abolitionists favour the end of human relationships with DAs, through their gradual extinction.

can present an onslaught against which the vulnerable have little power to say 'Stop!' 'Enough!' It is easy to imagine how this could operate in the case of DAs as well. Thus it is crucial to include opportunities for contestation into the process of supporting and interpreting agency – on the part of the party concerned, as well as third parties.

We have obviously just scratched the surface here in thinking about issues of interpretation, but we hope to have said enough to show that we are not operating in an epistemological void. DAs try to communicate with us, when we take the time to listen and learn and respond, and we already have some well-developed bodies of knowledge that help us understand this communication.

Conclusion

In this chapter, we have discussed a number of ways in which animal advocates can learn from the citizenship struggles of children and people with CD, including issues of macro-agency, the scaffolding of choice and the challenges of interpreting subjective good. But in conclusion, we'd like to step back and make a more general point about the value of these literatures for the animal question.

For the past 40 years, animal ethics has often wavered between two extremes. In its pessimistic Foucauldian moments, the relation between humans and DAs is seen as inherently and always already oppressive and dominating (disciplining and policing), with no potential for fundamental change. Interspecies relations are fundamentally locked into a framework of violence, with humans asserting a right to dominate animals as a continuing spoil of inter-species war (Wadiwel 2013). Against this background, the extinction of DAs (and a commitment to leave wild animals alone) appears as the only hope for ending the carnage.

In a more naïve (or self-serving) moments, animal ethicists search for and celebrate evidence of animals' micro-agency, reflected in the rise of free-range farms, or cooperative training methods, or 'enrichment' for zoo and lab animals – all of which are taken as evidence of 'partnership', 'cooperation', even 'love' (e.g., Rudy 2011; Haraway 2008). Yet they leave untouched, and indeed are complicit in, the systematic exploitation of animals to serve human interests, in large part because they take as given that the purposes of human–animal relations are always already fixed by humans.[42]

[42] We describe this as an alternative to the Foucauldian story, but of course in another sense, the provision of micro-agency is a central part of Foucault's story of how domination works.

What has been largely absent is any serious attempt to explore the vast territory in-between extinction and micro-agency, a territory in which DAs would be seen as co-authors of their relations with humans, and co-members of a shared society, in which cooperative activities would be as responsive to their interests and purposes as ours. And it is here, above all, that animal advocacy has much to learn from the citizenship struggles of children and people with CD. The shift to citizenship in the children's rights and disability rights literatures, we would argue, is precisely driven by the need to explore this territory in-between micro-agency and Foucauldian domination. And the key innovation that makes this possible is a new model of citizenship premised on ideas of membership and participation.

It is perhaps not surprising that animal rights theory has lagged behind children and disability studies in theorizing this territory. After all, in the case of DAs, it is still possible – however implausibly – to deny that they count as members of our shared society. In relation to children and CD, there is no credible way to deny membership, and so no credible alternative to including children and people with CD in our account of the demos and of citizenship.

In time, we believe, DAs will also be recognized as members of our society, and when this happens, the citizenship struggles of children and people with CD will have bequeathed a much richer set of concepts and practices for thinking about their membership and participation rights.

8 Hannah Arendt and Disability: Natality and the Right to Inhabit the World

Lorraine Krall McCrary

The thought of Hannah Arendt is rarely mined for its insights into disability.[1] This isn't shocking: Arendt says almost nothing directly about disability and its implications for politics. In fact, her silence on the matter is somewhat striking, given that her work responds to the persecution of Jewish people during the Holocaust, when the Nazis were also persecuting disabled people. Arendt understands the Nazi treatment of the Jews to be a rejection of their right to inhabit the earth; the Nazis similarly attacked the right of the disabled to inhabit the earth, a right that is still not sufficiently protected for people with disabilities today. While Arendt does not write explicitly about disability, she does write about what it means to be human, arguing that all humans should be welcomed into the world and into political community, while recognizing the existence of profound difference within humanity.[2]

There are several points at which Arendt's thought can be developed in a way that contributes to disability theory. Where disability studies has faced difficulties in arguing for the human dignity of those with disabilities, Arendt provides a unique and innovative way to understand what it means to be human: Natality, or the possibility of political action that is rooted in the action of being born, recognizes that action itself is always social; it is always informed by the community in which it occurs. In fact, action requires the existence of difference, which Arendt calls "plurality." Natality distinguishes itself in significant ways from other understandings of what it means to be human, from those based on religious reasons, speciesist arguments, and rationality (which has itself been repeatedly used to exclude those with profound intellectual impairments from politics). While Arendt denigrates the body in ways that are problematic for disability theory, her theory can be adapted and developed by

[1] Notable exceptions include Ruth Hubbard (2006), Seibers (2008), and Titchkosky (2000), all of which will be discussed in the course of this chapter.

[2] I want to thank Cynthia Barounis for her helpful comments on an earlier version of this paper, as well as members of the Workshop on Politics, Ethics, and Society at Washington University in St. Louis. Thanks are also due to Kathryn Krall and Lewis McCrary.

integrating disabilities studies' insights into the intrinsic connection of the person to the body. Although she was writing about "the right to have rights" in response to the Holocaust and the Nazi exclusion of the Jewish people, her comments have relevance for other people whose right to have rights has been called into question, including those with disabilities. In *Eichmann in Jerusalem*, she addresses the infamous perpetrator of Nazi genocide:

> Just as you supported and carried out a policy of not wanting to share the earth with the Jewish people and the people of a number of other nations – as though you and your superiors had any right to determine who should and who should not inhabit the world – we find that no one, that is, no member of the human race, can be expected to share the world with you. This is the reason, and the only reason, you must hang. (Arendt 1968b: 130)

Arendt's assertion of the right to inhabit the world, which she founds on human natality, intervenes today in debates over the ethics of prenatal testing. An Arendtian approach to prenatal testing not only draws attention to the need to create a public sphere in which all, including those with disabilities, can contribute to the creation of the world, it is also critical of attempts to restrict difference.

Human Dignity and Disability

The human dignity of disabled people is often denigrated, both in popular opinion, as well as in scholarly writing. The immensely popular *Girlfriends' Guide to Pregnancy*, which has been reprinted more than 40 times, widely translated, and which has 1.5 million copies in print, for instance, articulates an implicitly critical view of disabled children. The author writes of the fears that women face while expecting:

> As soon as you think that your baby is spared the traumas of Tay-Sachs disease or Down syndrome, you creatively come up with other things to obsess about, such as whether it is going to have crossed eyes or ears like Prince Charles's... Eventually, God willing, the baby is born in robust good health. But for those of you who are not completely distracted by the outrageous experience of having a full-size baby come out of your insides, there will be a moment after that last push, or when the doctor reaches into your cesarean section, when you steel yourself for the possibility that you are going to be presented with a baby that looks more like Bubbles the Chimp than the Gerber baby. (Iovine 2007: 63–4)

The author, Vicki Iovine, is right: fearing that one's child will be disabled is only one instance of a broader category of fear, emerging from parents' desire to control every aspect of their children's lives, a control that is impossible. However, rather than provide information about disability, information that would almost certainly help to moderate women's fears, Iovine dismisses their fears as unlikely to be actualized. This denies the ubiquity of disability – the fact that, if we live long enough, each of us will experience disability. It implies that if disability is avoided in the fetus, if "the baby is born in robust good health," the parent can then just worry about less-significant physical characteristics.

When considering the fraught question of whether or not to choose prenatal genetic testing, Iovine quickly jumps to the most extreme case – that of a non-viable fetus – almost entirely avoiding the more complicated issue of a viable fetus with a disability. And then she returns to her recurring dismissal of complicated situations, appealing to normalcy: "There, now that I have you ready to slit your wrists, let me rush to reassure you that your odds are incredibly good of having a perfectly normal baby" (2007: 91). Iovine's elevation of "normal" as a preferable category and her description of fear as an appropriate and ubiquitous response to disability are disheartening. The need for far more information than a genetic diagnosis and the potential that the home and community can be a welcoming place for both disabled and non-disabled members are possibilities that Iovine does not entertain.

Not only is a disregard for the human dignity of disabled people evident in popular culture, but also in scholarly literature. In his article, "Speciesism and Moral Status," and elsewhere, noted opponent of the disability movement Peter Singer philosophically critiques and dismisses arguments for the equal value of all human life: First, there are arguments on religious grounds for human dignity, but these ought not be the basis of law in a pluralist regime (Singer 2010: 335). Second, there are arguments on speciesist grounds, such as Bernard Williams' defense of the position that humans can prefer their own kind because they are the ones doing the judging (Singer 2010: 336). Speciesism does not consider what it is about humans that gives them moral worth and dignity. To this, Singer (2010: 336–7) asks: What is it that unites us? Are we really more like all humans than like anything else? Moreover, in what other ways is it morally licit to prefer what we are just because we are the ones judging? Third, there are arguments on the grounds of the superiority of humans' cognitive abilities (2010: 337). However, this basis for equal moral worth excludes those with severe cognitive impairments. Many contractarian views of morality have similar problems: they are unprepared to include those who cannot reason politically and consent to the contract (2010: 338). Singer argues that we ought to consider abandoning "the idea of the equal value of all humans, replacing that with a more graduated view in which moral status depends on some aspects of cognitive ability" (2010: 338). From the perspective of disability studies, this is unacceptable. What Singer's article does reveal, however, is the inadequacy of grounding human dignity in rationality, religious arguments, and speciesism.

It is clear that popular culture and academic affirmations of rationality threaten the human dignity of people with disabilities. Disability scholars have engaged with human dignity in ways that range from seeing it as a useful but limited social construct to tying it to human functioning in ways that continue to exclude some people with severe cognitive disabilities. Other theories appear to be overly inclusive, providing insufficient grounds for separating humans from animals.

Michael Bérubé, for instance, focuses on the openness of society to human potential, clearly a necessary aspect of ensuring the recognition of human dignity, rather than on the objective existence of human dignity in the person. He writes:

> [I]t might be a good idea for all of us to treat other humans as if we do not know their potential, as if they just might in fact surprise us, as if they might defeat or exceed our expectations... That might be one way of recognizing and respecting something you might want to call our human dignity. (Bérubé 2003: 53)

Indeed, an objective human dignity in the person is nearly useless without the corresponding recognition of that dignity by political society. However, I will argue with Arendt that there is a close connection between the subjective recognition of humanity and its objective presence.

One of the most discussed articulations of human dignity in disability studies is that of Martha Nussbaum. She advocates a capabilities theory that seeks to remedy both Rawls' exclusion of the disabled from the original position and that of the social contract tradition more broadly. Rather than relying on rationality as the central human capacity, Nussbaum identifies ten different capabilities of humans that she argues should all be supported. In doing so, she moves from understanding distributive justice as a process to understanding it as an outcome (Silvers and Stein 2007: 1642). While her theory includes within it many more disabled people than Rawls' social contract theory does, it does not recognize some people with severe cognitive disabilities as reaching minimal human functioning, including philosopher Eva Kittay's daughter, Sesha. Nussbaum writes:

> Try as it will, society cannot bring her up to the level at which she [Sesha] has in any meaningful sense the capabilities in question. It now would appear that the view that emphasizes the species norm [Nussbaum's own view] must choose: either we say that Sesha has a different form of life altogether, or we say that she will never be able to have a flourishing human life, despite our best efforts. (Nussbaum 2006: 187)

While Nussbaum's capabilities approach is more inclusive than Rawls', she has still laid out an understanding of human dignity that does not include some humans with severe cognitive disabilities. Kittay (2005a: 110) responds to Nussbaum, arguing that her daughter's life is not, as it is portrayed by Nussbaum, tragic. Anita Silvers and Michael Stein (2007: 1646) articulate a similar critique when they worry that Nussbaum's capabilities theory "could invite oppression" by stigmatizing those who fail to reach minimal standards of human flourishing set by her ten basic capabilities.

In another article, Michael Stein (2007: 101) further critiques Nussbaum's approach, arguing that her capabilities approach "does not go far enough towards empowering disabled persons with the 'right to be in the world,'" language reminiscent of Arendt's own critique of Eichmann. In order to secure human dignity for those he understands Nussbaum's theory as neglecting, Stein advocates instead cultivating individual talents, whatever those talents are, rather than (as Nussbaum does) understanding only those who express capabilities from her list at at least minimal levels as living a life worthy of human dignity (Stein 2007: 106–7). While Stein's disability human rights paradigm helpfully focuses on the individual as an end, rather than as a means to contributing to the social order, his approach raises questions: How is cultivating talents a uniquely human action? Might this not be applicable to animals, as well, many of which might be said to have talents? Moreover, how should the human be treated in the case that talents are difficult, or perhaps even impossible, to identify? It is clear that talents and capabilities are different, but aren't talents, like capabilities, about achievement? And couldn't talents, like capabilities, make humans into a means rather than an end? Beyond asserting that the development of talent is a moral imperative that societies owe their citizens, Stein does not argue for *why* human dignity requires this, nor on what foundation this human dignity rests.

In "Disability, Self Image, and Modern Political Theory," Barbara Arneil also critiques Nussbaum, defending a much broader human dignity that does include every person: Arneil (2009: 234) proposes a theory of "interdependency," advocating a reconciliation of profound dependence and claims to independence, both of which she claims are important to people with disabilities and to all people. One difficulty of Arneil's notion of interdependence is that, while it includes all disabled people, it seems to include non-human animals, as well, as Stefan Dolgert (2010) develops in his response to Arneil. Arneil's response is that the aspiring to independence aspect of human interdependence is not applicable to animals: "While almost all children wish to become independent of their parents (as true of children with disabilities as nondisabled children to the extent that they are able to be independent and society makes accommodations to support it), pets do not seek independence" (Arneil 2010: 866–7). This raises further, unanswered, questions for her theory: Do all humans, including severely cognitively disabled people, aspire to independence? If they do not, would her theory have the same problem as Nussbaum's and Stein's of not including all humans? Despite these questions, Arneil's theory is important in emphasizing both dependence and independence as unshakable aspects of being human. Arendt's understanding of humanness will support Arneil's articulation of humanness in highlighting both of these.

Eva Kittay proposes an alternative basis for moral obligation and equal human dignity. For her, it is located in the shared human experience of being a mother's child. She writes, "I came to recognize that the locutions 'I am also a mother's child' or 'He, too, is some mother's child' can be heard as 'We are all – *equally* – some mother's child'" (1999: 25). This is not an individualistic claim or an assertion of rights, but rather acknowledges human connectedness: her own mother "is the child of a mother only because another person is (or was) someone who mothered her" (Kittay 1999: 25). She develops this idea further: "The proposal is that rather than an equality based on properties that adhere to individuals, we develop an equality wherein the condition of its possibility is the inevitability of human interdependence: The interdependence that is featured both literally and metaphorically in the aphorism that we are all some mother's child" (1999: 50). This idea that we are all some mother's child is in the tradition of the feminist ethic of care – that moral obligation arises from affection and concern, not from contractual or purely voluntary relations (Kittay 1999: 53). Kittay's notion of each person being a mother's child is perhaps closest to Arendt's natality: it results from one's birth. Moreover, it requires a recognition on the part of the mother/family and of the wider society into which one is born. While, like Kittay, Arendt is in tune with human interdependence, Arendt more explicitly ties natality to political participation: because of the action of being born physically and inserting ourselves into the world, humans ought to be given the opportunity to likewise insert themselves into the political community. This corresponds with Arneil's critique of Kittay's point – that while she aptly grasps human dependence, it may be at the expense of human independence (Arneil 2009: 233).

Hannah Arendt on Being Human

With her conception of natality, Hannah Arendt offers an imaginative and unique understanding of what it means to be human, providing a basis for human dignity and the right to inhabit the world that avoids many of the problems that other conceptions of human dignity encounter: natality is neither a religious grounding nor a speciesist one; it is not an appeal to rationality, although it does intersect with rationality. Natality emphasizes both dependence and independence in ways that still differentiate humans from animals. Natality is relevant to more than the Jewish people: it can also be appealed to as a grounding for the rights of those with disabilities.

Natality is a complicated concept, one that admits of different interpretations among Arendt's readers, and one that is derived from and implies other of Arendt's concepts. Natality is the event of being born. It is both biological and political – humans are first born as babies; later, because of their first birth into the physical world, they are able to enter the political sphere through action, a sort of second birth.[3] It is to this political natality that Arendt refers when she writes, "With word and deed we insert ourselves into the human world, and this insertion is like a second birth, in which we confirm and take upon ourselves the naked fact of our original physical appearance" (Arendt 1998: 176–7). It is the fact of our birth that is confirmed through our participation in politics. Natality is "the beginning which came into the world when we were born and to which we respond by beginning something new on our own initiative" (Arendt 1998: 177). Natality is not something humans *have*, but something that they *are*. Patricia Bowen-Moore articulates this when she writes: "By virtue of his natality, then, man can exercise his capacity to begin exactly because he not only is in possession of this faculty but also because he is this crucial reality" (Bowen-Moore 1989: 25). Humans are this reality – a being who initiates – because of their birth. Birth is the action in which later human actions are rooted and by which they are inspired (Arendt 1965: 214).

In order to best understand natality and its implications for disability, we must turn to some interconnected ideas in Arendt: givenness, action, plurality and the pariah, the social aspect of natality, and the need for political guarantees for the right to have rights. For natality to be an effective foundation for human dignity, it needs to point to something that is stable and unchanging about what it means to be human; it needs to show what makes humans different from animals. Arendt's idea of "givenness" does this work. It explains the content of human natality or

[3] Patricia Bowen-Moore, in *Hannah Arendt's Philosophy of Natality*, distinguishes between two senses in which Arendt uses natality: the first, she calls primary natality, and the second, political natality. "Primary natality" refers to man's birth and his resulting capacity to initiate, and "political natality" refers to man's entrance into the public sphere through political action in the exercise of his freedom (Bowen-Moore 1989: 22, 24). Bowen-Moore also introduces a third kind of natality, which is tangential to our purposes here: "tertiary natality," or birth into the life of the mind.

birth: humans do not give birth to giraffes or kittens or dolphins. Natality does not simply refer to birth (or else it would be as applicable to crickets as to human babies), but to a specifically human birth. So what makes a human, human? Arendt identifies as given both the common humanity, which is characterized by the capacity to act, as well as what makes us different from other humans, the specific facts about individuals. Both what is universally true about humans, as well as diversity, are central parts of the human condition. Arendt's examples of givenness include not only existence, but also being a woman and being Jewish, facts that contribute to the plurality of the world and that allow her and others to be pariahs. Disability is another example of givenness, particularly when the disability is present from one's birth, but even where it emerges in the course of life.

Arendt argues that what is given – existence itself, as well as the individual content of that existence – deserves a response of respect and gratefulness. Givenness would matter little if we could and should change everything about ourselves. Modern man resents everything given, but should do the opposite – they should exhibit "a fundamental gratitude for the few elementary things that indeed are invariably given us, such as life itself, the existence of man and the world" (Arendt 1951: 438). They also ought to accept other facts about themselves. Respect for givenness does not imply that there is one way to live one way to live in the world as a woman, or as a Jewish person, or as a disabled person. Rather, Arendt is hopeful that people will take the chance to express through action their individual givenness among other individuals. She maintains that this is the meaning of a line from Dante that she translates as "Thus, nothing acts unless [by acting] it makes patent its latent self" (Arendt 1998: 175). What is given is the latent self that is actualized by acting; this includes both the capacity for action, as well as the individual characteristics of the self. In this sense, then, givenness allows for the existence of plurality, of difference among humans, and, as a result, for the possibility of action.[4]

[4] In *Hannah Arendt and Human Rights*, Peg Birmingham argues that natality and givenness are connected against interpretations of Arendt (rooted in *The Human Condition*) that understand Arendt to be separating givenness from politics and relegating it to the private sphere. Birmingham writes: "Rather than emphasizing natality as the capacity for action and for beginning something new, Arendt points approvingly to the Augustinian insight that the event of natality is also about that which is given – indeed, mysteriously given – and which cannot be changed" (2006: 72). And again: "[I]n the event of natality each of us is miraculously and gratuitously given as inescapably alien, singular, and embodied presence that can never be justified or represented, only affirmed and praised" (2006: 93). Birmingham recognizes that natality is simultaneously something that is shared by all humans, as well as something that is singular and unique. My own reading of the relationship between natality and givenness is in accord with Birmingham's on the connection between natality and givenness; this is crucial because it impacts whether or not there is something stable about being human, which I argue there is.

Givenness, then, is both a universal part of the human condition and individual, specifying our difference from others. Our natality and givenness, insofar as that refers to our mere existence, the universal aspect, allows us the capacity for action. This is the supreme human capability; it is what separates us from animals. It is our ability to begin or to initiate what is unpredictable, revealing each person's unique distinctiveness (Arendt 1998: 178). Action, according to Arendt, is distinctly political: action can establish the public realm or, if the public realm is already established, action occurs within it. Moreover, action is always social: it requires acting with and among others. Arendt explains:

> What makes man a political being is his faculty of action; it enables him to get together with his peers, to act in concert, and to reach out for goals and enterprises that would never enter his mind, let alone the desires of his heart, had he not been given this gift – to embark on something new. (Arendt 1970: 82)

The capacity for action, then, is a given and stable part of the human condition. While this chapter argues that natality as the capacity for action is a foundation for human dignity that can benefit disability studies, attending to disability also questions the close relationship between action and politics that Arendt articulates; as we shall see, taking into account the experience of people with disability draws attention to other realms than politics that are conducive to creation and action.

Our givenness, insofar as that refers to those things that make us different and distinct, contributes to another requirement of action – the existence of plurality. Difference or plurality is a necessary precondition for action, because revealing oneself to others requires the existence of the other (Arendt 1998: 7). Arendt describes plurality as "the fact that men, not Man, live on the earth and inhabit the world" (1998: 7). Differences in ethnicity, nationality, gender, disability, among other things, contribute to human uniqueness, which is the basis of plurality: "we are all the same, that is, human, in such a way that nobody is ever the same as anyone else who ever lived, lives, or will live" (Arendt 1998: 8). This, too, is part of the givenness that we experience as a result of our birth. While Arendt does not identify disability as an example of plurality, it clearly fits within her framework. Recognizing that difference is necessary in order for action to be possible is a strong argument for welcoming people with disabilities to contribute to and reshape political spaces.

A natality that includes givenness and requires plurality also implies the existence of what Arendt calls the pariah, a person whose individual difference can provide a privileged view of politics. One becomes a pariah by accepting the (given) facts about oneself; through that acceptance, one gains the additional perspective that difference offers. Arendt's pariah is set in contrast to the parvenu, the one who assimilates, a response to difference that she critiques. Arendt treats the pariah and parvenu in *Rahel Varnhagen*, her work about a Jewish woman who hosted a salon in Berlin at the turn of the nineteenth century. Rahel is Jewish and a woman; Arendt presents these facts about her, not as things to be escaped, but rather as things that Rahel must comprehend as part of her distinctiveness within her historical and social context. Arendt, like Rahel, understands that attempting to deny facts about herself is nonsensical. She writes about that fact that she is Jewish: "The truth is I have never pretended to be anything else or to be in any way other than I am, and I have never even felt tempted in that direction. It would have been like saying that I was a man and not a woman – that is to say, kind of insane" (Arendt 2007: 466). This is not to say that Arendt argues that to be Jewish or to be a woman means one thing and not another: Arendt understood those differences to be a starting point, which the person could develop in many different ways.

Arendt develops this idea further when she writes that it is through understanding oneself, including in one's difference, that one can contribute most effectively to politics and that one can most effectively reveal oneself among others:

> The history of humanity is not a hotel where someone can rent a room whenever it suits him; nor is it a vehicle which we board or get out of at random. Our post will be for us a burden beneath which we can only collapse as long as we refuse to understand the present and fight for a better future. Only then – but from that moment on – will the burden become a blessing, that is, a weapon in the battle for freedom. (Arendt 2007: 150)

This offers the pariah a "view of the whole," a broader perspective on political society, as well as a position from which to fight for change, for instance changes in society's understanding of what being a woman or being Jewish or being disabled means (Arendt 1997: 249). Being a pariah, then, and the homelessness that it involves, allows for a critical understanding that those who are not homeless may miss. The pariah is a critic at two levels: he critiques the rest of society from the position of his difference; in addition, he critiques even those who share his differences. Disability, due to the great diversity within it, especially questions a monolithic identity. Here we see that what is given about people through the event of their birth will inform even their engagement in the social and political world.[5] While Arendt does not apply her notion of the pariah to people with disabilities, the relevance

[5] This runs counter to the harsh separation between public and private that Arendt advocates in *The Human Condition*. *Rahel Varnhagen*'s critique of this absolute separation is a reading of Arendt that has much to offer disabilities studies.

is obvious: disabilities are a given difference; this difference, when acknowledged, can provide people with impairments with a wider perspective, one that may enrich politics. Unless one's disability is recognized, one cannot participate in constructing the meaning of that disability. Susan Wendell gives a picture of what applying Arendt's notion of the pariah to disabilities might look like in *The Rejected Body*:

> What would it mean, then, in practice, to value disabilities as differences? It would certainly mean not assuming that every disability is a tragic loss or that everyone with a disability wants to be "cured." It would mean seeking out and respecting the knowledge and perspectives of people with disabilities. It would mean being willing to learn about and respect ways of being and forms of consciousness that are unfamiliar. And it would mean giving up the myths of control and the quest for perfection of the human body. (Wendell 1996: 84)[6]

Natality is not only a capacity in the individual person in its universal and individual senses: it is also fundamentally social in both its biological sense and its political sense. Arendt's recognition of the need for social uptake of the actions of the individual is particularly relevant to disability: it is consistent with the insights of the social model of disability that disability is not simply a bodily impairment, but that the social context of the bodily difference can be more disabling than the bodily difference itself. The social aspect of natality is apparent in both public and private. In the biological realm, it is procreation that leads to natality: "[M]an was created with the power of procreation, that not a single man but Men inhabit the earth" (Arendt 1951: 439). Procreation itself is social – it requires two people and creates a third, allowing for plurality among humans. Humans do not multiply through cloning identical versions of themselves, but rather through the creation of an entirely new human person. "Procreation," even more than "natality," reminds us that birth is the creative act of two people together. Procreation respects the plurality of persons – the difference of a man and a woman is required to create a child. And, as this chapter will discuss in its conclusion, the practice of prenatal testing makes all the more apparent the importance of social uptake to the welcoming of people with disabilities into the world. Procreation is not the only aspect of the private realm that is social: from friendship to family, Arendt recognizes the fundamental dependence

[6] While she cautions downplaying "the 'Otherness' of people with disabilities by overextending the category of disability," Wendell also writes that she prefers "to speak of disability as a form of difference, while recognizing that both stigma and being 'the Other' are aspects of the social oppression of people with disabilities" (1996: 66). This is an important tweak of Arendt's notion of the pariah: people with disabilities should not be made into 'the Other' or seen as "exotic" "curiosities" (1996: 66–7). Wendell praises writing about disability that simultaneously does not minimize the suffering of the disabled, as well as is attentive to the intrinsic value of the differences that they experience (1996: 67).

humans have on others, perhaps especially for developing and living out their own unique identities. This social beginning is the foundation for later political action, which is similarly social – one person is always acting in the midst of others.

Political natality, like biological natality, is social. Participating in politics requires being permitted into the political sphere at all: Arendt writes in response to the exclusion of the Jewish people; people with disabilities have also been excluded – from being acknowledged in political theories, from being permitted to participate in politics, and sometimes simply logistically, from a lack of accommodation. Political participation also occurs in the context of what Arendt calls the "web" of human relationships, which are themselves the result of previous actions. Arendt is clear that political action does not happen in isolation, but is the insertion of one's self in a pre-existing set of relations and actions, which affect one's actions: "It is because of this already existing web of human relationships, with its innumerable, conflicting wills and intentions, that action almost never achieves its purpose" (Arendt 1998: 184). This web of human relationships affects how actions are received and whether or not they achieve their intended purpose (Arendt 1998: 183–4). Participants in the disability movement are, of course, aware of the way in which previous actions of others can thwart their ability to achieve their desired outcome. In both the political and private aspects of natality, then, Arendt recognizes the social aspect of human action. Likewise, as we shall see, Arendt recognizes that humanness is not only something present in the individual person, but also something that, in order to be enjoyed, must be recognized by political society; she is attentive to both independence (in the capacity for action) and dependence (in the always social context necessary for that action).

Because Arendt is so interested in keeping alive human difference – the existence of plurality and of pariahs and of the social context for action – she is skeptical of any appeals to human nature, which she worries will imply that that there is one way to live and restrain the potentiality of human action. Because she roots natality in the human as a result of birth, it is ontological; but because she makes clear that it is different from a human nature, she emphasizes that it is not teleological. Humans can only be revealed by action; they cannot be constrained to follow a particular nature in advance of their own choices (Arendt 1998: 10–1).[7]

[7] She writes, "nothing entitles us to assume that man has a nature or essence in the same sense as other things" (Arendt 1998: 10). If we did have one, then only a god could know what it was – "attempts to define human nature almost invariably end with some construction of a deity" (Arendt 1998: 10). Arendt writes, "The question about the nature of man is no less a theological question than the question about the nature of God; both can be settled only within the framework of a divinely revealed answer" (Arendt 1998: 11).

While she is adamant that natality is not a feature of human nature, the question that Arendt struggles with (and changes her mind about in her revisions to *The Origins of Totalitarianism*) is whether or not natality is a stable part of the human condition – whether biological natality inherently implies political natality or whether the human possibility for action is limitless and could even disconnect biological natality from political natality. On the one hand, Arendt jealously eliminates the possibility of natality being anything that might resemble human nature in its stability and fecundity. This position is reflected in the original edition of *The Origins of Totalitarianism*. On the other hand, Arendt wants to say that action will be a perpetually recurring possibility for humans; this position is reflected in her later revisions to *Origins*. Her shift has significant implications: The first position maintains that the possibilities of human's actions are entirely open and unlimited, and that humans can even act in a way to close down the possibility for action of future humans – humans are so free that they can shut down the possibility of future freedom. The second position allows for the constant future existence of freedom by limiting the ability of others to permanently suppress that freedom. However, this position also makes natality more akin to the human nature that Arendt rejects; regardless of whether action is a form of human nature, this second position limits the full range of possibilities open to man in a way that Arendt previously shied away from. The interpretation of Arendt on this point is crucial for the appropriation of her thought for disability studies. If, as in the first position, not engaging in political action means that you are not fully human, then Arendt would not offer a way to understand the humanness of those with severe cognitive impairments who are not always able to participate in politics. If, as in her revised position, however, which I adopt, natality is a stable part of the human person, present since birth, whether or not the person has the political opportunity to practice action, then an Arendtian approach becomes helpful for disability theory: particularly if we are not only attentive to political impediments to action, but also to physical impediments to action.

In the original *Origins of Totalitarianism*, published in 1951, Arendt argues that man's freedom, deriving from natality, is the origin of both political action and of what attempts to suppress and prevent the possibility of that action, totalitarianism. She writes: "The victory of totalitarianism may coincide with the destruction of humanity; wherever it has ruled, it has begun to destroy the essence of man" (Arendt 1951: viii). Because the essence of man is rooted in an action, if that action is made impossible through totalitarianism's destruction of the place and opportunity for politics, human essence could be destroyed (Arendt 1951: 293). This is the goal of totalitarianism – "the transformation of human nature itself. The concentration camps are the laboratories where changes in human nature are tested" (Arendt 1951: 432).[8]

In her second edition of *The Origins of Totalitarianism* (1958), Arendt retreats from the position that she took in her earlier editions and makes a stronger argument for the persistence and stability of natality. She writes at the very end of the new *Origins*:

> But there remains also the truth that every end in history necessarily contains a new beginning; this beginning is the promise, the only "message" which the end can ever produce. Beginning, before it becomes a historical event, is the supreme capacity of man; politically, it is identical with man's freedom. *Initium ut esset homo creates est* –"that a beginning be made man was created" said Augustine. This beginning is guaranteed by each new birth; it is indeed every man. (Arendt 1966: 478–9)[9]

This is much more hopeful than the conclusion of the previous edition. She sees action as something stable that will endure as long as man endures. In this reading, she seems to indicate that primary and political natality are inseparable – that the possibility of political beginning is

[8] Eric Voegelin, in a now-famous exchange with Arendt in *The Review of Politics* in response to *The Origins of Totalitarianism*, offers a serious critique of her use of the concept of nature in the book. He quotes Arendt, "Human nature as such is at stake, and even though it seems that these experiments succeed not in changing man but only in destroying him... one should bear in mind the necessary limitations to an experiment which requires global control in order to show conclusive results" (Arendt 1951: 433 in Voegelin 1953: 74). He then responds: "'Nature' is a philosophical concept; it denotes that which identifies a thing as a thing of this kind and not of another one. A 'nature' cannot be changed or transformed; a 'change of nature' is a contradiction of terms; tampering with the 'nature' of a thing means destroying the thing" (Voegelin 1953: 74–5). Changing human nature, then, is not possible. If there is something essential in what it means to be human, then that thing cannot be permanently eliminated from humans. If, on the other hand, what it means to be human is in flux and constantly developing, then on what basis can we critique totalitarianism for attempting to destroy the human ability to act? Arendt's focus on natality and action is caught in between these two positions. Arendt's revised position in the later edition of *The Origins of Totalitarianism* is closer to Voegelin's critique.

[9] In the new edition, Arendt removes the previous final section, "Concluding Remarks" and adds a new chapter: "Ideology and Terror: A Novel Form of Government." Elaborating on the end of the revised *Origins of Totalitarianism*, Bowen-Moore writes, "Totalitarianism is rehabilitated by the promise of freedom announced by human birth and the capacity for beginning again. Political natality, therefore, stands in resolute defiance against absolute domination; its indomitable factuality counters the utter bankruptcy of totalitarian tactics aimed at liquidating the gift of freedom. Each time a human being acts politically from the vantage point of the potentiality for a positive worldly beginning, he enlarges the field of political experience and creates the reality of freedom. When this happens, the initiator of action experiences a kind of 'second birth' and takes his place on the stage of the public world" (Bowen-Moore 1989: 47). Again, to be clear, this Bowen-Moore's read of Arendt's position is only accurate if you take her revised *Origins of Totalitarianism* to be the best articulation. This later conception of action undermines Arendt's earlier critiques of nature.

guaranteed by each new birth. Insofar as new human beings are born, there is action. Natality is "[t]he miracle that saves the world" (Arendt 1998: 247). Here Arendt affirms that biological and physical natality are, indeed, connected: A lack of political space for action could temporarily, but not completely, suppress this ability. Totalitarianism is a gravely unjust form of government and ought to be opposed; however, we do not need to fear that it will succeed in its attempt to change or destroy human nature, for it never can. The one thing that action cannot do, according to Arendt, is permanently wipe out freedom. This chapter will later examine whether the body itself, like totalitarian political regimes, could also be an impediment to action in a way that still allows us to recognize the presence of natality, although not its practice, in the person.

Even though natality is a stable fact about humans, Arendt is clear that the biological presence of natality is not a sufficient guarantee that a space for the political practice of natality will be created for any individual. As a result, it is crucial that natality and the possibility for action be politically guaranteed, otherwise people may be deprived of the one most fundamental human right. In *Between Past and Future*, Arendt writes:

> [W]herever the man-made world does not become the scene for action and speech – as in despotically ruled communities which banish their subjects into the narrowness of the home and thus prevent the rise of a public realm – freedom has no worldly reality. Without a politically guaranteed public realm, freedom lacks the worldly space to make its appearance. To be sure it may still dwell in men's hearts as desire or will or hope or yearning; but the human heart, as we all know, is a very dark place, and whatever goes on in its obscurity can hardly be called a demonstrable fact. (Arendt 1968a: 149)

Freedom requires a politically guaranteed public realm. Without that, it may be said to exist in the sense that the people who are not allowed to practice it are still human, but it is not a demonstrable fact. This freedom is fragile: "There are no institutions and revolutions, however radical, that can secure human freedom over the long term" (Arendt 2007: 174). Man's freedom, the right to have rights, is not secured once and for all, but rather must be continually secured through political means.[10] Once

[10] Arendt is focused primarily on the right to have rights – the right to participate in politics. She warns that we ought not "mistake civil rights for political freedom, or to equate these preliminaries of civilized government with the very substance of a free republic. For political freedom, generally speaking, means the right 'to be a participator in government,' or it means nothing" (Arendt 1965: 221). This is freedom to "to be master over one's own necessities of life and therefore potentially to be a free person, free to transcend his own life and enter the world all have in common" (Arendt 1998: 65). Freedom is only to be found, then, in the equality of the public realm (Arendt 1998: 32). Arendt's political participation is much thicker than that typically experienced in America. In fact, Arendt says that the only real political action in American is in town hall meetings

again, we see that political and social relationships are crucial to natality; natality is not only something that exists in the individual person, but is also something that is dependent upon relationships among other humans for its very existence.[11] Where disability is concerned, too, the assertion of human dignity is not sufficient – we must also be concerned with creating political institutions and laws that are responsive to that dignity.

It is humanity that must guarantee the right to participate in politics to others, but she is not naively optimistic:

> This new situation, in which "humanity" has in effect assumed the role formerly ascribed to nature or history, would mean in this context that the right to have rights, or the right of every individual to belong to humanity, should be guaranteed by humanity itself. It is by no means certain whether this is possible. (Arendt 1966: 298)

Disability scholar Tobin Seibers is attentive to Arendt's hesitancy about the effectiveness of political institutions to include all people within them. He sees in this recognition of the fragility of institutions a kinship with disability studies. He writes:

> I want to revisit Arendt's melancholia [about the fragility of human institutions that make human freedom possible] as a positive foundation for the right to have rights – a goal that requires disability to play a universal role as the guarantor of human rights. This guarantee is necessary because all known theories of human rights, whether based on humanity, social contract theory, utilitarianism, or citizenship, exclude individuals from the rights-bearing community if they do not possess the specific abilities required for membership. To acknowledge melancholia as a philosophical intuition about the fragility of human bonds and

and juries (Hill 1979: 317). In order to allow all humans the possibility of a political participation more involved than voting, more decisions would need to be made and more resources allocated at local levels. While the centralization of political power decreases the opportunities for political action for all people, it perhaps disproportionately disadvantages persons with disabilities, who face additional barriers to participation in national politics.

[11] In *Hannah Arendt and the Challenge of Modernity*, Serena Parekh (2008: 122) divides human rights advocates into "essentialists," "all those people who believe that human rights are grounded in some essential feature of the human being" and "anti-essentialists," for whom "human rights cannot be grounded in human nature or morality, and so search for a different kind of justification." She sees Arendt's discussion of human rights as situated between the two, arguing that the only stable thing about humans is that they are conditioned beings, "that everything we make in turn conditions us" (2008: 146). This is in contrast with Peg Birmingham (2006), who ties givenness to natality and maintains that Arendt advocates a respect for what is given; I come down on Birmingham's side in this debate. One problem with Parekh's analysis is that she sees essentialism deemphasizing the institutions that guarantee human rights (2008: 135). For Arendt at least there is no conflict: she simultaneously grounds human rights in something that is stable about humans – natality – and says that without political structures that recognize human natality, it only dwells in men's hearts.

institutions is equally to acknowledge the fragility of human beings – a fragility long recognize by disability scholars – since the vulnerability of human bodies and minds underlies as a first cause that of human institutions. It is also to understand that human-rights discourse will never break free from the ideology of ability until it includes disability as a defining characteristic of human beings. (Seibers 2008: 178)

Seibers looks to expand Arendt's description of the right to have rights beyond her application of the idea to the Jewish people. He recognizes that understanding disability as a defining characteristic of human beings is a logical extension of her argument, and that the centrality of the right to have rights, as well as a humility about the shortcomings of our political institutions, can drive disability theory forward. Moreover, the experience of the denigration of the human rights of people with disabilities, like the experience of totalitarianism under Nazism, can point us to the need to rethink human rights.[12]

While Arendt's natality connects physical birth and political birth in helpful ways that encourage thinking about citizenship and humanity together, one way in which Arendt's theory of natality is not well suited to contribute to disability theory is in its low view of the body; in fact, bringing Arendt's natality into dialog with feminist and disability theory could strengthen Arendt's ideas. This low view of the body is perhaps best articulated in *The Human Condition's* tripartite division between labor, work, and action: labor "corresponds to the biological process of the human body"; work "provides an 'artificial' world of things"; action "is the political activity par excellence" (Arendt 1998: 7, 9). Arendt connects labor to necessity and maintains that it should be part of the private, rather than the public, world; labor is what needs to be done in order for man to engage in work and action. Rather than relegating the body to the private sphere, feminist and disability theory is attentive to the way that the body itself is influenced by and given meaning through cultural constructs, and reciprocally questions and critiques those constructs. Rosemarie Garland Thomson describes this as Foucauldian "discipline": "Such disciplining is enacted primarily through the two interrelated cultural discourses of

[12] Patchen Markell is similarly attentive to the way in which Arendt's philosophy emerges from a particular political situation. His position is stronger: according to Markell, Arendt's politics, not her philosophical foundations, does the human rights work of her theory. Markell writes, "could Arendt, in 1951, have been trying to anchor a broader stance toward human existence *in* a concrete set of postwar political possibilities – to 'found' a philosophy on a politics, rather than the other way around?" (Markell 2008). While I see a philosophical founding of human rights rather than a political one in Arendt, it is clear that both a political crisis gave rise to the need for human rights and political institutions are a crucial part of the solution.

medicine and appearance" (Thomson 2006: 262). But the body is not just something that is disciplined; Seibers writes: "It is not inert matter subject to easy manipulation by social representations. The body is alive, which means that it is as capable of influencing and transforming social languages as they are capable of influencing and transforming it" (Seibers 2006: 180). Moreover, disability theory is in tune with the ways in which bodily experience, including the experience of disability, can inform one's identity. Wendell writes:

> I feel heartsore when I hear about someone being diagnosed with [myalgic encephalomyelitis]; how could I not want a cure for everyone else who suffers with it? Yet I cannot wish that I had never contracted ME, because it has made me a different person, a person I am glad to be, would not want to have missed being, and could not imagine relinquishing, even if I were "cured." (Wendell 1996: 83)

Wendell's bodily experience is obviously not something that is relegated to the private sphere, nor is it merely the realm of necessity. It informs her politics and her work.

Disability theory is in touch with the ongoing and reciprocal dialogue between the body and the cultural forces that influence how the body is perceived; it understands the centrality of the body to the development of the person in ways that inevitably transcend the private sphere. Natality can be developed further in light of a richer understanding of the body and its impact: Not only can a political system that does not allow for the participation of all citizens limit the expression of natality (as Arendt perceives totalitarianism to be attempting), but the body itself can impede or even prohibit entirely the expression of natality. The beginning that is there in the person as a result of birth might not be able to be acted out in the political sphere; this does not mean that natality is not present, but rather that it is, through no fault of the actor, temporarily or permanently unable to be displayed.[13] This bodily interference in the communication of the ability to begin, although she herself has begun with her birth, might explain the humanity that Eva Kittay recognizes in her daughter, Sesha:

[13] Certainly this extension of Arendt's thought will be unpalatable to some of her readers: I emphasize democratic aspects of Arendt's thought over the more hierarchical themes that emerge from her attention to the Greeks. Nonetheless, Arendt's emphasis on the political space as a place for distinction in addition to equality can be preserved without returning to the Greeks' "agonal spirit, the passionate drive to show one's self in measuring up against others" (Arendt 1998: 194). While everyone is not equally politically excellent for Arendt and plurality itself presupposes distinction, neither does the Greeks' search for immortal fame alone capture the equality that is a condition of Arendt's politics.

I have since learned – from her, from the disability community and from my own observations – that she is capable of having a very good life, one full of joy, of love, of laughter: a life that includes the appreciation of some of the best of human culture, great music and fine food, and the delights of nature, water, the scent of flowers, the singing of birds. No, she cannot participate in political life, she cannot marry and have children, she cannot read a book or engage in moral reasoning, but her life is richly human and full of dignity. (Kittay 2005a: 110)

Not only can theorizing about disability provide a helpful correction to Arendt's view of the body, but it also problematizes her deference to action over other places in which natality manifests itself, such as in the private sphere and through work and creativity in the public sphere. In fact, Arendt herself gives us reason to hope for a more substantial recognition in her work of the different places in which natality can manifest itself: "In this sense of initiative, an element of action, and therefore of natality, is inherent in all human activities" (Arendt 1998: 9). Because natality connects labor, work, and action, as well as the private and public spheres, it is an even more fundamental concept for Arendt than action. An attention to other expressions of natality than simply political action as revealing the humanness of the actor will allow for the recognition of the diverse expressions of humanity in those with disabilities who can communicate their ability to act and begin better outside of politics than within it. From the labor of cooking with my friend Pauleen, a resident at the L'Arche community in St. Louis, which involves a sort of beginning, to the colorful hot pad she made as a wedding gift for my husband and me, to her work in creating the world and helping to construct the human artifice through her artwork, which ranges from paintings to cards to banners, Pauleen exhibits natality in many non-political ways that nonetheless capture her humanity. A capacity to begin, although expressed through imagination rather than in the political world, also seems to be what Michael Bérubé noticed in his young son, Jamie, who has Down's syndrome. Bérubé recounts Jamie pretending that he is the waiter at a restaurant, meditating on its import:

[T]he distinct little person with whom I went to the restaurant that evening – a three year old whose ability to imitate is intimately tied to his remarkable ability to imagine, and whose ability to imagine, in turn, rests almost entirely on his capacity to imagine *other people*… the ability to imagine what other people might life, what other people might need – that seems to me a more crucial, more *essential* ability for human beings to cultivate. (Bérubé 1996: xviii)

Some people with disabilities act and help to create the world through actions in the private sphere and in the public sphere, but not always in the political realm. These expressions of natality, too, communicate their humanness.

Disability scholar Tanya Titchkosky gives another example of a natality that is not only political. According to Titchkosky, who cites Arendt, participating in disability studies itself is a sort of natality, an insertion of oneself into the world. She writes first about the inescapably social aspect of natality:

> There is a common character to each and every person's first birth, including those of us who are disabled. We are brought into the world as the consequence of other peoples' words and deeds and our beginning in the world is marked first and foremost with what those others have already begun, already thought, and have already understood. We come into the world as subjects of others' interpretations of our naked physical existence. The meaning and significance of our race, class, gender, and abilities are inscribed and reinscribed by others from the moment of our birth and forever onwards... In all these ways, our physical existence is a social one. With our first birth, the meaning of our physical self is given to us. (Titchkosky 2000: 218)

She then writes about the a second natality that confirms the first:

> Disability Studies has taken it upon itself to confirm the exact character of that which is given to disabled people at birth. Such confirmation, Arendt suggests, is like a second birth inasmuch as it requires words and deeds that insert the self into the world of ascribed meanings that were begun before and will continue after the birth and death of disabled people. With word and deed we insert our self into the meanings already provided to us. We insert our self in relation to the history of disability. In these ways, we insert into the world the possibility of beginning something new. (Titchkosky 2000: 218–9)

This second natality confirms the first in the sense of confirming the physical self, not the given meaning. Rather, according to Titchkosky, the insertion of the disabled self into the world critiques normate culture. Titchkosky is subtly revising Arendt: for whom this second natality comes through political action; for Titchkosky it is a much broader project that involves engagement in the academic and cultural discourse. She provides a model here for how natality might be expanded.

Natality and the right to have rights avoid Singer's critiques: it is not religious, rationalist, or speciesist, although all of those elements do influence her theory. Arendt derives her understanding of natality from Augustine, often citing his "*Initium ergo ut esset, creates est homo* – 'That there be a beginning, man was created'" (for instance 1994: 167; 1998: 177). Arendt secularizes Augustine's account of creation by taking it out of its controversial context of creation by a God who is outside of that creation and in whose image man is made and acts. Rather, she focuses on what no one denies: the fact of birth. Now man's creation becomes the first human action. That beginning carries within itself its own principle – "the principle inspires the deeds that are to follow and remains apparent as long as the action lasts" (Arendt 1965: 214). Arendt's natality is not about a "first beginner," God, as Augustine's was; rather, Arendt focuses on the birth of a human, which is both a beginning and a principle, or inspiration to further action. Arendt's argument for humanness, then, is an argument that is not limited to any religious tradition.

Arendt's understanding of what it means to be human is not limited by the capacity for rationality. Arguments for human distinctiveness from animals on the grounds of superior cognitive abilities, specifically in the human capacity to reason, are common in the history of political thought – from Plato's and Aristotle's praise of reason and physical exclusion from the polity of infants in whom reason is not perceived, to Hobbes' and Locke's social contract in which those in whom reason is not perceived are excluded from participation in the contract on the grounds that their lack of reason prevents them from consenting to the contract and being governed by the laws. Unlike common characterizations of reason and cognitive ability, natality is present in every person. While an argument can be made against the presence of reason in those with severe cognitive disabilities, it is much more difficult to argue that those people were not born. In Arendt's account, that birth alone requires that that person be allowed the opportunity to participate in politics. This position is sensitive to the fact that the presence of the ability to contribute to politics – the ability to act – is not always clear-cut. Disability is a category that includes vast and diverse conditions: persons with impairments may develop the ability to participate in politics over time, but the rate of development and the end of that development are unpredictable. The ability to contribute constructively to politics may wax and wane over the course of one's life. It is better that the political sphere err on the side of welcoming potential contributors, rather than prematurely excluding them.

Natality is also not speciesist, at least in Singer's conception of speciesism: "What is it about human beings that gives them moral worth and dignity? If there is no good answer forthcoming, this talk of intrinsic worth and dignity is just speciesism in nicer terms" (Singer 2010: 337). While natality is not reducible to reason, the human capacity for action is certainly present in natality, although it is not necessary that that capacity for action be communicated or displayed in order to verify one's humanity. This innate capacity for action, given in the action of our birth, is presumed to be present, whether or not it is able to be practiced. The capacity for action may be thwarted by a political regime that is not democratic or by the physical body.

Natality and Prenatal Testing

Focusing on both natality and the capacity for action inherent in it, as well as on the right to have rights, with its implicit critique of those who believe that they have the right to determine who can and cannot inhabit the world, lead naturally into a consideration of a fraught issue within disability studies: the ethics of prenatal testing. One position is to avoid this question by positing Arendt's natality, birth itself, as the foundation of rights. Another interpretation of Arendt, one offered by Ruth Hubbard in "Abortion and Disability: Who Should and Who Should Not Inhabit the World?" sees a parallel eugenic ideology underlying prenatal testing and the Nazi attempt to eliminate the Jewish people (Hubbard 2006: 99).[14]

I suggest that the important contribution of Arendt's theory to the debate over the ethics of prenatal testing is the social requirements of natality: that social and political institutions are an essential part of welcoming new members. Even physical natality is social: it requires parents to create and a community to recognize and welcome new members, including new members with disabilities. On what basis, however, should new members be welcomed into the world if they have not experienced the natality of birth that Arendt describes? Perhaps natality is longer than the hours of labor: it might be more aptly described as a process of beginning that starts before delivery and that continues for months or years afterward, when the child is vulnerable and could not live without its parents' care. And parents should not be caring for the child alone, without any support: we need a polity that cares for those who are incapable of surviving on their own. Moreover, the givenness that prenatal testing rejects – the disability – precedes the actual birth, but is present as a result of its own sort of coming into being and natality. This "coming into being," although not yet accompanied by birth, implies its own capacity for action, both in birth and later in political society. So givenness is already there, even though the birth hasn't occurred.

In addition, Arendt's focus on the need for plurality and pariahs itself is a reason to welcome people with disabilities into the world, rather than exclude them on the basis of their difference. Rosemarie Garland Thomson writes about the pernicious tendency of society to discipline bodies to get them to fit into societally acceptable forms; the most extreme version of this is to discipline them out of existence (2006: 262). As Stanley Hauerwas (2004: 87–106) writes, seeking to

[14] She explicitly refers to Arendt's response to Eichmann both in the title and body of her chapter.

prevent intellectual disability (which he calls "mental retardation") often in practice means preventing the existence of people with intellectual disabilities themselves.

Rather than disciplining disabled bodies out of existence, we should strive to create supportive communities that welcome people with disabilities, a world that is as inclusive of their uniqueness and as responsive to their needs as possible. First, there is not enough information available for women and families. Disability scholar Martha Saxton calls it a void of information about disability (2006: 106). People have the idea that the "enjoyment of life for disabled people is necessarily inferior," an idea that many people with disabilities dispute (2006: 106). People believe that "raising a child with a disability is a wholly undesirable experience" and that "we as a society have the means and right to decide who is better off not being born" (2006: 106). This void of information leads to many misunderstandings about disability and to unwelcoming physical and social spaces for those who are disabled. In fact, disability scholars Adrienne Asch and Gail Geller (1996: 339) worry that this could "ultimately erode our tolerance of difference as a society."

While prenatal testing is associated with decreasing tolerance of difference, an Arendtian approach to natality insists that, rather than seek to eliminate difference, we should seek to welcome difference both in the private and public spheres. This leads to the second thing that I argue we can do: we should work harder to support and empower women and families to raise whatever child they bear. Women and families should not be alone in navigating new challenges, but should be supported by their communities and through government services. This involves both attentiveness to physical sites of exclusion in the built environment, as well as to both explicit and subtle social discrimination. But it also involves providing flexible and individualized services in healthcare, education, and job training and placement services, over the course of the child's life. This list is by no means exhaustive: supporting women and families who bear disabled children is a multifaceted endeavor, and there is much work to be done. An essential aspect of providing women with unbiased and broad choices is making available ample information and support.

We should focus on making the world a place that welcomes difference and create spaces, in culture and politics, in which those with disabilities can themselves act and begin, can practice natality. Engaging in the process of creating the world together with people with disabilities will itself help to lessen the void of information about disability in which decisions about disability are made. In my own experience, helping to organize a week-long conference with a blind participant, getting to know her, and watching her navigate new spaces far more skillfully than I could have imagined, helped supplement my lack of information. Similarly, spending time at a L'Arche community and getting to know one of the residents, Jim, and seeing him joke and play and bring joy to the community with more wit than I could have imagined, also helped supplement my lack of information. Neighborliness and friendship are one obvious way to both rectify information deficiencies and to welcome people with disabilities into the world. Arendt writes about friendship's ability to welcome givenness into the world:

> This mere existence, that is, all that which is mysteriously given us by birth and which includes the shape of our bodies and the talents of our minds, can be adequately dealt with only by the unpredictable hazards of friendship and sympathy, or by the great and incalculable grace of love, which says with Augustine, "*Volo ut sis* (I want you to be)," without being able to give any particular reason for such supreme and unsurpassable affirmation. (Arendt 1951: 301)

9 Connecting the Disconnect: Mental Disorder and Political Disorder

Theresa Man Ling Lee

Locating the Problematic

According to the *World Report on Disability*, prepared jointly by the World Health Organization and the World Bank in 2011, six of the "top 20 causes" of disability worldwide are mental disorders (WHO 2011: 296). High on the list is depression (98.7 million), followed by "alcohol and problem use" (40.5 million), bipolar disorder (22.2 million), schizophrenia (16.7 million), panic disorder (13.8 million) and "drug dependence and problem use" (11.8 million) (WHO 2011: 296–7). These figures add up to a total of 203.7 million, which is about 26 percent of all those considered to have "moderate" to "severe" disability, as defined in the report;[1] or 3.17 percent of the world population. In addition, the same report indicates that there is a huge gap in the number of disabled people between the developed and the developing countries. Take the case of depression: of the global figure of 98.7 million, 82.4 million come from low- to middle-income countries (77.6 million under the age of 60, compared to 15.8 in high-income countries) (WHO 2011: 297). While the *World Report* identifies poverty as the main cause of disability (WHO 2011: 12), it should be noted that many countries in the developing world are also either rebuilding from war-torn conditions or engaging in wars. Added to this is the reality that since the Second World War, there has not been any war that actually took place in high-income countries even though they were and continue to be involved in wars elsewhere. In other words, the poorer countries are disproportionately bearing the human cost of wars. It is no wonder that Iran and Afghanistan were recorded to have among the highest number of "years of health lost due to disability (YLD)"; with Iran at 19.4 "YLDs per 100 persons in 2004" (WHO 2011: 273) and Afghanistan at 15.3 (WHO 2011: 271), compared to an average of 7 YLDs among the developed countries.

[1] For a detailed explanation on how the degree of severity was measured in surveys conducted across the world, see WHO (2011: 290–2).

To the extent that prosperity and peace are generally accepted across the ideological spectrum as vital indicators of good governance, these statistical data provided by the *World Report* show in concrete terms the correlation between (dis)ability and political (dis)order. But even without the statistical evidence, there is no denial that poverty is demeaning and war is traumatic. In short, humans can only suffer under these conditions. In the field of politics, suffering as a political subject typically falls under the framework of social justice. Unlike what is now a readily identifiable body of medical and humanitarian expertise on human suffering as experienced by concrete lives, there is no comparable body of comprehensive knowledge among students of politics.

This chapter is an attempt to address the problem of political disorder and its relation to human suffering. Max Weber, in his study of world religions, observed that all religions stemmed from our primordial need to make sense of human suffering (Weber 1946: 270–7).[2] Thus situated, making sense of human suffering, religious and otherwise, is fundamental to our being. At risk is none other than our mental health. The disproportionate share of mental disability among those who suffer from poverty and war is therefore a potent indicator of the difficulty in making sense of one's suffering when there is a breakdown in political order. Against such reality, this chapter sets out to explore the connection by asking how mental disorder as experienced by a given individual can be understood in political terms. It does not make claim to any comprehensive theory of mental disability. Rather it is an attempt to put together an analytical framework that aims to locate the connection between mental disorder and political disorder and its political ramifications by engaging the works of Franz Fanon, Karl Jaspers and Hannah Arendt. The selection of these thinkers suggests a phenomenological approach that "studies conscious experience as experienced from the subjective or first person point of view" (Smith 2013: 1.2). Specifically, all three were involved in varying degrees in phenomenology as a distinctive twentieth-century philosophical movement that began with Edmund Husserl. Fundamental to the Husserlian phenomenology is the postulation of intersubjectivity as "the most basic quality of human existence, which is constitutive of the

[2] Weber was by no means the first to provide a sociopolitical account of the origin of religion. Weber's view was no doubt influenced by the respective critiques of religion by Marx and Nietzsche. However, Marx's denouncement of religion as the "opium of the people" and Nietzsche's condemnation of religion as "slave morality" consign religion into an ideological tool that both manipulates and oppresses the believers. While Weber himself had noted the social hierarchy that emerged as organized religions began to take root in premodern societies, it is important to note that Weber, in contrast to Marx and Nietzsche, took religion as the embodiment of an existential angst that affects us all (Weber 1946: 282–8).

Subject and of the very notion of an objective world" (Duranti 2010: 1). The American anthropologist Alessandro Duranti puts forth the following interpretation of intersubjectivity:

> [I]ntersubjectivity in a truly Husserlian fashion means to think of it as, first and foremost, the possibility of human interaction and human understanding, a possibility that is at times realized by the mere evoking of an Other's presence (as when we perceive the surrounding natural world as a cultural world that has been touched, modified, exploited, or enjoyed by other human beings), and at other times it is presupposed by the presence of tools and artifacts that were made by humans. This means that intersubjectivity should be conceptualized as including an original or primordial level of participation in a world that is co-habited even when no one is visible or hearable. (Duranti 2010: 10–11)

At stake for Duranti is a conceptualization of intersubjectivity that is sufficiently expansive to address "the theoretical issue" of "whether we *should* distinguish among different ways or levels of being together" and "the empirical issue" of "whether we *can* distinguish, that is, find the evidence of categorical differences in and of co-presence" (Duranti 2010: 13, emphasis in original). As a conceptual tool, intersubjectivity is therefore "the starting point for a truly interdisciplinary study of human sociality… and could turn out to be just as important but hopefully not as vague as the notion of culture" (Duranti 2010: 11). Leaving aside the question of whether Duranti's interpretation of intersubjectivity is sufficiently warranted by Husserl's original writings, I consider Duranti's definition to be just as relevant to the study of politics. Intersubjectivity thus conceived means that we experience ourselves through interacting and communicating with others. While this existential condition is not necessarily coeval with politics, I argue that politics is essential to its realization. Stated differently, political disorder means, among other things, a breakdown in intersubjectivity. Individuals faced with such a challenge are no longer able to interact and communicate with others and, thereby, with their own self. Disconnection comes to define the (non-)existence of individuals as they confront the stark reality of living under an inhuman condition in which the presence of the Other can no longer be assumed.

Anti-psychiatry and Its Limits

I want to start by differentiating this study from the various positions associated with what is known as anti-psychiatry. Anti-psychiatry is used here to refer to the body of work that challenges mental disorder as a medical condition that can be established objectively by way of scientific methods. Instead, mental disorder is seen as a social construct that has both ethical and political bearing. Arguably the most widely known views and also representative of two very different positions under the rubric of anti-psychiatry are the works of Thomas Szasz (1920–2012) and Michel Foucault (1926–84) (Bracken and Thomas 2010).[3]

In a highly controversial book originally published in 1961–*The Myth of Mental Illness: Foundations of a Theory of Personal Conduct* – the American psychiatrist Thomas Szasz argued that there is neither physiological basis nor biological causes to mental illness (Szasz 2010: xvii–xxiiii, 285–300). It is therefore not a disease that can be readily treated through pharmaceutical or surgical intervention. Accordingly, Szasz was critical of psychiatry on the following grounds:

> My critique of psychiatry is two-pronged, partly conceptual, partly moral and political. At the core of my conceptual critique lies the distinction between the literal and metaphorical uses of language – with mental illness as a metaphor. At the core of my moral-political critique lies the distinction between relating to grown persons as responsible adults (moral agents) and as irresponsible insane persons (quasi-infants or idiots) – the former possessing free will, the latter lacking this moral attribute because of "mental illness." (Szasz 2010: 278)

Mental illness is for Szasz no more than a myth that is used to justify government intervention in what should have been a totally personal matter (Szasz 2010: xxx). What an "insane" person needs most is to learn to take responsibility of one's life (Szasz 2010: 262; Bracken and Thomas 2010: 220–3). As such, only the individual can determine when intervention is needed and it is best achieved through psychotherapy rather than what Szasz characterized as the pseudo-scientific medical intervention of psychiatry (Szasz 2010: 260–1). Speaking as a psychoanalyst (although critical of its founder, Sigmund Freud), Szasz professes that "the aim of psychoanalytic therapy is, or should be, to maximize the patient's choices in the conduct of his life... by enhancing his knowledge of himself, others, and the world [about] him, and his skills in dealing with persons and things" (Szasz 2010: 259). In short, Szasz' anti-psychiatry is quintessentially libertarian in that it aims to maximize the autonomy of the individual against any involuntary interventions of one's behavior. Psychiatrists as psychotherapists do not treat mental illnesses. Rather, "they deal with personal, social, and ethical problems in living" (Szasz 2010: 262).

In the case of Foucault, his critique of the rise of the asylum and with it the medicalization of one's mental conditions, is part of his broader

[3] The comparison between Szasz and Foucault in this section takes its cue from Bracken and Thomas (2010). But the analysis that follows is based on my own reading of the respective works of Szasz and Foucault for the purpose of illustrating what anti-psychiatry is about and how my concern is different from that of anti-psychiatry. In contrast, the analysis in Bracken and Thomas (2010) on the differences between Szasz and Foucault is considerably more comprehensive and nuanced than the one offered here.

critique of the Enlightenment and modernity. The binary distinction between "reason and non-reason" is predicated on the valorization of the human capacity for rational thought into truth itself (Foucault 1988: ix–x). Only then can there be insane persons to become objects of observation, surveillance and judgment (Foucault 1988: 241–78). From the "Ship of Fools" to the birth of the asylum in the eighteenth century was the categorical transformation of madness into mental illness. But the book *Madness and Civilization* is no simple chronicle of that history. In Foucault's words,

> [T]he constitution of madness as a mental illness, at the end of the eighteenth century, affords the evidence of a broken dialogue, posits the separation as already effected, and thrusts into oblivion all those stammered, imperfect words without fixed syntax in which the exchange between madness and reason was made. The language of psychiatry, which is a monologue of reason *about* madness, has been established only on the basis of such a silence.
>
> I have not tried to write a history of that language, but rather the archaeology of that silence. (Foucault 1988: x–xi, emphasis in original)[4]

Such transformation embodied a new form of power which Foucault later identified as disciplinary power (Foucault 1980a: 104–8). It works by modifying our conduct toward oneself and others through the discourse of normalization. New categories of individuals are henceforth created as new subjects of power, such as the mentally ill and the sexually deviant (Foucault 1983: 208, 212). Foucault argued that historically, disciplinary power facilitated the emergence of biopolitics that marked the birth of the modern state. The modern state is distinctive by making life itself the object of rule (Foucault 1978: 138, 142–3).

This brief survey of the respective positions held by Szasz and Foucault suggests that while both were critical of modern psychiatry, their views are fundamentally different.[5] Szasz was convinced that it is both possible and desirable to affirm individualism against the power of the state. His critique of psychiatry as a medical science that can cure the so-called mental illness of an individual is based on this conviction. Foucault was critical of psychiatry not because it is possible for individuals to be free from power – after all, Foucault is known for staking out the controversial claims that "power is everywhere" (Foucault 1978: 93) and that the

[4] Readers are reminded that this was early Foucault writing – before he adopted "genealogy" to describe his work. Archaeology, as defined by Foucault, postulates truth as "a system of ordered procedures for the production, regulation, distribution, circulation and operation of statements" (Foucault 1980b: 133).

[5] Bracken and Thomas (2010: 224) provide an informative table that summaries the key differences between Szasz and Foucault under the following headings: "attitude toward the Enlightenment," "individualism," "psychotherapy," "biomedicine," "truth and power" and "role of critical thought."

individual is no more than "an effect of power" (Foucault 1980a: 98). Foucault's anti-psychiatric stance is therefore not about freeing individuals from power. Instead, it is specifically about countering the power of reason as embodied in psychiatry that divides the sane from the insane for the purpose of excluding the latter because of its apparent incomprehensibility. The incomprehensible is inaccessible to reason and thus has no place in the discourse of truth.

Differences aside, the anti-psychiatric approach should be credited for using what is in effect the social model of disability to understand mental disorder long before the model was adopted to replace the medical model of disability. By this I mean the view that disability is a contextual rather than an absolute condition that can be readily identified by way of some generalizable criteria applicable to all. Disability as such represents a breakdown in what should have been an interactive condition between an impaired individual and the environment, which can be social and/or physical. In the case of mental disability, and specifically conditions such as depression, schizophrenia, bipolar disorder and panic disorder, that breakdown is first and foremost one of communication. A person with any one of these conditions is generally understood to be someone who can no longer make sense of the environment surrounding oneself. Likewise, others cannot make sense of the state of mind that the person is in. While anti-psychiatry has heightened our awareness that the context in which the breakdown occurs is hardly natural, it is not primarily concerned with the experience of the disconnection itself. Take the case of Szasz: while he maintained that there is still a therapeutic role for the psychotherapists as I have already noted, and said that it is important to establish a non-hierarchical relation between the therapist and the client (as opposed to the patient), that relation is about nullifying the client's experience. In other words, the experience is only valid to the extent that it shows the moral failing of the individual in question. Madness is the acting out of that failure, and hence it cannot be taken seriously. In the case of Foucault, with the exception of the memoir of Herculine Barbin (Barbin 1980; Foucault 1980c: xi–xvii), Foucault's own work is not so much about letting the excluded speak for themselves, but rather how categories of exclusion are constructed and thereby exposed.

To sum up, the kind of critical stance afforded by anti-psychiatry in fact leaves no room for madness as a subjective experience that constitutes the lives of more than just a handful of isolated individuals, as documented in the *World Report*. In proposing a study of the experience of mental illness in political terms, this chapter aims to go beyond anti-psychiatry. The problematic that it sets out to explore is not about madness as a site of power and control over the individual, but rather madness as a form of human experience. Experience as such has both empirical and normative dimensions. In the words of Arthur Kleinman, an American psychiatrist and medical anthropologist: "Experience is *moral*, as I define it, because it is the medium of engagement in everyday life in which things are at stake and in which ordinary people are deeply engaged stake-holders who have important things to lose, to gain, and to preserve" (Kleinman 1999: 362, emphasis in original). I mentioned in the introduction that there is a distinct lack of study on suffering as life in the field of politics. There is, however, one notable exception and that is the work of Franz Fanon.

Franz Fanon – Psychiatry and the Colonized

In his famous work, *The Wretched of the Earth*, Fanon provided a scathing account of human suffering as mental disorder among individuals during the Algerian War of Independence (1954–62). There was no doubt in Fanon's mind that the colonial war made Algeria "a favorable breeding ground for mental disorders" (Fanon 1963: 251). But even without the war, colonization had already created what was in effect an existential crisis for the colonized. In Fanon's words:

> Because it is a systematic negation of the other person and a furious determination to deny the other person all attributes of humanity, colonialism forces the people it dominates to ask themselves the question constantly: "In reality, who am I?" (Fanon 1963: 250)

The final chapter, "Colonial War and Mental Disorders," is where Fanon set out to ascertain the human cost of colonization by drawing upon his medical practice to provide an account of selected clinical cases that were classified as '"reactionary psychoses"' (Fanon 1963: 251). Accordingly, "prominence is given to the event which has given rise to the disorder," including "the bloodthirsty and pitiless atmosphere, the generalization of inhuman practices, and the firm impression that people have of being caught up in a veritable Apocalypse" (Fanon 1963: 251). The cases were divided into four groups. "Series A" included five cases of "Algerians or Europeans who had very clear symptoms of mental disorders of the reactionary type" (two were members of the National Liberation Army whose family members had suffered at the hands of the French as a result of their military involvement; another two were European officers involved in the interrogation and torture of Algerian prisoners; one was an Algerian civilian who survived a mass murder in his home village) (Fanon 1963: 254–70). "Series B" covered "certain cases or groups of cases in which the event giving rise to the illness is... the atmosphere of total war which reigns in Algeria" (Fanon 1963: 270). What distinguishes the second group from the first is that under Series B, none of the patients was directly engaged in the war (two Algerian teenage boys who killed their European classmates in cold blood; a suicidal Algerian male civilian in his twenties haunted by thought of being a traitor to his own people; the daughter of a high ranking French civil servant – a young woman in her twenties – suffering from anxiety disorder; "behavior disturbances" among children refugees whose parents were killed by the French either as soldiers or as civilians; women refugees along the Moroccan and Tunisian frontiers suffering from puerperal or postpartum psychosis) (Fanon 1963: 270–9). Cases under "Series C" involved patients "in a fairly serious condition whose disorders appeared immediately after and during the tortures" (Fanon 1963: 280). Fanon observed that "characteristic morbidity groups correspond to different methods of torture employed" (Fanon 1963: 280). For example, among those who had been tortured by electricity were three cases of "localized or generalized coenesthopathies" where patients "felt 'pins and needles' throughout their bodies; their hands seemed to be torn off, their heads seemed to be bursting, and their tongues felt as if they were being swallowed" (Fanon 1963: 283). The final group – "Series D" – consisted of cases involving psychosomatic disorders (Fanon 1963: 289–93). These were patients who had physical symptoms deemed to be "psychic in origin," such as stomach ulcers among younger adults (18 to 25 years old) and menstruation irregularities among women (Fanon 1963: 290).

This collection of cases prompted Fanon to make the following observation: "The hitherto unemphasized characteristics of certain psychiatric descriptions given here confirm... that this colonial war is singular even in the pathology that it gives rise to" (Fanon 1963: 252). Moreover, Fanon questioned "the notion of the relative harmlessness of these reactional disorders" (Fanon 1963: 252). Here he was referring to "certain secondary psychoses, that is to say cases where the whole of the personality is disrupted definitively" and can persist for a protracted period, rendering the patients to become visibly weak (Fanon 1963: 252). Based on "all available evidence," Fanon pronounced that "the future of such patients is mortgaged" (Fanon 1963: 252–3).

In addition to documenting the human cost of colonization, Fanon challenged one of the most commonly used doctrines to justify colonization – the inherent moral inferiority of the colonized. Specifically, the doctrine was expressed through the view that "the Algerian is a *born* criminal" (Fanon 1963: 298, emphasis added); a view that was supposedly validated by medical research carried out by French psychiatrists based in Algiers in the 1930s. Instead, Fanon offered a sociopolitical explanation of why Algerians violated one another as they got reduced to fighting among themselves to survive in an extremely deprived milieu. In Fanon's words,

> When, tired out after a hard sixteen-hour day, the native sinks down to rest on his mat, and a child on the other side of the canvas partition starts crying and prevents him from sleeping, it so happens that it is a little Algerian. When he goes to beg for a little semolina or a drop of oil from the grocer, to whom he already owes some hundreds of francs, and when he sees that he is refused, an immense feeling of hatred and an overpowering desire to kill rises within him: and the grocer is an Algerian. When, after having kept out of his way for weeks he finds himself one day cornered by the caid who demands that he should pay "his taxes," he cannot even enjoy the luxury of hating a European administrator; there before him is the caid who is the object of his hatred – and the caid is an Algerian. The Algerian, exposed to temptations to commit murder every day – famine, eviction from his room because he has not paid the rent, the mother's dried-up breasts, children like skeletons, the building-yard which has closed down, the unemployed that hang about the foreman like crows – the native comes to see his neighbor as a relentless enemy. If he strikes his bare foot against a big stone in the middle of the path, it is a native who has placed it there; and the few olives that he was going to pick, X-'s children have gone and eaten in the night. For during the colonial period in Algeria and elsewhere many things may be done for a couple of pounds of semolina. Several people may be killed over it. You need to use your imagination to understand that. (Fanon 1963: 307)

Under these oppressive conditions, "living does not mean embodying moral values or taking his place in the coherent and fruitful development of the world" (Fanon 1963: 308). Rather, for a colonized man "to live" means no more than "to keep on existing" (Fanon 1963: 308). Fanon observed, "Every date is a victory: not the result of work, but a victory felt as a triumph for life. Thus to steal dates or to allow one's sheep to eat the neighbor's grass is not a question of the negation of the property of others, nor the transgression of a law, nor lack of respect. These are attempts at murder" (Fanon 1963: 308–9). The harsh reality of everyday life for the colonized enabled Fanon to ascertain that the alleged "Algerian's criminality, his impulsivity, and the violence of his murders" were "not the consequence of the organization of his nervous system or of characterial originality, but the direct product of the colonial situation" (Fanon 1963: 309).

One obvious conclusion to draw from Fanon's writing is that there is a direct causal relation between political disorder through the exercise of colonial power and mental disability, as evident in his analysis of the mentally ill and accounts of daily lives in colonial Algeria. But what is perhaps less obvious is how Fanon validated his claim and its bearing on the question that this chapter sets out to explore, which is to understand the suffering experienced by the mentally ill in political terms. In this regard we need to consider seriously the disclaimer that Fanon made at the start of the chapter, in which he said, "we are not concerned with producing a scientific work. We avoid all arguments over semiology, nosology, or therapeutics. The few technical terms used serve merely as references" (Fanon 1963: 251). Yet it is clear that as one reads on, it is Fanon the psychiatrist speaking. In recounting his clinical cases to the readers, Fanon had importantly validated the experiences of these patients and victims to us, the laypersons, who otherwise would not be able to make sense of these experiences.[6] Moreover, Fanon did not appear to have any reservations about psychiatry per se.[7] It was after all modern medicine, which was invented by the West. While the science itself might not be by definition colonizing, it had certainly lent itself as a tool for colonization. As mentioned, Fanon was highly critical of the kind of medical research conducted by French psychiatrists in Algeria and, more generally, Western psychiatrists across Africa. Together as a group of medical experts, these psychiatrists had helped to propagate the view that Africans had a different nervous make-up from Europeans and an inborn propensity to aggression and violence (Fanon 1963: 298–304).

Fanon's study of colonialism and its impact on mental health demonstrates that much is indeed at stake in how to make connection with the disconnected among us – a problematic that anti-psychiatry simply evades by its uncompromising reconstitution of psychiatry as the site of power and control. In *The Wretched of the Earth*, however, Fanon did not elucidate on how he, as the psychiatrist, made his connection with his patients and what was entailed in that connection. In his earlier work, *Black Skin, White Masks*, there was a brief discussion on the challenge of analyzing

[6] According to Miraj Desai, it is only recently that there has been a growing interest among psychologists on Fanon's clinical insights into the relation between politics and psychology "despite Fanon's training as a psychiatrist and consistent use of psychological concepts" in his political analysis (Desai 2014: 59). Similarly, political theorists/philosophers have yet to explore the connection between Fanon the psychiatrist and Fanon the political thinker.

[7] In the last two chapters of *Black Skin, White Masks* ("The Negro and Psychopathology" and "The Negro and Recognition"), Fanon set out to investigate whether "the conclusions of Freud and of Adler can be applied to the effort to understand the man of color's view of the world" (Fanon 1967: 141). While Fanon showed that black persons and their white counterparts indeed had very different psychological experiences as they navigated the world around them, these differences were accounted for within the framework of psychoanalysis. David Macey, who wrote the authoritative biography of Fanon, made the following observation about Fanon at the start of his career: "He tried to humanize the hospital and to introduce new techniques, but remained within the parameters of psychiatry and did not challenge the existence of the institution itself. The radical – and soon to become revolutionary – psychiatrist remained in some ways a very conventional one" (Macey 2012: 208).

the "real" as experienced from the point of view of the investigator. On this important point, Fanon turned to Karl Jaspers who, like Fanon, was first trained as a psychiatrist. Citing Jaspers, Fanon observed that "What matters for us is not to collect facts and behavior, but to find their *meaning*" (Fanon 1967: 168, emphasis added; also cited in Desai 2014: 63). Hence, "What is important in phenomenology is less the study of a large number of instances than the intuitive and deep understanding of a few individual cases" (Fanon 1967: 168). Following Fanon, we shall now turn to Karl Jaspers to explore his distinctive approach to psychiatry.

Karl Jaspers – Psychiatrist as Phenomenologist

Karl Jaspers is better known among political theorists as a German philosopher who was once a teacher of Hannah Arendt and remained her close friend even after Arendt left Germany in 1933 to escape the Nazis. What is less known in this context is the fact that Jaspers was, as mentioned above, originally trained as a psychiatrist and that his first major work was an expansive volume published in 1913, titled *General Psychopathology*. In more than 800 pages of writings, Jaspers laid out a comprehensive study of psychopathology that spans psychiatry, psychology and philosophy. The breadth of this work shows that Jaspers did not confine himself to knowledge of the medical sciences. In particular, three thinkers – Edmund Husserl in philosophy, Wilhelm Dilthey in history, and Max Weber in politics – appeared to have substantial influence on Jaspers (McHugh 1997: vii; see also Leoni 2013). The book therefore represents a multidisciplinary approach to psychiatry, and Jaspers was convinced that both the sciences and the humanities are needed to understand the human psyche (Jaspers 1997: vol. 1, 37, 45–6). Paul McHugh, the psychiatrist who wrote the new forward to the 1997 edition, remarks that Jaspers considered psychiatry as inhabiting "a middle ground between science, where laws of nature are discerned, and history, where fateful events are conceived as emerging from human choices and actions" (McHugh 1997: vii).

Jaspers was clear that the "subject-matter" of psychopathology is the "actual conscious psychic events" themselves (Jaspers 1997: vol. 1, 2).[8] This means that what needs to be considered is the "full range

[8] As defined in *Oxford English Dictionary*, the term psychopathology refers to "the study of pathological mental and behavioural processes" and first appeared in English in 1847 as a translated term from German. Giovanni Stanghellini and Thomas Fuchs (2013: xviii) note that "psychopathology is not a specialty in the field of mental health, but the basic science in psychiatry and clinical psychology." In both Jaspers' time and now, the relevance of psychopathology to psychiatry is "threefold": 1) it serves as the "common language"

of psychic reality," which goes beyond "pathological phenomena" and include what "people experience in general and how they experience it" (Jaspers 1997: vol. 1, 2). There is therefore "no unitary concept of what is morbid" and no insistence "on any precise definition of mental illness" (Jaspers 1997: vol. 1, 2). In other words, at the very beginning of his study Jaspers was already preparing his readers for a contextual approach to mental phenomena. Nonetheless, psychopathology has an ambitious agenda of formulating a comprehensive analytical framework for the study of psychic experiences, including investigating the "causes and conditions" that are at work in these "actual" experiences, "as well as the relationships and the modes in which the experience comes to expression" (Jaspers 1997: vol. 1, 2). To achieve these objectives, "the preliminary work of representing, defining, and classifying psychic phenomena" must first be carried out (Jaspers 1968: 1314). But the task is hardly easy to complete. Jaspers observed that "the difficult and comprehensive nature of this preliminary work makes it inevitable that it should become for the time being an end in itself" (Jaspers 1968: 1314). Consequently, it is "pursued as an independent activity" and "constitutes phenomenology" proper (Jaspers 1968: 1314). This representation of psychopathological investigation suggests that in Jaspers' view, a psychiatrist is by definition a phenomenologist.[9]

Phenomenology demands its practitioners to be free from preconception of any kind in order to turn their attention "only to that which we [they] can understand as having real existence, and which we [they] can differentiate and describe" (Jaspers 1968: 1316). The stipulation is in fact more challenging than it may appear initially. This is because all psychologists and psychopathologists tend to "go through a stage where we [they] form our [their] own ideas... of psychic events, and only later acquire an unprejudiced direct grasp of these events as they really are" (Jaspers 1968: 1316). Hence, "this particular freedom from preconception which phenomenology demands is not something one possesses from the beginning, but something that is laboriously acquired after prolonged critical work and much effort" (Jaspers 1968: 1316). The "phenomenological

that enables "specialists" from "different schools... to understand each other"; 2) "it is the ground for diagnosis and classification in a field where all major conditions are not aetiologically defined disease entities, but exclusively clinically defined syndromes"; 3) it is indispensable to the attainment of "understanding" in psychiatry by making intelligible "the meanings of personal experiences" (Stanghellini and Fuchs 2013: xviii). It can be observed that all three are present in Jaspers' book, in both content and purpose.

[9] Toward the end of *General Psychopathology*, Jaspers said in more general terms the following: "the contemporary psychotherapist... *has to be a philosopher*, consciously or no, methodically or haphazardly, in earnest or not, spontaneously or following contemporary fashions" (Jaspers 1997: vol. 2, 806, emphasis in original).

attitude" can only be attained "by ever-repeated effort and by the ever-renewed overcoming of prejudice" (Jaspers 1968: 1316).

By focusing on "actual experiences," the psychiatrist as a phenomenologist is concerned with the "perceptible and concrete" rather than with factors "that may be thought to underlie psychic events and are the subject of theoretical constructs" (Jaspers 1968: 1322). The investigative questions that should be guiding the phenomenologist are therefore as follows: "has this actually been experienced? Does this really present itself to the subject's consciousness?" (Jaspers 1968: 1322) To answer these questions, the psychiatrist-cum-phenomenologist needs to utilize the "methods of phenomenological analysis" to "determine what patients really experience," that is, "subjective psychic experience" (Jaspers 1968: 1317–18). These methods include immersing oneself in the "gestures, behaviour, expressive movements" of patients; exploring through "direct questioning of the patients" and "accounts which they themselves… give of their own experiences" under guidance; and finally, drawing from "written self-descriptions" of the patients (Jaspers 1968: 1317–18). Importantly, Jaspers observed that while these self-descriptions are "seldom really good," they are "all the more valuable" and can be of use even if one has not known the writer personally (Jaspers 1968: 1317). "Good self-descriptions" are thus given the "highest value" in ascertaining the "actual experiences" of patients. Accordingly:

> Phenomenological findings derive their validity from the fact that the various elements of the psychic reality can be evoked repeatedly. Its findings can thus only be refuted if the facts of a case have previously been wrongly represented or are not represented correctly; *they can never be refuted by demonstrating their impossibility or error on the basis of some theoretical proposition.* Phenomenology can gain nothing from theory; it can only lose. The accuracy of a particular representation cannot be checked by its conformity to general criteria; phenomenology must always find its standards within itself. (Jaspers 1968: 1322, emphasis added)

This insight led Jaspers to observe that a well-executed psychopathological finding is one that yields "understanding" (*Verstehen*) "from within," as opposed to "explanation" (*Erklären*) "from without" (Jaspers 1997: vol. 1, 28).[10] More specifically, what is achieved is "empathic understanding" rather than "rational knowledge" (Jaspers 1997: vol. 1, 304). The latter enables the psychiatrist to make "a rational connection" of the "psychic content" but it is not "the psychic connection itself" (Jaspers 1997: vol. 1, 304). It is the former that "leads directly into the

[10] This is a distinction that originates in Dilthey's thought on the differences between the "natural" and the "cultural" sciences. The former aims to explain; whereas the latter aims to understand (Phillips 1996: 61). See also Hoerl (2013).

psychic connection itself" (Jaspers 1997: vol. 1, 304). What becomes known is the meaning of the psychic event under investigation, facilitated by three different dimensions of empathic understanding. First, it establishes a "meaningful content" that reveals "an individual relationship to the world" and then identifies the "basic forms of the meaningful" (Jaspers 1997: vol. 1, 316). These are indispensable steps in achieving understanding because, in Jaspers' view:

> The individual reaches his fulfilment and finds his place, meaning and field of activity in the community in which he lives. The tensions between himself and the community are one of the understandable sources of his psychic disturbances. Every moment of the day the community is effectively present for every individual. Where the community has become consciously rationalised, organised and has taken a specific shape we speak of "society." (Jaspers 1997: vol. 2, 710)[11]

Finally, understanding establishes "self-reflection" as the "basic phenomenon of all meaningfulness" (Jaspers 1997: vol. 1, 316). Much is at stake in affirming the primacy of self-reflection. Jaspers observed:

> [A]ll that an individual does, knows, desires, and produces will indicate how he understands himself in the world. What we have termed the "*psychology of meaningful connectedness*" is then an understanding of *his* understanding. But it is a basic human characteristic that man as man understands his own understanding and gains a knowledge of himself. *Self-reflection is an inseparable element in the understandable human psyche*... The psychology of meaningful connections must understand self-reflection, which it practices itself. As practitioners of this psychology, we either achieve for another what he has not yet achieved by his own self-reflection or else we understand his self-reflection, share and expand it. (Jaspers 1997: vol. 1, 347, second emphasis in original, first and third added)

Hence, "psychological understanding cannot be used mechanically as a sort of generalised knowledge" (Jaspers 1997: vol. 1, 316). Instead, "a fresh, personal intuition is needed on every occasion" (Jaspers 1997: vol. 1, 316). Thus situated, what empathic understanding offers is interpretation, which is "a science only in principle, in its application it is always an art" (Bleuler, cited in Jaspers 1997: vol. 1, 313).

While this study of Jaspers' work on psychopathology is limited in engaging the comprehensiveness of the book itself, it enables us to apprehend how a psychiatrist-cum-phenomenologist comes to identify what it is that needs to be attended to when faced with a mentally ill patient. It is clear that for Jaspers, science alone is insufficient in understanding the

[11] Sebastian Luft and Jann Schlimme (2013: 346) note, "In his existential-philosophical works, he calls community 'an original phenomenon of our human existence'... In this sense, human beings can only be human in the full sense of the term in community."

condition itself, let alone its treatment. As noted by McHugh, at the core of Jaspers' approach to psychiatry is that the patient must be treated as a subject who is capable of self-expression and can therefore speak for oneself (McHugh 1997: vii). However, that discourse may not be readily intelligible to the self or others when self-reflection, as defined by Jaspers, is absent. Yet this apparent unintelligibility by no means implies that what is said is not worth listening to, both literally and metaphorically. The onus is on the listener to understand what is being communicated by calling upon psychopathology "to give a searching presentation of *rare connections with abnormal meaning* as they appear in individual, concrete cases" (Jaspers 1997: vol. 1, 315, emphasis in original). Only then can there be context for self-reflection, which in turn forms the basis for self-expression.

Thus, I would argue that the key to Jaspers' model of psychiatric care is intersubjectivity, although Jaspers himself did not use the term in the book, nor did he develop a general theory of intersubjectivity after he became a full-blown philosopher (Luft and Schlimme 2013: 346). An intersubjective approach to psychiatric care means importantly that the psychiatrist cannot simply regard the patient as an object to be examined and treated. Such an approach can only lead to an explanation of the patient's experience from without, which is what Jaspers cautions against. Rather, the challenge for the psychiatrist is to make sense of the patient's experience when self-reflection can no longer be assumed and thereby signaling an existential rupture in the individual's relation to the world. To reiterate, the psychiatrist's task is to locate the appropriate context in which the patient's subjectivity, as expressed, can be understood meaningfully, both to oneself and to others. In rendering the patient's subjectivity meaningful and thereby intelligible through an interpretive act, the psychiatrist's own subjectivity is established. The psychiatrist, as psychiatrist, is now immersed in at least a community of two in which "*existential communication*" becomes feasible (Jaspers 1997: vol. 2, 798, emphasis in original). Jaspers was emphatic about drawing "a fundamental difference in meaning between depicting a patient as a particular case of some general disorder and describing him as his unique self" (Jaspers 1997: vol. 2, 675). According to Jaspers, "*Every good case-history grows into a biography*" and no single biography is identical to another (Jaspers 1997: vol. 2, 671, emphasis in original).

Although Jaspers insisted on the uniqueness of subjective experience, he dedicated an entire section of the book (albeit the shortest among six) to what he called the "social and historical aspects of the psychoses and personality disorder" and assessed various common factors that come into play in psychical disorder (Jaspers 1997: vol. 2, 709–43).

Of particular relevance here are the two full pages on "typical" social situations and "times of security, revolution and war" (Jaspers 1997: vol. 2, 718–20). Having observed that the "*uprooting* of people is a fate which has become increasingly common in our modern world," Jaspers identified "the heavy pressure of hopeless social conditions; chronic physical distress; persistent burdening of the psyche by unending worry and the need to get a livelihood and the lack of any element of fight, élan, aim or plan" as "typical" situations that "will often lead to states of apathy, indifference and extreme psychic impoverishment" (Jaspers 1997: vol. 2, 718, emphasis in original). Immediately following the list of problems facing people in the modern world is a brief discussion on psychic life in "times of security" (life before 1914), "revolution" (specifically the French and the Russian revolutions) and war (unspecified, although one paragraph on the First World War was added in subsequent editions of the book) (Jaspers 1997: vol. 2, 718–20). Yet the discussion is disappointingly inadequate from a psychiatrist who repeatedly emphasized the need to take into account a patient's entire life to the point that "a thorough *social anamnesis*" must be obtained from the patient; without which the social and historical context is incomplete (Jaspers 1997: vol. 2, 711, emphasis in original).

Arendt – Totalitarianism and Disconnectedness

To fill this gap in Jaspers' psychiatric work, I turn to Hannah Arendt, even though they came to know each other as professor and student in philosophy rather than psychiatry and there was no subsequent correspondence between them that made explicit references to Jaspers' earlier psychiatric work (Arendt and Jaspers 1992). In Anglo-American Arendtian scholarship in the past two decades, much has been written about the relationship between Arendt and Heidegger but not that between Arendt and Jaspers. However, an earlier work by Lewis Hinchman and Sandra Hinchman made a convincing case on Jaspers' influence by arguing for an "'existentialist' reading" of Arendt whereby Jaspers' philosophical categories "reappear, politicized, in Arendt's own thought" (Hinchman and Hinchman 1991: 435). In support of this interpretation, I want to draw upon Arendt's own words in the essay "What is Existenz Philosophy?", originally published in 1946 in *Partisan Review*. With respect to Jaspers' place in German existentialism among others (Kant, Schelling, Kierkegaard, and Heidegger), Arendt remarked:

Existence itself is, by its very nature, never isolated. It exists only in communication and in awareness of others' existence. Our fellowmen are not (as in

> Heidegger) an element of existence that is structurally necessary but at the same time an impediment to the Being of Self. Just the contrary. Existence can develop only in the shared life of human beings inhabiting a given world common to them all. In the concept of communication lies a concept of humanity new in its approach though not yet fully developed that postulates communication as the premise for the existence of man... [H]uman beings live and act with each other; and in doing so, they neither pursue the phantom of Self nor live in the arrogant illusion that they constitute Being itself.
>
> The movement of transcendence in thought... and the failure of thought inherent in that movement bring us at least to a recognition that man as "master of his thoughts" is not only more than what he thinks – and this alone would probably provide basis enough for a new definition of human dignity – but is also constitutionally a being that is more than a Self and wills more than himself. With this understanding, existential philosophy has emerged from its period of preoccupation with Self-ness. (Arendt 1994: 186–7)

With these words, it is only logical for Arendt to go on and write *The Human Condition*, arguably her most widely read work. Indeed, Hinchman and Hinchman described Arendt's mature political thought as a "brilliant but unstable synthesis" of Jaspers' existentialism and Aristotelian theory (Hinchman and Hinchman 1991: 436). Among the themes that Jaspers and Arendt shared was concern over the emergence of "mass society" as indicative of an existential crisis, which for Arendt, now in her Aristotelian framework, is ultimately destructive of politics as action (Hinchman and Hinchman 1991: 450–5).

To build on the interpretation by Hinchman and Hinchman, I turn to an earlier work of Arendt – *The Origins of Totalitarianism* – to further explore the problematic that this chapter sets out to study through the juxtaposition of Jaspers and Arendt. The focus is on Arendt's analysis of the "mass man" whose "chief characteristic" is "isolation and lack of normal social relationships" (Arendt 1973: 317). In considering this work for such purpose, I observe that the "mass man" is perhaps Jaspers' patient. Just as Jaspers set out to comprehend the isolated individual deemed to be incommunicable in *General Psychopathology*, Arendt embarked on a comparable task in political terms in an equally massive book. And just as Jaspers insisted that he had to begin by finding out what it is that he was investigating, Arendt started her study by noting that totalitarianism represented an unprecedented breakdown of political order in the twentieth century and, as such, she needed to first sort out what it is that she was attempting to explain (Arendt 1973: xiv–xv).

Arendt began the book by staking out the controversial claim that both Nazism and Stalinism were totalitarian systems and, hence, comparable.

Moreover, both were more than just radical ways of conducting racial politics or class struggle. Arendt noted:

> Totalitarian politics, far from being simply antisemitic or racist or imperialist or communist, use and abuse their own ideological and political elements until the basis of factual reality, from which the ideologies originally derived their propaganda value, the value of struggle, for instance, or the interest conflicts between Jews and their neighbours, have all but disappeared. (Arendt 1973: xv)

Therefore, what makes totalitarianism characteristically totalitarian is its capacity to orchestrate a radical disjunction with what Arendt identified as "factual reality." It is this capacity that sets totalitarianism apart from previous forms of "political oppression" such as despotism, tyranny and dictatorship (Arendt 1973: 460).

Arendt further argued that this new form of political oppression is necessarily sustained by "ideology," understood as the "logic of an idea" that lends itself to "ideological thinking." Ideological thinking is a distinctive mode of political reasoning defined by several characteristics. Its first unique feature lies in providing a "total explanation" of all happenings that cover the entire historical spectrum, that is, the past, the present and the future (Arendt 1973: 470). Yet despite its claim to account for "factual reality" in its totality, ideological thinking is characteristically divorced from reality and experience (Arendt 1973: 470–1). This is because experience is by definition rooted in specificity and cannot possibly account for all of reality. It follows that another distinctive aspect of ideological thinking is its capacity to "emancipate" thought from the limitation imposed by experience through a "specific method of demonstration" (Arendt 1973: 471). Within this framework, facts are rearranged by way of an "absolutely logical procedure" that starts from an "axiomatically accepted premise" (Arendt 1973: 471). Stated differently, ideological thinking is in effect logical thinking at the service of politics. As it proceeds from a premise through deductive reasoning to reach a necessary conclusion, the "logicality of ideological thinking" provides the basis for "total explanation," which in turn serves as the "principle of action" for totalitarian movement (Arendt 1973: 471–2).

Based on this insight into totalitarianism as a closed system of thought supported solely by formal logic, Arendt staked out yet another contentious claim, which is that at the heart of totalitarian appeal to its followers is precisely the form rather than the content. Specifically, the kind of consistency offered by totalitarian thinking is appealing to those who have lost a sense of bearing in the real world (that is, the world in which we inhabit) (Arendt 1973: 353). Arendt noted:

> The ideal subject of totalitarian rule is not the convinced Nazi or the convinced Communist, but people for whom the distinction between fact and fiction (that is, the reality of experience) and the distinction between true and false (that is, the standards of thought) no longer exist. (Arendt 1973: 474)

The term that Arendt used to describe this "ideal subject of totalitarian rule" is the "mass man," who is a highly isolated and atomized individual (Arendt 1973: 323). The "mass man" is found where people are "superfluous or can be spared without disastrous results of depopulation" (Arendt 1973: 311). Moreover, these people are otherwise unable to be "integrated into any organization based on common interest" (Arendt 1973: 311). In other words, the "mass man" has lost his/her uniqueness and sociality; both of which are essential to intersubjective existence. Expressed in the language of psychopathology, the "mass man" experiences a pathological mental condition that renders him/her incommunicable and thereby existentially disabled. Indeed, Arendt described the "mass man" as believing in what "'normal people' refuse to believe," and considered the "SS-men" (presumably they constituted a subgroup of "mass man") as "inanimate men, *i.e.* men who can no longer be psychologically understood" (Arendt 1973: 441).

Although not a psychiatrist, Arendt the political thinker was clear on what would have constituted the "social anamnesis" for the case at hand, which in Jaspers' view is an essential component in putting together the life history of a patient, as previously noted. Arendt maintained that by the end of the First World War, "the breakdown of class society," coupled with massive unemployment and displacement of population, facilitated the makeup of "the psychology of the European mass man" (Arendt 1973: 311–15). This suggests that the interwar years were part of the spectrum of extraordinary political disorder epitomized by the two world wars. The "mass man" emerged consequent to the First World War and in turn facilitated the Second. Confronted with absolute chaos, the mass man is someone who is "obsessed by a desire to escape from reality" (Arendt 1973: 352). For in his "essential homelessness," the mass man is no longer able to bear the "accidental, incomprehensible aspects" of reality (Arendt 1973: 352). This longing for escape from reality is a "verdict against the world" in which one is "forced to live" but "cannot exist" (Arendt 1973: 352). Such an escape, when executed *en masse*, is what Arendt called the "revolt of the masses" against "common sense," which in inter-war Europe was "the result of their atomization, of their loss of social status" (Arendt 1973: 352). A revolt of this kind means that the "whole sector of communal relationships in whose framework common sense makes sense" is lost (Arendt 1973: 352).

The collapse of common sense has a direct bearing on the effectiveness of totalitarian propaganda. It offers the mass man a substitute reality validated by the "logic of an idea" rather than by reality as experienced. This is how totalitarianism makes it possible for a completely isolated individual to live in a world where the condition of plurality has disappeared. Logical reasoning, which is the essence of ideological mode of thought, is characteristic of the human mind in singularity; one that is devoid of the self, the other and the world (Arendt 1973: 477). According to Arendt, when faced with "the anarchic growth and total arbitrariness of decay," the mass man will likely succumb to "the most rigid, fantastically fictitious consistency of an ideology" (Arendt 1973: 352). A world created by ideology is most attractive not because the "mass man" is "stupid and wicked" (Arendt 1973: 353). Rather, such a world provides "a minimum of self-respect" through conjuring up "a lying world of consistency which is more adequate to the needs of the human mind than reality itself" (Arendt 1973: 353). The unique capacity of ideological thinking to guarantee consistency against the unpredictability of a relentlessly chaotic reality is what enables a totalitarian movement to demand "total, unrestricted, unconditional and unalterable loyalty" from its followers (Arendt 1973: 323).

In Arendt's view, the fabricated world of logical consistency is most destructive of politics because it displaces opinion, which is at the very heart of politics as "action." Returning to *The Human Condition* at this point will therefore enable us to see its connection with *The Origins of Totalitarianism* from an intersubjective perspective. In *The Human Condition*, Arendt famously pronounced that speech is the prototype of human action. "Action" as "speech" is the only form of human activity that occurs "directly between men without the intermediary of things or matter" and thus, corresponds to the "human condition of plurality, to the fact that men, not Man, live on the earth and inhabit the world" (Arendt 1998: 7). Following Aristotle, Arendt was convinced that speech is "what makes man a political being" (Arendt 1998: 3). Dana Villa notes that speech for Arendt is always "speech with others" and that "genuine political action" is "a certain kind of talk" (Villa 1996: 31). Specifically, as political beings talking to one another, humans are engaged in debate, which Arendt considered to be the "very essence of political life" (Arendt 1977b: 241). Since debate is by definition an exchange of "opinion," opinion becomes in effect the substance of political action.

According to Arendt, opinion requires "representative" thinking, which in turn implies the capacity to consider "a given issue from different viewpoints" and to make present in one's mind "the standpoints of those who are absent" (Arendt 1977b: 241). However, representative thinking is "not a question of empathy, as though I tried to be or to feel like somebody else," or of "counting noses and joining a majority" (Arendt 1977b: 242). Rather, it is achieved by "being and thinking in my own identity where actually I am not" (Arendt 1977b: 242). Representative thinking therefore requires an "enlarged mentality," which entails situating oneself in a world of "universal interdependence" while suspending "one's own private interests" (Arendt 1977b: 242). Stated differently, thinking in the mode of enlarged mentality is not an exercise in abstract thinking that can be carried out by individuals in isolation. It can only be realized through "imagination, reflection, and storytelling" (Borren 2013: 248); all of which require the capacity to engage beyond oneself in an environment that is conducive to such engagement.

In her final lectures on Kant, Arendt affirmed the view that this capacity for an "enlarged mentality" is what enables us to make judgments (Arendt 1982). This means that an opinion, as an act of judgment, cannot simply be personal and subjective. For to judge is to disclose oneself to others, which requires "sharing-the-world-with-others" (Arendt 1977a: 221). Hence, "when one judges, one judges as a member of a community" and as such, judgment presupposes "common sense," which is in effect "community sense, *sensus communis*" (Arendt 1982: 72). As noted by Marieke Borren, "common sense avoids the traps of both subjectivism or relativism on the one hand, and universalism on the other. Instead, the kind of validity that common sense judgments achieve is intersubjectivity, or what could be called situated impartiality, or representativeness" (Borren 2013: 244; Disch 1994: 162). Judgment for Arendt is therefore necessarily intersubjective (Lee 1997: 126).

In addition, Borren observes that common sense for Arendt is neither an *a priori* capacity nor an *a posteriori* capacity. I suggest extending Borren's observation to incorporate intersubjectivity as an existential condition that is neither *a priori* nor *a posteriori*. It is not *a priori* in the sense that intersubjectivity is not about realizing some "universal and immutable human nature" (Borren 2013: 246). It occurs only in "the particular historical-political context and situation at hand, and simultaneously constitutes the context within which human beings act, speech, judge and make sense of the world" (Borren 2013: 246). But the situatedness of intersubjectivity does not thereby render it *a posteriori*. In Borren's words:

> Common sense always also needs critical appropriation – the operations of representation and reflection, the imaginative anticipation of others' views and *Selbstdenken* [thinking for oneself] – to accomplish sound understanding and judgment. Otherwise, the exchange of viewpoints would simply come down to conformism to the arbitrary *communis opinio* and the replacement of one's own subjective point of view or those of others. (Borren 2013: 246)

What is being put forth here is that common sense, to the extent that it is embedded in intersubjectivity, enables the distinctiveness of the self to be affirmed in the presence of others.

Arendt's study of totalitarianism illustrates that political breakdown marks the loss of common sense among a community of people, rendering them to become no more than a multitude of "mass man," or what Arendt referred to as the "masses." Existentially, it means that intersubjectivity – so essential to psychological health and healing, as Jaspers has shown – can no longer take place. Individuals are left to themselves without the means to connect with themselves and with others. This is when they become receptive to the kind of ideological thinking that totalitarianism deploys to recruit its followers.

Arendt's insight into totalitarianism and its subjects – the masses – is a powerful case of why politics matters. Its breakdown poses no less than an existential threat to everyone. By fabricating a substitute reality that enables individuals to develop a false sense of connectedness to the world around them, totalitarianism offers an exit to those who are otherwise disconnected. Although Arendt stopped short of using the term "collective madness" to describe the kind of collective actions taken by followers of totalitarianism, words such as "insanity" (Arendt 1973: 411) and "mad unreality" (Arendt 1973: 445) are used in the text. What makes sense to the followers of totalitarian movement does not make sense to those who are outside. The self-contained system of ideological thinking that Arendt used to analyze totalitarianism is in fact comparable to what Jaspers had to say about delusion, which he described "as a whole coherent world of appropriate behaviour apparent in a personality that is... by common standards not otherwise to be considered ill" (Jaspers 1997: vol. 1, 411). As such "the *incorrigibility of delusion has something over and above the incorrigibility of healthy people's mistakes*" (Jaspers 1997: vol. 1, 411, emphasis in original). Jaspers remarked:

> In principle... untruth can always be overcome by the great process of human reason which amongst a welter of mistakes, falsifications, obscurities, sophisms and bad intentions pursues truth. In the case of delusion, however, we may see someone irretrievably lost in untruth – an extreme situation which we may not be able to correct yet would much like to comprehend. (Jaspers 1997: vol. 1, 411)

Juxtaposed with Jaspers' view, Arendt's ideological thinking is delusion *en masse*. Moreover, in "politicizing" Jaspers, as suggested by Hinchman and Hinchman, Arendt argued that it is the disconnected who are most vulnerable to delusional thought and can therefore be manipulated to serve political purposes that feed upon political disorder. The stakes in maintaining a world where meaningful human connectedness is both feasible and sustainable have never been so high. This is because the triumph of totalitarianism would mean "the destruction of humanity" as it destroys "the essence of man" (Arendt 1973: viii). In short, totalitarianism represents a disabling environment in which no humans can thrive.

Conclusion – Mental Well-Being and Political Responsibility

To sum up, the thoughts of Fanon, Jaspers and Arendt point to intersubjectivity as an existential condition that is vital to one's sense of connectedness, both within the self and with others as an ongoing relational mode. To recognize the centrality of political order in creating and maintaining both the social and political space for intersubjectivity to take place means to be committed to a vision of politics in which the well-being of individuals, both physical and mental, is of utmost priority. This chapter begins with the observation that there is a need to study human suffering as experienced by individuals in political terms. My focus throughout the chapter has been human suffering in the form of mental disorder and its relation to political disorder. In this regard, Fanon made the most obvious connection by validating the experiences of his patients who were suffering from the protracted colonial war in Algeria in his position as a psychiatrist. Through his clinical work, Fanon maintained that there is a direct correlation between mental health and political order. Much is at stake as the psychiatrist negotiates the line between the medical and the sociopolitical. Yet Fanon did not explain how he handled the challenge. Prompted in part by Fanon, I turned to Jaspers, from whom we learn that the mentally ill are individuals whose subjectivity is no longer readily accessible. Accordingly, the task of the psychiatrist is first and foremost to relocate a plausible point of interface between the psychiatrist and the patient to enable reconnection with the disconnect. This is where attending to the patient as the experiencing subject becomes critical and where there is no ready-made diagnostic tool to facilitate the interaction. Jasper's insight into the unique role of psychiatry shows the centrality of intersubjectivity in determining connectedness among individuals. From Arendt, we ascertain that when intersubjectivity breaks down, individuals become vulnerable to making false connection with a fabricated world supported by a closed system of abstract reasoning that leaves no room for the concrete affirmation of one's subjectivity through what Arendt described as "sharing-the-world-with-others." While Arendt, in contrast to Fanon, was primarily focused on individuals as a social force, her work illustrates why we cannot simply remain indifferent to those who are indeed slipping. Against these considerations, I want to draw on a clinical case in contemporary psychiatric care to shed light on the challenge of making mental disorder a political concern that matters to us all.

The case involved a former Vietnamese refugee (identified as "BN") in his forties who, during the clinical diagnostic investigation, had been living in the United States for two decades.[12] He was arrested in the state of New Mexico on charges of domestic violence.[13] During arraignment, the man became mute and acted disrespectfully in court. He was then admitted to the hospital for psychiatric assessment but proved to be uncooperative. After several failed attempts to diagnose the patient, the physicians in charge of the case decided to bring in a "trusted member of the local Vietnamese community" to facilitate communication with the patient (Hollifield et al. 2003: 332). The narrative approach adopted by this person during interview turned out to be enormously decisive in breaking the silence. BN began talking. It turned out that shortly after the fall of Saigon (Ho Chi Minh City), BN's home was raided by Vietnamese communists. They seized his belongings, interrogated him and "violently arrested him" (Hollifield et al. 2003: 332). According to BN, this was exactly what happened one month before "when the police came to his house with his wife and her male friend, served him with a restraining order" (Hollifield et al. 2003: 333). As a result of this disclosure, the doctors eventually diagnosed BN with post-traumatic stress disorder (PTSD). The following observation was made by the clinicians involved in the case:

> [T]he beliefs and social forms created by the particular war and events experienced by BN are more relevant in this case than BN's ethnicity. Ethnicity may be associated with many customary beliefs, social forms, and material traits, and thus to 'culture,' but is often not the most important cultural domain in clinical

[12] The article does not provide the date of the case. Given the year of its publication (2003) and the most recent citation in the article, which is 2000, it is reasonable to assume that it occurred in the early 2000s.

[13] During BN's hospitalization, his wife and her family were interviewed. Apparently, it was a marriage "according to custom" rather than "a legal union" (Hollifield et al. 2003: 333). Moreover, both the wife and the family "denied that the patient had been physically abusive" (Hollifield et al. 2003: 333). But the wife did say that she moved out with her child because "she was afraid of BN and did not want to be controlled by him" (Hollifield et al. 2003: 333). The wife and his male friend were subsequently banned from the ward after they demanded the hospital to "give them BN's money and belongings, and insisted that BN be kept in the hospital or in jail" (Hollifield et al. 2003: 333–334). But most importantly, "the petitions for a treatment guardian and commitment were canceled as BN agreed to stay as a voluntary patient" (Hollifield et al. 2003: 333). He was eventually discharged and all his "seized belongings," including money, were returned to him (Hollifield et al. 2003: 334).

medicine... The general phenomena of war trauma and later re-traumatization were the primary socio-cultural forms responsible for BN's illness, not the fact that he was Vietnamese. There were certainly other aspects of his being Vietnamese – such as the traditional relationship and ideas about money, familial hierarchies and ownership – that were important to his personhood and clinical status. However, BN's illness originated primarily from trauma contextualized by the Vietnam–U.S. war, and the multiple betrayals and their mnemics that he experienced were more powerful predictors of his clinical status than his ethnic origin. (Hollifield et al. 2003: 334–5)

When placed in the context of war trauma, BN's behavior was determined to be typical of victims of war. It is well established that "people traumatized by war and political oppression are steeped in processes of anonymity, asymmetry, inequality, mistrust, and insecurity about time and place that are used to break mind and body" (Hollifield et al. 2003: 337). They tend not to "reveal themselves to people they do not know as a result of the mistrust created by trauma experiences in general and by the rational, learned mistrust of authority" (Hollifield et al. 2003: 337). Moreover, it is noted that while "war trauma and political oppression have common features across time through history, there are also different sociopolitical forces working in each war context" (Hollifield et al. 2003: 337–8). Specifically, during the Vietnam War, men, in contrast to women, were "more likely... to be imprisoned" (Hollifield et al. 2003: 338). Hence, it is reasonable to conclude that "this Vietnamese man had a history of severe traumatization contextualized by a specific war, including loss of autonomy and respect, loss of material wealth, betrayal, separation and isolation, displacement and physical detention and abuse." Such a personal history meant that BN was highly vulnerable to the "acute social stressor" that he was under at the time of the arrest and the resulting incarceration and mandated hospitalization (Hollifield et al. 2003: 338).[14]

These clinicians also reflected on why they were unable to obtain information from BN earlier. In their view, the scientific paradigm that American doctors are trained under means that doctors tend to focus on "obtaining data about the illness than about the person who has the illness, implying that data collection about non-contextualized signs and symptoms will suffice for understanding what is wrong with the patient" (Hollifield et al. 2003: 335). The resulting impersonal and interrogative

[14] The authors briefly brought up the factor of gender in discussing "trauma type, symptoms and coping style" (Hollifield et al. 2003: 337). This, along with the remark that the wife subsequently disclaimed any physical abuse from BN (see note 13 above), seem to suggest that these clinicians had no reason to think that the wife was suffering from comparable trauma. Among other things, it is not known to the readers if the wife was a refugee like BN.

style of interview can be counterproductive, as demonstrated in this case. The clinicians remarked as follows:

> With this patient, asking questions about events and symptoms in a way that he interpreted as interrogation served as a re-traumatizing event. Thus, these questions were met with the logical and conditioned, protective response of not hearing and not talking: "I will not be heard, so I will not speak"... When the clinician adopted a narrative approach to align more with the patient as person than with the impersonal biomedical and social notions about recent events and symptoms, new data emerged. Any attempt on the clinician's part to revert to an "interrogative" style resulted in BN reverting to an interrogated, traumatized patient. (Hollifield et al. 2003: 335–6)

It is therefore of utmost importance that clinical assessment is based on "an authentic relationship," in which "the clinician is attentive to the patient as a person, so that trust and understanding allow the clinician to treat the person with the illness" (Hollifield et al. 2003: 338). Although these clinicians did not make any reference to Jaspers (or, for that matter, Fanon or Arendt), it is reasonable to extrapolate from the case that intersubjectivity holds the key to psychiatrist–patient relation. Only when there was actual engagement between the two could there be insight into the case; namely, that the patient was suffering from extreme dislocation, both when he was arrested in Vietnam after the fall of Saigon and when he was charged with alleged domestic violence in his adopted country, the United States. The subsequent diagnosis of PTSD confirmed BN's disconnection with the world around him and the relation between political and mental disorder.

Commenting on what he regards as a disturbing trend in research funding priorities that disfavors psychotherapy, Richard A. Friedman, an American psychiatrist, argued that psychotherapy as opposed to psychopharmaceutical treatment has proven to be far more effective in the attainment of clinical outcomes for a range of mental conditions, including PTSD (Friedman 2015: SR5). However, Friedman was by no means the first psychiatrist in recent years to call for the need to revisit the issue of psychiatry as a purely scientific medical enterprise. Unlike those who fall under anti-psychiatry, these psychiatrists hold the view that psychiatry is a bona fide medical practice whose aim is no different from all others – to restore a patient's health. But because mental problems are not readily tractable through techno-medical testing and processing, these problems need to be accessed through non-scientific venues.[15] This means, first and foremost, the need for the psychiatrist to

[15] Friedman remarked, "There is often no substitute for the self-understanding that comes with therapy. Sure, as a psychiatrist, I can quell a patient's anxiety, improve mood and

get to the bottom of the problems that are destabilizing a patient's mental health. The clinical case of BN shows that such an investigation could only be conducted productively when the patient's "actual experiences" (see p. 199), to borrow Jaspers' term, are attended to through sharing with the psychiatrist.

But the case also shows importantly that the recovery of BN was ultimately dependent on his reintegration into the community (Hollifield et al. 2003: 339). The works of Fanon, Jaspers and Arendt remind us that an individual can only be disconnected in a community of others. In the context of current global "bio-psycho-social" model of disability, which postulates disability "as a dynamic interaction between health conditions and contextual factors, both personal and environmental" (WHO 2011: 4), each of us, as a member of this community of others, has in fact a direct role in sustaining each other's mental health. Stated differently, understanding mental disability as an interactive rather than a static condition requires all to become better listeners to one another.[16] This means that the obligation to listen is no longer confined to just the psychiatrist treating the patient, nor to listening without what Jaspers called "understanding." Indeed, we cannot simply shrug our shoulders by saying that unlike the psychiatrist, we are the untrained ears. We live in the condition of plurality. There can be no political order when that plurality is disrupted, whether by outright oppression, as Fanon had shown, or by maneuvering reality itself, as Arendt had argued. As citizens, we are all obliged to maintain political order. This chapter shows that such an obligation entails a genuine effort from each of us to attend to others as subjects with disparate lived experiences, even those who may appear to be out of touch with the rest. Only then can we begin to overcome one of the biggest challenges of our times, which is the exceptional marginalization and discrimination of the mentally ill. It is one concrete step that we can all adopt in order to partake in the precarious task of reconnecting with the disconnect.

clear psychosis with the right medication. But there is no pill – and probably never will be – for any number of painful and disruptive emotional problems we are heir to, like narcissistic rage and paralyzing ambivalence, to name just two" (Friedman 2015: SR5). In Bracken et al. (2012), a group of British psychiatrists argued for a "post-technological" psychiatry. In their words: "A post-technological psychiatry will not abandon the tools of empirical science or reject medical and psychotherapeutic techniques but will start to position the ethical and hermeneutic aspects of our work as primary, thereby highlighting the importance of examining values, relationships, politics and the ethical basis of care and caring" (Bracken et al. 2012: 432).

[16] As noted on p. 199, the word "listen" is to be understood both literally and metaphorically.

10 Disability and Violence: Another Call for Democratic Inclusion and Pluralism

Joan Tronto

Violence as a Serious Problem for Disabled People

Consider this example: in 2013, law enforcement officials beat a mentally ill man they were holding in the Beltrami County, Minnesota, jail. County authorities then persuaded a judge to temporarily release him from their custody in order to avoid responsibility for his medical bills. Deputies then put the man in a car and drove him 200 miles and 3½ hours to drop him outside of the emergency room door of a Minneapolis hospital (McEnroe 2014).

Violence against disabled people occurs frequently[1] and is often bitterly cruel. The UN Convention on the Rights of Persons with Disabilities (adopted in 2008) provides in Section 14 that "State parties shall ensure that persons with disabilities, on an equal basis with others, (a) Enjoy the right to liberty and security of person; (b) Are not deprived of their liberty unlawfully or arbitrarily." This lofty language, which echoes the venerable French *Declaration of the Rights of Man* by including "security" among natural and imprescriptible rights,[2] differs from the Anglo-American tradition where liberty is rarely discussed in conjunction with "security of person." Safety is not such an important concept in contemporary political theory,[3] and in a moment when many intrusive acts are

[1] Disabled people are frequently subject to physical violence. In the United States, 1.3 million persons with disabilities experienced violent victimizations in 2013. This was more than twice the rate of violent victimization for persons with disabilities (36 per 1,000), controlling for age. Twenty-four percent of those believed that they had been victimized because of their disability (US Bureau of Justice Statistics 2015). Globally, even working with relatively uneven data, scholars have noted a high prevalence of violence against both children and adults with disabilities (Hughes et al. 2012; Jones et al. 2012).

[2] "The aim of all political association is the preservation of the natural and imprescriptible rights of man. These rights are liberty, property, security, and resistance to oppression." Article 2. *Declaration of the Rights of Man and Citizen*, 1789. Further, Article 16 of the Convention on the Rights of Persons with Disabilities explicitly addresses "Freedom from exploitation, violence and abuse" by requiring State Parties to "take all appropriate legislative, administrative, social, educational and other measures to protect persons with disabilities, both within and outside the home, from all forms of exploitation, violence and abuse, including their gender-based aspects."

[3] Although "fear" is frequently discussed now, compare (Robin 2004).

carried out in the name of protection (e.g., by the US government to protect the American people), "security of person" hardly seems to be the right concept on which to think productively in a progressive political direction. In this chapter, I suggest that violence against disabled people requires us to rethink the meaning of violence and security from the standpoint of democratic citizens in pluralistic societies.

Many recent essays about the relationship of disabilities to political theory have begun from a concept or theoretical argument that is important to contemporary thought to show how that concept or argument is limited by not considering it from the standpoint of disability.[4] The approach of this chapter is a bit different. Violence against disabled people is real. Indeed, violence itself (whether it is organized by states, is part of civil conflict, or is a result of "criminal" activity or the vicissitudes of life) often creates disability among its victims. Within much of contemporary liberal political theory, such violence does not seem very theoretically interesting; it is part of the misfortunes of the world that exist beyond the boundaries of political theory's orderly constructions of democracy and citizenship.[5] Violence is wrong. The story ends. On another level, however, violence raises many serious political questions, such as why are some people more subject to violence than others? The confounding questions about violence and disability, however, help us to see more clearly the needs for a pluralistic democracy in which all people are comfortable.

Violence and Models of Disability

Disability studies have gone through several transformations in the past generation.[6] Beginning from a "medical model" of disability, which viewed disability as an unfortunate condition for individuals, the social movement for disabled people's rights took a new approach, arguing that what made people disabled was not their bodies or brains but a social order that was incapable of accommodating them. This social model of

[4] Among especially helpful analyses, see Hirschmann (2012) Arneil (2009) and Clifford (2012).

[5] Perhaps, in this regard, we still follow John Stuart Mill (1998) in assuming that political theory is an activity for those societies that have passed their "nonage" and eschew the use of violence as a means for settling disputes. Obviously, postcolonial theorists have focused much more on the violence intrinsic to colonialism; see, for example, Fanon (1963). For work on the intersection of postcolonial and disability theories, see, inter alia, Parekh (2007), Barker and Murray (2010) and Meekosha (2011). Young (1990) is a notable exception to this neglect of violence, and is discussed later in this chapter.

[6] For a more extensive discussion, see, inter alia, Arneil (2009). One additional point: while 80 percent of disabled people live outside the high-income nations, this chapter draws, given my limits as a scholar, primarily on scholarship from this portion of the world.

disability provided an important starting point for the disability rights movement. Proponents argued that institutions that hid away disabled people made them less visible and more vulnerable to abuse. Rejecting a model that presumed that professionals and medical personnel knew best about their lives and treatment, they proclaimed, through the slogan "Nothing about us without us" (Charlton 2000), that any care that was not responsive to the way in which disabled people themselves understood their needs, rights and desires was harmful. The social model afforded a political movement to grow.

Nevertheless, by the mid-2000s, it became clear that the rigid insistence that to place all of the problems encountered by disabled people at the doorstep of social institutions would no longer suffice (Shakespeare 2006; Schur et al. 2013). Such approaches had to downplay the realities of bodily pain and suffering and to adhere to a rigid distinction between "impairment" and "social" harm. Indeed, even authors who claim to adhere to a social model sometimes make arguments that are not, strictly speaking, operating entirely within this perspective. Thiara et al. (2012), for example insist that they are applying the "social model," but they also raise concerns that do not fit within this paradigm. At one point they describe the problem of a spouse who decides to leave an abusive relationship as the "bring me my scooter so I can leave you" problem (Thiara et al. 2012: 28). While social structures may exacerbate it, the problem of "exit" here is genuinely made more serious by mobility impairment. In addition to the medical and social models, a "family of social-contextual approaches to disability" (Shakespeare 2006: 9) has emerged that emphasize postmodern, relational and universalistic claims about disability (compare Corker and Shakespeare 2002). Schur et al. (2013) suggest that among these possible new approaches are to think of (1) "universalist" alternatives stress that disabled people are a group deserving of human rights and rights protections, (2) another universalist approach that emphasizes that all humans are potentially disabled (and will surely become so if they live long enough), (3) the "human variation" approach (disabled people are just further variations on the spectrum of human normality) and (4) various "relational" and postmodern approaches.

This reassessment of approaches to disability is welcome, especially for considering such matters as violence. Many writings within the social model of disability ignored or downplayed this question. Until recently, however, disability scholars have not dwelled upon violence.[7] In a review

[7] Erevelles (2011) has written eloquently about the ways in which war itself *produces* disabled bodies and implicates the state in a number of ways in the creation of disability.

essay called "Disability Worlds," that argues for greater attention to disability issues in anthropology, Ginsberg and Rapp (2013) never mention violence in their survey of the discipline. Susan Wendell's important book *The Rejected Body* (Wendell 1996) mentions that much disability is produced by violence and refers to the historic violence against women by men as a part of the frame of feminist theory. McRuer's *Crip Theory* makes passing reference to gang violence and violence endemic in gay men's lives, but does not treat the subject systematically (McRuer 2006). Amartya Sen's *Identity and Violence* discusses identity as a cause of violence, but ignores the question of violence against disabled people (Sen 2006). Kim Q. Hall's (2011) recent edited volume does include an essay by Nirmala Erevelles about state violence (Erevelles 2011), but not about more common forms of violence. Rosemarie Garland Thomson's immensely important book, *Extraordinary Bodies* introduced the concept of the "normate," but did not consider the role of violence in constructing it, although perhaps the normate is itself a kind of violence (Thomson 1997). This gap makes sense insofar as scholars of disability have moved away from approaches that see persons with disabilities as victims. But the real limits to the philosophical starting points of the medical model (for which violence is a kind of risk) should not obscure the reality of the serious violence against disabled people.

Violence against disabled people is a real concern. That disabled people are more likely to be subject to violence than others is well established through numerous studies and through meta-analyses of these studies (Fuller-Thomson and Brennenstuhl 2012; Jones et al. 2012). Arneil's (2009) essay in *Political Theory* discussed a case that is much too familiar in this literature, the killing of a disabled woman by her father. Horrific instances of violence against disabled people are ubiquitous and have long constituted an area for study (Sobsey et al. 1995).[8] Yet it is complicated to study violence against disabled people, given both the variety of people who fall within the category of disabled people, the various ways we might define violence,[9] and the variety of settings in which such violence is encountered. There are at least three main sites of violence against people with disabilities: in the public at large, in institutions and in intimate settings.[10]

[8] "International research suggests that patients within mental health services are up to eleven times more likely to have experienced recent violence than the general population" (Khalifeh and Dean 2010: 536).

[9] For the most part, I limit violence in this chapter to the use of physical violence, not including various types of "structural" or economic violence. For a conceptual justification for this more limited usage, see Bufacchi (2007).

[10] For a description of the ways in which intimate violence, institutional violence and at-large violence are all problematic, see, inter alia, Sherry (2010), Thiara et al. (2012) and Roulstone and Mason-Bish (2013).

One important effort to deal with violence has been through hate crimes legislation. Violence against disabled people is included as a hate crime in the US in 32 states and since 2009 in federal hate crime legislation as well. In the UK, violence against disabled people was legally defined as a hate crime in 2003. The everyday interactions of social life in complex societies provide the opportunity for slightly more intimate forms of hate crimes, which the British have named "mate crimes."[11] Here, an "able" person befriends a person with a disability in order to take advantage of that person, often involving them in criminal enterprises, and sometimes then inflicting violence upon them. In one famous case in the UK, the murder of Brent Martin, one of the murderers later expressed his contempt for his victim: "I am not going down for a muppet" (Thomas 2013: 140). As Mark Sherry points out, however, Martin's murder was not considered a hate crime and on appeal the three murderers' sentences were reduced (Sherry 2010: 2–3).

Many people with physical and mental disabilities require intimate "hands-on" care from others, and other disabled people are in intimate relationships with others. While the UK law that permits individuals to hire their own personal caregivers has contributed to some decline in the extent of abuse in such cases, nonetheless a very large percentage of cases of abuse still occur (Hague et al. 2011).

From the standpoint of the three different "models" of disability, violence against disabled people calls for different kinds of responses. To the medical model, disability can be described as a "risk factor" for being a victim of crime, and medical teams have worked out with some precision additional "risk factors" that make it more likely that a particular disabled person will become a victim of crime. Not surprisingly, many non-medical but social conditions figure in these risk factors (Hughes et al. 2012; Jones et al. 2012).

From the standpoint of the social model, violent crimes against disabled people lie on a continuum of violations and impositions that are part of their everyday existence. Such prodding and touching becomes normalized so that it becomes difficult for a person with a disability to draw a line and say that some forms of interaction are abusive; here an informant remarks:

> I also think that, like other disabled people, I lacked a sense of my own body belonging to me, and being private, of not having to be touched if I didn't want it to be... I remember being paraded in front of doctors with very little on and feeling I was a thing for discussion rather than a person in my own right... This lack of a sense that your body belongs to you is an issue that non-disabled children do

[11] For an important reflection of the nature of such crimes, see Thomas (2013).

not have to face. And, again, I can't say that this makes us more of a target, but it does make us better victims as we are less likely to object or tell. – *May*. (French and Swain 2012: 49)

In more formal institutions, violence seems endemic and little is done to stop it. The *New York Times* had run an exposé of the abuse suffered by patients in state institutions to aid people with developmental disabilities or mental illnesses in 2011. On August 9, 2013, the *Times* followed up their story and discovered that not much had changed in the intervening years (Hakim 2013). Patients are still being abused and the offenders seem to act with impunity; only 23 percent of the workers recommended for termination lost their jobs. It looked as if something had happened, the state had passed "Jonathan's Law," legislation that "forced the state to start disclosing abuse reports to parents," and Governor Andrew Cuomo "has put much stock in a new state bureaucracy" the "Justice Center for the Protection of People With Special Needs." His appointee to lead this Justice Center, however, is a lobbyist for private disabled-care providers and had lobbied against Jonathan's Law. Hundreds of thousands of people are under state supervision in New York alone; the promising Justice Center has hired 40 more investigators to oversee all of these workers and to investigate these abusive workers. Governor Cuomo asserted, "We will work around the clock to safeguard the rights and protections of our most vulnerable citizens" (Hakim 2013: A14).

From such a perspective, violence against disabled people appears as a fact about how social institutions enable violence against disabled people through their disregard of those left in their care. Thus, in the example provided above about New York State's lackadaisical response to violence committed by state workers against disabled people, one sees the argument for de-institutionalization.

From the standpoint of relational or contextual models, however, such violence takes on another valence. Instead of treating the victim as the "problem,"[12] such approaches suggest that the perpetrators of such violence, as well as the victims, are worth closer examination. Indeed, if we think about violence against disabled people from a relational model – that is, that violence is not only about disabled people but also about those who perpetrate violence – then the approach opens up new sets of questions that need to be explored. From a relational model, if we wish to think about the relationships or conditions that create the opportunities for and conditions of violence, when we need to explore both the

[12] Recall W. E. B. DuBois' (1999) question at the beginning of *The Souls of Black Folk*: "How does it feel to be a problem?"

psychic and interpersonal qualities of violence as well as the larger social forms that are forms not only of exclusion but also of domination.

If one takes these stubborn "facts" about violence against disabled people as the starting point for an investigation about the place of disabilities in political theory, then where do they lead? As Mark Sherry's recent subtitle asked, "Does Anyone Really Hate Disabled People?" His answer, through exhaustive reading of various internet sites, is that there is a great deal of license to speak of hatred towards disabled people (Sherry 2010).

Violence as Oppression and Vulnerability

Relational approaches to the problems of violence against disabled people take two different forms: one can conceive of the problem faced by disabled people as a problem of oppression or of vulnerability. Both of these perspectives are useful and both conceptions are also problematic in some ways. Let's consider each in turn.

In the first place, we might think of such violence as a kind of oppression. After cataloging the extent to which violence occurs against many oppressed groups Iris Young considered why violence is not just a moral wrong but a question of social injustice. She argued:

> What makes violence a face of oppression is less the particular acts themselves, though these are often utterly horrible, than the social context surrounding them, which makes them possible and even acceptable. What makes violence a phenomenon of social injustice… is its systemic character.
>
> Violence is systemic because it is directed at members of a group simply because they are members of that group… The oppression of violence consists not only in direct victimization, but in the daily knowledge shared by all members of oppressed groups that they are *liable* to violation, solely on account of their group identity. (Young 1990: 61–2)

Although Young did not include persons with disabilities among the examples of groups oppressed by violence in this passage, her analysis does apply to them as well. The circumstances of disabled people, who often have to put themselves into the hands of caregivers, make them even more "liable to violation." But although such violence is, by Young's account, systemic, it is not necessarily organized. She asserts: "Acts of violence or petty harassment are committed by particular individuals, often extremists, deviants, or the mentally unsound [sic]. How can they be said to involve the sorts of institutional issues I have said are properly the subject of justice?" (Young 1990: 61).

If Young's analysis is accurate, it would imply that violence is a kind of oppression. It only occurs if other forms of oppression have already marked a group off for exclusion, domination, and so forth. Her argument implies that if only other forms of discrimination ended against people with disabilities, then one could expect that *inclusion*, i.e., ending the exclusion of the group "people with disabilities" would suffice to end the violence against them.

The argument about oppression also grows out of an understanding of the problem faced by people with disabilities as being hated. As Barbara Faye Waxman put it:

> The contention that vulnerability is the primary explanation for disability-related violence is too superficial. Hatred is the primary cause, and vulnerability only provides an opportunity for offenders to express their hatred. Indeed, people who are respected and considered equal are not generally abused. (Waxman 1991: 191)

Waxman's argument that hatred and oppression are the cause of violence against disabled people fits well with the social model. What makes disabled people likely to experience violence are the pre-existing social institutions that make them targets of violence. The language of oppression also suggests that the solution to the problem of violence against disabled people results from legal action to end discrimination. Abuse will end when disabled people are respected and considered equal, invoking legal notions of equality to solve the problem. Thus, one important effort to deal with violence has been through hate crime legislation, as was discussed above.

Barbara Perry puts the point this way:

> [Hate crime] is a means of marking both the Self and the Other in such a way as to re-establish their 'proper' relative positions, as given and reproduced by broader ideologies and patterns of social and political inequality. (Perry 2001: 10, quoted in Chakraborti and Garland 2012)

Nevertheless, there is a problem with conceiving of the problem this violence as a form of oppression that returns us to the original meaning of oppression. To oppress derives from the verb "to press," "Something pressed is something caught between or among forces and barriers which are so related to each other that jointly they restrain, restrict or prevent the thing's motion or mobility" (Frye 1983). Thus, oppression implies an oppressor. Does it make sense to speak of a kind of oppressor here? Furthermore, framing violence against disabled people as a hate crime can also be disempowering, as Piggott explained, because it requires too much of them: "to ask disabled people to define themselves individually as objects of hatred in the eyes of the law demands a great deal in a culture which is often unthinkingly disabling" (Piggott 2011: 32).

On the other hand, the framework of vulnerability has become increasingly important in recent political theory, and in feminist theory in particular. This is partly a reaction to the work of Judith Butler. In her reaction to the American post-9/11 wars, Butler wrote a reflection on violence and vulnerability.[13] After reflecting that loss and vulnerability are connected, she observes that, "each of us is constituted politically in part by virtue of the social vulnerability of our bodies" (Butler 2006: 20). Understanding that, in general, violence begets further violence, Butler raised this question:

> But perhaps there is some other way to live such that one becomes neither affectively dead nor mimetically violent, a way out of the circle of violence altogether. This possibility has to do with demanding a world in which bodily vulnerability is protected. (Butler 2006: 42)

Butler was not discussing disabled people in this setting, and subsequent thought about vulnerability has shaped this point into a larger dilemma. As Jackie Leach Scully (2014) makes clear, discussions of vulnerability in recent years have bifurcated between those who think of vulnerability as somehow universal (for example, Butler 2006; Fineman 2008; Tronto 2013) and those who think of vulnerability as particular to some people, for example, in Robert Goodin's famous claims about "protecting the vulnerable" (Goodin 1985). Scully observes that some people are globally vulnerable (e.g., infants) while other especially vulnerable people are often vulnerable because of the situation in which they find themselves. Scully notes that undergraduates are not usually considered vulnerable but become vulnerable when they are asked to participate as research subjects for a grade. Scully thus concludes every understanding of vulnerability "pushes some features of vulnerability to the fore while necessarily obscuring others" (Scully 2014: 206).

For Scully, thinking of disabled people in terms of vulnerability creates a problem for them. She calls this problem "ascribed global vulnerability"; that is, "the tendency on the part of the nondisabled to extrapolate a genuine vulnerability in one area of a disabled person's life (e.g., physical weakness, economic precariousness) to a globally increased vulnerability stretching over the entirety of that person's life" (Scully 2014: 209, footnotes omitted). Thus, what might seem to be a way to universalize the experience of disability becomes another way in which disabled people become especially disempowered (Chakraborti and Garland 2012). What the analysis of violence against disabled people through the lens of

[13] I am indebted to Stacy Clifford for her thoughtful paper on violence and care read at the Western Political Science Association meeting in 2013 (Clifford 2013b). I follow Clifford in invoking Butler's work on this subject.

vulnerability suggests, then, is that vulnerability needs to be expressed in more universal and pluralistic terms. One needs both to recognize all people's potential vulnerabilities and to see particular vulnerabilities in their specificity.

Thus, while both oppression and vulnerability seem to capture some elements of the reasons why disabled people are subject to so much violence, neither analysis alone seems entirely adequate. The examination of the perpetrators of such violence needs to attract our attention next.

Violence and Vulnerability

Sara Ruddick wrote in *Maternal Thinking:* "Children are vulnerable creatures and as such elicit either aggression or care. Recalcitrance and anger tend to provoke aggression" (Ruddick 1995: 166). On its face, this claim seems plausible. Some children cruelly injure a small animal that they find, others respond by taking it home to care for it. Because her concern is to remark upon mothers' usual restraint from using violence, she adds that "Recalcitrance and anger tend to provoke aggression and children can be angrily recalcitrant" (Ruddick 1995: 166). Ruddick's short list of recalcitrance and anger can probably be expanded to include a number of other actions and emotions that provoke violence. Indeed, there may be a gendered dimension to the quickness with which men or women respond to vulnerability with aggression. In her original experimental work that led to *In a Different Voice*, Carol Gilligan administered the "thematic apperception test" and was surprised by the frequency (about 20 percent) with which young men responded to the photographs that portrayed intimacy with a tale of violence (Gilligan 1982: 39). James Gilligan posits that the most violent members of society often function within a moral code of shame and honor, in which status matters greatly. A threat to one's status provokes violence (Gilligan 2011).

But if this is a psychic response of aggression to vulnerability, it is also a trope that is well established in society more broadly. It is the kind of attitude that Cynthia Enloe might call "militarized," (Enloe 2002, 2007) and it also accords with the concerns of a society in which there is much "risk." Calculations of such vulnerability can easily be overexaggerated; indeed, "security studies" seems to posit the idea that vulnerability provokes aggression, one reason why defense must be impregnable.[14]

[14] I am indebted for this point to Carol Cohn, who expressed it orally at the panel on Ruddick's work at the 2012 International Studies Association Meeting. Private communication.

Neither Ruddick (nor anyone else) much discusses *why* vulnerability engenders a response of care. Clearly the vulnerable *need* care. Fisher and Tronto (1990) simply presumed that the question of motivation was beside the point, people are always already engaged in care relations. As more findings point out the caring begins very early in life (Bråten 2003; Mullin 2005), care seems also to be an almost "natural" response to need. But it does not seem very convincing to accept a naturalistic explanation: if that were so, then why would vulnerability sometimes elicit care and sometimes elicit aggression? Early feminist object relations theorists argued that the "reproduction of mothering" made women more "caring" (Chodorow 1978).

A few other feminist scholars might be helpful here. Butler does not think of care as so automatic; she believes that "A vulnerability must be perceived *and recognized* in order to come into play in an ethical encounter" (Butler 2006: 43) and recognizing the vulnerability inscribes it as a vulnerability. Diemut Bubeck (1995) has argued that given the nature of caring (including demands for attentiveness and receptiveness, and for the kind of work that it is), care workers are disproportionately vulnerable themselves. But this is not an explanation for why vulnerability elicits care. We are still left with this question: why does vulnerability elicit aggression? Why does vulnerability elicit care?

But even if we suppose that there is some answer to it, matters are still more complicated. After all, in many of the settings of care for persons with disabilities, the response is not one of care *or* aggression, but care *and* aggression. Caregivers are sometimes, perhaps often, the ones who abuse disabled people. The personnel in institutions, and intimate caregivers, both family members and others, sometimes treat their disabled charges violently. Does the ambivalence between care as "naturalized" and as a professional obligation prove to be too much? Do those who are lower-level employees in non-prestigious institutions lose sight of their caring nature? Do they have such kindness driven out of them? Or do they find themselves in such impossible situations that violence seems the only recourse?

This last set of observations require us to turn our focus away from disabled people as victims of violence and ask, instead, about the conditions under which some people commit violence against disabled people. We can then ask what can be done to reduce violence against disabled people.

Violence and the Ideology of Ability

Thus far, this chapter has surveyed a number of possible explanations for the elevated levels of violence against disabled people. For some, the medical model suggests risk assessment as the appropriate form of analysis. For others, the social model leads to an indictment of social institutions. The situation of disabled people can be seen as a form of oppression or an aggression-inviting vulnerability. But we need not resolve all of the issues about which of these approaches is best in order to consider more practical ways to think about this violence. Rather than thinking of the difference between rights-based responses to oppression or paternalistic care-based responses to vulnerability, it is more useful to think about perpetrators and victims alike as caught in other systematic forms of domination and to try to address them.

A good analogy to the approach considered next is the argument of Charles Mills about the nature of white supremacy (Mills 1997). Mills not only argues that blacks are oppressed, but that there is a system, white supremacy, that holds that oppression in place. Similarly, disability studies scholars make some parallel arguments that a larger form of domination is actually at work in the characterization of disabled people. Tobin Siebers describes "the ideology of ability," which "is at its simplest the preference for able-bodiedness." He continues: "Disability defines the invisible center around which our contradictory ideology about human ability revolves. For the ideology of ability makes us fear disability" (Siebers 2011: 8–9).

In a similar yet more chilling vein, Sharon L. Snyder and David T. Mitchell suggest that the force of the eugenics movement in the United States has not been fully appreciated.

> As eugenics came increasingly to delineate a concept of substandard labor capacities – then identified largely through classifications such as idiocy, feeblemindedness, or subnormalcy – it started to give the category of disability a coherence... Eugenics, as an influential hegemonic formulation, increasingly struck us as not "over." (Snyder and Mitchell 2006: x)

The end result was the creation of "cultural locations of disability," where, "[e]ven in the face of benign rhetoric about disabled people's best interests, these locations of disability have resulted in treatment, both in the medical and cultural sense, that has proven detrimental to their meaningful participation in the invention of culture itself" (Snyder and Mitchell 2006: 3). As they trace the horror of eugenics through Western cultures and its close connection with racist ideologies of the nineteenth and twentieth centuries, it is difficult to dispute their findings. They end by suggesting that we are now experiencing "a new form of cultural onslaught galvanized by new media environments... all collude together in constituting a bereft subject as disabled – as properly the subject for eugenic care, control, rehabilitation, evaluation, roundup, exclusion, and social erasure" (Snyder and Mitchell 2006: x).

Some political theorists reject the broadening of violence to cover systematic forms of oppression; they argue that such accounts of structural violence make it difficult to discuss the conditions under which violence becomes an injustice (Bufacchi 2007). But if violence is ever domination, then surely we should describe a system for the creating of "bereft subjects as disabled" as such a systemic deployment of violence?

We come back then to a point made earlier, but that now gains greater salience. The universalism that might be most relevant here is not the same as the universal subject of human rights, which we now know includes persons with disabilities. Instead, what might make us universal is the way in which "the ideology of ability" has the capacity to make almost all of us equally unable to function in this world. Consider the starting assumption of Robert McRuer:

> Throughout *Crip Theory*, I take neoliberal capitalism to be the dominant economic and cultural system in which, and also against which, embodied and sexual identities have been imagined and composed over the past quarter century… Above all, through the appropriation and containment of the unrestricted flow of ideas, freedoms, and energies unleashed by the new social movements, neoliberalism favors and implements the unrestricted flow of corporate capital. (McRuer 2006: 2–3)

On the other hand, those who are unable to keep up with the flows of these new energies are likely to be left bereft. And as bereft subjects, we may then ourselves be seen as "disabled" and subject to the new versions of eugenics to come. "I'm not going down for a muppet" are the words of a bereft subject.

Or, on the other hand, we may be able to stop hating, fearing, avoiding, misrecognizing, using violence against disabled people, and see the promise that the challenge disability poses to the ideology of ability. In a defense of a new kind of "identity politics," Siebers argues that the key quality of disability is that

> Disability creates theories of embodiment more complex than the ideology of ability allows, and these many embodiments are each crucial to the understanding of humanity and its variations, whether physical, mental, social, or historical. (Siebers 2011: 9)

In *Justice and the Politics of Difference*, Iris Young had already discussed the non-rational ways in which the psychology of hatred of "ugly bodies" could be transformed into violence by relying upon Kristeva's account of the "abject." She wrote: "The abject provokes fear and loathing because it exposes the border between self and other as constituted and fragile, and threatens to dissolve the subject by dissolving the border" (Young 1990: 144). This incapacity to deal with ambiguity (in Kristeva's term) underpins the aggressive response to vulnerability that we discussed before. What is important about this psychological account, however, is that it breaks us out of the framing of some as "privileged" and others as oppressed. Those who are not vulnerable to attack because of their physical frailty are likely not to feel privileged in society in many other ways. Asking them to think of themselves as powerful oppressors will not succeed, whether appealing to them to cease being violent or to them to care for others.

In noting the existence of an ideology of ability, the challenge of understanding violence against disabled people takes us full circle. It may have to do with the starting point of focusing on safety. Those who are not "able" are likely to be bypassed for advantages in an unjust society (Dorling 2011).

Tom Shakespeare, longtime scholar of disabilities who is now at the World Health Organization (WHO), has remarked that violence is a "preventable disease" (quoted in Quarmby 2011). Faced with describing how to prevent violence, WHO listed, among other criteria, these: "developing safe, stable and nurturing relationships between children and their parents and caregivers; developing life skills in children and adolescents; reducing the availability and harmful use of alcohol, promoting gender equality to prevent violence against women, and changing cultural and social norms that support violence" (Mikton et al. 2014: 3222). But these steps require an enormous political will to end a whole series of profound cultural, psychological and political changes. How can they happen?

The key to solving the problem of violence against disabled people, if the problem is oppression, is to be more inclusive. The key to solving the problem of violence against disabled people, if the problem is vulnerability, is to be more pluralistic. These two answers are not mutually exclusive ways to pursue a solution, but must be undertaken together. The more precarious the social order becomes, the more difficult it is to act with openness and generosity towards those excluded or even to think about others at all. In the end, then, only in an inclusive and pluralistic democratic order that provides for the "liberty and security of the person" for all can this problem be addressed.

11 Rethinking "Cure" and "Accommodation"

Nancy J. Hirschmann and Rogers M. Smith

The tensions between responding to disability by searching for "cures," versus providing "accommodation" for persons' differing abilities and situations, reflect central debates in disability studies, with most disability scholars and activists favoring accommodation approaches (Oliver and Barnes 2012; Shillmaier 2007).[1] These tensions reflect the struggles within and between various disability groups and other political actors over where to spend resource dollars. Do we accept impaired conditions as they are and try to shape the material world in ways that better respond to the needs posed by bodily difference, or do we seek to modify impairment, or even undo it altogether?

In addition to competition for resources, tensions also come, perhaps more fundamentally, from attitudes toward persons with disabilities, as well as differing experiences of disability, by disabled persons, by their family members, and by unrelated persons who are not disabled. One example is the controversy over an "Autism Speaks" video portraying autism as a horrible condition that unilaterally ruins lives – prompting a

[1] We recognize the changing preferences over time for "disabled persons" versus "persons with disabilities," and we are aware of the advantages and disadvantages of both (See Oliver and Barnes 2012 for the argument in favor of "disabled persons"; see Epp 2001 for the "person first" argument for "persons with disabilities"; see Linton 2006: 161–5 for changing uses of language over time). We will use both of these terms throughout, letting syntax, sentence structure and writing flow determine the term choice. We also are aware that, in the social model view, "disability" is a term that should refer exclusively to the disadvantages and obstacles that social attitudes, the built environment, and other contextual factors create for persons with impairments, but we use "disability" and "disabled" in a more inclusive sense to acknowledge that there are some physical impairments that create disabilities for the affected person regardless of the context. We agree with Michael Shillmaier that "disability can be understood neither exclusively as an individual bodily impairment *nor* solely as a socially attributed disability" (2007: 195). For instance, there are some things that a person without any arms cannot do – although the number of things that he could do with some accommodation and support is much greater than often assumed by most able-bodied persons. Thus, we use the term "disability" in its larger sense that includes both the socially manufactured and the intrinsic disadvantages to which some impairments place people, given that we share a commitment to lessening those disadvantages as much as possible if not ending them altogether.

"parody" response (by a group called "Autism Speaks Speaks") suggesting that the Autism Speaks group is what is responsible for ruining lives by creating false hope and exaggerating the stigma of autism (Diament 2009; Wallis 2009; Willingham 2013).[2] We see these tensions as arising from real, legitimate, but often conflicting concerns. We agree with many disability advocates and scholars that in contemporary America, the dominant response to the tensions has been a one-sided focus on seeking "cures" when productive accommodations are more realistic and available. That is gradually changing, as disability scholarship is reaching a wider and wider audience. But in this chapter, we argue that the tendency to pose "accommodation" and "cure" as opposed alternatives, between which individuals, families, and societies must definitively choose, is a barrier to finding ways to give people the broadest possible opportunities and resources to live what they define as fulfilling lives.

As Eric Barnes and Helen McCabe (2012) suggest, autism has been one of the most contentious grounds in this controversy. Other prominent examples include the late movie actor Christopher Reeve's advocacy of a cure for the spinal cord injury he experienced in a horse-riding accident, leaving him quadriplegic; Michael J. Fox's advocacy for a cure for Parkinson's disease; and the movement for cochlear implants. Some of these may seem less controversial than others to a non-disabled reader – the cochlear implant controversy, for instance, is sometimes viewed by hearing people as not a controversy at all, because they dismiss the passionate defense of deaf culture as being "radical" or "fringe." But despite advances in disability awareness brought about by the ADA, divides persist between people who perceive and experience disability as tragedy, loss, and suffering and those who perceive and experience it as a valuable difference that enriches our social lives together.[3] Of course, many disabilities are plausibly seen as falling in complex ways somewhere between these two positions. Thinking about the relationship between cure and accommodation would benefit from similar complexity.

The cleavage lines running through this debate are multiple. The contrast often drawn between persons with disabilities versus persons with illnesses may seem the most obvious. More clearly than many conceptions of "disability," the very notion of "illness" contains within it the

[2] The dueling videos can no longer be found on YouTube, since Autism Speaks pulled theirs down and "privately apologized to a number of disability organizations" (Diament 2009). But see Wallis (2009) and Willingham (2013). We also wish to acknowledge that we approach this topic from the perspective of personal experience with disabilities for which we are not opposed to a cure: as will be mentioned in the text, one of us has a child with autism, the other has diabetes.

[3] As Thomson (1996, 2009) and others note, some even see disability as perversion or freakery.

desirability of a cure. Illness is often viewed as a state of disorder in the body, a thing gone wrong within the body itself. If disability is an illness – as it often tends to be viewed on what disability scholars call the "medical model" – then the most appropriate approach is to seek to cure it, or even prevent it through genetic screening and selective abortion (Drake 1999). By contrast, on what scholars term the "social model," disability is produced by the way the built environment is structured to favor certain bodies over others: disability is either wholly within the environment and/or it is a specific bodily difference that makes the world more challenging to navigate because that world is designed for a body other than the ones that some people have. Some disability scholars today believe that neither model alone tells the whole story of disability, and we agree with them (see, for example, Wolff 2009). But when talking about cures, it is difficult not to remember a long history of medicalization of disability prior to the entry of the social model (e.g., Burch and Joyner 2015), and thus positions can be hardened that otherwise would be more flexible. As Wolff (2009: 52) puts it, "a social policy requiring individuals to undergo physical change in order to function well encourages the idea that there is something wrong with such people, and that they need to be cured."

Moreover, disability scholars and activists have argued forcefully that "disability" should not be conceived as illness – a concept that more "naturally" lends itself to "cure." Although some illnesses can be disabling, and some disabilities can be the result of disease, as was generally the case with polio, many disabilities are caused by accidents, mutations, and other causes that clearly have no genesis in disease. Disabilities characterize bodies that, like all bodies, can do some things and not others, but they are often not at all "sick" bodies. This view is linked to the related view that disability should not be seen as an intrinsically negative condition but rather one that is made negative by a hostile society. Illness, in contrast, is overwhelmingly perceived as intrinsically negative. Few people wish future generations of children would get polio, for instance, even among people for whom polio caused physical impairments that they now value and appreciate, or at least are not concerned about changing. Parents in the anti-vaccine movement do not want their children to contract the diseases the vaccines are supposed to prevent; they instead believe that the vaccines themselves will produce other medical problems (Kirkland 2012). Most people who have MS wish it would be cured and do not look forward to increasing mobility impairment. Very few people with diabetes, a group that includes one of this paper's co-authors, are glad that they have the disease – even if they are adjusted to it, have developed networks of friends they would otherwise not have had, receive adequate accommodation at work with breaks to check blood sugars, take medication and eat snacks, have developed healthy eating and exercise habits they would likely not have otherwise had, and through these measures are in excellent health.[4]

By contrast, many wheelchair users do not wish they could walk; they only wish for a more accessible society (Linton 2006). Many deaf people not only do not wish to be hearing, they want to have deaf children and to live in deaf communities where deaf culture is shared and celebrated. They do not consider deafness a disability at all. And even many who do view themselves as disabled see a value in their condition. As Harriet McBride Johnson (2006) argues, the insights her disability has given her into the human condition, not to mention the ways she has developed as a person shaped by her disability, make her disability not something to be regretted or mourned, much less something she wishes had never existed, but rather something to value and appreciate.

To be sure, the relationship between illness and disability is more complicated than a simply negative/positive valence, as scholars such as Susan Wendell have argued (2001). In the first place, the three illnesses we have mentioned (polio, diabetes, and MS) all involve physical impairments that are classified as disabilities under the Americans with Disabilities Act and other federal legislation, thus raising important questions about where one draws the line between disability and illness. These blurred edges are shared by others such as those with fibromyalgia and chronic fatigue syndrome, diseases whose defining features include the fact that they disable the affected person from engaging in a variety of common significant activities in which they were formerly able to partake. Thus, the question of what constitutes a "disability" must recognize that some conditions that are undeniably illnesses are included under the dominant legal definition.

Second, many such illnesses share with many disability conditions a high degree of improbability that a "cure" will occur in our lifetimes – thus making the stress on cure as potentially misleading as Autism Speaks Speaks suggests. As an example, the Juvenile Diabetes Research Foundation (JDRF), which was formed explicitly for purposes of finding a cure for diabetes, has been using promises of a cure in the near future in its promotional material for decades. Yet despite the flurry of excitement at the turn of the twenty-first century over stem cell therapies holding out the hope of replacing insulin-producing beta cells without the need

[4] This may be because the vast majority of diabetics are diagnosed well into childhood, or adulthood, after living a more conventional or "normal" life. See Bernstein (2009), who argues that being diagnosed within the first few years of life creates a different identity and relationship to the condition.

for immunosuppressive drugs, a cure still remains far out of reach and is highly unlikely to be attained in the lifetime of most readers of this volume.[5]

At the same time, the phenomenal technological progress resulting in insulin pumps, continuous glucose monitors, and indeed, pumps and monitors that communicate with one another, creating what some call an "artificial pancreas," all have made diabetes a highly manageable disease with which people can lead completely "normal" lives (if "normal" is a word appropriate to describe Olympic and professional athletes, marathon runners, actors, leading politicians, and other celebrities).[6] But because this progress in technological aids does not make diabetes disappear, it is not viewed as a cure. Instead, "accommodation," or developing a built environment to address the needs of diabetic bodies, has far outpaced progress toward a "cure." These circumstances suggest that if JDRF had gone in the "accommodation" direction from the beginning rather than cure, such technology might well be even further advanced today; although private companies today are producing such devices, the basic research that led to these developments had to be funded without JDRF support. And still today, many diabetics and parents of diabetic children, such as the founders of JDRF, want diabetes to "go away," not to accommodate it through cyborg technology. The JDRF website proclaims: "Together, we are creating a world without diabetes," not "a world where diabetes can be so easily managed that disabling symptoms and complications are a thing of the past."[7]

A second difficult division is between those with disabilities themselves and family members of persons with disabilities, particularly parents and

[5] Whether the restrictions on embryonic stem cell research instituted by President George W. Bush (in disagreement with his father and many leading conservative Republicans), causing many young US scientists to flee from this field of research altogether in the first decade of the twenty-first century, did irreparable damage to the field is impossible for us to assess; although many agree that the field was set back.

[6] The incidence of diabetes is so surprising among professional athletes in particular that the categorization of diabetes as a disability is readily called into question. See http://integrateddiabetes.com/athletes-with-type-1-diabetes. Yet it is a disease that tends to be associated with disabling conditions, such as blindness and amputation. As monitoring and insulin technologies improve, such disabilities will become less and less frequent, and are generally associated with adults whose Type II diabetes went undetected and untreated for many years.

[7] This point presents a different angle on the "social model" of disability. It is not always the case that society must be reconfigured to remove *barriers* from particular bodies. Often social aspects of the disease – ranging from improved medical access to better technology to improved financial access (successful maintenance of diabetes is generally expensive) – have a literal impact on the body, enabling it to maintain more capabilities. Providing a motorized wheelchair does not change the fact that my legs cannot support me; providing an insulin pump and continuous glucose monitor can prevent my feet from being amputated. See https://jdrf.org.

other caretakers on whom some disabled persons may depend (or are seen to depend). The controversy over cochlear implants is the most notable. The implants produce only an approximation of "normal" hearing. But hearing parents who want their children to "hear" more like they do have the devices surgically implanted in their children's skulls long before the children are able to choose for themselves, because the younger a child receives the implant, the easier it is for her to adapt to it. Deaf parents who want their children to be like them, live in their deaf communities and communicate by sign, are sometimes seen as selfish and ideological by other family members.[8]

Similarly, many parents of autistic children, including one of this paper's co-authors, want their children's autism to "go away" – a view for which others in the disability community criticize them, at times inaccurately likening this desire to the obviously abhorrent view that all disabled *people* (thereby logically including their autistic children) should "just go away" (Johnson 2003). The question of how central autism is to the identity of a person on the autistic disorder spectrum is one that different autistic individuals will answer differently – some regarding it as inessential, others as fundamental to who they are and want to be (e.g., Grandin 2006) – and ideally each such individual should be able to decide the issue for herself. But few believe that very early in life, autistic children – or any other children – can or should make their own decisions competently. In those years, parents must take responsibility for their child's development. Parents also often must make significant sacrifices – above and beyond the "normal" sacrifices all parents must make for their children – in order to care for children with disabilities. These responsibilities and these sacrifices give them a particular standing in the debate. Many parents do not believe that they can or should defer all the choices that will greatly affect the future lives and identities of their children and themselves to the judgments of advocacy groups or medical experts whose experiences and skills lead them to uphold certain policies as generally desirable, even obligatory.

That is not to say that parents should be regarded as sovereign over their children. The parents who authorized medical procedures to prevent puberty and limit physical growth in the infamous "Ashley X" case are widely criticized by disability scholars and activists (Kittay 2011). Still, the fact is that caring for a developmentally disabled child, not to mention children with a variety of other disabilities, can be overwhelming.

[8] Josh Aronson's 2000 documentary film *Sound and Fury* details precisely such a division in several families, although arguably is biased toward the hearing perspective as we discuss below.

Parents – particularly women, since mothers often bear responsibility for the majority of such care – may be prevented from pursuing careers and developing their lives as individuals, something the feminist movement has fought for long and hard, compounded by the degree to which community or public forms of support are available to them. As Allison Carey's work has shown, parents have undertaken difficult fights for rights for their disabled children, but also for rights for themselves *over* their children against the claims of state and private agencies. This is particularly significant given that parents are often the primary caretakers of disabled persons once they are out of school and are designated as adults. Our point again is that it is often difficult to separate out those two advocacies (Carey 2015).

We offer these examples not to take a stand either pro or con "cure" or "accommodation," for or against an "illness/disability" distinction, or favoring or opposing parental rights in any and all circumstances. Instead, we stress the need to acknowledge that both sides of these arguments *have* arguments with legitimate reasons that require us to pay attention.

What is a Cure?

These divisions, however, call out for a theoretical consideration of what "cure" means and entails, as well as attention to its historical and political development as a concept and a practice, in order to gain a better appreciation of its positive and negative potential. The dominant but least defensible understanding of cure in the modern history of disability seems to entail the notion of restoring a diseased or deformed body to its former and "true" state. Following Rosemarie Thomson's idea of the "normate" – the Platonic ideal of the strong healthy body in perfect physical shape, accompanied by the "normal" rational mind – the notion of a "cure" similarly seems to operate from a presupposition of an ideal individual that exists beneath a disability and only needs a "cure" to be revealed (Thomson 1997). If disability is a distortion of the individual's *telos*, its highest purpose and true essence, cure is what restores the *telos*, purpose and essence. Disability is seen on this view as a wholly negative distortion that cure can restore.

In the nineteenth and twentieth centuries, the language of "rehabilitation" to some degree supplanted or even replaced that of "cure," following the recognition that World War I had produced many disabilities (Stiker 2000; Linker 2011).[9] But as with cures, "the goal of rehabilitation

[9] Stiker in fact argued that rehabilitation discourse was a direct result of the large numbers of disabilities created by the First World War, an idea that Linker (2011) supports.

was to fix or improve the 'performance' of broken bodies and thus make them 'fit' once again to carry out their social roles and responsibilities" (Hughes 2002: 62–3). Probably not coincidentally, the rise of this view corresponded with the industrial capitalist shift to an economy of wage labor from which disabled bodies were widely excluded (Hughes 2002: 61). The "uniformity of labor" needed to operate in mechanized forms of production where machines determined the speed and specificity of each worker's task meant that many of the disabled were excluded by virtue of their bodily differences (Marks 1999: 80).[10] In such an economy there are powerful economic incentives to pursue "cures" or "rehabilitations" that make more people into productive workers. As Cathy Kudlick puts it, "'cure' meant erasing disability without calling definitions of normality into question" (Kudlick 2014).

The irony is that in some cases "cures" can prove disastrous, with gains that are outweighed by high costs. Most dramatically, some blind people whose sight has been restored have sometimes subsequently become depressed and in some cases even killed themselves (Lester 1971, 1972). Similarly, we now know that the intensive therapies directed at polio survivors, meant to build up muscular strength, actually damaged the muscles, hastening or heightening mobility impairments later in life (Marks 1999: 64). Yet even when the outcome is more positive, it is always mixed; as Karen Beauchamp-Pryor notes about the restoration of her vision, as much as she is "mesmerized by the stars and the moon," she is "shocked" by facial imperfections. It is not an unadulterated joy for her to be part of the sighted world, as many non-disabled people might imagine. Indeed, she had lenses implanted on her eyes that required her to wear glasses, so that "when I am unable to cope, I can take off my glasses and revert to a familiar security and safeness" (Beauchamp-Pryor 2011: 12).

The hostility and suspicion of "cure" among disability scholars and activists is understandable in light of these experiences and in the context of twentieth-century medical practice and eugenics, which overwhelmingly conveyed an attitude of "fixing" bodies that were regarded as "inferior," "perverted" and "distorted" (Borsay 2005). The idea of cure was a function of, or expression of, the shift of medicine into a "form of social control rather than a value-free technology for helping people," and higher status became attached to curing than to the provision of chronic care needs, as is the case today (Marks 1999: 63–4). Accordingly, "In the quest to cure and change disabled people, radical programmes of surgical intervention and therapy were exerted… often result[ing] in excruciating surgery and treatment" (Beauchamp-Pryor 2011: 6). Medical

[10] This was also one of Engels' (2009) main points, although from a different direction.

professionals regarded procedures that would today be likened to torture as "cutting edge" and visionary ways to treat disability. Many seemed to see the disabled body as not worth inhabiting, so any amount of suffering was worth being rid of the body's impairment. Often such treatments took a "millenarian" tone, to borrow from Michael Oliver, holding forth the idea of the "miracle cure," complete and uncompromisingly restorative, accomplished within a set frame of time in the near future (Oliver 1993: 21; see also Oliver 1996). As Oliver acerbically points out:

> If able-bodied children were taken from their local school, sent to a foreign country, forced to undertake physical exercise for all their waking hours to the neglect of their academic education and social development, we would regard it as unacceptable and the children concerned would rapidly come to the attention of the child protection mafia. But in the lives of disabled children (and adults too), anything goes as long as you call it therapeutic. (Oliver 1996: 107)

On his view, this millenarian search for "cure" involves, at least implicitly, a drastic devaluing of the lives of persons with impairments – which are assumed to be so awful that the individual would gladly put up with extreme regimens in order to be ride of them.

From the March of Dimes telethons to the aforementioned Autism Speaks commercial to the current cleft palate campaigns – regardless of whatever good these have done to raise money for research and treatment or provide information and resources – the message of the cure has indeed frequently been that life with these impairments is tragic, horrible, perhaps not worth living. In the move to develop the social model of disability, and to understand the ways in which certain traits *became* disabilities through an inaccessible built environment, prejudicial and discriminatory attitudes, and other hostile aspects – including these excruciating surgeries that often did more harm than good – it is, again, not just understandable but for the most part admirable that disability activists and scholars have resisted notions that the answers for all "disabilities" are "cures" (Wendell 1996: 83; Shakespeare 1992: 40–2).[11]

[11] Perhaps ironically, as the social model became more accepted and non-disabled people became more aware of socially constructed barriers facing disabled persons and viewed disability less and less in terms of "deviancy" (although many still regard the disabled as uncomfortably "Other"), disability scholars and activists were freed to talk more about the actual physical limitations of impairments, such as pain. Shakespeare (1992) points out the risk that the view of disability being exclusively a negative limitation will be reinscribed by such discussions, and so the number of disability scholars who have written about these issues remains relatively small. But rarely do even these scholars engage the concept of "curing." Part of the problem is that when disabled people say that want to be cured or rid of their impairments, such a desire is read by non-disabled persons to mean not just that the impairment is disagreeable, but that it is so disagreeable as to make the life of the person who has the impairment not worth living. As Wendell (1997) notes, this "places the self-respect of people with disabilities in conflict with any desire to be 'cured.'"

But this notion of cure that the social model critiques is a relatively recent understanding, associated with the rise of the medical model of disability. The word "cure" comes from the Latin *cura*, which referenced a kind of "care" and involved a broader notion of help. The first several definitions of "cure" in the Oxford English Dictionary mirror this notion, referring to ideas that entail easement of many sorts of discomfort, including "spiritual oversight." This definition is followed by more medical understandings of the term that involve a restoration or return to a former, better self, again suggesting the recentness of this particular locution of the term. Henri-Jacques Stiker's history of disability suggests, in fact, that many kinds of disability were viewed quite variably over the centuries, ranging from exposure of "deformed" infants in ancient societies and Plato's declaration in *The Laws* that "the insane should not appear in the city" but rather at home, to Cicero's identification of the positive effects of blindness and deafness, to the honoring of dwarves in ancient Egypt. Madness in medieval times was often viewed as a kind of special wisdom, whereas in the early modern period the mentally and physically disabled were often seen as struck by afflictions from God, which must be faithfully borne by those individuals and cared for by their families and communities with Christian charity, rather than "cured." As part of this way of thinking about disability, Stiker indicates, disabled people were also – indeed thereby – fairly well integrated within the "normal" community throughout seventeenth-century Europe (Stiker 2000: 167; see also Arneil 2009: 219).

Rushton's consideration of official court records similarly suggests that although some persons were put in jail and houses of correction in early modern England, significant percentages of cognitively disabled individuals lived in the custody of relatives, while others "were left in virtual independence… with no hint of custody or care by others" (Rushton 1988: 43). Additionally, the prevalence in this era of one-story buildings, and the absence of high-curbed sidewalks, motor vehicles with narrow doors, and other manifestations of industrial society, as well as the lack of stigma for those with "peg legs," eye-patches, and crutches, all may have meant that the medieval and early modern world was not as hard to navigate for the disabled as much of our world has become today. Consequently, many may have viewed disability differently than we do today. Rather than needing to be cured, many accepted disability as not especially abnormal, or as God's will, with a corresponding human duty of care, generally within the family and community (see Hirschmann 2013a).

Much of this changed in the eighteenth century where cognitive and physical disabilities came to be viewed as a disorder or form of illness that needed to be treated and, if possible, cured, which often required segregation of disabled persons from "normal" society. Foucault (1988) dates "the great confinement" of the insane, which often included individuals with only physical impairments, to the seventeenth and eighteenth centuries.[12] Not coincidentally, this is around the time that medicine started to intervene in disability, perhaps as a result of notions inspired by the Enlightenment that suggested the power of human action to change and intervene in matters of health:

> The intellectual revolution of the Renaissance and Enlightenment contributed to fundamental changes in the relationships between humans, society, and God. For the first time, people were deemed to be capable of intervening in what had been perceived to be the immutable natural order: a belief that society and human beings could be perfected. This revolution in thinking stimulated extensive efforts to develop treatment interventions for people with disabilities, including the deaf, blind, and people with mental disabilities, and it led to the ascendancy of a professional class of physicians, educators, and caretakers. The medicalization and professionalization of disability reinforced the development and proliferation of institutions and schools across Europe and subsequently in North America. (Albrecht et al. 2001: 29)

Although Stiker's history shows that disability always entailed the intermingling of the biological and the social – when disabilities were seen as punishments for or negative commentary on a society by the gods, for instance (2000: 39–40) – Foucault notes, in a further twist on the dichotomy between medical and social models, that the rise of medicine as a scientific field coincided with its rise as a social field. Enlightenment thought and the French Revolution in particular generated a rethinking of humans' relationship to disease, such that rather than merely accepting the fate God had decreed, man could intervene and shape health. Indeed, Foucault traces a vision in eighteenth-century France – never realized – in which medicine would do away with itself: "in a society that was free at last, in which inequalities were reduced, and in which concord reigned, the doctor would have no more than a temporary role: that of giving legislator and citizen advice as to the regulation of his heart and body. There would no longer be any need for academies and hospitals" (Foucault 1994: 33–4). Yet at the same time this different understanding of a social model produced the ideological and political visions that give rise to the problematic foundations of later versions of the medical model, namely the "healthy man" who becomes linked, through

[12] Porter (1990) maintains, however, that in England the mentally disabled were not institutionalized in great numbers until the late eighteenth and more likely nineteenth centuries.

the connections of "health, happiness, and virtue," to "the model man" (Foucault 1994: 34).

For in Foucault's view, the birth of the clinic sees, at the same time, an abstraction of illness from the patient; "the patient is only an external fact; the medical reading must take him into account only to place him in parentheses" (Foucault 1994: 8). Because of this view, Foucault quotes an eighteenth-century French doctor, "the success of the cure depends" not on the patient, but only "on an exact knowledge of the disease" (Foucault 1994: 8). This reflected a shift, according to Foucault's analysis, that objectified the patient even further than was already the case: "In the hospital, the patient is the *subject* of his disease, that is, he is a *case*; in the clinic, where one is dealing only with *examples*, the patient is the accident of his disease, the transitory object that it happens to have seized upon" (Foucault 1994: 59).

While on the one hand, then, this signals a break with the earlier focus on care for the afflicted who had to be accepted within "regular" society, Foucault also points out that the "care" dimensions of cure have reflected the "restorative" dimensions of religion and have always assumed, at least implicitly, the goal of restoring an ideal body, just as Foucault suggests that the job of the "curate" was to restore people's pure souls so they could realize an ideal perfection in the afterlife. The notion of cure on earth may seem to echo these ideals within a medical framework. Foucault indeed suggests that "pastoral power" is a dominant form of power in the modern era, part of the interaction of institutions such as church, state, and hospital that pursue the end of "the production of truth – the truth of the individual himself" (1983: 214). As Sullivan notes, the focus on curing disabilities has in Foucauldian terms placed disabled persons within the "grid" of biopower – "a network of disciplinary and regulatory practices… of various institutions – educational, industrial, military, medical, and psychiatric, the police, assorted apparatuses of the state" (Sullivan 2005: 28). This grid of biopower, in Foucault's view, deploys common standards of "normality," or what Foucault calls "normalization" and "normalizing judgment" which identifies "the abnormal" for which appropriate rehabilitation methods can be prescribed (Foucault 1977: 184; 2003). The circularity Foucault identifies – creating the norms from which difference constitutes "deviation" which must be "corrected" – is the essence of "disciplinary power. Foucault uses the term "carceral archipelago" (Foucault 1977: 297) to describe this phenomenon because through it the logic of the prison is extended to all other social institutions: as he famously notes, "Is it surprising that prisons resemble factories, schools, barracks, hospitals, which all resemble prisons?" (Foucault 1977: 228).

In the nineteenth and twentieth centuries, Foucault notes, criminal behavior was compared to illness, because similarly a "normalization technique" developed that "consist[ed] in singling out dangerous individuals and of taking responsibility for those that are accessible to penal sanction in order to cure them or reform them" (2003: 25). As Foucault then later notes in "The Subject and Power," the hospital – and medicine more broadly – is a key carceral practice that engages in a process of separating persons into mutually exclusive dualities of "the mad and the sane, the sick and the healthy, the criminals and the 'good boys'" (1983: 208). The application of cure becomes "a form of power which makes individuals into subjects" (Sullivan 2005: 30).[13] For as Foucault notes, the different meanings of the term intertwine, as the medical focus of study – the illness or disability – turns the person affected by it into a subject of observation, thereby subjecting the person, in the sense of "control and dependence." And this, in turn, helps produce the person's subjectivity, "his own identity by a conscience or self-knowledge" (Foucault 1983: 212).

Although not all scholars are convinced that the institutions comprising "biopower" operated in quite so unified a fashion as Foucault suggests, or that all conceptions of cure were akin to carceral responses to criminal conduct, there is little doubt that in the late-modern era ideas of "illness" and "criminality," "cure" and "rehabilitation," and the institutions of hospitals and prisons have often been closely intertwined. The notion of "cure" is further complicated by the fact that the idea has also often been commingled with disturbing notions of prevention or "elimination." For instance, work on Werdnig-Hoffman disease consists in identifying the gene that causes it, leading to the abortion of fetuses displaying that gene, rather than to an actual cure of the disease in a person who is born with it (Basen 1992). The primary focus on Down's syndrome, similarly, does not entail *in utero* therapies but rather *in utero* testing to enable parents to decide whether to abort the pregnancy. We do not enter into the abortion debate here except to note the fraught moral dilemma between insuring that women having absolute rights to bodily integrity – including the right to abort for reasons that others view as morally unacceptable – and disabled persons having a right to not have their lives devalued and seen as intrinsically eliminable. The point, however, is that the notion of "curing" or preventing has often been tied to eugenics by disability scholars (Thomson 2015). This has taken a new valence with genetic engineering in which, as one cell biologist put it, "biological modification of people who do not yet exist [is conflated]

[13] Foucault discusses this theme throughout Foucault (1983: esp. 208–14).

with medical treatment of actual sick people" (Scolding 2013; see also Comfort 2015). The death in 1999 of Jesse Gelsinger, a teenager who died of organ failure in response to an attempt to cure his rare liver disorder by a genetically engineered virus, meant to correct a defective gene in his body, showed however that genetic engineering is very much still tied to attempts to cure, as is often invoked in these arguments.

The complex importance of this linkage between curing and eugenics is shown by the fact that it is visible even in the thought of those who seek to resist it. Scott Woodcock, for instance, declares that we have "a *prima facie* obligation to maintain a diversity of moral agents and to therefore avoid seeking to eliminate human kinds" (2009: 252). Yet a few sentences after saying this he offhandedly notes: "the claim that it is never permissible to eliminate any human kind is a nonstarter. The successful eradication of Huntington's Disease would presumably be a good thing, though research aimed at doing so would consist in seeking to prevent a particular human kind from existing" (Woodcock 2009: 252). He nowhere in his article details what he sees as the relevant differences between Huntington's and Werdnig-Hoffman disease, which he thinks it wrong to eradicate via abortions. His distinction is particularly difficult to grasp because Huntington's tends to manifest in adulthood, whereas Werdnig-Hoffman disease "has a mortality rate greater than sixty percent by age two, and this mortality rate rises to nearly eighty percent by age five" (Woodcock 2009: 251). It is not clear why the fact that a small number of individuals with Werdnig-Hoffman do live into adulthood with productive lives makes the disease more worth preserving than Huntington's, where symptoms never manifest *until* adulthood.

Our point is not to insist on Woodcock's incoherence. It is to suggest that the desire to eliminate various disabling conditions and illnesses seems unavoidable for many advocating a cure perspective, and that the arguments on both sides of the "elimination" debate are often marred by imprecise reasoning and selective evidence.[14] Consider, for instance, that everyone agrees that cognitive damage resulting from lead poisoning is uniformly a bad thing, and that lead paint should be removed. But any critical engagement about what precisely enables us to make a unilaterally negative assessment of this kind of cognitive impairment, while at the same time respecting other sorts of cognitive impairments as valuable difference, seems to be missing. We all tend to make assumptions: we all

[14] We prefer "elimination" to "eugenics" because the latter is already morally charged in ways that settle judgment and forestall disagreement. We do not here take a position whether it would be better to eliminate from the possibility of existence persons with certain physical conditions. Although we do tend toward the side of biodiversity, we think that such arguments often distort, in both directions, the effects of suffering.

think cancer should be cured, and the reason is that it is associated with suffering and often with death. But given that other disabling conditions similarly result in suffering and early death, we think that more critical questioning is in order: what makes some "differences" worth more than others, such that the "less worthy" differences can be eliminated without controversy? We urge greater theoretical attention to these sorts of questions and distinctions.

Barnes and McCabe's consideration of the ethical status of curing autism illustrates some of these prejudices on the part of "cure" advocates and the failure to critically engage these deeper theoretical questions about *why* some differences are more valued than others. They argue against views favoring neurodiversity by insisting: "diversity itself adds nothing useful to the discussion" (Barnes and McCabe 2012: 264). They maintain that "any reason why the kind of diversity created by autism is good can be considered on its own," that is, through case-by-case basis consideration of the value of the particular "difference" offered by a particular autistic individual (2012: 264). But precisely because we cannot be certain about our judgments of the value of all different types of minds, there is a strong argument that neuro-diversity will prove valuable over time for reasons that we may overlook in case-by-case considerations. And indeed, specific differences that now appear valueless may in the future be appreciated.

Similarly, Barnes and McCabe seem to reject the argument that autism can help generate particular "talents and perspectives" by claiming: "a small proportion (less than 10 percent) of PWA possess special skills, such as arithmetic calculation, music skills, etcetera" (2012: 258). It is doubtful, however, that the potential of any persons, abled or disabled, to make worthwhile contributions can be gauged accurately simply by summing their "special" technical skills. They also reject the argument that persons with autism may generate a valuable distinctive "culture" by saying: "since the hardships associated with autism are quite evident, the burden of proof falls on those shunning a cure to show that the value of autistic culture itself (not contributions of individual PWA...) outweighs the value of curing autism" (Barnes and McCabe 2012: 263).

In contrast to Lauren Young (2012), who maintains that autobiographies of those with autism destabilize preconceptions of autism in very positive ways, Barnes and McCabe do not consider the various articles, books, and memoirs that make such a case. Indeed they seem to dismiss the possibility outright: "This strikes us as a difficult argument to make persuasively, and so the culture argument is unlikely to justify shunning a cure" (Barnes and McCabe 2012: 263). A parallel argument is offered by Jaarsma and Welin, who maintain that the "difference" argument is invalid when one advocates a "broad version of the neurodiversity claim, covering low-functioning as well as high-functioning autism" (2012: 20). Instead, they believe that only "a narrow conception of neurodiversity, referring exclusively to high functioning autists, is reasonable," thereby including a relatively small percentage of people with autism (2012: 20).

Many disability activists and scholars – not to mention political theorists – can see the bias that is built into such dismissive arguments: *a priori*, only a narrow range of differences is declared to be conceivably valuable, and such value is measured by particular technical abilities, such as mathematical skills. Autistic people are presumed not to be able to form a distinctive, viable community but rather constitute at best a collection of individuals with limited capacities. Their evaluations are generally rooted in an ethic that prizes capabilities to choose above all, arguing that shunning cures prevents affected individuals from developing capacities to choose their pursuits. These authors do not consider that in many cases the most important developmental choices will be made, and often must be made, by non-autistic parents for their autistic children (just as cochlear implants are selected by hearing parents for their deaf infants). Although especially in a child's early life, parental choices are unavoidable, it cannot be denied that whatever the parents decide, it is their choices, not the child's, that are shaping the affected child's identity and future. Hence the claim that "cures" uniquely provide capabilities for personal "choices" later in life is belied by the reality that whatever parents do inescapably precludes some options for their children in the future.

It is problematic "cure" views like these, expressive of unreflective presumptions and dismissive judgments, that have led some disability scholars to eschew the concept of cure altogether. Philosopher Eva Kittay argues that neurodiversity, including many forms of cognitive disability, presents the ultimate challenge to the putatively liberal ideal of the rational self that feminists and other critical theory scholars have long repudiated. The existence of neurodiversity thus provides us with a positive good in terms of understanding who we are as human beings and what an ethical system requires of us (Kittay 1999). She disparages the notion of "curing" in favor of a morality of "caring" that offers more promise to value more human lives. Thomson goes even further, comparing arguments for "curing" disability to Nazism and pointing out that the Nazis began by putting disabled persons, not Jews, in concentration camps that soon became death camps (Thomson 2010; Miller and Levine 2013).[15] Woodcock (2009) similarly suggests that the attempt to

[15] Miller and Levine also invoke images of genocide when they suggest that linking "curing" to eugenics is not unreasonable, for the stress on cure goes hand in hand with the denigration of those "uncured" who are left behind with even greater stigma.

cure certain conditions entails the limitation of those conditions from the gene pool, by preventing infants with such conditions from being born. The UN Convention on the Rights of Persons with Disabilities never once mentions the word "cure."

Many disability scholars will agree that it is unproductive to assimilate all notions and forms of "cure" to genetic testing and abortion. To take our own two experiences as an example, few if any parents of an autistic or diabetic child wishes their child had never been born. Most adore their children. But they also want their child, as she is with her talents and abilities, both active and latent, to be free of conditions that may prevent the latent abilities from blooming. Such parents do not believe that their child's particular disability is an essential, ineradicable feature of the child's identity, much less her defining feature. Some disability analysts may find this goal of reducing barriers to a child's development a problematic fantasy that can ignore or downgrade the talents that such children *already* display. But we think that such goals are defensible, indeed they may represent the only defensible position from which to begin a reconsideration of the concept of "cure." We recognize the thorny paradox that in curing certain conditions, such as bipolar disorder and autism, "it may not be possible to eliminate the relevant disability without eliminating the unique contributions of those who exhibit it" (Woodcock 2009: 269). But that will not always be the case.

Hence, as Tom Shakespeare (2004) argues, "while a sceptical assessment of medical hype is necessary for balance, total rejection of the concept of cure seems self-defeating." There is "no reason why disabled people can't support medical research, as well as campaigning for civil rights and barrier removal. We should prevent impairment, as well as preventing disability." Shakespeare rightly seeks to disaggregate disability identity, as well as the suffering caused by poorly designed and inaccessible social space, from the negative effects of some disabling conditions: "aiming to prevent or minimise impairment effects is not like trying to turn black people white, or gay people straight. It's not an attack on disability identity, it's a rational response to forms of embodiment that are often painful or limiting" (Shakespeare 2004).

Rethinking "Cure"

We agree with Shakespeare's position. Even so, the historical connections between "curing" and eugenics, as well as the reductive medicalization of disability when a reconfigured – or even minimally attentive – social environment would eliminate many such limits, means that taking such a position also requires us to think more deeply about what "cure" means and how it operates within a disability framework. Accordingly, we maintain that curing must not entail the notion of elimination, if that is understood as pursuing a world in which the disability in question is gone and has left no traces. Disease and disability occur within bodies attached to consciousness and personality, which are formed, shaped, and influenced by their experiences. Those experiences may or may not be the central defining features of people's lives, but they will always be part of who they are, and they can be sources of enduring insights and benefits. They cannot in any case be eliminated.

Consequently, a "cure" cannot be thought of in terms of a simple model of "taking a magic pill so that the condition will go away" (Hahn and Belt 2004: 455). Such hypotheticals are as ideologically biased as are studies that claim that most able-bodied people would rather be dead than disabled (Silvers 1995; Stone 1984). The notion that a condition such as autism or spinal injury or diabetes would "go away" is a backward-looking gesture; a longing for an unrecoverable past, a vision of how the present would appear differently in an alternate universe where the disability or illness never occurred. It suggests not just a cessation of the impairment or condition, but also a complete removal of it from our history. But if an autistic person, or a diabetic, or someone with cerebral palsy were *cured*, would he or she ever be "normal," if "normal" means never having experienced those conditions? Would memory of how their brains used to work, or of severe low blood sugar or other bodily experiences be obliterated? If not, would it really be possible to operate in the world as if those insights didn't matter? We think that it would not be possible.

Cures therefore should be conceived as more forward-looking. They involve a transformation to a new state of being that carries with it changes that result from *both* the condition and the cure. To be sure, cures are often not benign, and as we have noted, they can be traumatic. The "slash and burn" approach to cancer makes the treatment, in some cases, worse than the disease itself, even as it may make the difference between life and death (Frank 1991). By that we do not mean to suggest that staying alive is not a worthy goal for individuals to choose in agreeing to undergo such treatment, only that the prolonged agony of cancer treatment may well cause more suffering than the end stage of the disease – and of course such treatment may fail, thereby reducing or even depleting the quality of life that remains.

Cancer is undeniably an illness, and so it might seem to be different from disability, especially since it can be fatal (although increasingly less so, just as cancer treatments are often less horrific than in the past). But consider again diabetes, categorized as a disability under the Americans with Disabilities Act; some claim it *can* be "cured" through pancreas transplants, as opposed to accommodated via insulin pumps and "closed loop" systems. This procedure requires, however, a lifetime of anti-rejection drugs that make the individual vulnerable to a wide range of other infections, and other side-effects ranging from weight gain and (ironically) elevated blood sugar, to kidney toxicity, gastro-intestinal distress, depression and mood swings, hair loss, tremors, and headaches. The "cure" is certainly not benign – which is why such transplants are offered only to those who would die without them. Even when successful, and absent such grueling procedures and side-effects, the process of being cured has profound effects on the cured person that in many cases changes them forever.

So the way we talk about cures in disability studies needs to be separated from the desire that an impaired condition "go away." Physical conditions like diabetes, autism, cerebral palsy, and post-polio syndrome shape who we are, how we see and understand the world – a perspective that "curing" the disease is not likely to ever eliminate, nor should it. Rather, a "cure" must be conceived as a transformation to a new state of being that will carry within it elements that result from both the condition and the cure. One enters a new stage in one's relation to one's body, a body that contains memory of the disability condition. Cancer survivors who have cleared the five-year mark often acknowledge a fundamental change in their attitude toward life, relationships, the physical world around them, and to their bodies, even if the superficial details of their lives seem the same.

Recall the example of Karen Beauchamp-Pryor's chronicles of her experience of having her sight surgically restored. She found that her "cure" did not simply "restore" her to a status quo ante self, nor was her blindness made to "go away." Rather, she holds the memory of her experiences as a vision-impaired person in a society geared toward the fully sighted. She holds her understanding of "the shared experience of oppression," which leads her to continue to identify with vision-impaired persons, and indeed disabled persons more broadly defined (Beauchamp-Pryor 2011: 15). Harlan Hahn and Todd Belt (2004) found that the reluctance of many disabled persons to accept a "cure" for their condition was based on the perception that it would pose a threat to their positive constructions of themselves, constructions that had been built on the identity of being disabled. For many this loss of self would be far worse than any benefits a "cure" might provide. It is vital that "cures" come to be understood to mean adaptions in, but not repudiation of, valued features of persons' pre-"cure" identities.

Relatedly, in a small study of disabled persons, Nancy Weinberg found that when asked whether they would be willing to undergo a surgery that would "completely cure your disability (with no risk)," half of the subjects who had been disabled from birth or very early in life said no, because they "felt that they could reach satisfying goals without it," while half desired such surgery "because they felt their disability substantially interfered with their achieving desired goals." Weinberg concludes that the difference between these responses "had nothing to do with either their disabilities or with what each was able to achieve. What distinguished them was how they construed their situations – what they set as their goals and whether they considered themselves capable of reaching these goals" (Weinberg 1988: 45).

Political theorists familiar with theories of freedom, choice, and desire might immediately point out that the Stoic position – the idea that in order to be free in restrictive conditions, one only need reduce, constrict, or alter one's desires in order to be free – could help explain this difference: some people are better than others at rationalizing and accepting their limitations (Berlin 1971). This response, however, from the start dismisses the possibility of a meaningful life for persons with disabilities, which we reject. Other political theorists might note that the social construction of desire in different people – such as women versus men – suggests that disabled persons' desires may themselves be structured by the limiting conditions imposed, whether biologically or socially, by their impairments or disabilities (Hirschmann 2003). Although we believe this argument has more traction, Weinberg contends that the differences between these two groups "is no different from one middle-class family that is discontent because they are unable to be upper class, while another middle-class family is delighted to be economically secure" (1988: 146). That is, we are all socially constructed, and how we evaluate constructions differently is a political and social matter. Moreover, insofar as the dissatisfactions expressed by the group that *would* opt for surgery are the product of a discriminatory and unjustly limiting environment that makes living with their physical differences more difficult, we can hardly blame these persons' bodies or anything intrinsic to the impairments, but must look to the social environment as the cause of limitations on their freedom and satisfaction. That is, what needs to be "cured" is the social and built environment as much as – if not more than – individual bodies. But to deny that some people want their bodily conditions changed, or impairments "fixed," is to put ideology and politics before goals of individual choice and freedom, for which most disability scholars and advocates have long fought.

This means that "cures" should often be seen as matters of degree, and we should recognize as well that they may represent ambivalent choices: not just because the "restoration" of the physical status quo ante is never complete, often leaving behind scars, residual effects, and further complications to deal with, but also because the identity of the "cured" self is conceptualized and experienced in ways it could not have been otherwise. A cure must be seen as something driven by care, going back to its etymological origins, which affects not just specific medical conditions but a person's whole existence and identity; and identities, which are notoriously difficult to change, generally can and should be transformed only partially. People cannot be expected to give up what they see as most valuable in who they are in order to become something others see as better. In this sense any kind of cure is about self-care.

The Politics of Curing

Beauchamp-Pryor contends: "the search for a miraculous cure is about choice" (2011: 11). We agree, but exactly the same can be said for the provision of accommodation. Even though "accommodation" may convey a more immediate sense of care for people as they are now, whereas "cure" suggests a future possibility that may never be attained, these are choices that we make as a society, particularly about how to allocate public funding. And it may be the centrality of money to both accommodation and cure that sometimes causes the relationship between the two to appear to be zero-sum, particularly in an era where public funding for basic scientific research is declining and the role of private investment in marketable products has gained prominence in guiding such research. These financial considerations may be particularly stressed in works of political theory and philosophy, because a dominant theme in such work is the justice of "resource allocation," which almost always refers to public resources (Wolff 2009). If one is rich enough, it seems to be implied, one can buy whatever accommodations one wants. Of course, this ignores that many accommodation resources – such as curb cuts, "talking" crosswalk signals, and elevators in public buildings – can only be provided through public policy choices. And such choices will often produce zero-sum thinking on the part of policymakers. But at their best, quests for cure and accommodation overlap; and so the pursuit of the most promising routes to achieve both should hold a high priority in public as well as private philanthropic budgeting. For despite the role of private industry in enhancing accommodation devices, many of these are expensive, requiring subsidy from health insurance (which thereby indirectly has financial effects on non-disabled persons via higher premiums) and frequently public or philanthropic funding. This fact sometimes lends the "cure versus accommodation" discussion a zero-sum flavor.

But a more critical questioning of the larger context allows us to recast the conversation to compare the (public) money spent on *both* approaches to that spent on other priorities for public spending, from public sports arenas to space exploration to military weaponry, not to mention taxation policies that indirectly make policy judgments about how people should spend the money they have acquired.[16] In this shift, we also shift the political framework. Questions of resource allocation often make many implicit and conservative assumptions about the ways resources are already allocated. For example, some part of the hundreds of billions of dollars the US spends on the military for wars that produce many impairments, funds that many believe can now safely be reduced, should be reallocated in ways that reduce the incidence of disability and allow more resources to flow *both* to medical research *and* to improving access. Such suggestions may seem "impractical," but they are not any more so than many other current uses of public spending.

In conclusion, we suggest that "curing" properly conceived does not entail elimination, repudiation, or erasure of disability or disability identity. If cure is understood to be not a "return" to some prior "normal" condition but rather a form of care that serves the best interests of the individual, different ways of thinking and theorizing cure and accommodation, not to mention disability, open up. Many forms of cure and accommodation can coexist. Both can and should be pursued, because the desire for a better future should never come at the sacrifice of a better present.

[16] Luxury taxes are a good example of this, but tax breaks and supports for certain kinds of industries also reflect social choices. See for instance Fineman (2005).

Bibliography

Aaltola, Elisa. 2012. *Animal Suffering: Philosophy and Culture*. Basingstoke, UK: Palgrave.

Abrams, Lindsay. 2012. "Is Anxiety Overdiagnosed?" *The Atlantic*, August 1. Available online at www.theatlantic.com/health/archive/2012/08/is-anxiety-overdiagnosed/260549.

Acampora, Ralph. 2004. "*Oikos* and *Domus*: On Constructive Co-Habitation with Other Creatures." *Philosophy & Geography* 7, no. 2: 219–35.

Ackerly, Brooke A. 2008. *Universal Human Rights in a World of Difference*. Cambridge: Cambridge University Press.

Ahmed, Sara. 2008. "Some Preliminary Remarks on the Founding Gestures of the 'New Materialism.'" *European Journal ofWomen's Studies* 15, no. 1: 23–39.

Albrecht, Gary L., Katherine D. Seelman, and Michael Bury. 2001. *Handbook of Disability Studies.* Thousand Oaks, CA: Sage Publications.

Alderson, Priscilla. 2008. *Young Children's Rights: Exploring Beliefs, Principles and Practice*, 2nd edition. London: Jessica Kingsley Publishers.

Alger, Janet and Steven Alger. 2005. "The Dynamics of Friendship Between Dogs and Cats In the Same Household." Paper presented at the Annual Meeting of the American Sociological Association, Philadelphia, PA, August 13–16.

Allison, Henry. 1990. *Kant's Theory of Freedom*. Cambridge: Cambridge University Press.

Andrews, Jonathan. 1996. "Identifying and Providing for the Mentally Disabled in Early Modern London" in *From Idiocy to Mental Deficiency: Historical Perspectives on People with Learning Disabilities*, edited by David Wright and Anne Digby, 65–92. London: Routledge.

1998. "Begging the Question of Idiocy: The Definition and Socio-Cultural Meaning of Idiocy in Early Modern Britain: Part 2." *History of Psychiatry* 9, no. 34: 179–200.

Andrews, Kristin. 2011. "Beyond Anthropomorphism: Attributing Psychological Properties to Animals" in *The Oxford Handbook of Animal Ethics*, edited by Tom L. Beauchamp and R.G. Frey, 469–94. Oxford: Oxford University Press.

Angell, Marcia. 2011. "The Epidemic of Mental Illness: Why?" *The New York Review of Books* 58, no. 11: 2–4.

Anthony, Lawrence. 2009. *The Elephant Whisperer: My Life with the Herd in the African Wild*. New York: Thomas Dunne Books.

APA. 2000. *Diagnostic and Statistical Manual of Mental Disorders: DSM-IV-TR*. Washington, DC: American Psychiatric Association.

2013. *Diagnostic and Statistical Manual of Mental Disorders (DSM-5)*, 5th edition. Arlington, VA: American Psychiatric Association.
Arendt, Hannah. 1951. *The Burden of Our Times*. New York: Schocken Books.
1959. *The Human Condition*. Chicago: University of Chicago Press.
1965. *On Revolution*. New York: Penguin.
1966. *The Origins of Totalitarianism*, new edition. New York: Harcourt, Brace & World, Inc.
1968a. *Between Past and Future: Eight Exercises in Political Thought*. New York: Penguin.
1968b. *Eichmann in Jerusalem: A Report on the Banality of Evil*. New York: Viking Press.
1970. *On Violence*. New York: Harcourt, Brace & World.
1973. *The Origins of Totalitarianism*, revised edn. New York: Harcourt Brace Jovanovich.
1977a. "The Crisis in Culture: Its Social and Its Political Significance" in *Between Past and Future: Eight Exercises In Political Thought*, 194–222. New York: Penguin.
1977b. "Truth and Politics" in *Between Past and Future: Eight Exercises in Political Thought*, 223–59. New York: Penguin.
1982. *Lectures on Kant's Political Philosophy*. Edited by Ronald Beiner. Chicago: University of Chicago Press.
1994. "What is Existential Philosophy?" in *Essays in Understanding: 1930–1954*, edited by Jerome Kohn, 163–87. New York: Harcourt Brace and Company.
1997. *Rahel Varnhagen: The Life of a Jewess*. Edited by Liliane Weissberg. Translated by Richard and Clara Winston. Baltimore: Johns Hopkins University Press.
1998. *The Human Condition*, 2nd edition. Chicago: The University of Chicago Press.
2007. *The Jewish Writings*. Edited by Jerome Kohn and Ron H. Feldman. New York: Schocken Books.
Arendt, Hannah and Karl Jaspers. 1992. *Hannah Arendt/Karl Jaspers Correspondence, 1926–1969*. Edited by Lotte Kohler and Hans Saner. Translated by Robert and Rita Kimbe. New York: Harcourt Brace Jovanovich.
Arneil, Barbara. 2009. "Disability, Self Image, and Modern Political Theory." *Political Theory* 37, no. 2: 218–42.
2010. "Animals and Interdependence: A Reply to Dolgert." *Political Theory* 38, no. 6: 866–9.
2011. "The Meanings of Disability/Illness in Political Theory." Paper presented at the Annual American Political Science Association Meeting, September 1–4.
Asch, Adrienne and Gail Geller. 1996. "Feminism, Bioethics, and Genetics" in *Feminism & Bioethics: Beyond Reproduction*, edited by Susan M. Wolf. New York: Oxford University Press.
August, Rick. 2009. *Paved With Good Intentions: The Failure of Passive Disability Policy in Canada*. Available online at www.caledoninst.org/Publications/PDF/763ENG.pdf.
Augustine. 1964. *On Free Choice of the Will*. Translated by Anna Benjamin and L. H. Hackstaff. New York: Bobbs-Merrill.

Avrich, Paul 2006. *The Modern School Movement: Anarchism and Education in the United States*. Oakland, CA: A. K. Press.

Ayers, John. 1981. "Locke Versus Aristotle on Natural Kinds." *The Journal of Philosophy* 78, no. 5: 247–72.

Bagenstos, Samuel. 2003. "The Americans with Disabilities Act as Welfare Reform." *William and Mary Law Review* 44, no. 3: 921–1027.

Bailey, Christiane. 2013. "Zoopolis: A Political Renewal of Animal Rights Theories." *Dialogue* 52, no. 4: 725–37.

Balcombe, Jonathan. 2009. "Animal Pleasure and Its Moral Significance." *Applied Animal Behaviour Science* 188, no. 3–4: 208–16.

Barbin, Herculine. 1980. *Herculine Barbin: Being the Recently Discovered Memoirs of a Nineteenth-Century French Hermaphrodite*. Intro. Michel Foucault. Translated by Richard McDougall. New York: Pantheon Books.

Barclay, Linda. 2010. "Disability, Respect and Justice." *Journal of Applied Philosophy* 27: 154–71.

Barker, Clare and Stuart Murray. 2010. "Disabling Postcolonialism: Global Disability Cultures and Democratic Criticism." *Journal of Literary & Cultural Disability Studies* 4, no. 3: 219–36.

Barnes, C. 1991. *Disabled People in Britain and Discrimination*. London: Hurst and Co.

2003. "Disability, the Organization of Work and the Need for Change" in *Transforming Disability Welfare Policies*, edited by Bernd Marin, Christopher Prinz, and Monika Queisser, 133–8. Surrey: Ashgate.

Barnes, R. Eric and Helen McCabe. 2012. "Should We Welcome a Cure for Autism? A Survey of the Arguments." *Medicine, Health Care and Philosophy* 15, no. 3: 255–69.

Basen, Gwynne. 1992. *On the Eighth Day: Perfecting Mother Nature*. Montreal: National Film Board of Canada.

Baumgold, Deborah. 2010. *Contract Theory in Historical Context: Essays on Grotius, Hobbes, and Locke*. Leiden: Brill Press.

Beauchamp-Pryor, Karen. 2011. "Impairment, Cure and Identity: 'Where Do I Fit In?'" *Disability & Society* 26, no. 1: 5–17.

Becker, Lawrence. 2005. "Reciprocity, Justice and Disability." *Ethics* 116, no. 1: 9–39.

Beitz, Charles. 2005. "Cosmopolitanism and Global Justice." *The Journal of Ethics* 9, no. 1–2: 11–27.

Benn, Stanley. 1988. *A Theory of Freedom*. New York: Cambridge University Press.

Bergson, Henri 1911. *Matter and Memory*. Translated by Nancy Margaret Paul and W. Scott Palmer. London: Allen and Unwin.

Berlin, Isaiah. 1971. "Two Concepts of Liberty" in *Four Essays on Liberty*, 118–72. New York: Oxford University Press.

1979. "From Hope and Fear Set Free" in *Concepts and Categories: Philosophical Essays*. New York: Viking Press.

Bernstein, Jessica. 2009. *The Diabetes World: The Development of Sense of Self and Identity in Adults with Early Onset, Type 1 Diabetes*. Saarbrücken: VDM Verlag.

Bérubé, Michael. 1996. *Life as We Know It: A Father, a Family, and an Exceptional Child*. New York: Pantheon Books.

2003. "Citizenship and Disability." *Dissent* 50, no. 2: 52–7.

2009. "Equality, Freedom, and/or Justice for All: A Response to Martha Nussbaum." *Metaphilosophy* 40, no. 3–4: 353–65.

Bigby, Christine. 2008. "Known Well By No-one: Trends in the Informal Social Networks of Middle-Aged and Older People with Intellectual Disability Five Years After Moving to the Community." *Journal of Intellectual and Developmental Disability* 33, no 2: 148–57.

Birke, Linda, Arnold Arluke, and Mike Michael. 2007. *The Sacrifice: How Scientific Experiments Transform Animals and People*. West Lafayette, IN: Purdue University Press.

Birmingham, Peg. 2006. *Hannah Arendt and Human Rights: The Predicament of Common Responsibility*. Indianapolis: Indiana University Press.

Block, Laurie, Jay Allison, and John Crowley. 1998. "Beyond Affliction." *The Disability History Project, The Overdue Revolution*. National Public Radio. Available online at www.npr.org/programs/disability/ba_shows.dir/revoluti .dir/prg_3_tr.html.

Böhme, Hartmut and Gernot Böhme. 1996. "The Battle of Reason with the Imagination" in *What is Enlightenment: Eighteenth-Century Answers and Twentieth-Century Questions*, edited by James Schmidt, 426–52. Berkeley, CA: University of California Press.

Boni-Saenz, Alexander. 2015. "Sexuality and Incapacity." *Ohio State Law Journal* 76: 1206–1216.

Bordo, Susan. 1993. *Unbearable Weight: Feminism, Western Culture and the Body*. Berkeley, CA: University of California Press.

Borren, Marieke. 2013. "'A Sense of the World': Hannah Arendt's Hermeneutic Phenomenology of Common Sense." *International Journal of Philosophical Studies* 21: 225–55.

Borsay, Anne. 2005. *Disability and Social Policy in Britain Since 1750*. Basingstoke: Palgrave Macmillan.

Botting, Eileen Hunt. 2016. *Wollstonecraft, Mill, and Women's Human Rights*. New Haven: Yale University Press.

Boucher, David and Paul Kelly. 1994. "The Social Contract and Its Critics: An Overview" in *The Social Contract From Hobbes to Rawls*, edited by David Boucher and Paul Kelly, 1–34. New York: Routledge.

Boucher, Joanne. 2005. "Male Power and Contract Theory: Hobbes and Locke in Carole Pateman's *The Sexual Contract*." *Canadian Journal of Political Science* 36, no. 1: 23–38.

Bourdillon, Michael, Ben White, and William Myers. 2009. "Re-assessing Minimum-Age Standards for Children's Work." *International Journal of Sociology and Social Policy* 29, no. 3: 106–17.

Bowen-Moore, Patricia. 1989. *Hannah Arendt's Philosophy of Natality*. New York: St. Martin's Press.

Bracken, P. and P. Thomas. 2010. "From Szasz to Foucault: On the Role of Critical Psychiatry." *Philosophy, Psychiatry, & Psychology* 17: 219–28.

Bracken, Pat, Philip Thomas, Sami Timimi, Eia Asen, Graham Behr, Carl Beuster, Seth Bhunnoo, Ivor Browne, Navjyoat Chhina, Duncan Double, Simon Downer, Chris Evans, Suman Fernando, Malcolm R. Garland, William Hopkins, Rhodri Huws, Bob Johnson, Brian Martindale, Hugh Middleton, Daniel Moldavsky, Joanna Moncrieff, Simon Mullins, Julia Nelki, Matteo Pizzo, James Rodger, Marcellino Smyth, Derek Summerfield,

Jeremy Wallace, and David Yeomans. 2012. "Psychiatry Beyond the Current Paradigm." *The British Journal of Psychiatry* 201: 430–4.

Bråten, Stein. 2003. "Participant Perception of Others' Acts: Virtual Otherness in Infants and Adults." *Culture & Psychology* 9, no. 3: 261–76.

Bray, Anne. 2003. *Effective Communication for Adults with an Intellectual Disability*. Wellington, New Zealand: National Advisory Committee on Health and Disability.

Brekhaus, Wayne H. 2003. *Peacocks, Chameleons, Centaurs: Gay Suburbia and the Grammar of Social Identity*. Chicago, IL: University of Chicago.

Brett, Annabel S. 2011. *Changes of State: Nature and the Limits of the City in Early Modern Law*. Princeton, NJ: Princeton University Press.

Brown, Brene. 2012. *Daring Greatly: How the Courage to Be Vulnerable Transforms the Way We Live, Love, Parent, and Lead*. New York: Gotham Books.

Brown, Jenny. 2012. *The Lucky Ones: My Passionate Fight for Farm Animals*. New York: Avery.

Brown, Lerita Coleman. 2013. "Stigma: an Enigma Demystified" in *The Disability Studies Reader*, edited by Lennard J. Davis, 147–60. New York: Routledge.

Brown, Rita Mae. 2009. *Animal Magnetism: My Life with Creatures Great and Small*. New York: Ballantine.

Bubeck, Diemut. 1995. *Care, Justice and Gender*. Oxford: Oxford University Press.

Buchanan, Allen. 1990. "Justice as Reciprocity versus Subject-Centered Justice." *Philosophy & Public Affairs* 19, no. 3: 227–52.

Budiansky, Stephen. 1999. *The Covenant of the Wild: Why Animals Chose Domestication*. New Haven, CT: Yale University Press.

Bufacchi, Vittorio. 2007. *Violence and Social Justice*. New York: Palgrave Press.

Burch, Susan and Hannah Joyner. 2007. *Unspeakable: The Story of Junius Wilson*. Chapel Hill, NC: University of North Carolina Press.

2015. "The Disremembered Past" in *Civil Disabilities: Theory, Membership, and Belonging*. Philadelphia: University of Pennsylvania Press.

Burns, Matthew K. 2010. "Response-to-Intervention Research: Is the Sum of the Parts as Great as the Whole?" *Perspectives* 36, no. 2: 13–17.

Busfield, Joan. 1989. "Sexism and Psychiatry." *Sociology* 23, no. 3: 343–65.

Butler, Judith. 1993. *Bodies that Matter: On the Discursive Limits of 'Sex'*. New York: Routledge.

2006. *Precarious Life: The Politics of Mourning and Violence*. New York: Verso.

Butler, Melissa. 1978. "Early Liberal Roots of Feminism: John Locke and the Attack on Patriarchy." *The American Political Science Review* 72, no. 1: 135–50.

Callahan, Michael, Cary Griffin, and Dave Hammis. 2011. "Twenty Years of Employment of Persons with Significant Disabilities: A Retrospective." *Journal of Vocational Rehabilitation* 35, no. 3: 163–72.

Callicott, J. Baird. 1992. "Animal Liberation and Environmental Ethics: Back Together Again" in *The Animal Rights/Environmental Ethics Debate*, edited by Eugene C. Hargrove, 249–62. Albany: SUNY Press.

Camp, Joe. 2008. *The Soul of a Horse: Life Lessons From the Herd*. New York: Three Rivers Press.

Campbell, Tom. 2011. "From Aphasia to Dyslexia, a Fragment of a Genealogy: An Analysis of the Formation of a 'Medical Diagnosis'." *Health Sociology Review* 20, no. 4: 450–61.

Carey, Allison. 2009. *On the Margins of Citizenship: Intellectual Disability and Civil Rights in Twentieth-Century America*. Philadelphia, PA: Temple University Press.

2015. "Citizenship and the Family: Parents of Children with Disabilities, the Pursuit of Rights, and Paternalism" in *Civil Disabilities: Citizenship, Membership and Belonging*, edited by Nancy J. Hirschmann and Beth Linker. Philadelphia: University of Pennsylvania Press.

Carlson, Licia. 2009. "Philosophers of Intellectual Disability: A Taxonomy." *Metaphilosophy* 40, no. 3–4: 552–66.

2010. *The Faces of Intellectual Disability: Philosophical Reflections*. Indianapolis, IN: Indiana University Press.

Carlson, Licia and Eva Feder Kittay. 2009. "Introduction: Rethinking Philosophical Presumptions in Light of Cognitive Disability." *Metaphilosophy* 40, no. 3–4: 307–30.

Chakraborti, Neil and Jon Garland. 2012. "Reconceptualizing Hate Crime Victimization Through the Lens of Vulnerability and 'Difference'." *Theoretical Criminology* 16, no. 4: 499–514.

Chambers, Clare. 2008. *Sex, Culture, and Justice: The Limits of Choice*. Pittsburg, PA: Penn State University Press.

Charlton, J. I. 2000. *Nothing About Us Without Us: Disability Oppression and Empowerment*. Berkeley, CA: University of California Press.

Chodorow, Nancy. 1978. *The Reproduction of Mothering: Psychoanalysis and the Sociology of Gender*. Berkeley, CA: University of California Press.

Clark, J. J. 2009. "The Slave Whisperer Rides the Frontier" in *Animals and Agency: An Interdisciplinary Exploration*, edited by Sarah E. McFarland and Ryan Hediger, 157–80. Leiden, Netherlands: Brill.

Clifford, Stacey. 2012. "Making Disability Public in Deliberative Democracy." *Contemporary Political Theory* 11, no. 2: 211–28.

2013a. "A Narrative Inquiry of Self Advocacy: Rethinking Empowerment from Liberal Sovereignty to Arendtian Spontaneity." *Disability Studies Quarterly* 33, no. 3: 12.

2013b. "When Care and Violence Converge: Dependency, Opacity and Disability in Judith Butler and Joan Tronto's Moral Ethics" in *Annual Conference of the Western Political Science Association*. Hollywood, CA.

Clifford, Stacy. 2014. "The Capacity Contract: Locke, Disability, and the Political Exclusion of 'Idiots'." *Politics, Groups, and Identities* 2, no. 1: 90–103.

Clutton-Brock, Juliet. 2012. *Animals as Domesticates: A World View Through History*. East Lansing, MI: Michigan State University Press.

Cohen, Gerald A. 1979. "Capitalism, Freedom, and the Proletariat" in *The Idea of Freedom: Essays in Honor of Isaiah Berlin*, edited by Alan Ryan. Oxford: Oxford University Press.

Comfort, Nathaniel. 2015. "Can We Cure Genetic Diseases Without Slipping Into Eugenics?" *The Nation*, July 16. Accessed online at www.thenation.com/article/can-we-cure-genetic-diseases-without-slipping-into-eugenics.

Connolly, William E. 2002. *Neuropolitics: Thinking, Culture, Speed*. Minneapolis, MN: University of Minnesota Press.

2008. *William E. Connolly: Democracy, Pluralism and Political Theory*. Edited by Samuel Chambers and Terrell Carver. New York: Routledge.

Coole, Diana. 1994. "Women, Gender and Contract: Feminist Interpretations" in *The Social Contract From Hobbes to Rawls*, edited by David Boucher and Paul Kelly, 193–212. New York: Routledge.

Corker, Mairian. 1999. "Differences, Conflations and Foundations: The Limits to 'Accurate' Theoretical Representations of Disabled People's Experience?" *Disability & Society* 14: 627–642.

Corker, Mairian and Tom Shakespeare, eds. 2002. *Disability/Postmodernity: Embodying Disability Theory*. New York: Continuum.

Cornell, Drucilla. 1998. *At the Heart of Freedom*. Princeton: Princeton University Press.

Crow, L. 1996. "Including All Our Lives" in *Encounters with Strangers: Feminism and Disability*, edited by J. Morris. London: Women's Press.

Daniels, Norman. 1987. "Justice and Health Care" in *Health Care Ethics*, edited by Donald Van DeVeer and Tom Regan. Philadelphia: Temple University Press.

1990. "Equality of What: Welfare, Resources, or Capabilities." *Philosophical and Phenomenological Research* 50: 273–96.

David-Ménard, Monique. 2000. "Kant's 'An Essay on the Maladies of the Mind' and *Observations on the Feeling of the Sublime*." Translated by Alison Ross. *Hypatia* 15, no. 4: 82–98.

Davidson, Michael. 2007. "Introduction" in "Disability and the Dialectic of Dependency." *Journal of Literary Disability* 1, no. 2: i–vi.

Davis, Lennard J. 1995. *Enforcing Normalcy: Disability, Deafness, and the Body*. London: Verso.

1997. "Constructing Normalcy: The Bell Curve, the Novel, and the Invention of the Disabled Body in the Nineteenth Century" in *The Disability Studies Reader*, edited by Lennard J. Davis, 9–28. New York: Routledge.

2002. *Bending Over Backwards: Disability Dismodernism and Other Difficult Positions*. New York: New York University Press.

Desai, Miraj U. 2014. "Psychology, the Psychological, and Critical Praxis: A Phenomenologist Reads Franz Fanon." *Theory & Psychology* 24: 58–75.

De Vos, Jan. 2013. "Interpassivity and the Political Invention of the Brain: Connolly's Neuropolitics versus Libet's Veto-right." *Theory & Event* 16, no. 2.

Diament, Michelle. 2009. "Autism Speaks Pulls Video as Critics Turn Up Heat." *Disability Scoop*, 2 October. Accessed online at www.disabilityscoop.com/2009/10/02/autism-speaks-apology/5624.

Dionne, Emilie. 2011. "Dangerous Discourses of Disability, Subjectivity, and Sexuality [Review]." *Hypatia* 26, no. 3: 658–62.

Disch, Lisa. 1994. *Hannah Arendt and the Limits of Philosophy*. Ithaca: Cornell University Press.

Dolgert, Stefan. 2010. "Species of Disability: Response to Arneil." *Political Theory* 38, no. 6: 859–64.

Donaldson, Sue and Will Kymlicka. 2011. *Zoopolis: A Political Theory of Animal Rights*. Oxford: Oxford University Press.

2012. "Do We Need a Political Theory of Animal Rights?" Paper presented at Minding Animals International conference, Utrecht, Netherlands, July 4–6.

2015. "Farmed Animal Sanctuaries: The Heart of the Movement?" *Politics and Animals* 1: 50–74.

Donovan, Josephine and Carol J. Adams, eds. 2007. *The Feminist Care Tradition in Animal Ethics*. New York: Columbia University Press.

Dorling, Daniel. 2011. *Injustice: Why Social Inequality Persists*. Bristol, UK: Policy Press.

Drake, R. F. 1999. *Understanding Disability Policies*. Basingstoke: Macmillan.

DuBois, W. E. B. 1999. *The Souls of Black Folk*. New York: W. W. Norton.

Dunayer, Joan. 2004. *Speciesism*. Derwood, MD: Ryce Publishing.

Duncan, Grant. 2000. "Mind–Body Dualism and the Biopsychosocial Model of Pain: What Did Descartes Really Say?" *Journal of Medicine and Philosophy* 25, no. 4: 485–513.

Duranti, Alessandro. 2010. "Husserl, Intersubjectivity and Anthropology." *Anthropological Theory* 10: 1–10.

Dworkin, Ronald. 2005. "Equality, Luck, Hierarchy." *Philosophy and Public Affairs* 31, no. 2: 190–8.

Edenberg, Elizabeth and Marilyn Friedman. 2013. "Debate: Unequal Consenters and Political Illegitimacy." *The Journal of Political Philosophy* 12, no. 3: 347–60.

Emens, Elizabeth F. 2012. "Disabling Attitudes: US Disability Law and the ADA Amendments Act." *The American Jounral of Comparative Law* 60: 205–34.

Engels, Frederick. 2009. *The Conditions of the Working Class in England*, edited by David McLellan. Oxford: Oxford University Press.

Enloe, Cynthia. 2002. "Demilitarization – Or More of the Same? Feminist Questions to Ask in the Postwar Moment" in *The Postwar Moment: Militaries, Masculinities and International Peacekeeping Bosnia and the Netherlands*, edited by C. Cockburn and D. Zarkov. London: Lawrence & Wishart.

2007. *Globalization and Militarism: Feminists Make the Link*. Lanham, MD: Rowman & Littlefield.

Epp, Timothy. 2001. "Disability: Discourse, Experience and Identity." *Disability Studies Quarterly*, 134–44.

Erevelles, Nirmala. 2011. "The Color of Violence: Reflecting on Gender, Race and Disability in Wartime" in *Feminist Disability Studies*, edited by K. Q. Hall. Bloomington: Indiana University Press.

Ettore, Elizabeth. 1998. "Re-shaping the Space Between Bodies and Culture: Embodying the Biomedicalized Body." *Sociology of Health and Illness* 20, no. 4: 548–55.

Eze, Emmanuel Chukwudi. 1995. "The Color of Reason: The Idea of 'Race' in Kant's Anthropology" in *Anthropology and the German Enlightenment*, edited by Katherine Faull, 200–41. Lewisburg, PA: Bucknell University Press.

Fanon, Frantz. 1963. *The Wretched of the Earth*. Translated by C. Farrington. New York: Grove Press.

1967. *Black Skin, White Masks*. Translated by Charles Lam Markmann. New York: Grove Press.

Feinberg, Joel. 1986. *Harm to Self*. New York: Oxford University Press.

Ferguson, Kathy E. 2008a. *A Resource Guide about Dyslexia for People in Hawai'i*. Honolulu: HIDA.

2008b. "Thinking Dyslexia with Connolly and Haraway" in *The New Pluralism: William Connolly and the Contemporary Global Condition*, edited by David Campbell and Morton Schoolman, 221–49. Chapel Hill, NC: Duke University Press.

Feuerstein, N. and J. Terkel. 2008. "Interrelationship of Dogs (*canis familiaris*) and Cats (*felis catus L.*) Living Under the Same Roof." *Applied Animal Behaviour Science* 113, no. 1: 150–65.

Fine, Michelle and Adrienne Asch, eds. 1988. *Women with Disabilities: Essays in Psychology, Culture and Politics*. Philadelphia, PA: Temple University Press.

Fineman, Martha Albertson. 2005. *The Autonomy Myth: A Theory of Dependency*. New York: The New Press.

2008. "The Vulnerable Subject: Anchoring Equality in the Human Condition." *Yale Journal of Law and Feminism* 20, no. 1: 1–24.

Finkelstein, Victor. 1980. *Attitudes and Disabled People*. New York: World Rehabilitation Fund.

Fisher, Berenice and Joan C. Tronto. 1990. "Toward a Feminist Theory of Caring" in *Circles of Care*, edited by E. K. Abel and M. Nelson. Albany, NY: SUNY Press.

Flathman, Richard E. 1984. *The Philosophy and Politics of Freedom*. Chicago: University of Chicago Press.

Flores, Noelia, Cristina Jenaro, M. Begoña Orgaz, and M. Victoria Martín. 2011. "Understanding Quality of Working Life of Workers with Intellectual Disabilities." *Journal of Applied Research in Intellectual Disabilities* 24, no. 2: 133–41.

Foot, Philippa. 1995. "Does Moral Subjectivism Rest on a Mistake?" *Oxford Journal of Legal Studies* 15, no. 1: 1–14.

Forrester-Jones, Rachel, John Carpenter, Pauline Coolen-Schrijner, Paul Cambridge, Alison Tate, Jennifer Beecham, Angela Hallam, Martin Knapp, and David Wooff. 2006. "The Social Networks of People with Intellectual Disability Living in the Community 12 Years after Resettlement from Long-Stay Hospitals." *Journal of Applied Research in Intellectual Disabilities* 19: 285–95.

Foucault, Michel. 1977. *Discipline and Punish: The Birth of the Prison*, translated by Alan Sheridan. London: Allen Lane.

1978. *The History of Sexuality, Vol. 1: An Introduction*. Translated by Robert Hurley. New York: Vintage Books.

1980a. "Two Lectures" in *Power/Knowledge: Selected Interviews and Other Writings 1972–1977*, edited and translated by Colin Gordon, 78–108. New York: Pantheon Books.

1980b. *Power/Knowledge: Selected Interviews and Other Writings 1972–1977*. Edited and translated by Colin Gordon. New York: Pantheon Books.

1980c. "Introduction" in Herculin Barbin: Being the Recently Discovered Memoirs of a Nineteenth-Century French Hermaphrodite, translated by Richard McDougall. New York: Pantheon Books.

1983. "The Subject and Power" in Herbert Dreyfus and Paul Rabinow, *Michel Foucault: Beyond Structuralism and Hermeneutics*, 2nd edn, 208–28. Chicago: University of Chicago Press.

1988. *Madness and Civilization: A History of Insanity in the Age of Reason*. Translated by Richard Howard. New York: Vintage Books.

1994. *Birth of the Clinic*, translated by A. M. Sheridan Smith. New York: Vintage Books.
2003. *Abnormal: Lectures at the Collège de France*, 1974-75. Ed. Valerio Marchetti and Antonella Salomoni, trans. Graham Burchell. New York: Picador.
2008. *Psychiatric Power: Lectures at the Collège de France, 1973–1974.* Translated by Graham Burchell. London: Picador.
Francione, Gary L. 2007. *Animal Rights and Domesticated Nonhumans.* Blog. Available online at www.abolitionistapproach.com/animal-rights-and-domesticated-nonhumans.
Francis, L. P. and Anita Silvers. 2007. "Liberalism and Individually Scripted Ideas of the Good: Meeting the Challenge of Dependent Agency." *Social Theory and Practice* 33, no. 2: 311–34.
Frank, Arthur W. 1991. *At the Will of the Body: Reflections on Illness.* New York: Houghton Mifflin Company.
Fraser, Nancy. 1981. "Foucault on Modern Power: Empirical Insights and Normative Confusions." *Praxis International* 1: 272–87.
Frazee, Catherine, Joan Gilmour, and Roxanne Mikitiuk. 2006. "Now You See Her, Now You Don't: How Law Shapes Disabled Women's Experience of Exposure, Surveillance, and Assessment in the Clinical Encounter" in *Critical Disability Theory: Essays in Philosophy, Politics, Policy, and Law*, edited by Dianne Pothier and Richard Devlin, 223–47. Vancouver, BC: University of British Columbia Press.
Freeman, Samuel, ed. 1999. *Collected Papers.* Cambridge, MA: Harvard University Press.
French, Sally. 1993. "Disability, Impairment or Something In-Between?" in *Disabling Barriers, Enabling Environments*, edited by John Swain, Vic Finkelstein, Sally French, and Mike Olive, 17–25. London: Sage.
French, Sally and John Swain. 2012. *Working With Disabled People in Policy and Practice.* New York: Palgrave Macmillan.
Friedman, Milton. 1962. *Capitalism and Freedom.* Chicago: University of Chicago Press.
Friedman, Richard A. 2015. "Psychiatry's Identity Crisis." *The New York Times*, July 19, SR5. Available online at www.nytimes.com/2015/07/19/opinion/psychiatrys identity crisis.html.
Frye, Marilyn. 1983. *The Politics of Reality: Essays in Feminist Theory.* Trumansburg, NY: Crossing Press.
Fuller-Thomson, Esme and Sarah Brennenstuhl. 2012. "People with Disabilities: The Forgotten Victims of Violence." *The Lancet* 379, no. 9826: 1573–4.
Garner, Robert. 2013. *A Theory of Justice for Animals: Animal Rights in a Nonideal World.* Oxford: Oxford University Press.
Gasson, Ruth and Chris Linsell. 2011. "Young Workers: A New Zealand Perspective." *International Journal of Children's Rights* 19, no. 4: 641–59.
Gauthier, David. 1986. *Morals by Agreement.* Oxford: Oxford University Press.
Gert, Bernard. 2001. "Hobbes on Reason." *Pacific Philosophical Quarterly* 82, no. 3–4: 243–57.
Gilligan, Carol. 1982. *In a Different Voice: Psychological Theory and Women's Development.* Cambridge, MA: Harvard University Press.

Gilligan, James. 2011. *Why Some Politicians Are More Dangerous Than Others*. Malden, MA: Polity Press.

Ginsburg, Faye and Rayna Rapp. 2013. "Disability Worlds." *Annual Review of Anthropology* 42, no. 1: 53–68.

Gladstone, David. 1996. "The Changing Dynamic of Institutional Care: The Western Counties Idiot Asylum, 1864–1914" in *From Idiocy to Mental Deficiency: Historical Perspectives on People with Learning Disabilities*, edited by David Wright and Anne Digby, 134–60. London: Routledge.

Goodey, C. F. 1994. "John Locke's Idiots in the Natural History of Mind." *History of Psychiatry* 5, no. 18: 215–50.

1996. "The Psychopolitics of Learning and Disability in Seventeenth-Century Thought" in *From Idiocy to Mental Deficiency: Historical Perspectives on People with Learning Disabilities*, edited by David Wright and Anne Digby, 93–117. London: Routledge.

2011. *A History of Intelligence and 'Intellectual Disability': The Shaping of Psychology in Early Modern Europe*. Surrey, UK: Ashgate.

Goodey, C. F. and Tim Stainton. 2001. "Intellectual Disability and the Myth of the Changeling Myth." *Journal of the History of the Behavioral Sciences* 37, no. 3: 223–40.

Goodin, Robert E. 1985. *Protecting the Vulnerable: A Reanalysis of Our Social Responsibilities*. Chicago: University of Chicago Press.

Goodyear-Ka'ōpua, Noelani. 2013. *The Seeds We Planted: Portraits of a Native Hawaiian Charter School*. Minneapolis, MN: University of Minnesota Press.

Gorman, Christine 2003. "The New Science of Dyslexia." *Time* 162, no. 4: 52–9.

Grandin, Temple. 2006. *Thinking in Pictures: My Life with Autism*. New York: Vintage Press.

2011. "Avoid Being Abstract When Making Policies on the Welfare of Animals" in *Species Matters: Humane Advocacy and Cultural Theory*, edited by Marianne DeKoven and Michael Lundblad. New York: Columbia University Press.

Gray, John. 1980. "On Positive and Negative Liberty." *Political Studies* 28, no. 4: 510–13.

Grove, Nicola, Karen Bunning, Jill Porter, and Cecilia Olsson. 1999. "See What I Mean: Interpreting the Meaning of Communication by People with Severe and Profound Intellectual Disabilities." *Journal of Applied Research in Intellectual Disabilities* 12, no. 3: 190–203.

Guyer, Paul. 2000. *Kant on Freedom, Law, and Happiness*. Cambridge: Cambridge University Press.

Hague, Gill, Ravi Thiara, and Audrey Mullender. 2011. "Disabled Women, Domestic Violence and Social Care: The Risk of Isolation, Vulnerability and Neglect." *British Journal of Social Work* 41, no. 1: 148–65.

Hahn, Harlan. 1985. "Towards a Politics of Disability: Definitions, Disciplines and Policies." *Social Science Journal* 22, no. 4: 87–105.

1988. "The Politics of Physical Differences: Disability and Discrimination." *Journal of Social Issues* 44, no. 1: 39–47.

Hahn, Harlan D. and Todd L. Belt. 2004. "Disability Identity and Attitudes Toward Cure in a Sample of Disabled Activists." *Journal of Health and Social Behavior* 45: 453–64.

Hakim, Danny. 2011. "At State-Run Homes, Abuse and Impunity." *New York Times*, March 12.

2013. "State Lagging on Dismissals In Abuse Cases." *New York Times*, August 9.

Hall, Kim. 1997. "*Sensus Communis* and Violence: A Feminist Reading of Kant's *Critique of Judgment*" in *Feminist Interpretations of Immanuel Kant*, edited by Robin May Schott, 257–74. University Park, PA: The Pennsylvania State University Press.

Hall, Kim Q., ed. 2011. *Feminist Disability Studies*. Bloomington: Indiana University Press.

Hampton, Jean. 1999. "The Failure of Hobbes's Social Contract Argument" in *The Social Contract Theorists: Critical Essays on Hobbes, Locke, and Rousseau*, edited by Christopher W. Morris, 41–57. Oxford: Rowman & Littlefield.

Handley, Peter. 2001. "Theorising Disability: Beyond 'Common Sense'." *Politics* 23, no. 2: 109–18.

Haraway, Donna J. 2008. *When Species Meet*. Minneapolis, MN: University of Minnesota Press.

Hartley, Christie. 2009. "Justice for the Disabled: A Contractualist Approach." *Journal of Social Philosophy* 40, no. 1: 17–36.

2011. "Disability and Justice." *Philosophy Compass* 6, no. 2: 120–32.

Hartsock, Nancy. 1990. "Foucault on Power: A Theory for Women?" in *Feminism/Postmodernism*, edited by Monique Leyanaar et al. Leiden, Netherlands: Vakgroep Vrouwenstudies.

Harvey, Jean. 2008. "Companion and Assistance Animals: Benefits, Welfare and Relationships." *International Journal of Applied Philosophy* 22, no. 2: 161–76.

Hauerwas, Stanley. 2004. "Suffering the Retarded: Should We Prevent Retardation?" in *Critical Reflections on Stanley Hauerwas' Theology of Disability: Disabling Society, Enabling Theology*, edited by John Swinton. Binghamton, NY: Haworth.

Hayek, H. A. 1978. *The Constitution of Liberty*. Chicago: University of Chicago Press.

Hearne, Vicki. 2007 [1986]. *Adam's Task: Calling Animals by Name*. New York: Skyhorse Publishing.

Held, Virginia. 2006. *The Ethics of Care: Personal, Political, Global*. Oxford: Oxford University Press.

Hill, Melvyn A., ed. 1979. *Hannah Arendt: The Recovery of the Public World*. New York: St. Martin's Press.

Hillsburg, Heather. 2010. "My Pet Needs Philosophy: Ambiguity, Capabilities, and the Welfare of Domestic Dogs." *Journal for Critical Animal Studies* 8, no. 1: 33–46.

Hinchman, Lewis P. and Sandra K. Hinchman. 1991. "Existentialism Politicized: Arendt's Debt to Jaspers." *Review of Politics* 53: 435–68.

Hirschmann, Nancy J. 2003. *The Subject of Liberty: Toward a Feminist Theory of Freedom*. Princeton, NJ: Princeton University Press.

2008. *Gender, Class, and Freedom in Modern Political Theory*. Princeton, NJ: Princeton University Press.

2009. "Stem Cells, Disability, and Abortion: A Feminist Approach to Equal Citizenship" in *Gender Equality: Dimensions of Women's Equal Citizenship*, edited by Linda McClain and Joanna L. Grossman, 154–73. Cambridge: Cambridge University Press.

2011. "A Question of Justice? A Question of Rights? Or a Question of Freedom?" Paper presented at the Annual Meeting of the American Political Science Association, Seattle, WA, September 1–4.

2012. "Disability as a New Frontier for Feminist Intersectionality Research." *Politics & Gender* 8, no. 3: 396–405.

2013a. "Freedom and (Dis)Ability in Early Modern Political Thought" in *Recovering Disability in Early Modern England*, edited by Allison P. Hobgood and David Houston Wood, 167–86. Columbus, OH: Ohio State University Press.

2013b. "Rawls, Freedom, and Disability: A Feminist Rereading" in *Feminist Interpretations of John Rawls*, edited by Ruth Abbey. University Park, PA: The Pennsylvania State University Press.

2013c. "Queer/Fear: Disability, Sexuality, and the Other." *Journal of Medical Humanities* 34, no. 2: 139–47.

2015. "Invisible Disability: Seeing, Being, Power" in *Civil Disabilitites: Citizenship, Membership, and Belonging*, edited by Nancy J. Hirschmann and Beth Linker. Philadelphia: University of Pennsylvania Press.

2016. "Disability Rights, Social Rights, and Freedom." *Journal of International Political Theory* 12, no. 1: 42–57.

Hirschmann, Nancy J. and Beth Linker, eds. 2015. *Disabilitites: Citizenship, Membership, and Belonging*. Philadelphia: University of Pennsylvania Press.

Hirschmann, Nancy J. and Kirstie M. McClure, eds. 2007. *Feminist Interpretations of John Locke*. University Park, PA: The Pennsylvania State University Press.

Hirschmann, Nancy J. and Joanne H. Wright. 2013. "Hobbes, History, Politics, and Gender: A Conversation with Carole Pateman and Quentin Skinner" in *Feminist Interpretations of Thomas Hobbes*, edited by Nancy J. Hirschmann and Joanne H. Wright, 18–43. University Park, PA: The Pennsylvania State University Press.

Hobbes, Thomas. 1985. *Leviathan*. Edited by C. B. Macpherson. New York: Penguin.

1991. "De Cive" In *Man and Citizen: De Homine and De Cive*, edited by Bernard Gert. Indianapolis, IN: Hacket.

1999. "The Questions Concerning Liberty, Necessity, and Chance" in *Hobbes and Bramhall on Liberty and Necessity*, edited by Vere Chappel. New York: Cambridge University Press.

2010a. *Leviathan, or the Matter, Forme & Power of a Common-Wealth Ecclesiasticall and Civill*. Edited by Ian Shapiro. New Haven, CT: Yale University Press.

2010b. *On the Citizen*. Edited by Richard Tuck and Michael Silverthorn. Translated by Michael Silverthorn. Cambridge: Cambridge University Press.

Hoerl, Christoph. 2013. "Jaspers on Explaining and Understanding in Psychiatry" in *One Century of Karl Jaspers' General Psychopathology*, edited by Giovanni Stanghellini and Thomas Fuchs, 107–20. Oxford: Oxford University Press.

Hollander, Eric and Daphne Simeon. 2008. "Anxiety Disorders: Introduction." *American Journal of Psychiatry* 165, no. 9: 1210.

Hollifield, Michael, Cynthia Geppert, Yuam Johnson, and Caol Fryer. 2003. "A Vietnamese Man with Selective Mutism: The Relevance of Multiple Interacting 'Cultures' in Clinical Psychiatry." *Transcultural Psychiatry* 40: 329–41.

Hooran, R. H., V. A. Widdershoven, H. W. Borne, and L. M. Curfs. 2002. "Autonomy and Intellectual Disability: The Case of Prevention of Obesity in Prader-Willi Syndrome." *Journal of Intellectual Disability Research* 46, no. 7: 560–8.

Höpfl, Harro and Martyn Thompson. 1979. "The History of Contract as a Motif in Political Thought." *The American Historical Review* 84, no. 4: 919–44.

Hribal, Jason. 2007. "Animals, Agency, and Class: Writing the History of Animals from Below." *Human Ecology Review* 14, no. 1: 101–12.

2010. *Fear of the Animal Planet: The Hidden History of Animals Resistance.* Oakland, CA: Counter Punch Press.

Hruby, George G. and George W. Hind. 2006. "Decoding Shaywitz: The Modular Brain and Its Discontents." *Reading Research Quarterly* 41, no. 4: 544–56.

Hubbard, Ruth. 2006. "Abortion and Disability: Who Should and Who Should Not Inhabit the World?" in *The Disability Studies Reader*, 2nd edition, edited by Lennard J. Davis, 93–103. New York: Routledge.

Hughes, Bill. 2002. "Disability and the Body" in *Disability Studies Today*, edited by Colin Barnes, Mike Oliver, and Len Barton. Cambridge: Polity Press.

Hughes, Karen, Mark A. Bellis, Lisa Jones, Sara Wood, Geoff Bates, Lindsay Eckley, Ellie McCoy, Christopher Mikton, Tom Shakespeare, and Alana Officer. 2012. "Prevalence and Risk of Violence Against Adults with Disabilities: A Systematic Review and Meta-Analysis of Observational Studies." *The Lancet* 379, no 9826: 1621–9.

Hume, David. 2000. *An Enquiry Concerning Human Understanding.* Oxford: Oxford University Press.

Hurst, Rachel. 1995. "Choice and Empowerment –Lessons from Europe." *Disability & Society* 10, no. 4: 529–34.

Hutchinson, Alex. 2012. "Why Humans are Wired to Run – and Ferrets are Not." *Globe and Mail*, April 16: L4.

Inclusion International. 2009. *Priorities for People with Intellectual Disabilities in Implementing the United Nations Convention on the Rights of People with Disabilities.* London: Inclusion International. Available online at http://inclusion-international.org/priorites-for-people-with-intellectual-disabilities-in-implementing-the-un-crpd.

International Dyslexia Association. 2002. http://eida.org/definition-of-dyslexia.

Iovine, Vicki. 2007. *The Girlfriends' Guide to Pregnancy*, 2nd edition. New York: Pocket Books.

Irvine, Leslie. 2004. "A Model of Animal Selfhood: Expanding Interactionist Possibilities." *Symbolic Interaction* 27, no. 1: 3–21.

Jaarsma, Pier and Stellan Welin. 2012. "Autism as a Natural Human Variation: Reflections on the Claims of the Neurodiversity Movement." *Health Care Analysis* 20, no. 1: 20–30.

Jamison, Beth. 2003. *Real Choices: Feminism, Freedom, and the Limits of Law.* Pittsburg, PA: Penn State University Press.

Janara, Laura. 2012. "Nonhuman Animals, Political Theory, Power." Presentation at the Annual Meeting of the Canadian Political Science Association, Edmonton, Alberta, June 13–15.

Jans, Marc. 2004. "Children as Citizens: Towards a Contemporary Notion of Child Participation." *Childhood* 11, no. 1: 27–44.

Jaspers, Karl. 1968. "The Phenomenological Approach in Psychopathology." *The British Journal of Psychiatry* 114: 1313–23.

1997. *General Psychopathology*, 2 vols. Translated by J. Hoenig and Marian W. Hamilton. Baltimore: John Hopkins University Press.

Jaworska, Agnieszka. 2009. "Caring, Minimal Autonomy, and the Limits of Liberalism" in *Naturalized Bioethics: Toward Responsible Knowing and Practice*, edited by Hilde Lindemann, Marian Verkerk, and Margaret Walker. Cambridge: Cambridge University Press.

Johannesen, Jennifer. 2011. *No Ordinary Boy: The Life and Death of Owen Turney.* Toronto, ON: Low to the Ground Publishing.

Johnson, Harriet McBryde. 2006. *Too Late to Die Young: Nearly True Tales from a Life.* New York: Picador.

Johnson, Mary. 2003. *Make Them Go Away: Clint Eastwood, Christopher Reeve and the Case Against Disability Rights.* Louisville, KY: Avocado Press.

Jones, Lisa, Mark A. Bellis, Sara Wood, Karen Hughes, Ellie McCoy, Lindsay Eckley, Geoff Bates, Christopher Mikton, Tom Shakespeare, and Alana Officer. 2012. "Prevalence and Risk of Violence Against Children with Disabilities: A Systematic Review and Meta-Analysis of Observational Studies." *The Lancet.* 380, no. 9845: 899–907.

Jones, Pattrice. 2008. *Strategic Analysis of Animal Welfare Legislation: A Guide for the Perplexed.* Springfield, VT: Eastern Shore Sanctuary & Education Center, Strategic Analysis Report. Available online at http://pattricejones.info/blog/wp-content/uploads/perplexed.pdf.

Kafer, Alison. 2013. *Feminist, Queer, Crip.* Bloomington: Indiana University Press.

Kahn, Jeffrey. 2014. "Lessons Learned: Challenges in Applying Current Constraints on Research on Chimpanzees to Other Animals." *Theoretical Medicine and Bioethics* 35, no. 2: 97–104.

Kant, Immanuel. 1960. *Education.* Ann Arbor: University of Michigan Press.

1996 [1784]. "An Answer to the Question: What is Enlightenment?" in *Practical Philosophy,* edited and translated by Mary J. Gregor. Cambridge: Cambridge University Press.

1996 [1793]. "Religion within the Boundaries of Mere Reason." Translated by George di Giovanni. In *Religion and Rational Theology*, edited by Allen W. Wood and George di Giovanni. Cambridge: Cambridge University Press.

1996 [1797]. *The Metaphysics of Morals* in *Practical Philosophy.* Edited and translated by Mary J. Gregor. Cambridge: Cambridge University Press.

1997. *Lectures on Ethics.* Translated by Peter Heath. Edited by Peter Heath and J. B. Schneewind. Cambridge: Cambridge University Press.

2000 [1790]. *Critique of the Power of Judgment.* Translated by Paul Guyer and Eric Matthews. Edited by Paul Guyer. Cambridge: Cambridge University Press.

2005. "Notes on Metaphysics." Translated by Paul Guyer and Curtis Bowman. In *Notes and Fragments*. Edited by Paul Guyer. Cambridge: Cambridge University Press.

2006a. *Fundamental Principles of the Metaphysic of Morals*. Lenox, Massachusetts: Lenox Hard Press.

2006b. *Toward Perpetual Peace and Other Writings on Politics, Peace, and History*. Translated by David L. Colclasure, edited by Pauline Kleingeld. New Haven, CT: Yale University Press.

2007 [1764a]. "Essay on the Maladies of the Head." Translated by Holly Wilson. In *Anthropology, History, and Education*, edited by Günter Zöller and Robert B. Louden, 63–77. Cambridge: Cambridge University Press.

2007 [1764b]. "Observations on the Feeling of the Beautiful and Sublime." Translated by Paul Guyer. In *Anthropology, History, and Education*, edited by Günter Zöller and Robert B. Louden, 18–62. Cambridge: Cambridge University Press.

2007 [1784]. "Idea for a Universal History with a Cosmopolitan Aim." Translated by Allen W. Wood. In *Anthropology, History, and Education*, edited by Günter Zöller and Robert B. Louden, 107–20. Cambridge: Cambridge University Press.

2007 [1786]. "Conjectural Beginnings of Human History." Translated by Allen W. Wood. In *Anthropology, History, and Education*, edited by Günter Zöller and Robert B. Louden, 160–75. Cambridge: Cambridge University Press.

2007 [1798]. "Anthropology from a Pragmatic Point of View." Translated by Robert B. Louden. In *Anthropology, History, and Education*, edited by Günter Zöller and Robert B. Louden, 227–429. Cambridge: Cambridge University Press.

2007 [1803]. "Lectures on Pedagogy." Translated by Robert B. Louden. In *Anthropology, History, and Education*, edited by Günter Zöller and Robert B. Louden, 434–485. Cambridge: Cambridge University Press.

2012. *Lectures on Anthropology*. Trans. Robert R. Clewis, Robert B. Louden, G. Felicitas Munzel, and Allen W. Wood. Edited by Allen W. Wood and Robert B. Louden. Cambridge: Cambridge University Press.

Kavka, Gregory. 1999. "Hobbes's War of All Against All" in *The Social Contract Theorists: Critical Essays on Hobbes, Locke, and Rousseau*, edited by Christopher W. Morris, 1–22 Oxford: Rowman & Littefield.

Kelly, Duncan. 2010. *The Propriety of Liberty: Persons, Passions and Judgement in Modern Political Thought*. Princeton, NJ: Princeton University Press.

Kerasote, Ted. 2007. *Merle's Door: Lessons from a Free-thinking Dog*. New York: Harcourt.

Khalifeh, Hind and Kimberlie Dean. 2010. "Gender and Violence Against People With Severe Mental Illness." *International Review of Psychiatry* 22, no. 5: 535–46.

Kirby, Jeffrey. 2004. "Disability and Justice: A Pluralistic Account." *Social Theory and Practise* 30, no. 2: 229–46.

Kirkland, Anna. 2012. "Credibility Battles in the Autism Litigation." *Social Studies of Science* 42, no. 2: 237–61.

Kittay, Eva. 1999. *Love's Labor: Essays on Women, Equality, and Dependency*. New York: Routledge.

2001. "When Care Is Just and Justice is Caring: The Case of the Care for the Mentally Retarded." *Public Culture* 13, no. 3: 557–79.
2002. "When Caring is Just and Justice is Caring: Justice and Mental Retardation" in *The Subject of Care: Feminist Perspectives on Dependency*, edited by Eva Feder Kittay and Ellen K. Feder, 257–76. New York: Rowman & Littlefield.
2005a. "Equality, Dignity and Disability" in *Perspectives on Equality: The Second Seamus Heaney Lectures*, edited by Mary Ann Lyons and Fionnuala Waldron, 95–122. Dublin: Liffey Press.
2005b. "At the Margins of Moral Personhood." *Ethics* 116, no. 1: 100–31.
2009a. "Ideal Theory Bioethics and the Exclusion of People with Severe Cognitive Disabilities" in *Naturalized and Narrative Bioethics*, edited by Hilde Lindemann, Marian Verkerk, and Margaret Walker, 218–37. Cambridge: Cambridge University Press.
2009b. "The Personal is Political is Philosophical: A Philosopher and Mother of a Cognitively Disabled Person Sends Notes From the Battlefield." *Metaphilosophy* 40, no. 3–4: 607–27.
2011. "Forever Small: The Strange Case of Ashley X." *Hypatia: Journal of Feminist Philosophy* 26, no. 3: 610–31.
Kleege, Georgina. 1999. *Sight Unseen*. New Haven: Yale University Press.
Kleingeld, Pauline. 1993. "The Problematic Status of Gender-Neutral Language in the History of Philosophy: The Case of Kant." *The Philosophical Forum* 25, no. 2: 134–50.
Kleinman, Arthur. 1999. "Experience and Its Moral Modes: Culture, Human Conditions, and Disorder" in *The Tanner Lectures on Human Values*, Vol. 20. Salt Lake City: University of Utah Press.
Klonsky, Ed. 2007. "The Functions of Deliberate Self-injury: A Review of the Evidence." *Clinical Psychology Review* 27, no. 2: 226–39.
Knight, Amber. 2014. "Disability as Vulnerability: Redistributing Precariousness in Democratic Ways." *The Journal of Politics* 76: 15–26.
Krause, Sharon. 2011. "Bodies in Action: Corporeal Agency and Democratic Politics." *Political Theory* 39, no. 3: 299–324.
2012. "Plural Freedom." *Politics & Gender* 3: 238–45.
Kristin. 2015. *The Adventures of Anxiety Girl: Striving for Super Hero Courage in the Face of Fear*. Blog. Available online at www.theanxietygirl.blogspot.com.
Kristjánsson, Kristján. 1992. "What Is Wrong With Positive Liberty?" *Social Theory and Practice* 18, no. 3: 289–310.
Kudlick, Catherine J. 2003. "Disability History: Why We Need Another 'Other'." *The American Historical Review* 108, no. 3.
2014. "Disability and Survival: the Hidden Lives of Epidemics" in *Disability Histories*, edited by Susan Burch and Michael Rembis. Urbana, IL: University of Illinois.
Kuhn, Thomas S. 1996. *The Structure of Scientific Revolutions*, 3rd edition. Chicago: University of Chicago Press.
Kymlicka, Will. 1993. "The Social Contract Tradition" in *A Companion to Ethics*, edited by Peter Singer, 186–96. Cambridge: Blackwell.
Kymlicka, Will and Sue Donaldson. 2014. "Animal Rights, Multiculturalism and the Left." *Journal of Social Philosophy* 45, no. 1: 116–35.

Lange, Lynda, ed. 2002. *Feminist Interpretations of Jean Jacques Rousseau*. Pittsburgh, PA: Penn State University Press.

Lavoi, Rick. 2003. "On the Waterbed: The Impact of Learning Disabilities." Kapiolani Community College.

Lee, Theresa Man Ling. 1997. *Politics and Truth: Political Theory and the Postmodernist Challenge*. Albany: State University of New York Press.

Leoni, Federico. 2013. "Jaspers in His Time" in *One Century of Karl Jaspers' General Psychopathology*, edited by Giovanni Stanghellini and Thomas Fuchs, 3–15. Oxford: Oxford University Press.

Lerner, Richard. 2007. "Another Nine-Inch Nail for Behavioral Genetics!" *Human Development* 49, no. 6: 336–42.

Lester, David. 1971. "Suicide After Restoration of Sight: Part I." *Journal of the American Medical Association* 216: 678–97.

1972. "Suicide After Restoration of Sight: Part II." *Journal of the American Medical Association* 219: 757–76.

Levack, Brian. 2013. *The Devil Within: Possession and Exorcism in the Christian West*. New Haven: Yale University Press.

Lewis, Bradley. 2013. "A Mad Fight: Psychiatry and Disability Activism" in *The Disability Studies Reader*, edited by Lennard J. Davis, 115–31. New York: Routledge.

Leys, Ruth. 1993. "Mead's Voices: Imitation as Foundation, or the Struggle Against Mimesis." *Critical Inquiry* 19, no. 2: 277–307.

Libel, Peter, George Loewenstein, and Christopher Jepson. 2003. "Whose Quality of Life? A Commentary Exploring Discrepancies between Health State Evaluations of Patients and the General Public." *Quality of Life Research* 12, no. 6: 599–607.

Linker, Beth. 2011. *War's Waste: Rehabilitation in WWI America*. Chicago, IL: University of Chicago Press

Linton, Simi. 2006. *My Body Politic: A Memoir*. Ann Arbor: University of Michigan Press.

Lippold, T. and J. Burns. 2009. "Social Support and Intellectual Disabilities: A Comparison between Social Networks of Adults with Intellectual Disability and Those with Physical Disability." *Journal of Intellectual Disability Research* 53, no. 5: 463–73.

Lister, Ruth. 2007. "Why Citizenship? Where, When and How Children?" *Theoretical Inquiries in Law* 8, no. 2: 693–718.

Liu, K. P. Y., T. Lee, A. Yan, C. W. Siu, F. W. Choy, K. L. Leung, T. Y. Siu, and A. C. Kwan. 2007. "Use of the *Interact Short Form* as a Tool to Evaluate Emotion of People with Profound Intellectual Disabilities." *Journal of Intellectual Disability Research* 51, no. 11: 884–91.

Lloyd, Margaret. 1992. "Does She Boil Eggs? Towards a Feminist Model of Disability." *Disability, Handicap and Society* 7:207–21.

Lloyd, Sharon A. 2009. *Morality in the Philosophy of Thomas Hobbes: Cases in the State of Nature*. Cambridge: Cambridge University Press.

Locke, John. 1960 [1689]. *Two Treatises of Government*. Edited by Peter Laslett. Cambridge: Cambridge University Press.

1975 [1690]. *An Essay Concerning Human Understanding*. Edited by Peter H. Nidditch. Oxford: Clarendon Press.

1996. "Some Thoughts Concerning Education" in *Some Thoughts Concerning Education and of the Conduct of the Understanding*, edited by Ruth Grant and Nathan Tarcov. Indianapolis: Hackett Publishers.

Lohrmann-O'Rourke, Sharon and Diane M. Browder. 1998. "Empirically Based Methods to Assess the Preferences of Individuals with Severe Disabilities." *American Journal on Mental Retardation* 103, no. 2: 146–61.

Lonmore, Paul K. and Lauri Umansky, eds. 2001. *The New Disability History: American Perspectives*. New York: New York University Press.

Louden, Robert. 2000. *Kant's Impure Ethics: From Rational Beings to Human Beings*. Oxford: Oxford University Press.

2011. *Kant's Human Being: Essays on His Theory of Human Nature*. Oxford: Oxford University Press.

Luft, Sebastian and Jann E. Schlimme. 2013. "The Phenomenology of Intersubjectivity in Jaspers and Husserl: On the Capacities and Limits of Empathy and Communication in Psychiatric Praxis." *Psychopathology* 46: 345–54.

Luke, Allan 1994. *The Social Construction of Literacy in the Primary School*. South Melbourne: Palgrave Macmillan Australia.

Lyon, G. Reid. 2003. "Reading Disabilities: Why Do Some Children Have Difficulty Learning to Read? What Can Be Done About It?" *Perspectives* 29, no. 2: 17–18.

2004. "Why Scientific Evidence Must Guide Reading Assessment and Reading Instruction." Paper presented at the Pacific Basin Learning Disabilities, ADHD & Teen Conference, Waikiki, HI, February 13–14.

Macey, David. 2012. *Franz Fanon: A Biography*, 2nd edition. London: Verso Books.

MacIntyre, Alasdair. 1984. *After Virtue*. Notre Dame, IN: Notre Dame Press.

2001. *Dependent Rational Animals: Why Human Beings Need the Virtue*. Chicago: Open Court Publishing.

MacIntyre, Fergus Gwynplaine. 2004. "Happy in Her Work: Florence Foster Jenkins." *The Daily News*, June 23.

Malhotra, Ravi A. 2006. "Justice as Fairness in Accommodating Workers with Disabilities and Critical Theory: The Limitations of a Rawlsian Framework for Empowering People with Disabilities in Canada" in *Critical Disability Theory: Essays in Philosophy, Politics, Policy, and Law*, edited by Dianne Pothier and Richard Devlin, 70–86. Vancouver, BC: University of British Columbia Press.

Mansfield, C., S. Hopfer, and T. M. Marteau. 1999. "Termination Rates After Prenatal Diagnosis of Down Syndrome, Spina Bifida, Anencephaly, and Turner and Klinefelter Syndromes: A Systematic Literature Review." *Prenatal Diagnosis* 19, no. 9: 808–12.

Markell, Patchen. 2008. "Review Essay: Peg Birmingham," *Hannah Arendt and Human Rights: The Predicament of Common Responsibility*, and Serena Parekh, *Hannah Arendt and the Challenge of Modernity: A Phenomenology of Human Rights*." *Notre Dame Philosophical Reviews*. Available online at http://ndpr.nd.edu/news/23855/?id=14788.

Marks, Deborah. 1999. *Disability: Controversial Debates and Psycho-Social Perspectives*. London: Routledge.

McCarthy, Thomas. 2010. *Race, Empire, and The Idea of Human Development*. Cambridge: Cambridge University Press.
McEnroe, Paul. 2014. "Bipolar Man's Suit Claims Negligence." *Star Tribune*, October 8.
McHugh, Paul R. 1997. "Foreword to the 1997 Edition." *General Psychopathology*: v–xii.
McMahan, Jeff. 1995. "The Metaphysics of Brain Death." *Bioethics* 9, no. 2: 91–126.
1996. "Cognitive Disability, Misfortune, and Justice." *Philosophy & Public Affairs* 25, no. 1: 3–35.
2002. *The Ethics of Killing: Problems at the Margins of Life*. Oxford: Oxford University Press.
2009. "Cognitive Disability and Cognitive Enhancement." *Metaphilosophy* 40, no. 3–4: 582–605.
McRuer, Robert. 2006. *Crip Theory: Cultural Signs of Queerness and Disability*. New York: New York University Press.
McWhorter, Ladelle. 2009. *Racism and Sexual Oppression in Anglo-America: A Genealogy*. Bloomington, IN: Indiana University Press.
Mead, George Herbert. 1907. "Concerning Animal Perception." *Psychological Review* 14, no. 6: 383–90.
Meekosha, Helen. 2011. "Decolonising Disability: Thinking and Acting Globally." *Disability & Society* 26, no. 6: 667–82.
Mehta, Uday. 1990. "Liberal Strategies of Exclusion." *Politics & Society* 18: 431–6.
1992. *The Anxiety of Freedom: Imagination and Individuality in Locke's Political Thought*. Ithaca, NY: Cornell University Press.
1999. *Liberalism and Empire: A Study in Nineteenth-Century British Liberal Thought*. Chicago, IL: The University of Chicago Press.
Meynell, Letitia. 2008. "The Power and Promise of Developmental Systems Theory." *Les Ateliers de L'Ethique* 3, no. 3: 88–103.
Mikton, Christopher, Holly Maguire, and Tom Shakespeare. 2014. "A Systematic Review of the Effectiveness of Interventions to Prevent and Respond to Violence Against Persons With Disabilities." *Journal of Interpersonal Violence* 29, no. 17: 3207–26.
Mill, John Stuart. 1974 [1859]. *On Liberty*. Harmondsworth, UK: Penguin Books.
1998. *On Liberty and Other Essays*, new edition. New York: Oxford.
Miller, David. 1983. "Constraints on Freedom." *Ethics* 94: 66–86.
Miller, Paul Steven and Rebecca Leah Levine. 2013. "Avoiding Genetic Genocide: Understanding Good Intentions and Eugenics in the Complex Dialogue Between the Medical and Disability Communities." *Genetics in Medicine* 15, no. 2: 95–102.
Mills, Charles W. 1997. *The Racial Contract*. Ithaca, NY: Cornell University Press.
2005a. "'Ideal Theory' as Ideology." *Hypatia* 20, no. 3: 165–84.
2005b. "Kant's *Untermenschen*" in *Race and Racism in Modern Philosophy*, edited by Andrew Walls, 169–93. Ithaca, NY: Cornell University Press.
2007. "The Domination Contract" in *Contract and Domination*, by Charles Mills and Carole Pateman, 79–105. Cambridge: Polity Press.

2009. "Rawls on Race/Race in Rawls." *The Southern Journal of Philosophy* 47, no. S1: 161–84.

Mills, Charles W. 2012. "Liberalizing Illiberal Liberalism." Keynote address delivered at Political Theory and the "LiberaL" Tradition, University of Oxford Political Theory Graduate Conference, April 19–20.

Mitchell, David and Sharon Snyder. 2000. *Narrative Prosthesis: Disability and the Dependencies of Discourse*. Ann Arbor, MI: University of Michigan Press.

2003. "The Eugenic Atlantic: Race, Disability, and the Making of an International Eugenic Science, 1800–1945." *Disability & Society* 18, no. 7: 843–64.

Moats, Louisa Cook. 2010. *Speech to Print: Language Essentials for Teachers*, 2nd edition. Baltimore: Paul H. Brookes Publishing Co.

Moore, David. 2007. "A Very Little Bit of Knowledge: Re-Evaluating the Meaning of the Heritability of IQ." *Human Development* 49, no. 6: 347–53.

Morris, Jenny. 1991. *Pride Against Prejudice*. London: Women's Press.

1996. *Encounters with Strangers: Feminism and Disability*. London: Women's Press.

2001. "Impairment and Disability: Constructing an Ethics of Care That Promotes Human Rights." *Hypatia* 16, no. 4: 1–16.

Mullin, Amy. 2005. "Trust, Social Norms, and Motherhood." *Journal of Social Philosophy* 36, no. 3: 316–30.

Murderball. 2005. Henry Alex Rubin and Dana Adam Shapiro, Dir. Thinkfilm.

Myers, Gene. 1998. *Children andAnimals: Social Development and Our Connections to Other Species*. Boulder, CO: Westview Press.

National Council on Disability. 2003. *Addressing the Needs of Youth with Disabilities in the Juvenile Justice System: The Current Status of Evidence-Based Research*. Washington, DC: National Council on Disability.

Neale, Bren. 2004. "Introduction: Young Children's Citizenship" in *Young Children's Citizenship: Ideas into Practice*, edited by Bren Neale. York: Joseph Rowntree Foundation.

Nozick, Robert. 1974. *Anarchy, State, and Utopia*. New York: Basic Books.

Nurse, Angus and Diane Ryland. 2013. "A Question of Citizenship: Examining Zoopolis' Political Theory of Animal Rights." *Journal of Animal Ethics* 3, no. 2: 201–7.

Nussbaum, Martha C. 2000. *Women and Human Development: The Capabilities Approach*. Cambridge: Cambridge University Press.

2001. *Upheavals of Thought: The Intelligence of Emotions*. Cambridge: Cambridge University Press.

2004. "Beyond the Social Contract: Capabilities and Global Justice." *Oxford Development Studies* 32, no. 1: 331–51.

2006. *Frontiers of Justice: Disability, Nationality, Species Membership*. Cambridge, MA: Harvard University Press.

2009. "The Capabilities of People with Cognitive Disabilities." *Metaphilosophy* 40, no. 3–4: 331–51.

O'Brien, Ruth. 2001. *Crippled Justice: The History of Modern Disability in the Workplace*. Chicago, IL: University of Chicago Press.

2005. "Other Voices at the Workplace: Gender, Disability and an Alternative Ethic of Care." *Signs: Journal of Women in Culture and Society* 30, no. 2: 1529–55.

OECD. 2003. *Policy Brief: Disability Programmes in Need of Reform.* Paris: Organisation for Economic Co-operation and Development.

Okin, Susan Moller. 1979. *Women in Western Political Thought.* Princeton, NJ: Princeton University Press.

Oliver, Michael. 1990. *The Politics of Disablement.* Basingstoke: Macmillan.

1993. "What's So Wonderful About Walking?" Inaugural Professorial Lecture, University of Greenwich, London. Accessed online at http://disability-studies.leeds.ac.uk/files/library/Oliver-PROFLEC.pdf.

1996. *Understanding Disability: From Theory to Practice.* Basingstoke: Macmillan.

Oliver, Michael and Colin Barnes. 2012. *New Politics of Disablement.* New York: Palgrave Macmillan.

Ong, Walter J. 1982. *Orality and Literacy: The Technologizing of the World.* New York: Routledge.

Ostapczuk, Martin and Jochen Musch. 2011. "Estimating the Prevalence of Negative Attitudes Towards People with Disability: A Comparison of Direct Questioning, Projective Questioning and Randomised Response." *Disability and Rehabilitation* 33, no. 5: 399–411.

Oswell, David. 2013. *The Agency of Children: From Family to Global Human Rights.* Cambridge: Cambridge University Press.

Pallotta, Nicole R. 2008. "Origin of Adult Animal Rights Lifestyle in Childhood Responsiveness to Animal Suffering." *Society and Animals* 16, no. 2: 149–70.

Palmer, Clare. 2003. "Colonization, Urbanization, and Animals." *Philosophy & Geography* 6, no. 1: 47–58.

Panagia, Davide. 2009. *The Political Life of Sensation.* Chapel Hill, NC: Duke University Press.

Parekh, Pushpa. 2007. "Gender, Disability and the Postcolonial Nexus." *wagadu* 4.

Parekh, Serena. 2008. *Hannah Arendt and the Challenge of Modernity: A Phenomenology of Human Rights.* New York: Routledge.

Pateman, Carole. 1979. *The Problem of Political Obligation: A Critical Analysis of Liberal Theory.* Cambridge: Polity.

1988. *The Sexual Contract.* Cambridge: Polity.

2007. "On Critics and Contract" in *Contract and Domination,* by Charles Mills and Carole Pateman, 200–29. Cambridge: Polity Press.

Pateman, Carole and Teresa Brennan. 1979. "Mere Auxiliaries to the Commonwealth: Women and the Origins of Liberalism." *Political Studies* 27, no. 2: 183–200.

Patton, Paul. 2003. "Language, Power and the Training of Horses" in *Zoontologies: The Question of the Animal,* edited by Cary Wolfe, 83–99. Minneapolis, MN: University of Minnesota Press.

Perry, Barbara. 2001. *In the Name of Hate: Understanding Hate Crimes.* London: Routledge.

Pettit, Philip. 2001. *A Theory of Freedom: From the Psychology to the Politics of Agency.* New York: Oxford University Press.

2009. *Made with Words: Hobbes on Language, Mind, and Politics.* Princeton: Princeton University Press.

Phillips, James. 1996. "Key Concepts: Hermeneutics." *Philosophy, Psychiatry, & Philosophy* 3: 61–69.

Philpott, Michael J. 1998. "A Phenomenology of Dyslexia: The Lived-Body, Ambiguity, and the Breakdown of Expression." *Philosophy, Psychiatry, & Psychology* 5, no. 1: 1–19.

Piggott, Linda. 2011. "Prosecuting Disability Hate Crime: A Disabling Solution?" *People, Place & Policy Online* 5, no. 1: 25–34.

Pinheiro, Lucas G. 2012a. At the Margins of Contract: Intellectual Disability and the Limits of Justice in Locke and Kant. MPhil Dissertation. Cambridge: Faculty of History, University of Cambridge.

2012b. "Locke, Liberalism, and Disability: Towards an Ableist Contract." Paper presented at Political Theory and the "Liberal" Tradition, University of Oxford Political Theory Graduate Conference, April 19–20.

2012c. "Physical Disability and Materialism in Rousseau." Paper presented at The Rude Body, International History Conference for Postgraduates and Early Career Historians, University of Essex Postgraduate History Conference, September 14–15.

2014. "Colonizing Cognitive Disability: Progress, Development, and Confinement in Nineteenth-Century America." Paper presented at Subjectivity and the System, the Brown University History Graduate Student Association Interdisciplinary Conference, April 4–5.

2015a. "Disability in Nietzsche: A Critique of Brown's Deontological Identity Politics." Paper presented at the Annual American Political Science Association Meeting, September 3–6.

2015b. "The 'Idiot' Within the 'Cripple': Physical Disability and Materialism in Locke and Rousseau." Paper presented at the Annual Midwest Political Science Association Meeting, April 16–19.

Pitts, Jennifer. 2005. *A Turn to Empire: The Rise of Imperial Liberalism In Britain and France*. Princeton, NJ: Princeton University Press.

Planinc, Emma. 2012. "Animals as Citizens: A Democratic or Tyrannical *Zoopolis*?" Available online at http://utoronto.academia.edu/EmmaPlaninc.

Plato. 1991. *The Republic*, 2nd edition. Translated by Allan Bloom. New York: Basic Books.

Pogge, Thomas W. 2002a. "Can the Capability Approach Be Justified?" *Philosophical Topics* 30: 167–228.

Pogge, Thomas. 2002b. "Moral Universalism and Global Economic Justice." *Politics, Philosophy and Economics* 1, no. 1: 29–58.

Pongrácz, Péter, Ádám Miklósi, and Vilmos Csányi. 2005. "Human Listeners Are Able To Classify Dog Barks Recorded in Different Situations." *Journal of Comparative Psychology* 119, no. 2: 136–44.

Porcher, Jocelyne and Tiphaine Schmitt. 2011. "Dairy Cows: Workers in the Shadows?" *Society and Animals* 20, no. 1: 39–60.

Porter, Roy. 1990. "Foucault's Great Confinement." *History of the Human Sciences* 3, no. 1: 47–60.

Prince, Michael. 2009. *Absent Citizens: Disability Politics and Policy in Canada*. Toronto, ON: University of Toronto Press.

Quarmby, K. 2011. *Scapegoat: Why We Are Failing Disabled People*. London: Portobello Books.

Radoilska, L. and E. Fistein. 2010. *Intellectual Disabilities and Personal Autonomy*. Available online at www.phil.cam.ac.uk/news_events/intellectual_disabilities_autonomy.pdf.

Rancière, Jacques. 2004. *The Flesh of Words: The Politics of Writing*. Translated by Charlotte Mandell. Stanford, CA: Stanford University Press.

Randell, M. and S. Cumella. 2009. "People with an Intellectual Disability Living in an Intentional Community." *Journal of Intellectual Disability Research* 53, no. 8: 716–26.

Raphael, D. D. 1950. "Justice and Liberty." *Proceedings of the Aristotelian Society* 51: 167–96.

Raskind, Marshall. 2005. *Research Trends: Is There a Link between LD and Juvenile Delinquency?* Available online at www.schwablearning.org.

Rawls, John. 1999 [1951]. "Outline of a Decision Procedure for Ethics" in *Collected Papers*, edited by Samuel Freeman, 1–19. Cambridge, MA: Harvard University Press.

1999 [1963]. "Constitutional Liberty and the Concept of Justice" in *Collected Papers*, edited by Samuel Freeman, 73–95. Cambridge, MA: Harvard University Press.

1999 [1967]. "Distributive Justice" in *Collected Papers*, edited by Samuel Freeman, 130–53. Cambridge, MA: Harvard University Press.

1999 [1968]. "Distributive Justice: Some Addenda" in *Collected Papers*, edited by Samuel Freeman, 154–75. Cambridge, MA: Harvard University Press.

1999 [1971]. "Justice as Reciprocity" in *Collected Papers*, edited by Samuel Freeman, 190–224. Cambridge, MA: Harvard University Press.

2001. *Justice as Fairness: A Restatement*. Cambridge, MA: Belknap Press.

2003 [1971]. *A Theory of Justice*. Cambridge, MA: Belknap Press.

2005. *Political Liberalism*. New York: Columbia University Press.

Raz, Joseph. 1986. *The Morality of Freedom*. Oxford: Clarendon Press.

Reinders, J. S. 2002. "The Good Life for Citizens with Intellectual Disability." *Journal of Intellectual Disability Research* 46, no. 1: 1–5.

Richards, Todd L. and Virginia W. Berninger. 2008. "Abnormal fMRI Connectivity in Children with Dyslexia During a Phoneme Task: Before But Not After Treatment." *Journal of Neurolinguistics* 21, no. 4: 294–304.

Rioux, Marcia and Michael Bach, eds. 1994. *Disability Is Not Measles: New Research Paradigms in Disability*. North York: L'Institut Roeher Institute.

Roberts, Monty. 2000. *Horse Sense for People*. New York: Penguin Books.

Robertson, Janet, Eric Emerson, Nicky Gregory, Chris Hatton, Sophia Kessissoglou, Angela Hallam, and Christine Linehan. 2001. "Social Networks of People with Mental Retardation in Residential Settings." *Mental Retardation* 39, no. 3: 201–14.

Robertson, Janet, Eric Emerson, Lisa Pinkney, Emma Caesar, David Felce, Andrea Meek, Deborah Carr, Kathy Lowe, Martin Knapp, and Angela Hallam. 2005. "Community-based Residential Supports for People with Intellectual Disabilities and Challenging Behavior: The Views of Neighbors." *Journal of Applied Research in Intellectual Disabilities* 18, no. 1: 85–92.

Robin, Corey. 2004. *Fear: The History of a Political Idea*. New York: Oxford University Press.

Rome, Paula D. and Jean S. Osman. 2000. *Advanced Language Toolkit: Teaching the Structure of the English Language*. Cambridge, MA: Educators Publishing Service.

Roulstone, Alan and Hannah Mason-Bish, eds. 2013. *Disability, Hate Crime and Violence*. London: Routledge.

Rousseau, Jean-Jacques. 1953. *The Confessions*. London: Penguin Books.

1979. *Emile, or, On Education*. Translated by Allan Bloom. New York: Basic.

1991. "The Social Contract" in *The Social Contract and Discourses*, translated by G. D. H. Cole, revised and augmented by J. H. Brumfitt and John C. Hall. London: J. M. Dent.

1997a. *Julie, Or the New Heloise: Letters of Two Lovers Who Live in a Small Town at the Foot of the Alps*. Translated by Philip Stewart and Jean Vaché. Hannover, NH: Dartmouth Press.

1997b. *On the Social Contract and Other Later Political Writings*. Edited by Victor Gourevitch. Cambridge: Cambridge University Press.

Rowley, Dane. 2013. "Stigma and Sexism, Behind Psychiatry's Labels." *Bad Housekeeping*, 7 October. Accessed online at http://bad-housekeeping.com/2013/10/07/how-psychiatry-oppresses-women.

Ruddick, Sara. 1995. *Maternal Thinking: Toward a Politics of Peace*, revised edition. Boston: Beacon.

Rudy, Kathy. 2011. *Loving Animals: Toward a New Animal Advocacy*. Minneapolis, MN: University of Minnesota Press.

Rushton, Peter. 1988. "Lunatics and Idiots." *Medical History* 32, no. 1: 34–50.

1996. "Idiocy, the Family, and the Community in Early Modern North-East England" in *From Idiocy to Mental Deficiency: Historical Perspectives on People with Learning Disabilities*, edited by David Wright and Anne Digby, 44–64. London: Routledge.

Russell, Nerissa. 2002. "The Wild Side of Animal Domestication." *Society & Animals* 10, no. 3: 285–302.

Ryan, Michael. 1994. *The Other Sixteen Hours: The Social and Emotional Problems of Dyslexia*. Baltimore, MD: The Orton Dyslexia Society.

Salomon, Daniel. 2010. "From Marginal Cases to Linked Oppressions: Reframing the Conflict between the Autistic Pride and Animal Rights Movements." *Journal for Critical Animal Studies* 8, no. 1: 47–72.

Samuels, Ellen Jean. 2002. "Critical Divides: Judith Butler's Body Theory and the Question of Disability." *NWSA Journal* 14, no. 3: 58–76.

Sankar, Muthu. 2003. *Enlightenment Against Empire*. Princeton, NJ: Princeton University Press.

Sartre, Jean-Paul. 1981. *The Family Idiot: Gustave Flaubert 1821–1857*, Vol. I. Translated by Carol Cosman. Chicago: University of Chicago Press.

Satel, Sally and Scott O. Lilienfield. 2013. *Brainwashed: The Seductive Appeal of Mindless Neuroscience*. New York: Basic Books.

Savage-Rumbaugh, Sue, Kanzi Wamba, Panbanisha Wamba, and Nyota Wamba. 2007. "Welfare of Apes in Captive Environments: Coments On, and By, a Specific Group of Apes." *Journal of Applied Animal Welfare Science* 10, no. 1: 7–19.

Saxton, Martha. 2006. "Disability Rights and Selective Abortion" in *The Disability Studies Reader*, 2nd edition, edited by Lennard J. Davis. New York: Routledge.

Scholz, Sally and Shannon M. Mussett, eds. 2005. *The Contradictions of Freedom: Philosophical Essays on Simone de Beauvoir's Les Mandarins*. Albany, NY: SUNY Press.

Schott, Robin, ed. 1997. *Feminist Interpretations of Immanuel Kant*. Pittsburgh, PA: Penn State University Press.

Schriempf, Alexa. 2001. "(Re)fusing the Amputated Body: An Interactionist Bridge for Feminism and Disability" *Hypatia* 16, no. 4: 53–79.

Schröder, Hannelore. 1997. "Kant's Patriarchal Order" in *Feminist Interpretations of Immanuel Kant*, edited by Robin May Schott, 275–96. University Park, PA: Penn State University Press.

Schur, Lisa, Douglas Kruse, and Peter Blanck. 2013. *People With Disabilities: Sidelined or Mainstreamed?* New York: Cambridge University Press.

Schweik, Suan M. 2009. *The Ugly Laws: Disability in Public*. New York: New York University Press.

Scientific American Mind. 2013. "The Anxious Sex." *Scientific American Mind* 24, no. 3: 15.

Scolding, Neil. 2013. "Three-Parent Babies: Miracle Cure of Eugenics?" *Standpoint Magazine*. Accessed online at http://standpointmag.co.uk/node/5304/full.

Scott, James C. 2009. *The Art of Not Being Governed: An Anarchist History of Upland Southeast Asia*. New Haven, CN: Yale University Press.

Scott, Shelly R. 2009. "The Racehorse as Protagonist: Agency, Independence, and Improvisation" in *Animals and Agency: An Interdisciplinary Exploration*, edited by Sarah E. McFarland and Ryan Hediger, 45–65. Leiden, Netherlands: Brill.

Scully, Jackie Leach. 2014. "Disability and Vulnerability: On Bodies, Dependence, and Power" in *Vulnerability: New Essays in Ethics and Feminist Philosophy*, edited by C. Mackenzie, W. Roger, and S. Dodds. New York: Oxford.

Sedgwick, Sally. 1997. "Can Kant's Ethics Survive the Feminist Critique?" in *Feminist Interpretations of Immanuel Kant*, edited by Robin May Schott, 77–100. University Park, PA: The Pennsylvania State University Press.

Séguin, Édouard. 1866. *Idiocy and Its Treatments by the Physiological Method*. New York: William Wood & Co.

Seibers, Tobin. 2006. "Disability in Theory: From Social Constructionism to the New Realism of the Body" in *The Disability Studies Reader*, 2nd edition, edited by Lennard J. Davis. New York: Routledge.

2008. *Disability Theory*. Ann Arbor: The University of Michigan Press.

Seliger, Martin. 1968. *The Liberal Politics of John Locke*. London: Allen and Unwin.

Sen, Amartya. 1983. "Poor, Relatively Speaking, *Oxford Economic Papers* 35, no. 2: 153–69.

1990. "Justice: Means versus Freedoms." *Philosophy & Public Affairs* 19, no. 2: 111–21.

1999. *Development as Freedom*. New York: Alfred A. Knopf.

2006. *Identity and Violence: The Illusion of Destiny*. London: Penguin.
Shakespeare, Tom. 1992. "A Response to Liz Crow." *Coalition*: 40–2.
1994. "Cultural Representations of Disabled People: Dustbins for Disavowal?" *Disability and Society* 9, no. 3: 283–99.
2002. "The Social Model of Disability: An Outdated Ideology?" *Journal of Research in Social Science and Disability* 2: 9–28.
2004. "Christopher Reeve: You'll Believe a Man Can Walk." *BBC Ouch!* Accessed online at www.bbc.co.uk/ouch/features/christopher-reeve-you-ll-believe-a-man-can-walk.shtml.
2006. *Disability Rights and Wrongs*. New York: Taylor & Francis.
2013. "The Social Model of Disability" in *The Disability Studies Reader*, 4th edition, edited by Lennard Davis, 214–21. New York: Routledge.
Shakespeare, Tom and Nicholas Watson. 1997. "Defending the Social Model." *Disability and Society* 12, no. 2: 293–300.
Shapiro, Kenneth. 1990. "Understanding Dogs through Kinesthetic Empathy, Social Construction, and History." *Anthrozoös* 3, no. 3: 184–95.
Shapiro, Michael J. 1988. *The Politics of Representation: Writing Practices in Biography, Photography, and Political Analysis*. Madison, WI: University of Wisconsin Press.
2012. *Michael J. Shapiro: Discourse, Culture, Violence*. Edited by Terrell Carver and Samuel Chambers. New York: Routledge.
Shaywitz, Sally. 2003. *Overcoming Dyslexia: A New and Complete Science-Based Program for Reading Problems at Any Level*. New York: Knopf.
Sheldon, L., S. Swanson, A. Dolce, K. Marsh, and J. Summers. 2008. "Putting Evidence into Practice: Evidence-Based Interventions for Anxiety." *Clinical Journal of Oncology Nursing* 12, no. 5: 789–97.
Shelton, Jo-Ann. 2004. "Killing Animals that Don't Fit In: Moral Dimensions of Habitat Restoration." *Between the Species* IV, August. Available online at http://digitalcommons.calpoly.edu/bts.
Sherry, Mark. 2010. *Disability Hate Crimes: Does Anyone Really Hate Disabled People?* Burlington, VT: Ashgate Publishing.
Shilmaier, Michael. 2007. "Dis/Abling Practices: Rethinking Disability." *Human Affairs* 17.
Showalter, Elaine. 1987. *The Female Malady: Women, Madness, and English Culture, 1830–1980*. New York: Penguin.
Siebers, Tobin. 1995. *Disability Theory*. Ann Arbor, MI: University of Michigan Press.
2001. "In Theory: From Social Constructionism to Realism of the Body." *American Literary History* 13, no. 4: 737–54.
2011. *Disability Theory*. Ann Arbor, MI: University of Michigan Press.
Silvers, Anita. 1993. "Formal Justice" in *Disability, Difference, Discrimination: Perspectives on Justice in Bioethics and Public Policy*, edited by Anita Silvers, David Wasserman, Mary B. Mahowald, and Lawrence C. Becker. New York: Rowman & Littlefield.
1995. "Reconciling Equality to Difference: Caring (F)or Justice For People With Disabilities." *Hypatia* 10, no. 1: 30–55.
1996. "(In)Equality, (Ab)normality, and the 'Americans With Disabilities' Act." *The Journal of Medicine and Philosophy* 21, no. 2: 209–224.

1998. "A Fatal Attraction to Normalizing: Treating Disabilities as Deviations from 'Species-Typical' Functioning" in *Enhancing Human Traits: Ethical and Social Implications*, edited by Erik Parens, 95–123. Washington, DC: Georgetown University Press.

2005. "Justice through Trust: Disability and the 'Outlier Problem' in Social Contract Theory." *Ethics* 116, no. 1: 40–77.

2009. "No Talent? Beyond the Worst Off: A Diverse Theory of Justice for Disability." In *Disability and Disadvantage*, edited by Kimberley Brownlee and Adam Cureton. Oxford: Oxford University Press.

2011. "Moral Status: What a Bad Idea! Why Discard It? What Replaces It?" Paper presented at the workshop, "In From the Margins: New Foundations for Personhood and Legal Capacity in the 21st Century," University of British Columbia, Vancouver, British Columbia, April 29–May 1.

Silvers, Anita and Leslie P. Francis. 2005. "Justice Through Trust: Disability and the 'Outlier Problem' in Social Contract Theory." *Ethics* 116, no. 1: 40–76.

2007. "Liberalism and Individually Scripted Ideas of the Good: Meeting the Challenge of Dependent Agency." *Social Theory and Practice* 33, no. 2: 311–34.

2009. "Thinking About the Good: Reconfiguring Liberal Metaphysics (or Not) for People with Cognitive Disabilities." *Metaphilosophy* 40, no. 3–4: 475–98.

Silvers, Anita and Michael Ashley Stein. 2007. "Disability and the Social Contract." *The University of Chicago Law Review* 74: 1635–61.

Singer, Peter. 1990. *Animal Liberation*, 2nd edition. New York: HarperCollins.

1994. *Rethinking Life and Death: The Collapse of Our Traditional Ethics*. New York: St. Martin's Griffin.

2009. "Speciesism and Moral Status." *Metaphilosophy* 40, no. 3–4: 567–8.

2010. "Speciesism and Moral Status" in *Cognitive Disability and Its Challenge to Moral Philosophy*, 331–44. Oxford: Wiley-Blackwell.

Skinner, Quentin. 1996. *Reason and Rhetoric in the Philosophy of Hobbes*. New York: Cambridge University Press.

Skocpol, Theda. 1992. *Protecting Soldiers and Mothers: The Political Origins of Social Policy in the United States*. Cambridge, MA: Harvard University Press.

Smith, David W. 2013. "Phenomenology" in *The Stanford Encyclopedia of Philosophy*, edited by Edward N. Zalta. Available online at http://plato.stanford.edu/archives/win2013/entries/phenomenology.

Smith, Julie Ann. 2003. "Beyond Dominance and Affection: Living with Rabbits in Post-Humanist Households." *Society & Animals* 11, no. 2: 81–97.

Smith, Kerri. 2011. "Neuroscience vs. Philosophy: Taking Aim at Free Will." *Nature* 477: 23–5.

Smith, Kimberly K. 2012. *Governing Animals: Animal Welfare and the Liberal State*. Oxford: Oxford University Press.

Smuts, Barbara. 2001. "Encounters with Animal Minds." *Journal of Consciousness Studies* 8, no. 5–7: 293–309.

Snyder, Sharon L. and David T Mitchell. 2006. *Cultural Locations of Disability*. Chicago, IL: University of Chicago Press.

Sobsey, Dick, Don Wells, Richard Lucardie, and Sheila Mansell. 1995. *Violence and Disability: An Annotated Bibliography*. Baltimore: Paul H. Brookes Publishing.

Spiegelberg, Herbert. 1944. "A Defense of Human Equality." *The Philosophical Review* 53, no. 2: 101–24.

Stanghellini, Giovanni and Thomas Fuchs. 2013. "Editors' Introduction" in *One Century of Karl Jaspers' General Psychopathology*, edited by Giovanni Stanghellini and Thomas Fuchs, xiii–xxiii. Oxford: Oxford University Press.

Stark, Cynthia. 2009. "Respecting Human Dignity: Contract Versus Capabilities." *Metaphilosophy* 40, no. 3–4: 366–81.

Stein, Michael Ashley. 2007. "Disability Human Rights." *California Law Review* 95, no. 1: 75–121.

Steiner, Gary. 2013. *Animals and the Limits of Postmodernism*. New York: Columbia University Press.

Steinmetz, Erika. 2002. *Americans with Disabilities: 2002*. Current Population Reports, US Census Bureau.

Stiker, Henri-Jacques. 2000. *A History of Disability*. Translated by William Sayers. Ann Arbor, MI: University of Michigan Press.

Stone, Deborah. 1984. *The Disabled State*. Philadelphia: Temple University Press.

Sullivan, Martin. 2005. "Subjected Bodies: Paraplegia, Rehabilitation, and the Politics of Movement" in *Foucault and the Government of Disability*, edited by Shelly Tremain. Ann Arbor, MI: University of Michigan Press.

Swanton, Christine. 1992. *Freedom: A Coherence Theory*. Indianapolis, IN: Hackett.

Szasz, Thomas S. 2010. *The Myth of Mental Illness: Foundations of a Theory of Personal Conduct*, Harper Perennial edition. New York: HarperCollins

Taylor, Charles. 1984. "Foucault on Freedom and Truth." *Political Theory* 12: 152–83.

1994. "The Politics of Recognition" in *Multiculturalism: Examining the Politics of Recognition*, edited by A. Gutmann, 25–73. Princeton: Princeton University Press.

Taylor, Sunaura. 2011. "Disability Studies and Animal Rights." *Qui Parle: Critical Humanities and Social Sciences* 19, no. 2: 191–222.

2013. "Vegans, Freaks, and Animals: Toward a New Table Fellowship." American Quarterly 65, no. 3: 757–64.

2014. "Interdependent Animals: A Feminist Disability Ethic-of-Care" in *Ecofeminism: Feminist Intersections with Other Animals and the Earth*, edited by Carol Adams and Lori Gruen. London: Bloomsbury.

Temple, Elise, Russell A. Poldrack, Joanna Salidis, Gayle K. Deutsch, Paula Tallai, Michael M. Merzenich, and John D. E. Gabrieli. 2001. "Disrupted Neural Responses to Phonological and Orthographic Responses in Dyslexic Children: An fMRI Study." *Neuroreport* 12, no. 2: 299–307.

tenBroek, Jacobus. 1966a. "The Disabled in the Law of Welfare." *California Law Review* 54, no. 2: 809–40.

1966b. "The Right to Live in the World: The Disabled in the Law of Torts." *California Law Review* 54, no. 2: 841–919.

Thiara, Ravi, Gill Hague, Ruth Bashall, Brenda Ellis, and Audrey Mullender. 2012. *Disabled Women and Domestic Violence: Responding to the Experiences of Survivors*. London: Jessica Kingsley.

Thierman, Stephen. 2011. "The Vulnerability of Other Animals." *Journal for Critical Animals Studies* 9, no. 1–2: 182–208.

Thomas, Elizabeth Marshall. 1993. *The Hidden Life of Dogs*. Boston: Houghton Mifflin.

Thomas, Pam. 2013. "Hate Crime or Mate Crime? Disablist Hostility, Contempt and Ridicule" in *Disability, Hate Crime and Violence*, edited by A. Roulstone and H. Mason-Bish. London: Routledge.

Titchkosky, Tanya. 2000. "Disability Studies: The Old and the New." *The Canadian Journal of Sociology* 25, no. 2: 197–224.

Thomson, Rosemarie Garland. 1996. *Freakery: Cultural Spectacles of the Extraordinary Body*. New York: New York University Press.

1997. *Extraordinary Bodies: Figuring Physical Disability and American Culture and Literature*. New York: Columbia University Press.

2006. "Integrating Disability, Transforming Feminist Theory" in *The Disability Studies Reader*, 2nd edition, edited by Lennard J. Davis. New York: Routledge.

2009. *Staring: How We Look*. New York: Oxford University Press.

2010. "Senior Scholar Address." At the Society for Disability Studies Annual Meeting, Philadelphia, PA.

2015. "Eugenic World-Building and Disability: The Strange World of Kazuo Ishiguro's Never Let Me Go." *Journal of Medical Humanities*, online first edition, December 2, doi:10.1007/s10912-015-9368-y.

Torgeson, Joseph K. 1995. "Phonological Awareness: A Critical Factor in Dyslexia." Baltimore, MD: The Orton Dyslexia Society.

Tremain, Shelly, ed. 2002. *Foucault and the Government of Disability*. Ann Arbor: University of Michigan Press.

Trent, James. 1994. *Inventing the Feeble Mind: A History of Mental Retardation in the United States*. Berkeley, CA: University of California Press.

Tridas, Eric Q., ed. 2007. *From ABC to ADHD: What Parents Should Know about Dyslexia and Attention Problems*. Baltimore, MD: IDA.

Tronto, Joan C. 1993. *Moral Boundaries: A Political Argument for an Ethic of Care*. New York: Routledge.

2013. *Caring Democracy: Markets, Equality and Justice*. New York: NYU Press.

Tuana, Nancy. 2006. "The Speculum of Ignorance." *Hypatia* 21, no. 3: 1–19.

Ure, Michael. 2008. *Nietzsche's Therapy: Self-Cultivation in the Middle Works*. Lanham, MD: Lexington Books.

Valentini, Laura. 2011. "Canine Justice: An Associative Account." Unpublished

Vehmas, Simos. 1999. "Discriminative Assumptions of Utilitarian Bioethics Regarding Individuals with Intellectual Disabilities." *Disability and Society* 14, no. 1: 37–52.

Villa, Dana. 1996. *Arendt and Heidegger: The Fate of the Political*. Princeton: Princeton University Press.

Voegelin, Eric. 1953. "The Origins of Totalitarianism." *The Review of Politics* 15, no. 1: 74–5.

Vorhaus, J. 2005. "Citizenship, Competence and Profound Disability." *Journal of Philosophy of Education* 39, no. 3: 461–475.

Wadiwel, Dinesh. 2013. "Whipping to Win: Measured Violence, Delegated Sovereignty and the Privatised Domination of Non-Human Life" in *Law and the Question of the Animal: A Critical Jurisprudence*, edited by Yoriko Otomo and Edward Mussawir, 116–32. New York: Routledge.

Waldron, Jeremy. 1998. *The Right to Private Property*. Oxford: Clarendon Press.

2002. *God, Locke, and Equality: Christian Foundations in Locke's Political Thought.* Cambridge: Cambridge University Press.

Walker, Hill M., Carl Calkins, Michael L. Wehmeyer, Laura Walker, Ansley Bacon, Susan B. Palmer, George S. Jesien, Margarent A. Nygren, Tamar Heller, George S. Gotto, Brian H. Abery, and David R. Johnson. 2011. "A Social-Ecological Approach to Promote Self-Determination." *Exceptionality* 19, no. 1: 6–18.

Wall, John. 2011. "Can Democracy Represent Children: Toward a Politics of Difference." *Childhood* 19, no. 1: 86–100.

Wallis, Claudia. 2009. "'I Am Autism': An Advocacy Video Sparks Protest." *Time Magazine*, November 6.

Ward, Tony and Claire Stewart. 2008. "Putting Human Rights into Practice with People with and Intellectual Disability." *Journal of Developmental and Physical Disabilities* 20, no. 3: 297–311.

Warkentin, Traci. 2009. "Whale Agency: Affordances and Acts of Resistance in Captive Environments" in *Animals and Agency: An Interdisciplinary Exploration*, edited by Sarah E. McFarland, and Ryan Hediger, 23–43. Leiden, Netherlands: Brill.

Wasserman, David, Adrienne Asch, Jeffrey Blustein, and Daniel Putnam. 2012. "Cognitive Disability and Moral Status." *The Stanford Encyclopedia of Philosophy*. Available online at http://plato.stanford.edu/archives/fall2012/entries/cognitive-disability.

Waxman, Barbara Faye. 1991. "Hatred: The Unacknowledged Dimension in Violence Against Disabled People." *Sexuality and Disability* 9, no. 3: 185–99.

Weber, M. 1946. "The Social Psychology of World Religions" in *From Max Weber: Essays in Sociology*. Edited and translated by H. H. Gerth and C. Wright Mills, 267–301. New York: Oxford University Press.

Wehmeyer, Michael and Nancy Garner. 2003. "The Impact of Personal Characteristics of People with Intellectual and Developmental Disability on Self-Determination and Autonomous Functioning." *Journal of Applied Research in Intellectual Disabilities* 16, no. 4: 255–65.

Wehmeyer, Michael L., Wil H. E. Buntinx, Yves Lachapelle, Ruth A. Luckasson, Robert L. Schalock, Miguel A. Verdugo, Sharon Borthwick-Duffy, Valerie Bradley, Ellis M. Craig, David L. Coulter, Sharon C. Gomez, Alya Reeve, Karrie A. Shogren, Martha E. Snell, Scott Spreat, Marc J. Tassé, James R. Thompson, and Mark H. Yeager. 2008. "The Intellectual Disability Construct and Its Relation to Human Functioning." *Intellectual and Developmental Disabilities* 46, no. 4: 311–18.

Weinberg, Nancy. 1988. "Another Perspective: Attitudes of People with Disabilities" in *Attitudes Towards Persons with Disabilities*, edited by Harold E. Yuker. New York: Springer Publishing Co.

Weisberg, Zipporah. 2009. "The Broken Promises of Monsters: Haraway, Animals and the Humanist Legacy." *Journal for Critical Animal Studies* 7, no. 2: 22–62.

Wendell, Susan. 1996. *The Rejected Body: Feminist Philosophical Reflections on Disability*. New York: Routledge.

2001. "Unhealthy Disabled: Treating Chronic Illnesses as Disabilities." *Hypatia* 16, no. 4: 17–33.

White, Hayden. 1972. "The Forms of Wilderness: Archeology of an Idea" in *Wild Man: An Image in Western Thought From the Renaissance to*

Romanticism, edited by Edward Dudley and Maximillian E. Novak, 3–38. Pittsburgh, PA: Pittsburgh University Press.

White, Hillary. 2008. *Half of Americans would Choose Death over Disability: Survey.* Available online at www.lifesitenews.com/news/archive/ldn/2008/jul/08071505.

Willett, Cynthia. 2012. "Affect Attunement in the Caregiver-Infant Relationship and Across Species." *PhiloSOPHIA* 2, no. 2: 111–30.

Williams, Bernard. 1995. "Evolution, Ethics and the Representation Problem" in *Making Sense of Humanity*. Cambridge: Cambridge University Press.

Willingham, Emily. 2013. "Why Autism Speaks Doesn't Speak for Me." *Forbes Magazine* online, November 12. Accessed online at www.forbes.com/sites/emilywillingham/2013/11/13/why-autism-speaks-doesnt-speak-for-me.

Wingrove, Elizabeth. 2000. *Rousseau's Republican Romance*. Princeton, NJ: Princeton University Press.

Wolch, Jennifer. 2002. "Anima Urbis." *Progress in Human Geography* 26, no. 6: 721–42.

Wolf, Maryanne. 2007. *Proust and the Squid: The Story and Science of the Reading Brain*. New York: HarperCollins.

Wolff, Jonathan. 2009. "Disability, Status Enhancement, Personal Enhancement and Resources Allocation." *Economics and Philosophy* 25: 49–68.

Wollstonecraft, Mary. 1989. *The Works of Mary Wollstonecraft*. Marilyn Butler and Janet Todd. New York: New York University Press.

Wong, Sophia Isako. 2002. "At Home with Down Syndrome and Gender." *Hypatia* 17, no. 3: 89–117.

2009. "Duties of Justice to Citizens with Cognitive Disabilities." *Metaphilosophy* 40, no. 3–4: 382–401.

Wood, Allen. 1999. *Kant's Ethical Thought*. Cambridge: Cambridge University Press.

Woodcock, Scott. 2009. "Disability, Diversity, and the Elimination of Human Kinds." *Social Theory and Practice* 35, no. 2: 251–78.

WHO. 2011. *World Report on Disability*. Geneva: World Health Organization Press. Available online at www.who.int/disabilities/world_report/2011/report.

Yates, Roger. 2004. *The Social Construction of Human Beings and Other Animals in Human-Nonhuman Relations: Welfarism and Rights: A Contemporary Sociological Analysis*. PhD dissertation, University of Bangor, Wales. Available online at http://roger.rbgi.net.

Young, Iris Marion. 1990. *Justice and the Politics of Difference*. Princeton NJ: Princeton University Press.

2006. "Taking the Basic Structure Seriously." *Perspectives on Politics* 4, no. 1: 91–7.

Young, Lauren L. 2012. "Validating Difference and Counting the Cost of Exclusion in the Lives of People Who Identify as on the Autistic Spectrum." *Disability & Society* 27, no. 2: 291–4.

Young, Rosamund. 2003. *The Secret Life of Cows: Animal Sentience at Work*. Preston, UK: Farming Books.

Zaw, Susan Khin. 1998. "The Reasonable Heart: Mary Wollstonecraft's View of the Relation between Reason and Feeling in Morality, Moral Psychology, and Moral Development." *Hypatia* 13, no. 1: 78–117.

Zerilli, Linda. 1994. *Signifying Woman: Culture and Chaos in Rousseau, Burke, and Mill*. Ithaca, NY: Cornell University Press.

Index